PUBLIC LIBRARIES
IN NAZI GERMANY

PUBLIC LIBRARIES IN NAZI GERMANY

Margaret F. Stieg

THE UNIVERSITY OF ALABAMA PRESS

Tuscaloosa and London

LIBRARY OF CONGRESS CATALOGING-IN-PUBLICATION DATA

Stieg, Margaret F.
   Public libraries in Nazi Germany / Margaret F. Stieg.
      p.   cm.
   Includes bibliographical references and index.
   ISBN 0-8173-5155-8 (pbk. : alk. paper)
   1. Public libraries—Germany—History—20th century. 2. Libraries
and national socialism. 3. Libraries and state—Germany—
History—20th century. 4. Germany—Politics and
government—1933–1945. I. Title.
Z801.A1S924   1992
027.443—dc20   90-46771

To the memory of my mother,
who loved Germany

Contents

Contents

TABLES

Acknowledgments

A S DO MOST projects, this book has a long history. Many people have contributed to it and I am deeply grateful. It may be trite to say that without their help I could not have written it, but it is no more than the truth.

The idea for a study of public libraries in Nazi Germany came to me on a June day in 1977 as I sat in the Staatsarchiv in Berlin, doing the research for a book on the development of scholarly historical periodicals. I was reading the papers of Friedrich Meinecke, long-time editor of the *Historische Zeitschrift*, who was forced out by the Nazis. It had been a long day and my attention was wandering. Into my mind popped the question: If the Nazis did this to an obscure scholarly journal, what did they do to the public library, a much more useful institution from their point of view? When I returned home, I looked into it. No one had written anything on the subject; it seemed the perfect topic. Everything came together—an undergraduate concentration in government, my background in European history, and my education and experience as a professional librarian.

I began by improving my German. Although I had passed the required minimum for doctoral work, I knew I needed a better command of the language and especially the ability to speak and understand aurally. I was lucky enough to encounter a truly gifted teacher, Ellin Feld, who not only helped me acquire the firm foundation in grammar and vocabulary I needed but gave me a real affection for the language. Further study in the German department at Columbia University and in Austria with the Austrian-American Society was a pleasure.

Then there are the archivists and librarians. Because the records of the central organizations responsible for public libraries were destroyed in 1943, alternative sources needed to be found. I wrote to the archives at both Potsdam and Koblenz, to the archives of each Land, to some individual libraries, and to a variety of organizations with some relation to public libraries. The replies were uniformly helpful. When I appeared in person, archivists patiently explained procedures and did whatever was possible to smooth my path. I am especially grateful to those who went beyond the call of duty. Dr. Lent in Wolfenbüttel insisted I sit down with a directory of German manuscript collections. I might already have used it, but the importance of the Ackerknecht collection did not strike me until that day. Ackerknecht's papers turned out to be my most useful source on the internal politics of the profession during the 1930s. Dr. Saupe in Munich spent the better part of a morning making accessible to me that part of a closed file I could be allowed to see. Frau Morgenstern, director of the Beratungsstelle at Bayreuth, made those records available to me, and Erich Hodick, director of the Borromäus Verein, generously opened that organization's records. Dr. Karl-Heinz Jügelt, director of the library of the University of Rostock, shared the results of his own research, giving me an important piece of information I could not otherwise have obtained.

One of the most rewarding aspects of doing this book has been meeting many interesting people. To supplement written records, I tried to interview librarians who had worked in public libraries during the 1930s. Those with whom I spoke shared their memories, and their honesty helped me better understand the human side of a painful and difficult time.

Both personally and professionally I encountered much kindness from many individuals. I remember with particular gratitude Dr. Joerden and his wife in Hamburg, Dietrich Vorwerk of Bad Dürrheim, Hans E. Hofmann, son of Walter Hofmann, and his wife of Ludwigsburg, and, in Bayreuth, Kurt Wiegand and his wife and Brigitte Herrmann. Dr. Peter Vodosek, now rector of the Fachhochschule für Bibliothekswesen in Stuttgart, not only made available the Hofmann papers for this project but has helped me in numerous ways since. The Schriewer family, Jürgen Schriewer and his wife Elisabeth, the son and daughter-in-law of Franz Schriewer,

Acknowledgments

and Hanna Bieger, the older daughter of Franz Schriewer and herself a librarian, opened their homes to me and have become friends.

Institutionally speaking, I am grateful to the Deutsche Akademischer Austauschdienst for financing my second summer's research. The School of Library and Information Studies of The University of Alabama, Dean Philip Turner, and former dean James Ramer provided me with the support that is so necessary on a project of this scope. Ulrike Dieterle did a fine job entering the indexing of the records into a database. Martha Lux put the bibliography into proper form. Frances Wilson, our longtime typist, did her usual excellent work. And finally, Malcolm MacDonald and his staff at The University of Alabama Press have again been knowledgeable, helpful, and understanding.

Margaret F. Stieg
Tuscaloosa

Abbreviations

BSUK   Bayerisches Staatsministerium für Unterricht und Kultus

BuB   *Bücherei und Bildungspflege*

DAF   Deutsche Arbeitsfront

DB   *Die Bücherei*

DZ   Deutsche Zentralstelle für volkstümliches Büchereiwesen

EKH   Einkaufshaus

HfB   *Hefte für Büchereiwesen*

HJ   Hitler Jugend

PLVB   Preußische Landesstelle für volkstümliches Büchereiwesen

PMWKV   Preußisches Ministerium für Wissenschaft, Kunst und Volksbildung

RSK   Reichsschrifttumskammer

RV   Reichsstelle für volkstümliches Büchereiwesen; Reichsstelle für Volksbüchereiwesen

RWEV   Reichsministerium für Wissenschaft, Erziehung und Volksbildung

VDA   Verein für das Deutschtum im Ausland

VDV   Verband Deutscher Volksbibliothekare

Glossary

Altkämpfer: an early member of the Nazi party.

Anschluß: the annexation of Austria by Germany in March 1938.

Auslandsdeutsche: a German living outside the Reich; similar to Volksdeutsch, an ethnic German.

Bayerische Ostmark: region between the Danube and Naab rivers on the Bohemian border, including the Bohemian-Bavarian Forest and Upper Palatinate. The cities of Passau, Regensburg, and Hof lie within it.

Beratungsstelle: advisory center; generally used for the provincial public library agency.

Bezirk: an administrative district; the Bezirksamt is the district office.

Blut und Boden: literally, blood and soil. *See* Heimat literature.

Führer: leader; in the Third Reich, used as synonym for Hitler.

Gau: Nazi party administrative district, each of which was headed by a Gauleiter; not identical with the administrative divisions of the government.

Gleichschaltung: the coordination, especially during 1933, of all non-Nazi political, economic, and cultural organizations and institutions of Germany; the laws that brought this about were designed both to eliminate possible bases of opposition and to create a centralized, one-party state.

Grenzbüchereidienst: organization created in 1919 to strengthen libraries in border areas of the Reich; a reasonable anglicization is Border Book Service.

Heimat literature: *Heimat* is usually translated "homeland"; at the end of the nineteenth century an antiurban, antiindustrial literary movement that urged authors to write fiction about the region in which they lived and knew intimately. It could have a nationalistic and/or anti-Semitic bias and, under national socialism, was linked to the regime's racial policies.

Kreis: an administrative district of a Land in Germany and Austria; a Kreisbüchereipfleger was appointed to supervise the public libraries in a Kreis.

Land: a state in the Third Reich; more generally, a province.

Landesstelle: a provincial agency. *See* Beratungsstelle.

Leihbücherei: a subscription lending library, usually a commercial enterprise, often run jointly with a tobacconist's shop.

Machtergreifung: the seizure of power in 1933 by the Nazis.

Nebenamtlich: in addition to one's regular duties.

Oberregierungsrat: senior executive officer.

Referat: a departmental section in a ministry, usually a specialty area such as libraries.

Reich: empire; in the 1930s used to indicate Germany.

Reichsschrifttumskammer: literally, imperial literary chamber; the national cultural organization created to control authors, editors, newspapers, and so on.

Reichstag: the parliamentary body of Germany.

Richtung: direction; the Richtungsstreit was the philosophical conflict that dominated German public librarianship between 1912 and 1933.

Säuberung: cleaning or purging. In German public libraries refers to the successive waves of censorship when books not acceptable to the Nazi government were removed from the collections.

Tagung: meeting, conference, workshop.

Volk: people, nation; in national socialism a key concept that tied racial origin and identity to belonging to a nation.

Zentralstelle: central agency.

PUBLIC LIBRARIES
IN NAZI GERMANY

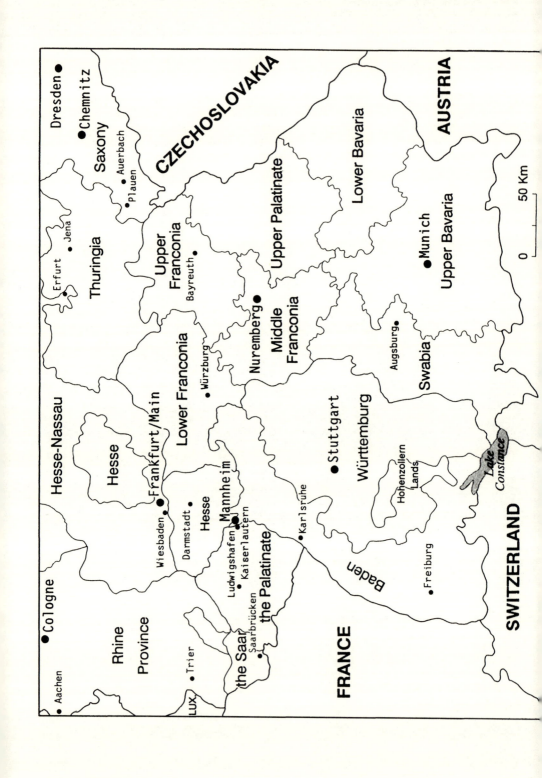

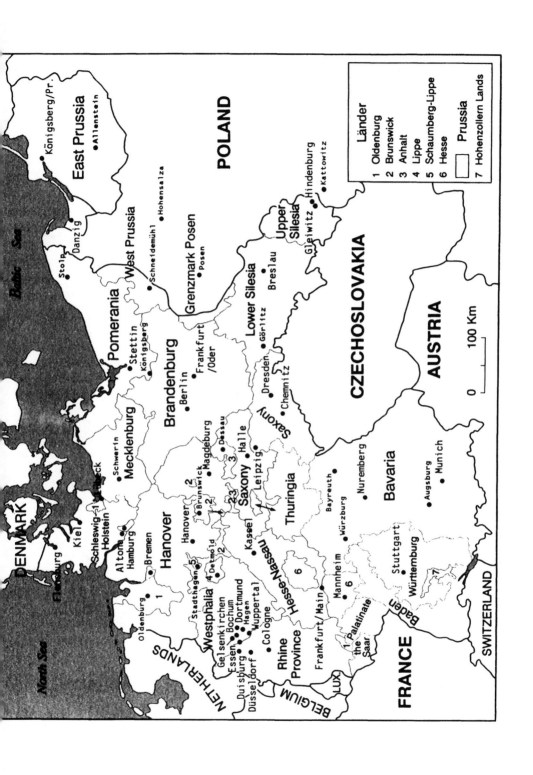

CHAPTER ONE

Introduction

ON MARCH 6, 1938, thirty new public libraries in the Rhenish border district of Germersheim formally opened. Of no particular importance in its own right, this routine event incorporates most of the major aspects of Nazi public librarianship. Those thirty new libraries were concrete evidence of librarianship militant. Without the organization of a national administrative network for public libraries in the Third Reich, an aggressive program to build libraries in culturally endangered border areas, and a new policy of competition with Catholic libraries, they would not have existed. The very occurrence of the self-promoting ritual expressed the importance of ceremony in Nazi Germany. The ostentatious warmth with which local government and party officials greeted the representatives of the Reich, Oberregierungsrat Dr. Heinz Dähnhardt of the Reichsministerium für Wissenschaft, Erziehung und Volksbildung und Oberstudiendirektor Dr. Fritz Heiligenstaedt of the Reichsstelle für Volksbüchereiwesen, communicated the harmony that was supposed to prevail in a one-party, federated state. Fundamental policy informed the generic speeches; the local party representative contrasted the dark (precensorship) days before 1933, when "un-German thoughts" tore the *Volk* asunder, with the present unity fostered by the "German book."[1]

In a sense the Germersheim festivities celebrated the supersession of the impoverished and demoralized public librarianship of 1933 by a strong and self-confident Nazi version. In 1933 public libraries were a depressed industry, scarce, small, and rather dreary. Already

1

divided internally by fierce theoretical quarrels, public librarianship had been hard hit by the depression. There was universal agreement that public librarianship needed something, but none on what that something should be. By 1938 the new regime had revised the profession's theoretical basis, organized an administrative structure, developed new programs, and begun building libraries in unserved areas. Most of all, they had proclaimed that public libraries were important and had forced local governments to translate this principle into tax support. Librarians might not have agreed with the Nazi prescription in 1933, but the solid accomplishments of 1938 had to be welcome.

Public libraries are institutions that preserve and disseminate culture. When culture is assigned an explicitly social role, they assume an important social function. Their primary task may be modified still further if, as they were under national socialism, they are defined as political instruments. The history of public librarianship in Nazi Germany is the record of an attempt to turn a cultural institution into a political one, to change an institution that primarily reflects societal values into one that shapes them. In its fully developed form the Nazi public library defines the political public library.

Those well acquainted with Nazi Germany will find many familiar elements in the history of public libraries. Much of what happened in public libraries was happening elsewhere in German society. Librarians proved no more able than other professions or groups to resist the conformity imposed upon them. Basically decent people were co-opted to develop both Nazi policies for their profession and programs to implement the new policies. Grandiose plans were laid, inflated accomplishments trumpeted. State control penetrated every aspect of librarianship, from the books in the collection to the hours of opening. But the history of German librarianship is more than just a minor variant of an old tale or a small piece of a larger puzzle. It is a microcosm of the Nazi experience, terrible because it was so very ordinary. It is also a cautionary tale. What occurred in German public libraries in the 1930s is the consequence when the political becomes the only standard, when political values control the entire constellation of customs, beliefs, attitudes, and behavior that underpin a society.[2]

2

Introduction

German public librarianship had its roots in the Enlightenment, but German public libraries, like those of other Western countries, were fundamentally a product of the nineteenth century. The first phase of development came in the 1840s. Friedrich Raumer, a Prussian ministry official and educator, visited England and the United States. Impressed by what he had observed, especially in the United States, he proposed that public libraries on the U.S. model be established. In 1850 four public libraries were opened in Berlin as a result of his efforts. Sometimes inspired by Raumer's writings or the Berlin example, sometimes acting independently, Frankfurt/Main, Dresden, Hamburg, Leipzig, and Breslau, as well as an assortment of smaller places, began libraries.

This early expansion was followed by stagnation. Library development, like other kinds of development, was inhibited by the consequences of the Revolution of 1848. Lack of leadership, resources, and interest prevented building on the foundation laid in the 1840s. The public library movement splintered, and growth tended to be within small interest groups instead of on a broad national or societal level. Catholic libraries, Protestant libraries, libraries for union members, and libraries for members of ethnic groups multiplied, all of them tiny.[3]

If public librarianship could point to few tangible accomplishments in the second part of the nineteenth century, it did develop a close relationship with the strong and vital adult education movement that prepared the way for later progress. In the 1880s and 1890s adult education flourished. Germany's rapid industrialization and urbanization had created a working class eager for educational opportunity and a bourgeoisie with money and a sense of obligation. The political unification of 1871 needed to be consolidated in other ways. Adult education seemed an obvious enterprise. Public librarianship benefited from its growth because the two endeavors shared the same goals, and public librarianship activities complemented those of adult education societies. Indeed, in many cases adult education groups found it necessary to organize libraries to support their other work if a public library did not already exist, libraries that would often then become the public library of the community. Several of the adult education associations that were most

3

active in promoting libraries were the Comenius Gesellschaft, the Gesellschaft für Verbreitung von Volksbildung, and the Gesellschaft für ethische Kultur.[4]

Toward the end of the century public librarianship was revitalized by a series of proposals for reform that allied it still more closely with adult education. The two men most prominently associated with this revival were Constantin Nörrenberg, a professor at the University of Kiel, and Eduard Reyer, a professor at the University of Vienna (Ger. Wien). Nörrenberg was a university librarian; Reyer, a geologist. Both had traveled extensively in the United States and were greatly influenced by what they saw there. The articles they wrote and the speeches they gave stressed the need for popular libraries to serve all classes, libraries that would provide the materials needed and wanted by readers, and be open at hours they could take advantage of. This conception was quite different from the old-fashioned city library found in most German towns, which was really a library for the clergy and other professions.[5]

Reyer's writings, which were slightly earlier than Nörrenberg's, laid the groundwork. He compared the poverty and abysmal condition of public librarianship in the German-speaking lands with that of England and the United States, hitting hard with statistics. Reyer went on to found a library organization in Vienna, the Verein Zentralbibliothek. Nörrenberg articulated the principle that became the credo of the new public library movement: The primary purpose of the public library is education. He claimed for the library an essential social role—that of minimizing class distinctions by bringing together all classes; as well as a political one—educating the Volk so that they could exercise their newly won right to vote with intelligence. To prevent the reading of poor novels, Nörrenberg encouraged the public library to satisfy the demand for entertainment by circulating novels in good taste.

These ideas guided the rapid expansion of public libraries that began in the 1890s. Called the Bücherhallenbewegung (reading room movement) after the reading room, a characteristic feature of the libraries opened at this time, this new phase of public librarianship emphasized service to the working class. Nörrenberg's ideas provided intellectual conviction and a program of action, replacing the earlier passivity. In the last decade of the century the pace of development accelerated dramatically, and by 1907 forty-two German cities had 179 public libraries.

Notwithstanding the enthusiasm for U.S. public librarianship and the great influence of U.S. models, German public librarianship differed from that in the United States in several significant ways. To begin with, German public libraries had no standard name; this is another way of saying that *public library* is the term used to translate a number of different words used for institutions approximating an English-speaker's idea of a public library. The variety of names reflected disparate origins or administrative arrangements, or both. The basic word was usually *Bibliothek* (library) or *Bücherei* (also library, but more likely to be, specifically, public library). A *Stadtbibliothek* was literally a city library; it could mean a popular—that is, public—library but was more likely to refer to a scholarly library, founded before 1890, that did not see adult education as its principal function. Many German cities and towns had had libraries of this kind since the eighteenth or nineteenth centuries, primarily serving the educated middle class. Often, such a library was the only library in a community and was described as a "public library" even if it did not act like one. An *Einheitsbibliothek* was a combined scholarly and popular library. Sometimes the popular library would be a separate department, sometimes not. There were also *Lesehallen* (reading halls or rooms) that dated from the 1890s and *Lesevereine* (reading societies) that might be the closest thing in terms of function to a public library that a community possessed. The Nazi regime eliminated this heterogeneity; what a public library was, was defined, and *Volksbücherei* (people's library) was prescribed as the preferred term.

An even more important difference from U.S. practices was in the area of financing. Local government did not accept responsibility for library service, which remained a private enterprise. "Public" libraries were, therefore, neither free nor tax-supported. Instead, they depended primarily on membership fees, circulation charges, and gifts. The local government might occasionally deign to grant a small subsidy, but for the most part the libraries had to generate their own support. Unlike many European countries, Germany did not have a library law that mandated public library service and established a tax basis for it.

Given the lack of a reliable and adequate financial base, it is not surprising that German public libraries remained weak. Some comparisons with U.S. libraries do not look bad: In Germany 69 percent of the population was served in 1934, compared to 67 percent in the United States in 1935; Germany had libraries in 9,494 communities, where there were only 6,235 libraries in the United States. But the differences in collections and financing indicate how poor the quality of those libraries was. German libraries, including traveling collections, held 10,502,467 volumes; U.S. libraries had ten times that many for a population of about the same size. In other words, Germans had 0.16 volumes for each inhabitant, and Americans 0.82 for each. Americans spent $46,375,695 or $0.38 per capita on their public libraries; Germans spent $2,037,425 or $0.03. Nor do the raw figures convey the total picture. Public libraries were often nonexistent in rural areas. Southern Germany was particularly ill served. Even relatively strong libraries such as those in Berlin and Hamburg compare unfavorably with those in British and U.S. cities of comparable size in collection, readership, funding, and personnel[6] (see Table 7.4, pp. 136–37).

Some problems might have been overcome had there been any kind of administrative structure for public librarianship, but this was another area in which Germany was deficient. Public librarianship was left to the *Länder*; until 1935 no national government body had any responsibility for it. The Länder usually assigned it to their ministers of education, few of whom had any interest in public libraries. Some provinces did organize a public library agency (Beratungsstelle), although these agencies had no real authority and were intended to provide professional advice and services rather than make decisions. Prussia (Ger. Preußen) was more advanced than most of the other Länder, but even there the picture was bleak.

As if these circumstances were not sufficiently dire, public librarianship exacerbated its own difficulties by internecine warfare. Early in the new century the Bücherhallenbewegung divided into two camps that called themselves the Alte Richtung (Old Direction) and Neue Richtung (New Direction), each, of course, claiming to be the true representative of the Bücherhallenbewegung. The official starting point of the division was Walter Hofmann's unfavorable review of Paul Ladewig's book, *Die Politik der Bücherei*. It did not end until the Nazi takeover rendered it irrelevant. By 1933 the war of words had

6

come to encompass virtually every aspect of library work, but most differences had their roots in a profound disagreement over the most fundamental issue: What is the purpose of the public library? Divergent definitions of education and culture, and dissimilar views of human nature produced very different answers to this question.[7]

The Alte Richtung, as its name implies, was the senior group, the established party. If the wider circulation of its journal is indicative, it was also the more generally accepted. The Alte Richtung was a loose association of most of the leading German public librarians of the pre–World War I period—Erwin Ackerknecht of Stettin, Paul Ladewig of the Krupp Library in Essen, and Eugen Sulz of Essen. Nörrenberg, too, the father of the Bücherhallenbewegung, worked with the group on occasion, an association that reinforced its claim to orthodoxy. In later years Ackerknecht, because he published the journal and trained so many librarians at Stettin, gradually assumed the leadership.

The Neue Richtung, on the other hand, was very much identified with one man, the prolific and combative librarian of Leipzig, Walter Hofmann. A self-educated man from the working classes, Hofmann was a distinctive figure in the higher reaches of German public librarianship where almost everyone else could sign himself "Doktor." He was possessed of an enormous energy, and under his leadership Leipzig became a national center of public librarianship, with a school and national professional institute in addition to a major library. The Neue Richtung is in many ways the more intellectually interesting of the two.

Where the Alte Richtung looked to England and the United States for inspiration, the Neue Richtung worshiped Germanness. The Alte Richtung stressed the individual, the Neue Richtung thought in collective terms such as "The Public" or "The Bourgeois Housewife." "Volkish" ideas were an important strand in Hofmann's thinking. The Alte Richtung saw education as a process, the means by which an individual could achieve full humanity. To the Neue Richtung education was a product, to be purveyed to the library user.

Although the two groups agreed that libraries should have good books, their respective views on library collections had little in common. The Alte Richtung regarded culture as diverse; while not happy that readers wanted light entertainment, they would make some effort to satisfy that demand in the hope of later guiding users to worthier reading. They were willing, even eager to include nonbook materials if that was what it took to reach some of the library's public. Ackerknecht at Stettin pioneered public library involvement with films early in the 1920s. Hofmann, on the other hand, held that culture had only one form. In his collections *only* good books were welcome. He emphasized the value of the classical German authors.

Attitudes to readers' advising reflect these different opinions. The Hofmannian readers' advisor was a teacher; it was his task to guide the reader to educationally appropriate books. The Alte Richtung did not articulate a position of its own on this subject, but it is clear from the numerous objections to Hofmann's ideas that its adherents favored a far less didactic, less structured approach. For them there was a greater difference between the school's version of education and the library's.

The dissension between Alte and Neue Richtung was the product of differing philosophies, values, and experiences, but style and personality also played important parts. Where the Alte Richtung was pragmatic and unsystematic in its thinking, Hofmann preferred the formal logic and argument so characteristic of German philosophy. With justice, the Alte Richtung accused him of rigidity. Hofmann was combative and constantly on the offensive, something of an intriguer.

The gulf that divided the two groups was wide and deep in 1933. Younger librarians had made an effort to bridge it toward the end of the 1920s, but animosities remained. The stage was set for an externally imposed solution. National socialism provided it.

The seizure of power by the Nazis in January 1933 immediately rendered the *Richtungsstreit* irrelevant. Within days the new ordering of public libraries had begun. Action characterized the Nazi approach to public librarianship, just as it did to all governance. The main lines of a public library program quickly began to emerge, sometimes through word, but more often by deed. The year 1933 was hectic for libraries: Censorship began; the Prussian ministry responsible for education successfully asserted its claim to jurisdiction of public libraries, over the Propaganda Ministry; the need for appropriate professional preparation in addition to political acceptability was affirmed; and a Prussian library agency was created. In 1934 the new Reichsschrifttumskammer incorporated the former organization of public librarians, the first step in the organization's gradual disappearance; a new professional journal replaced the two former journals; the Prussian Ministry of Education became the Reich Ministry of Education; and Heinz Dähnhardt was appointed to a new position with responsibility for adult education and public libraries in the new Reich ministry. The next year, 1935, saw a local government ordinance passed that assigned responsibility for cultural institutions to communities; the Prussian library agency became the Reich library agency; Franz Schriewer replaced Wilhelm Schuster, who had guided the profession's transition to national socialism, as director of the agency; and a second, more systematic wave of censorship removed still more books from collections. After that the pace of change declined. National guidelines were formulated in 1937, and Schriewer resigned as head of the Reich library agency. A library development plan was prepared for the Reich. In 1938 the development plan was formally mandated and its anti-Catholic purpose publicized. The war began in 1939, bringing new tasks and problems. A year later Catholic libraries were ordered to remove all nonreligious writings, destroying an important branch of community library service and bringing new responsibilities to the public libraries. From then until the defeat of the Third Reich the story was a simple one of diminishing resources and increasing difficulties.

German public librarianship has attracted relatively little scholarly interest, although that situation is gradually changing. The organization of the Wolfenbütteler Arbeitskreis für Bibliotheksgeschichte, a society devoted to library history, has institutionalized interest in the topic; its meetings offer an informed and serious audience for scholarly presentations. The session of 1988 and a supplementary session in 1989 both had as their theme librarianship under the Nazis.[8] The Fachhochschule für Bibliothekswesen in Stuttgart has begun to collect the personal papers of important librarians. As academic study in librarianship expands and more and more public librarians work toward a doctorate, the numbers of potentially interested parties increase steadily.

Another stimulus has been the appearance of some foundational works. In 1978 a general history of German public libraries was published. Some major aspects, such as the Bücherhallenbewegung, have been treated extensively. The West German public library journal, *Buch und Bibliothek*, has published a number of important scholarly articles on the subject. Significant work is also going on in East Germany, as, for example, that of Wolfgang Mühle and Felicitas Marwinski.

With respect to the Nazi period, the seminal work was a collection of documents edited by Friedrich Andrae, the librarian of the Hamburger Öffentliche Bücherhallen, that came out in 1970. A few reminiscences had previously appeared, but German librarians obviously had little interest in recalling this painful time and too many other urgent matters demanding their attention. The document collection sparked the interest of a younger generation, and several treatments of one or another feature of Nazi public library policy soon followed. In 1986 a monograph on public librarianship in Nazi Germany by Engelbrecht Boese treated the subject comprehensively from the German point of view.[9]

This book is the first discussion in English of public libraries under the Nazis, apart from a few contemporary comments on events in Germany by U.S. and English librarians. It covers all aspects of public librarianship, treating the governmental agencies responsible for public libraries, the internal operations of the libraries and their programs, the education of public librarians, and their professional organization and activities. Constantly in the background is the question of how librarians responded and were affected in human terms. German public librarianship is considered in the larger context of public librarianship in the world, taking cognizance of librarianship in other totalitarian countries, but especially of public librarianship in the English-speaking lands that have always been the leaders in this area.

Library history is an expression of the growth of interest in the cultural institutions that help shape the values and outlook of a people, a product of a heightened awareness of the inseparability of cultural values and political issues so obvious in our own times. The products of culture—the great books, poems, and symphonies—have been objects of study for centuries, but only recently have scholars begun to look at the social, economic, and institutional aspects of culture. Scholarly attention to popular culture parallels this new approach. The study of public libraries is an aspect of both.

The Nazi attempt to take over German public libraries is a subject at which several important historiographical questions intersect. In library history one of the most heated debates has been the extent to which public libraries have been instruments of social manipulation. The Nazi public library was the ultimate expression in theoretical terms of the library as a means of influence; the relationship to practice of this theory reveals something essential about the nature of the public library. In German historiography, a major issue has been whether nazism represented an aberration from German traditions or whether it was a logical development of those same traditions. Was the Nazi "revolution" a true revolution, with the massive reorientation of values, institutions, and individuals that that implies, or was it simply a power grab? The experiences of German public libraries illuminate these questions and illustrate even more directly the revolution in action, since the library itself was used as a mechanism of reorientation.

The history of Nazi public libraries offers some clarification of other questions as well. What, if any, were the sources of resistance to nazism? What was the relationship between central government, which essentially defined library policy, and local government, which implemented it and paid for it? What was the role of the party in this governmental activity? Were real changes made in librarianship and real gains achieved, or was the only reality of public librarianship, as it was for so many Nazi programs, publicity announcements in the *Völkischer Beobachter* and local newspapers.

From the vantage point of the historian of libraries the relevant questions are somewhat different. What were the values and priorities of German librarians, and how were they modified by nazism? How did a profession based on the proudest traditions of humanism lend itself to a system that was the antithesis of everything humane? In what way did Nazi views about the proper role of women affect this profession that was led by men, but in which most of the practitioners were women?

The Nazi period was dramatic, destructive, revolutionary, a critical phase in the development of German public libraries. To serve the ends of national socialism the new regime brought an institution adrift in a backwater into the mainstream. It ignored its past, erased its traditions, and challenged its professional ethos; public librarianship was redirected and transformed. Many positive achievements

11

can be credited to this time; Boese views it as an essential stage of modernization. But the history of the period also has all the elements of classic tragedy—pride, conflict with a superior force, and a disastrous outcome. In 1945 Nazi public librarianship was, like the regime it served, totally bankrupt. Little except ashes and rubble remained of its libraries. The worst damage, however, had come from within.

CHAPTER TWO

The Nazi Idea
of the
Public Library

WHEN THE National Socialists took control of Germany in January 1933, they owed their success to their political skill and to propitious circumstances. Few people, then or now, regarded that power seizure as the ineluctable triumph of a philosophy whose time had come; Germans acquiesced, not because they believed in national socialism, but because they wanted change. It is, indeed, questionable whether the Nazis had a philosophy. Certainly, the miscellany of slogans that passed for ideas among them was hardly either comprehensive or systematic. The wide-ranging emotional appeal of these ill-assorted, often incoherent pronouncements made them an effective political platform, but they provided only a limited theoretical foundation for the governance of a complex modern society.

What nazism offered was a collection of themes, many of which reflected the political alliances that had gone into the forging of the party. With one of the party's tenets being faith in action rather than reason, little energy went into abstract thought, and there is no document or documents that serve as an intellectual manifesto. *Mein Kampf*, the Nazi answer to Marx's *Das Kapital*, does not impart any organized system, but it does at least mention most of the themes in passing. The importance of racial purity, the dangers of racial impurity, veneration of all things German, glorification of militarism, the Volk as the foundation of the nation, and preference for rural over urban life are all present in Hitler's treatise.[1]

Although some historians have questioned how genuine the Nazi

13

dedication to volkish theory was, the idea of the Volk remains an important central organizing principle of nazism. Certainly, its annexation by nazism was what guaranteed immortality to volkish thinking. As Hitler stated in *Mein Kampf*, "from the basic ideas of a general folkish world conception the National Socialist German Workers' Party takes over the fundamental traits, and from them, with due consideration of practical reality, the times and the available human material as well as its weaknesses, forms a political creed which in turn, by the strict organizational integration of large human masses thus made possible, creates the precondition for the victorious struggle of this world view."[2]

The idea of the Volk was developed by Herder, Hegel, and some of the romantic philosophers. Herder was the first to replace the classical political-juridical state with the concept of an organic folknation. He could not define the Volk, but he wrote of a living organic force that fashioned organic units from the chaos of homogeneous matter. The place of the individual was derived from his connection with the folk heritage and the folk community.[3]

Karl Friedrich Schlegel made the Volk, as described by Herder, the basis of the nation, and the ideal nation was one that embraced all descendants of one tribe or members of one Volk. Schelling saw metaphysics as the means by which a mass of human beings could become of one heart and of one mind; that is, a Volk. In Schelling's writings we can also perceive the tendency to sacrifice the individual for the totality of the Volk, a concept the Nazis used the motto "Gemeinnutz vor Eigennutz" (the common good before individual good) to inculcate. All these ideas were brought together by Hegel and expressed in a form in which they had great influence. The basis of Hegel's nation was the Volk; he taught that "the Volk as state is the spirit in its substantial rationality and direct reality, hence the absolute power on earth." In the *Philosophy of History* he wrote, "The individuals vanish for the universal substantial [the folk spirit or the state], and this forms for itself the individuals which it requires for its own purposes."[4]

These mystical, magniloquent ideas were widespread in Germany and were to be found in groups across the political spectrum. Under national socialism, however, they became part of the basis of governance. The earliest statement of the party, the program of 1920, declared that "none but members of the nation may be citizens of the State. None but those of German blood, whatever their creed, may be members of the nation." It called for the creation of a strong central power and for unquestioned authority for the politically centralized parliament.[5]

After nazism became the official state philosophy, its rather crudely worded, undeveloped principles were elaborated and expanded. The idea of the Volk was repeated relentlessly, but with only minor variations. Ernst Rudolf Huber, the constitutional lawyer, made it central as he defined Nazi constitutional theory.

> In contrast to the state, the people form a true organism—a being which leads its own life and follows its own laws, which possesses powers peculiar to itself, and which develops its own nature independent of state forms. . . . This living unity of the people has its cells in its individual members, and just as in every body there are certain cells to perform certain tasks, this is likewise the case in the body of the people. The individual is bound to his people not only physically, but mentally and spiritually and he is influenced by these ties in all his manifestations.[6]

In the theory of the volkish Reich, people and state were conceived of as inseparable. Huber defined the state as a function of the Volk, molded out of itself as the form in which it achieved historic permanence. "It is the form in which the people attains to historical reality. It is the bearer of the historical continuity of the people which remains the same in the center of its being in spite of all changes, revolutions, and transformations."[7]

What made a Volk was beyond logical comprehension, but among the most important factors was shared blood. People were shaped by the lands they inhabited; Germany's central position between East and West determined the nature of the German people and the historical purpose of state activity. Their sense of a common destiny reinforced the sense of unity.

The Nazi version of volkish theory incorporated the idea of racial supremacy and a particularly virulent form of anti-Semitism. Other volkish groups were anti-Semitic, but nazism brought it to new heights. *Mein Kampf* is riddled with diatribes of hatred directed at the Jews; the Jews were held responsible for every evil from poverty to venereal disease. The official Nazi program excluded Jews from

15

the nation and then required membership in the nation for participation in social and economic life.

If the first pillar of national socialism was the concept of the Volk, the second was that of the *Führer*, or leader. Like the idea of the Volk, the idea of the Führer was a familiar theme of nineteenth-century German politicians and political theorists. The longing for a leader was rooted in the desire to have someone to follow: to whom could be attached feelings of loyalty; for whom the individual could sacrifice; and in whom one could believe. Huber gave the Nazi concept of the Führer its clearest exposition. "The Führer-Reich of the [German] people is founded on the recognition that the true will of the people cannot be disclosed through parliamentary votes and plebiscites but that the will of the people in its pure and uncorrupted form can only be expressed through the Führer." The Führer was independent of all groups and associations and had unlimited authority.[8]

In contrast to the idea of the Führer, the office of Führer had developed out of the Nazi party movement. It was originally not a state office but a party one and became part of the structure of the Reich only when the Führer took over the Office of Chancellor and then assumed the position of head of state. "The Führer unites in himself all the sovereign authority of the Reich; all public authority in the state as well as in the movement is derived from the authority of the Führer." He was infallible and required complete obedience.[9]

Most other Nazi themes are corollaries to the ideas of Volk and Führer. It was a very small step from asserting the importance of the Volk to asserting the superiority of the *German* Volk. All things German were automatically superior to all things not German, German being a flexibly interpreted characteristic. One application was the veneration of the rural life because it was held to embody German values in an especially pure form. By definition the peasantry were heroes.

Glorification of Germanness progressed naturally to imperialism. Mankind has long accepted that the superior receive a disproportionate share of the resources and rewards of a society because this arrangement works to benefit everyone. The Nazis generalized this to a nation. Military might was the way to enforce this view on nations who did not agree. A militarism more aggressive and more universal than that of Wilhelmine Germany was a constituent element of nazism.

Of equal importance with the ideas of nazism are its anti-ideas. Nazism was against communism, parliamentarianism, foreigners, Jews, and capitalism. It repudiated liberal ideas without offering anything in their place. It carried the romantic rejection of the excesses of rationalism one step further and rejected rationalism itself. It denied the fundamental principle of democracy, the equality of individuals. It discarded traditional moral and religious concepts about the nature of man and his essential human dignity, an act that had its logical consequence in the death camps. These negations removed some of the strongest individual and societal safeguards evolved by Western civilization.

Nazi cultural policy was as shallow as its political ideology. On the whole, Nazi leaders were not particularly well educated and had little more than superficial interest in art, literature, or music. Only if culture produced politically desirable results did it have worth. Under nazism the writer was reduced to one task, "to mold Germans to make them irresistible."[10]

Mein Kampf has very little to say on the subject of culture, despite Hitler's own artistic leanings. To the extent that Hitler treats culture as a concept, he treats it as a symbol of the nation. He complains that modern German cities, in contrast to those of the ancient world, lack the outstanding symbol of the national community, and that the national community sees no symbol of itself in the cities. A reference to the classical idea of *mens sana in corpore sano* is interposed between a diatribe on prostitution and syphilis and one on the ill health of German art and theater in which futurism, cubism, and dadaism are singled out for special denunciation. The reader is presumably supposed to draw an analogy between the individual and the nation, thus making culture into a kind of collective mind. The party program adds virtually nothing on the subject of culture, and the explanation by Gottfried Feder, one of the program's framers, is meaningless: "Our cultural aim is that all the sciences and fine arts shall flourish on the basis of a politically free, economically healthy state."[11]

Education also received minimal attention. Hitler declared, "If as the first task of the state in the service and for the welfare of its nationality we recognize the preservation, care, and development of the best racial elements, it is natural that this care must not only extend to the birth of every little national and racial comrade, but that it must educate the young offspring to become a valuable link in the chain of reproduction."[12] Nazism valued education, but education in a very special sense. Nazi education's first consideration was the breeding of healthy bodies and the promotion of forceful spirits. Mere knowledge, geniuses, and intellectuals were derided; courage, self-confidence, physical strength, and willpower praised. It was these latter qualities Nazi education was to foster, rather than burdening youthful minds with dates and declensions that would never be used. Only incidentally was education an intellectual process; ideas were largely limited to political conditioning.

After the Nazi takeover there was some effort to amplify these assertions to provide a better basis for educational or cultural decisions. In his speech to the Reichstag on March 23, 1933, outlining the new government's plans, Hitler promised that the government would conduct a moral purging as thorough as its intended political purging. All cultural institutions, the educational system, theater, cinema, literature, press, and radio, would be used as a means to that end and valued accordingly. Hitler declared, "They must all serve for the maintenance of the eternal values present in the essential character of our people." Blood and race were "once more" to be the source of artistic intuition. The government would assure that the nation's will to live found more-forceful cultural expression.[13]

A speech published in 1934 vowed great attention to the care of culture. Hitler decried foreign influence and warned those decadent artists now trying to present themselves as flag bearers of the National Socialist future. Culture was the expression of inner experience and must not endanger healthy thought in the Volk. A politically heroic age—Nazi Germany was by definition politically heroic—should seek to build bridges to the past by drawing upon it for artistic inspiration.[14]

Emphasis on what was culturally abhorrent was the expression in cultural terms of the hostility that was so much a part of national socialism. It gave cultural activity an inherent dynamism. In 1935 Hitler supplied a definitive list of the state's cultural enemies: rootless

18

bourgeois intellectuals; those who nostalgically looked backward rather than advocated progress; volkish ideologues; and opportunists. Aggression dominates a treatise on culture in 1940. The author proclaims the need to destroy bourgeois culture and describes the cultural "fighter" as "neither scholar nor philosopher, but only a soldier." Even culture could be militarized.[15]

Because cultural laws such as that establishing the Reichsschrifttumskammer left the definition of guiding principles to political bodies and leaders, they brought little coherence to the confusion. Their main contribution to clarity was the unequivocal assertion of the supremacy of the state in cultural affairs. In the National Socialist state "culture is an affair of the nation. It is a means for spiritual leadership and requires, therefore, to be positively manipulated that all may be educated to a sense of responsibility that promotes the shaping of the nation." There was no room for nonconformity.[16]

Painting and architecture were Hitler's preferred cultural forms, and literature, books, and reading received little attention from Nazi leaders, either before or after the *Machtergreifung*. Contempt for learning, of which the book is a symbol, combined with a reverence for the physical, further contributed to neglect. The Nazis understood that for their purposes the book was relatively ineffectual. As a cultural medium, the book suffered from the fact that its influence is likely to be slow and indirect. The nature of the act of reading encourages thought and reflection, undesirable activities in Nazi eyes. Because it has a more direct impact and evokes an immediate response, the spoken word was held in much higher esteem. Radio and film were the media of interest rather than the book.[17]

A fundamental ambivalence thus lies at the heart of all Nazi statements on the theme "reading is good." After the Machtergreifung librarians tried to portray Hitler as a lover of books by citing his statement that he had read widely on social issues. To make this likeness credible, they had to ignore his explanation of "correct" reading, which he defined as studying a book or magazine, immediately perceiving by instinct what is worth permanently remembering. Only this kind of reading, "organized along the lines of life," had meaning and purpose. They also had to ignore that for the Führer the only literature of any significance was political.[18] The poster for Book Week in 1936 illustrates their problem. It printed at the top the fol-

19

lowing quotation from Hitler: "Except for my architecture, the rare visit to an opera, I had books as my only friends. I then read insatiably and fundamentally. In a few years I created the basis of a knowledge on which I still draw."[19]

Joseph Goebbels, who as minister of propaganda was concerned more directly with the life of the mind, offered somewhat more useful grist. His oration inaugurating the book burnings of May 1933, in which he condemned what filled the libraries as Jewish asphalt literature,[20] post-Versailles rubbish and trash, and promised its replacement with German writings, was by implication a tribute to the power of the book. At the opening of Book Week two years later, Goebbels officially endorsed the book as a medium despite the indirect impression it made: "We recognize very well the immense, wideranging influence the book can achieve." He then spent some time elaborating on the theme that writers and thinkers had a vital role in the new state. He concluded by urging his hearers to "hold fast to the German book and treasure it as the valuable repository of our German spirit!" To Goebbels, librarians were indebted for the slogan "The book—the sword of the German spirit," a phrase that adorned many placards and publicity materials.[21]

For the most part, however, the redefinition of the public library in Nazi terms was left to the profession. No high-level party leader ever appears to have extolled libraries per se. It was the responsibility of librarians to apply the themes of nazism to the context of the public library, incorporating the few tributes they could cull on books and reading. Necessary if they were to survive, this task offered at the same time a great opportunity. Many prominent librarians used the occasion to try to ingratiate themselves with the new regime.

Imposition of a common philosophical basis had the immediate effect of terminating the Richtungsstreit abruptly. Old quarrels lost their relevance as members of the Alte and Neue Richtung competed to demonstrate their conversion to the new faith. To some extent this proceeding was the substitution of one form of incoherence for another, but, for better or worse, all models of the public library in the Third Reich were, at least in theory, built upon the same intellectual foundation of national socialism.

The attempt to offer a new-model public library required the repudiation of much of the old model. Librarians echoed the party's rejection of Weimar and all it represented. Perhaps most fundamentally, they abjured the Western tradition of humanism with its emphasis on the individual, although library service is inherently individualized. They scorned neutrality, a concept with many direct applications to the practice of librarianship. The pre-Nazi public library was execrated as a "bourgeois" institution, less on the grounds that it served the reading and information needs of the middle class than because it was one of their charitable activities. It conferred on the lower classes as a gift what should have been theirs by right and indoctrinated them with the wrong ideas.[22]

Rejecting neutrality was one aspect of the most striking change the National Socialist revolution brought to librarianship. Suddenly, the public library was a political institution in a totalitarian state dedicated to the creation of an unthinking, chauvinistic population. This politicization was more than a new orientation; it immediately became the ethos of the public library, an all-pervasive influence that informed and shaped its character. As the decree of December 1933, the first major edict of the new era relating to public libraries, put it: "All public libraries are to work in the spirit of the National Socialist state."[23]

Constant reiteration of the primacy of the political testifies to the magnitude of the change and its drastic character. Politicization was something to be recognized, accepted, and advocated. Franz Schriewer, a leading librarian of the time, was forthright: "The public library is a political library today, which word is to be understood in its breadth; that is, the public library is to be oriented to the Volk and state." In 1937 an article in a Braunschweig newspaper went so far as to say that the public library was *not* concerned with literature but was a *political* institution. More usually, however, statements were couched in terms that were both less uncompromising and less clear. Phrases that described the public library as a "cultural-political intermediary" were common.[24] This same insistence on the political character of the public library is the foundation of Soviet public librarianship.[25]

Librarians tried to use the heightened emphasis on political ends for their own purposes. One of their more extreme claims was that the public library was an important means of making the German people a world Volk of the first rank. More significant was the argument that to carry out its responsibilities of political education, the public library had to become a public responsibility. If libraries were a public responsibility, then they would be supported by tax revenues.[26]

How genuinely this reorientation was accepted is questionable. In private, librarians sometimes expressed the desire to keep the library apart from politics, an act that would have rejected the claims of the totalitarian state. Some tried to treat politics as a frame for their work, rather than the informing principle. Whether even those who advocated a political character for the library actually believed what they wrote is highly questionable; much was written for public consumption and recognized as such.

The new political public library incorporated the idea of the Führer as a separate and distinct component. It was one more means to bind the Führer and his people together. It could be conceived of as existing to serve the will of the Führer.[27]

The idea of education, however, remained fundamental to the concept of the public library. The familiar phrase "the purpose of the public library is education, not entertainment" was intoned on many occasions. Although there were many variations within that idea, librarians invariably used for their activity the word *Bildung*, a term meaning education in the sense of intellectual development, rather than *Schulung*, which is education in the sense of training.[28] At the official opening of the model Dietrich-Eckart-Bücherei in 1935 Bernhard Rust, the minister of education, whose department had jurisdiction over public libraries, declared: "Under liberalism our public libraries were warehouses. Under Marxism they looked at the destruction of everything truly German. National socialism has learned from both sides. Our public libraries are educational institutions." With this one statement Rust simultaneously affirmed what was then at issue in a power struggle between the Ministry of Education and the Ministry of Propaganda—that public libraries were indeed educational; rejected both democratic and Marxist definitions of the past; and allied himself with the dead Nazi hero-poet Dietrich Eckart to whom Hitler had dedicated *Mein Kampf*. Eckart had maintained, "The essence of the revolution is not the seizure of power but the education of men."[29]

Asserting that the primary purpose of the public library was education required some clarification. Education in Nazi terms meant education to the ideas of nazism and contradicted everything that German education had previously been. In 1934 Wilhelm Schuster, the president of the Verband Deutscher Volksbibliothekare (VDV, or Association of German Public Librarians), attempted to explain National Socialist education to the humanistically trained librarians. Education began with the ordering and classification of (German) mankind: "It places men in a particular place in the totality of the Volk, organizes them into a state and volkish structure, orders them there with respect to other men, and classifies them there with respect to other men. From this begins duties and rights." In this place it was possible for men to experience the idea of this ordering and to become conscious of it. They would therefore go further in the double direction of duties and rights.

For Schuster, education was the key to the individual and societal renewal the revolution promised. From this ordering would arise "a completely new moral code, a new and stronger placement of friend and foe, the joining of Führer and society, a new law of society and property, a new idea of guilt and punishment, of obligation to devotion, sacrifice, and action." He emphasized that this new model made ethical considerations central, but again, it was ethical with a difference. The new ethos discarded traditional Christian and humanistic features or gave them a new interpretation; ethical now meant ready for action, willing to sacrifice, loyal, like the Führer, and bound to the Volk.[30]

Soon after, Schriewer, in a comprehensive article that sought both to define the public library and to state what it ought to be, also addressed the issue of education. Schriewer's thesis is clear from the first statement he made under the heading "Educational Direction": "The public library is a political public library." But politics in a narrow sense is not sufficient; the public library should be concerned with basic political forces. Constant political dissemination and penetration, the strengthening of the political will, are necessary. Schriewer takes the rejection of an individualistic idea of education as a given. In a statement obviously directed at a general perception, he protests that this rejection does not mean that moral development

23

is not valued in comparison to the idea of state and Volk. It is, in fact, completely false to establish a dichotomy between collective and individual education.[31]

Education was further defined by negation. Heinz Dähnhardt, the official in charge of the public library section within the Ministry of Education, repudiated *Überpädagogisierung*, an overly pedagogical approach to librarianship. The book was not an object to be enthroned and admired. This negative assertion is closely akin to the repudiation of the public library as a scholarly library in miniature, a view public librarians had been disavowing since the 1890s.[32]

These new definitions of education rested on the new theory of man: Man achieves humanity only in the context of the Volk. Librarians used the term *Volk* as a catchword, a mystical, vague notion that yet had the force of a creed. The conception of the Volk was one theme of nazism that could be integrated relatively easily into theories of the public library. It had, after all, been a vital element in the thinking of Walter Hofmann, leader of the Neue Richtung. The advent of nazism changed only the degree of prominence; what had been one strand among many became a constant presence, intrinsic to all discussion. The ubiquity began with the name of the public library itself, Volksbücherei or *Volksbibliothek*, where Volk was a defining element. Rust used this semantic asset to claim "high authority" for the library, aligning it with the power of the larger concept.[33]

To some extent, *Volk* was a word ceaselessly reiterated in Nazi Germany to invoke convenient associations, and many uses of it by librarians do not bear rigorous scrutiny. They wrote of the need to develop a healthy volkish culture, of the need to strengthen the Volk intellectually and spiritually. They maintained that the public library belongs to the Volk, that its central idea was the volkish worldview. They described the library as grounded in the living spirit of the Volk.

The idea of the Volk is more, however, than empty words and phrases, even if it often failed to surpass that level of discourse. At its root is the assertion that collective society takes priority over the individual. This postulate could be used as a basis for a theory of public librarianship. Simplistic formulations appeared immediately. In a 1933 article in *Soziale Praxis* Dr. Rudolf Reuter, director of the Cologne (Ger. Köln) public library, contended that the public library was an important means to help members of the Volk achieve their highest potential, that highest potential being a worthwhile member of the Volk. The statement of Georg Narcisz was equally direct: He argued that education of the Volk must precede that of the individual. Interestingly, his views sound like a rejection of Reuter's. Narcisz claimed that the old free adult education had mistakenly sought to achieve the solidarity of the Volk through education of the individual. New librarians must recognize that precisely the opposite was the correct way: The politics of the Volk must always have first place in the cultural area. The positions of Reuter and Narcisz can be reconciled only if Reuter's member of the Volk is deprived of all individuality.[34]

Two years later Schriewer offered a more complex analysis. He began by asserting that "the determination of the nature [of the public library] proceeds from the original idea *Volk*, not from the summation of the individual classes and social strata. In the public library the Volk as an idea is powerful." He dissociated the library from the historic tradition of folklore. For Schriewer the core of the idea of Volk is philosophic, rooted in race and soil, yet at the same time he attempted to extend the idea beyond the peasantry, stressing that it was more than regional nostalgia and genealogy. Too much emphasis on parts of the Volk led to particularism and was regression to the individualistic epoch. Bearers of "Völkishness" could be found in all classes and the idea spanned all occupations. Völkishness was not a form but an inner working force and a principle that always applied. It could not be completely understood in rational terms; it was a matter of inner belonging.[35]

Underlying many of the attempts to assert and delineate the volkish character of the public library was the notion of unity. The public library was one more instrument to bind the Volk together. In general terms, it was to serve educational and cultural unity. More specifically, it was to bring together the educated and uneducated. Fritz Heiligenstaedt, director of the provincial library administration for Hanover (Ger. Hannover) until he became the director of the national library organization in 1937, described it as "the intellectual meeting place and collecting room of the nation."[36] This goal is also the goal of Soviet public librarianship, although it derives from a completely different theoretical basis and is interpreted quite differently.

Unity also appears in discussions of the public library in a very different sense. The public library itself was to achieve wholeness, to mirror the ordering, or rather absence of ordering, of the Volk. As Dähnhardt expressed it in a speech to a meeting of librarians in Würzburg: "Today this is our goal: the establishment of a unified, good and thoroughly prepared institution, the creation of a native public library-organism, a model." His use of the term *organism* is significant, both because it was another Nazi catchword, intended to prompt ideas of life and health, and because it implied wholeness.[37]

If it is generally accepted that the main purpose of the National Socialist public library was to facilitate the *Volkwerdung*—that is, the becoming of a Volk—of the German people, this formulation nonetheless left many details unspecified. One of the most important "details" was how the library was to accomplish this task. Although programs and procedures were frequently described, such discussions generally lacked a theoretical framework. Because the change in purpose brought by the revolution was not matched by any corresponding change in methods, much pre-Nazi thinking on procedural matters remained valid, and much undoubtedly was taken for granted.

Most discussions of the way in which the public library was to fulfil its goals assumed that the book would be the principal, if not the only, means. Consideration rarely went beyond the most general terms. Typical pronouncements were that the public library was to strengthen the Volk intellectually and spiritually through the book, or that the public library was to advance the reading of the Volk.

Schriewer's exhortation that the public library was to offer spiritual value, intellectual support, and practical help in living gave somewhat more guidance. Writing in 1938, Karl Taupitz, director of the provincial library administration in Saxony (Ger. Sachsen), an industrial region, elaborated on Schriewer's summary and somewhat extended it. The book improves the cultural, political, and economic position of the German Volk; it maintains and expands the capabilities of industries. The book serves external needs, but also those of the inner life of men. The right book is a helper and advisor on philosophic concerns and on questions of faith. Through it, the character of a man is formed and shaped and he is helped to find his place as a member of, and comrade in, the German volkish society. The public library disseminates this all-efficacious book in a regular way.[38]

Implicit in discussions of method is the question of intensity. How zealously should the public library prosecute its business? To this issue the Nazis brought a policy and tradition of activism, a characteristic they shared with the Soviets. The Nazi brand of activism may have been shallow and unthinking, but to the often dusty, somnolent world of public librarianship it brought a much needed breath of fresh air. Statements such as "the public library is a repository of the words of our ancestors" or "the public library is a storehouse of culture" could still be found in articles written during the Nazi period, but librarians were given new responsibilities, too, and expected to carry them out with energy. No longer were they to be passive keepers of the flame of German culture. Instead, "the German public librarian of our day should bring together reader and book. Prior to this, he has the duty and obligation to familiarize himself with the output of German writing and to organize it. Then, as his highest responsibility, he is to influence the readership philosophically and to lead them." A library that was a mere warehouse was not fulfilling its purpose. One unfortunate library earned the ultimate put-down when it was dismissed as a "cemetery" after it spent all its money on a new building.[39]

Changes in style and vigor were among the most notable changes brought by nazism. Perhaps their clearest expression was in a presentation made by the director of the Westphalian provincial library administration to a conference of local librarians in the fall of 1933. The new library had to become "more strongly directive, more strongly active, than the old, more strongly authoritative and—corresponding to the National Socialist principle of leadership—more strongly responsible in its work." With each iteration of "more strongly" the sense of forcefulness heightens until the phrase is almost an incantation.[40]

Regular employment of military terminology further enhanced the air of increased intensity. Time and time again, the book or the library was referred to as a weapon. On one occasion Dähnhardt characterized the library as a "weapon in the volkish life battle"; Schriewer called it "a defensive weapon against the spirit of Western civilization." It was considered a part of the educational "front."[41]

Although this chapter is titled "The Nazi Idea of the Public Library," it could equally well have been called "Ideas about the Public Library during the Nazi Period" or something similar that would emphasize the variations and complexities within thinking about the purpose and nature of public libraries. Diversity did exist. Schuster and Schriewer, for example, had different foundations for their views on education, Schuster's being traditional humanistic goals, Schriewer's a very practical, life-oriented approach. A general description also fails to bring out the different qualifications individuals made. No position other than that the library was a political instrument was possible in print, but debate continued over just how political it should be. With an eye to working-class readers, Karl Kossow argued that in the reading rooms of large-city public libraries political books should not be allowed to supplant instructional (presumably a euphemism for apolitical) nonfiction. Schriewer declared that if a work did not oppose national socialism, it should be allowed in the library.[42]

The importance of such distinctions depends upon the viewpoint of the individual. Contemporaries severed friendships and built careers on them. Fifty years later, however, the similarities and the results seem more significant than the differences.

Normally, variation develops as time passes, as well as being present between individual thinkers. Did the Nazi idea of the public library change over time? This is a problematic question because the answer varies with what is being considered. Because the profession was so small, few wrote on what the nature and purpose of the public library were. Opinions divide more naturally into Schuster's, Schriewer's, or Hofmann's than they do into early, middle, and late. An author had more in common with his own earlier writings than one publication did with others of a given year. The shortness of the Nazi period, a mere twelve years, of which five were wartime, militates against long-term development. On the other hand, programs and actions defined an increasingly politicized public library, but it was a conception that emerged out of practice, not literature.

Theoretical writing on the nature and purpose of public libraries too often has, to all except initiates, the appearance of being preoccupied with minor differences. It had this effect on Heinz Dähnhardt, whose opinion was of some consequence. In 1937 he, as the ministry official responsible for public librarianship in the Reich Ministry of Education, undertook to present an official version. He contended that the task of the public library could be derived neither from the professional nor from the traditional, conventional bases: It had to develop from, and be established upon, the political. "The German public library possesses no pedagogical autonomy and therefore may no longer, as it was earlier, be considered as the independent place of rendezvous of the intellect. Still less may it represent itself as a neutral no-man's-land between the philosophical fronts of the present. . . . The public library is today a weapon in the folkish life battle and therefore a political institution." His pronouncement hardly clarified the issue or treated it with any complexity, but it did at least stand as the official word on the subject.[43]

One may also criticize thinking about public libraries during the Nazi period in rational terms. Because it is rooted in a disorderly, often contradictory miscellany of ideas, thought on public librarianship is inevitably disorderly and contradictory. To deplore this want of logic, however, is to miss the essence. Nazism did not seek to cultivate reason, a commodity too easily turned against it, but instead appealed to emotion. Like the members of other professions, librarians attempting to accommodate librarianship to nazism sought to develop proper beliefs and feelings. Speeches and articles were almost invariably hortatory and inspirational. Words were piled on words, encouraging listeners or readers to suspend their critical faculties. The total impression was what mattered, not individual elements.

The speech made by Wilhelm Schuster, president of the VDV, to the association at its first conference after the takeover, in September 1933, provides an excellent illustration of this approach.[44] At the same time it conveys the flavor of the Nazi idea of the public library more accurately and more tellingly than does systematic examination. It was a speech planned to serve Schuster's personal ends by demonstrating his conversion to the new, and to assert his leadership, but it also tried to make a definitive intellectual statement.

Schuster began with a pious genuflection to the Nazi revolution: "Since we met in our last general convention, our Volk has had the great experience for which they and their state have been destined for centuries, the National Socialist revolution, and the beginning of the great struggle for freedom, which it will be the task of us and our sons to bring to a successful conclusion. In it lies the meaning and purpose of our most distant life and by it our work is determined." He then outlined the task ahead in very general terms. The librarian has to bring the skeptical, the uninvolved, and the many who had mindlessly cheered the flags and symbols of the revolution to an appreciation of its deeper meaning. The loyal and true also needed intellectual support. The motto of the society should be "Education to National Socialism."

Schuster urged his listeners to be inspired by German youth, by "its bold and pure will, its simple straightforwardness, its faithful loyalty to the chosen Führer, its unity despite all separating barriers, and the caste spirit of which it has taken possession." He called upon them for work, devotion, and sacrifice. His exhortation—"If you wish something professionally from us, show us what you have already done for the profession and what you can do for it"—anticipates John Kennedy's "Ask not what your country can do for you, ask what you can do for your country."

The mood established, Schuster then made a number of unconnected assertions that were often only tenuously related to his theme of "The Public Library and National Socialism"; among them, the public library was an important unit in the movement for National Socialist education. The librarian had the sacred responsibility to preserve the purity of the new educational ideals. Readers had faith in the leadership of the librarian. National Socialist thought was all-encompassing. National socialism unified philosophy and life.

Schuster touched on the task of the public library and declared its distinctiveness from the scholarly library. He affirmed yet again that entertainment was a legitimate function of the public library and denounced asphalt literature in passing. Rural life received its tribute. Schuster concluded with Hitler's words to the Nuremberg (Ger. Nürnberg) party rally, endorsing the importance of culture.

None of these ideas is important in itself; few of them were not already familiar to the audience. What was different was the way in which the political permeated the professional and took precedence over all other considerations. What was important was how nazism was treated as a religion, demanding total dedication.[45] Schuster's speech was a harangue, and even after decades its impact is emotional rather than intellectual. It was a harbinger of what was to come in librarianship and was absolutely typical of thinking on the public library during the Nazi period.

The Nazi Idea

No more than *Mein Kampf* or Rosenberg's *The Myth of the Twentieth Century* in the political arena, were the articles and speeches on public librarianship a blueprint for action. Although presented in numerous speeches, articles, and books, the idea of the Nazi public library remained vague and unconvincing, its policies and principles undefined. One of the few certainties was that the library was now one means to accomplish the complete penetration of the German Volk with National Socialist thought, feeling, and will. In a very real sense it was left to the librarians to determine the nature of the public library by action.

Imprecision and ambiguity deprive those who would comprehend the Nazi public library of a guide to its complexities, but their consequences were far more serious for contemporary librarians. With no clear direction in a volatile and dangerous situation, librarians could make no professional decision without risk. They were left to their own interpretative devices in applying National Socialist principles to their libraries. That same imprecision left decision makers free to alter interpretations to suit their convenience, and to react arbitrarily.

CHAPTER THREE

Politics, People,

and the Takeover

of the Profession

ARISTOTLE'S famous statement that man is by nature a political animal is a truth most of us begin to discover in childhood. Politics is not limited to the realm of statecraft and public governance but is present in every form of interaction when any decision is to be made or any kind of reward is at stake. Each group has its own rules, and when we elect to participate in a particular group, we must make decisions about the nature of our own political activity.

Politics had always been an omnipresent fact of life in German public librarianship. As had other countries, Germany had had struggles within the profession over such prestige and power as librarians could command, as well as competition for public resources that pitted librarians against others seeking funds from local and national governments. During the Third Reich politics was not only present in public librarianship, it became all-pervasive as previously apolitical issues were recast in political terms. The tone of life grew strident and all conflicts were exacerbated, this despite the Nazi promise that in the new Germany political rivalry would no longer exist.

The politics of public librarianship in Nazi Germany were complex, distinctive, and extremely unpleasant. New ideas, new terminology, and new participants were superimposed upon the old, not replacing the old but interacting with them. The quarrels of the Richtungsstreit continued to influence events, but at the same time new elements were becoming important. Some relationships held,

32

but many professional friendships became more cautious as distrust and intrigue became a way of life.

The politics of Nazi public librarianship are particularly confusing because conflict was occurring in so many different contexts. There was rivalry between individuals, debate over the primacy of professional concerns vis-à-vis political, a struggle for supremacy between ministries, and competition between the central Reich government and the traditional autonomy of different provinces. At the same time, politics often seemed to exist quite independently of any question of substance. Principles and personal alliances were important, but both changed constantly. Until 1937 everything and everybody seemed to be in constant flux. In 1937 it became clear that the most important points had been settled. New leaders had emerged, an organizational structure had been created, and policies had been decided.

To control public librarianship it was necessary to control librarians. Somehow librarians had to be coerced, persuaded, and molded into a force that could be relied on to carry out Nazi policies and programs. How this was accomplished is the central question of this chapter: How was a group of people whose profession was based on humanistic values induced to implement policies and programs that were the antithesis of humanism? This is a political question but it is also a fundamentally human one. It is not too much to say that what was at stake was the soul of the profession.

When Adolf Hitler became chancellor of Germany on January 30, 1933, it was as the head of a coalition government that had been patched together by opportunistic politicians and accepted by President Paul von Hindenburg after yet another of the political crises that marked the course of the Weimar Republic. With only three Nazis in the cabinet, nothing indicated that this regime would be significantly different from any of its recent, short-lived, and virtually impotent predecessors. Yet within six months, all other political parties had ceased to exist, and the Nazis controlled the machinery of government at every level.

During the months immediately following Hitler's assumption of the chancellorship, events moved with such rapidity that it was often difficult for contemporary observers to appreciate their significance.

33

What was clear was that the Nazis were eliminating all opposition, single-mindedly and in a fashion not overly concerned with legal niceties. The process was called *Gleichschaltung,* a term translated as "coordination." For the specifically Nazi use of the term, "bringing into line" or "elimination of opponents" is more precise. Some of the important landmarks along the Nazis' way to total control were the suppression of the leftist press for a week in February, the decree that followed the Reichstag fire in February, the election of March 5, and the passage of the Enabling Act of March 23. The comprehensiveness of Gleichschaltung is clear in the warning of the librarian most concerned with the coordination of libraries: "It is a mistake with painful and fatal consequences if individual organizations believe that they can continue to lead their own self-sufficient lives by voluntarily undertaking incorporation in the great plan for all areas."[1]

The Nazis used their power to attempt a remaking of society in the Nazi image. Historians debate whether the Nazi party was truly a revolutionary party, and whether it indeed carried through a revolution,[2] but neither party members nor contemporary observers doubted its revolutionary credentials. Having gained control of the mechanisms necessary to carry out change, Nazis set about effecting the transformation of Germany. In the various sectors of society, programs were hastily cobbled together to convert Nazi slogans into action.

The Nazi takeover of Germany was brought about as much by forces within the society and the economy as it was by the Nazis. Hitler had proclaimed the necessity of converting the masses, and, like so many other Germans, many librarians were ready to be converted. The Nazis promised change. In the early years it was possible for librarians to see the fluid situation as offering great opportunity to achieve long-cherished goals, and some public librarians did indeed hold this optimistic view. Others, trying to make the best of things, adopted this attitude. There is no doubt that genuine enthusiasm existed within the profession for much that was done in the Nazi period; it was not completely imposed from above.

One example of this state of mind is the section of the "Erklärung und Aufruf" (Explanation and call) signed by Max Wieser and published along with another section signed by Wilhelm Schuster and Wolfgang Herrmann on behalf of the association of German public librarians in both *Bücherei und Bildungspflege (BuB)* and *Hefte für Büchereiwesen (HfB)*. This document, dated March 25, 1933, exudes a sense of ripeness for change. Wieser deplored the policies of the past in which Marxist writers and others who had opposed the German Being were included in collections. He called for public librarians to dedicate themselves to the great work of German renewal.[3]

A readiness, even an eagerness, for change had been apparent for some time, particularly among younger librarians. In Western Europe World War I had exacerbated and sharpened throughout society the eternal conflict between youth and age. Although the younger generation of 1914 had become the older generation of 1933, a sense of generational division pervaded German librarianship. The Nazi emphasis on youth—they described themselves as "the organized will of youth"—had, therefore, considerable appeal to many younger librarians.[4] As Ackerknecht noted, the Nazi victory raised the hopes of many young librarians that the political changes would bring them professional opportunities. One of his friends interpreted Ackerknecht's own removal from the Stettin public library as a victory of the "junge Heißsporne" or young hotheads.[5]

This sense of distinction had existed well before the Nazi takeover, and the younger men had already demonstrated some independence from their elders. It might not have been quite as explicit as in 1934 when Georg Narcisz, director of the Breslau library, criticized Schuster in a rather pompous note to Ackerknecht on behalf of "we younger men" for having failed to set a clear goal, but it was real.[6] The 1928 flare-up of the Richtungsstreit had produced unmistakable evidence that younger librarians were trying to go beyond the polarized positions of the Richtungsstreit and to seek a common ground rather than pursue hostilities.[7]

Other evidence of a readiness to turn in new directions, especially in the direction of nazism, can be found. Johannes Beer, director of the library of Frankfurt/Main, wrote an essay titled "Authority and Adult Education." Intended as a discussion of the philosophical basis of adult education, it comes across as an indictment of democracy and of the Weimar constitution from an adult educator's perspective. It is worth considering in some detail because, although not published until 1933 when the views expressed were highly expedient, it was

35

actually written in 1932 and was thus a genuine attempt to reconcile the goals of adult education with a more effective state.

Beer began by posing what he perceived as the fundamental choice faced by educators: loosening[8] or consolidation. He found it difficult to define the purpose of adult education, a circumstance he attributed to the deficiencies of the German state. In Beer's view, the Weimar Republic lacked the support of its citizens. Beer's opinion was and is widely held, but Beer then proceeded to conclude that this absence of support deprived the state of authority and created a situation in which adult education was misused. On the failings of adult education Beer was unsparing; among the most serious were that it lacked purpose and that there were no standards for developing book collections.

As a solution, Beer proposed consolidation, but this new consolidated adult education could only be based on "authority." Beer's state had obvious resemblances to a Nazi one, as when he spoke of a Führer. He argued that human life was possible only in society, by which he meant that it was through the state that an individual received his being. Beer concluded by formulating a new purpose for adult education: It was *not* to develop individuality but was to help the individual recognize his place and his task in the state.[9]

Beer's essay was controversial and should not be taken as the judgment of the profession as a whole. Franz Schriewer summed it up as "not an essay about cultural questions, but a political essay about the badness of earlier adult education." Schriewer complained that he had not seen anything so formless and unclear in years. To publish it in the uncertain situation of 1933 was "complete idiocy." He felt that it discredited all adult education.[10] Kurd Schulz, on the other hand, felt that many of Beer's conclusions were correct; not coincidentally, in 1933 Schulz was expressing considerable admiration for nazism.[11]

Ackerknecht, the senior editor of *BuB*, had not been in favor of publishing. When Beer first told him in September 1932 about his essay, then titled "The State as Bearer and Educational Goal of Adult Education," he was enthusiastic, but his enthusiasm had cooled on actually reading it. He and Schuster, who was a co-editor of *BuB*, had done their best to keep it out of the journal but had ultimately yielded to Beer's insistence. Schuster found it difficult to take Beer seriously as a philosopher—he considered Beer industrious, ambitious, clever, and so shallow that he described him as "only a few centimeters beneath the surface"—but Beer was, after all, also a co-editor of *BuB*.[12] After its publication, Ackerknecht found himself in the awkward position of having to respond to complaints with which he essentially agreed. In his answer to a letter to the editor he made two important points about *BuB*: that the journal did not have a political position, and that publication of an article did not signify editorial endorsement.[13]

Although primarily an expression of a heightened awareness consonant with the growing strength of national socialism, a collective review of Nazi books by Wolfgang Herrmann is another example of the profession's interest in nazism. The review of the literature of the new nationalism was Beer's idea, and in the spring of 1932 Ackerknecht asked Max Wieser, one of the few party members at the time, if he would be interested. When Wieser failed to reply, he approached Herrmann.

Herrmann is a curious figure among German public librarians; Ackerknecht considered him a typical outspoken big-city intellectual. He had two professions, librarianship and journalism, between which he shuttled. At the time he wrote the review, he was at Halle an der Saale; by the spring of 1933 he was in Berlin, appointed to the Purification Committee by the mayor and to the acting chairmanship of the VDV by Schuster. Later in the year he became the public library commissioner for Berlin. Although he was already a party member in 1932, like so many "old fighters" he failed to achieve power and success under the new regime.

A major factor in Herrmann's failure was his review, "The New Nationalism and Its Literature."[14] Herrmann may have been a National Socialist, but he was not an unthinking one. Unhampered by blind loyalty to the Führer, he criticized *Mein Kampf* for "not containing a single intellectually original or theoretically well-considered thought." The accuracy of his judgment was irrelevant, as was his description of Hitler's book as "the most authoritative source on the 'movement'"; these words and other less than adulatory comments would haunt him and eventually get him dismissed from the party. Five years later Herrmann was badgering Ackerknecht to find something in the editorial correspondence that would "unburden" him of the *Mein Kampf* review.[15]

Association with Herrmann and his assessment was dangerous. Ackerknecht, Beer, and Schuster all liked the review but recognized that its publication was being used as an excuse to threaten *BuB*. In February 1933 Hans Engelhardt, another of the rare pre-1933 librarian party members, suggested that the wording be softened when the review was reprinted as a separate publication, a proposal with which Wilhelm Schuster concurred. Engelhardt argued, as it turned out correctly, that Hitler would achieve complete dominance and that criticism was highly impolitic. The reprint version was accordingly blunted but, even so, failed to redeem Herrmann. Schuster's subsequent appointment of him as acting chair of the VDV, a move designed to satisfy Nazi authorities that the organization was properly *gleichgeschaltet*, or coordinated, backfired, and association with Herrmann hurt rather than helped.

Despite evidence of new currents and rising men—or at least men attempting to rise—as of January 1933 the profession had neither been affected by nazism nor had its longtime leaders been replaced. The men who dominated the profession were still, as they had been in 1914, Erwin Ackerknecht and Walter Hofmann. Although both had withdrawn from polemics to devote their energies to other activities, their preeminence remained. Other leading librarians still grouped themselves either with the Alte or the Neue Richtung, adherents either of Ackerknecht or Hofmann.

Because so few public librarians and no library leaders were members of the Nazi party in January 1933, control of the profession could not be achieved by a few strategic substitutions. Instead, existing leaders had to be retooled until they could be replaced by a few, more properly indoctrinated and prepared individuals. A few pre-1933 members were eventually able to parlay their political perspicacity into professional advancement, but their success was distinctly limited and had no effect on the profession as a whole.

The significance of party membership changed through the years. Until 1933 it was a statement of conviction and commitment; after the seizure of power it gradually became little more than a formal gesture, a necessary qualification for professional achievement, required of all administrators. As early as January 1934 Ackerknecht was advising, "I don't need to emphasize in detail that today membership in the NSDAP [National Socialist German Workers' party],

38

preferably in the form of SA or SS service, is extremely desirable, not to say essential, for anyone who wants to obtain a leading cultural position."[16] The case of Rudolf Joerden, director of the Hamburger Öffentliche Bücherhallen from 1938 to 1940 and 1945 to 1970, illustrates the nature of the changes. In 1933 Joerden had a chance to be director of the public library of Lübeck but was unable to accept because he was not a party member. Joerden weighed the choice carefully: "On the one hand the immense national possibilities that the revolution offers, on the other, the injustice, the Machiavellianism and everything else one hears about. Finally, I see the solution to lie always in remaining true to oneself; one can only thereby do the new a favor. On the other side, again the danger suddenly offered of being unable to work for an unforeseeable time, perhaps for one's whole life, at the task of education and thereby for the Volk." Two years later Joerden became the director of the Wiesbaden library, even though the trustees knew he was not a party member. Eventually, the mayor of Wiesbaden informed him, as a fait accompli, that he had been enrolled in the party, and Joerden did not protest.[17]

In the spring of 1933, however, the decision to join the party was a conscious choice. It was also a decision that those who made it felt called upon to justify. Both Ackerknecht and Hofmann, neither of whom joined the party, received letters of explanation from colleagues who did. A common thread runs through these letters: The new members did it for the good of their institutions and librarianship. Occasionally, they also acknowledged that it was necessary for professional advancement. Erich Thier doubtless spoke for many: "I am convinced that at least we young ones will be able to accomplish useful work in the areas of culture and education and, it is hoped, in the broader frame of the NSDAP, and that we can hardly do it outside the framework in present circumstances."[18] Others, such as Walter Hofmann, made every effort to appear as Nazilike as possible without joining the party.

Party membership meant outward conformity. Few librarians seem to have changed any fundamental political values, and none went on to achieve prominence in the party. One must agree with the librarian who said of the two most important public librarians of the Nazi period, both party members, that "they weren't Nazis,"[19] but in another sense they obviously were. Librarians remained librarians, but they also provided the leadership that redirected the profession to serve Nazi ends.

The most strategically located librarian in 1933 was Dr. Wilhelm Schuster, librarian of the Hamburger Öffentliche Bücherhalle, associate editor of *Bücherei und Bildungspflege*, and since 1928 president of the national association of public librarians, the Verband Deutscher Volksbibliothekare. Born in 1888 in Stettin, the son of a pharmacist, he had studied German, philosophy, and philology at the universities of Göttingen, Kiel, and Berlin. Like most of his generation, he had fought in World War I, serving as a lieutenant in an artillery company. After the war he became a librarian, receiving his preparation under Ackerknecht at Stettin. By 1933 he had reached the top of his profession, having gained experience in rural librarianship in the border area of Upper Silesia (Ger. Oberschlesien) and in urban librarianship as an assistant director of the Berlin library under Dr. Gottlieb Fritz.

Dr. Wilhelm Schuster. (Courtesy, Dr. Adolf von Morzé.)

Schuster was a man of considerable intelligence and ability; as Ackerknecht put it, "of extraordinary diplomatic skill and a rich and versatile intellectuality." He was also a man of some political flexibility. Hostile to nazism in 1932, he rapidly accommodated himself and joined the party, a decision he made for essentially professional reasons. He would have been unable to continue in his position without doing so. Ackerknecht accepted his choice in those terms and wrote to him that he hoped Schuster would thereby be able "to prevent authoritatively those actions that would unnecessarily weaken and shake German public librarianship during the erection of the new state." Even his enemies agreed that he was motivated by the desire to save what he had worked for rather than by ambition. Schuster seems to have been true to his intentions and retained the respect of his colleagues; an obituary by his longtime colleague, Carl Jansen, paid tribute to his character. In Jansen's opinion Schuster "performed his duties cleanly, with spiritual responsibility." He attempted to stand for a new "social humanism" and helped endangered colleagues whenever possible.[20]

Another important leader was Franz Schriewer, in 1933 the librarian of the Stadtbibliothek in Flensburg and the director of the provincial library service for the border province of Schleswig. Schriewer was a native of Schleswig; his father was a carpenter in Rendsburg. Five years younger than Schuster, Schriewer, too, had studied at the universities of Kiel and Berlin and, after serving as a lieutenant in the war, had prepared as a librarian under Ackerknecht at Stettin. From Stettin he had gone directly to Flensburg where he had remained ever since.

Schriewer's career during the Third Reich was somewhat checkered. In 1933 he was ousted from his position in Flensburg by local Nazis but was able to find a new job as librarian in Frankfurt/Oder. He succeeded Schuster in 1935 as the director of the Preußische Landesstelle für volkstümliches Büchereiwesen that became in September of that year the Reichsstelle für volkstümliches Büchereiwesen, renamed to reflect the extension of its responsibilities to the entire Reich. Schriewer had accepted the position at the urging of his acquaintance Heinz Dähnhardt, the advisor in the Ministry of Education responsible for public libraries. Schriewer hoped to put through a national library law but was sufficiently

Dr. Franz Schriewer.
(Courtesy, Jürgen Schriewer.)

doubtful about his prospects for success that he did not resign, but only took a leave of absence from his position as librarian in Frankfurt/Oder. Less than two years later he returned. He spent most of World War II in the army as a transport officer in Frankfurt, which permitted him to remain involved with the direction of the library.

Schriewer was a different type of man than Schuster. A very private person, his most outstanding personal characteristic was reserve; Ackerknecht felt that he gave an "authoritarian" impression. Although he shared the hope that the Nazi regime would bring greater opportunities for public librarianship, he never joined the party.[21]

Several other directors of large-city libraries and provincial library administrations were also leading figures in the profession in 1933: Karl Taupitz in Saxony; Rudolf Reuter in Cologne; Johannes Beer in Frankfurt/Main; and Rudolf Angermann in Westphalia (Ger. Westfalen). Like Schuster and Schriewer, all were born in the last two decades of the nineteenth century. With the exception of Beer, an associate editor of *Bücherei und Bildungspflege*, all were adherents of Hofmann. Taupitz was considered Schriewer's probable successor at the Reichsstelle in 1937, but the others, while remaining professionally active, did not achieve any particular distinction during the Nazi years.

Nor can the elder statesmen of the profession, Ackerknecht and Hofmann, be forgotten. Ackerknecht remained on the fringes during the period but was in fairly close touch with what was going on. His former students and colleagues wrote and visited frequently; often his advice was sought. Hofmann attempted to take a more prominent role. He saw the situation as an opportunity to regain some of the influence he had enjoyed during the 1920s when Robert von Erdberg was the official responsible for adult education in Prussia. Hofmann was active on many fronts. His publications were designed to sway opinion and to demonstrate the essentially National Socialist cast of his thought. He promoted his own organization, the Deutsche Zentralstelle (DZ) for dominance. He used every contact he had and attempted to cultivate and manipulate the emerging powers. Alte Richtung adherents saw his influence at every turn; to judge by his correspondence, he was certainly trying to be there, even if he were less successful than his enemies would have believed.

The two men who eventually emerged as the most important figures in the world of public librarianship were Fritz Heiligenstaedt and Heinz Dähnhardt, neither of whom was a trained librarian. Dähnhardt, the more powerful, was born in 1897 in Berlin, the son of a vice admiral in the imperial navy. After passing an emergency examination at his gymnasium in August 1914, he joined a regiment of guards and was posted to the eastern front. Less than a year later, he was invalided out of the army, thanks to a severe case of polio. Until he was drafted in September 1917, he spent the war years teaching at his gymnasium and studying at the University of Berlin.

Dähnhardt became politically active while very young. According to his résumé, in 1911 he joined a troop of Boy Scouts whose leader was from the volkish movement and who introduced him to anti-Semitism. As a student, he joined the Deutschvölkisch Studentenverband, and after the war he was a member of one of the Freikorps. In 1924 he worked for a group seeking the election of conservative candidates that cooperated to some extent with the National Socialists and the Deutschvölkisch Freiheitspartei. Dähnhardt later joined the Stahlhelm, the veteran's organization of the Nationalist party, and in 1930, the Volkskonservative Vereinigung.

Dr. Heinz Dähnhardt.
(Courtesy, Akademie
Sankelmark.)

During the 1920s Dähnhardt completed his studies at the University of Hamburg in German and folklore, although his main interest was history. He began teaching history at the Fichtegesellschaft and continued his activity in the youth movement. In 1934 he taught briefly at a teacher-training institute in Cottbus and in October of that year, with the help of conservative friends, went to the Reichs- und Preußischesministerium für Wissenschaft, Erziehung und Volksbildung (RWEV) as the advisor (*Referat*) for adult education. By 1937 he had become an *Oberregierungsrat*, with increased responsibilities and power. Like so many, Dähnhardt had joined the party in April 1933.

The external facts of Dähnhardt's life testify to his political skill and adaptability; to have survived and prospered in the perilous politics of the Third Reich was no small accomplishment. Dähnhardt pleased the people who mattered but gained a reputation for being *zwiespältig*, or two-faced, among librarians. He courted both sides of the Richtungsstreit. Ackerknecht mistrusted him and treated him with extreme caution. Hofmann came away after a meeting with him in 1934 convinced that Dähnhardt was totally committed to

Hofmann's views. When Dähnhardt wished, he could be charming, as one previously unimpressed librarian found when forced to spend an hour seated next to him during an air raid.[22]

Fritz Heiligenstaedt had neither Dähnhardt's vitality, political skill, nor power and was informally if not officially Dähnhardt's subordinate. His letters and activities convey the picture of the consummate bureaucrat, cautious and bound by routine. He appears to have been selected as the director of the Reichsstelle für Volksbüchereiwesen (RV) precisely because he would follow Dähnhardt and make no attempt to exercise any initiative. In 1942 Ackerknecht commented that he had found that in critical situations Heiligenstaedt would not make any decision with which Dähnhardt disagreed.[23]

Heiligenstaedt had come to the RV from the provincial library administration of Lower Saxony (Ger. Niedersachsen), a position that because of the administrative organization of Lower Saxony entailed some direction and supervision over other provincial library administrations, as, for example, that of Braunschweig. He had been trained as a teacher and, except for service during World War I in the army news division that was primarily concerned with the Balkans, had been a teacher and school administrator. He, too, had been one of the "spring flowers" who joined the National Socialist party in 1933.

The advent of the Nazis and the consolidation of their power in local and national government brought another kind of political action to public librarianship that was quite new, at least in its scale and brazenness. Many librarians were dismissed from their jobs under nazism for political reasons. As soon as the Nazis seized power, they made an effort to purge the civil service and replace those dismissed with more-dependable recruits. Obviously, Marxists, pacifists, and Jews were their targets. Satisfying though this purge was to the party faithful, it quickly became apparent that professional expertise could not safely be ignored. As early as April 7, 1933, limits began to be established, when the Law for the Restoration of the Civil Service ended unregulated dismissals and put the process in the hands of state officials. Broszat estimates that in the end only 1 to 2 percent of civil servants were dismissed.[24]

Because so few librarians were civil servants, however, they only rarely came under the provisions by which the civil service was regulated. To redress this, two decrees from the Prussian minister of education were promulgated during the summer of 1933 that imposed similar requirements on librarians. That of September 2 read, "I request that it be observed, that only such persons be chosen by the local authorities to hold positions in public librarianship who are professionally educated, personally suitable, and politically reliable." Among the qualifications, "politically reliable" was underlined, but the requirement of professional education was at least as significant in the circumstances. Although both decrees had legal force only in the one-third of the Reich that was Prussia, it was expected that they would either be observed or serve as models for similar regulation in the other Länder.[25]

These decrees and the general nazification cost some librarians their jobs; the later decrees specifically directed at Jews brought further dismissals. The exact numbers affected cannot be determined because of the lack of reliable lists. Such lists would have been difficult to compile at best, given the absence of a uniform definition of public librarian, but in the circumstances it was impossible. Ackerknecht did talk in September 1933 about publishing a list of those dismissed, but it never appeared. Significance cannot always be measured in numbers, however, and it is clear that the dismissals had a demoralizing effect on librarians.[26]

A few directors, such as the director at Kiel, were Socialists and were immediately removed, but most librarians were women, and politically active women were rare. They were, moreover, predominantly middle class and both less likely to be Socialists and more inclined to the essential conservatism expressed by one elderly librarian: "We were raised to be *Kaiser-treu.*"[27] Nor were many public librarians Jews; unlike law or finance, librarianship simply was not a profession that had attracted many. An article, published after the war, paying tribute to former Jewish colleagues named only eight individuals, although the list was admittedly incomplete.[28]

The purge was erratic. Ackerknecht lost his job in 1933 as head of Stettin's popular library, although he was allowed to remain as the director of the scholarly city library. Ackerknecht was no Socialist, but the Nazis did not find him sufficiently sympathetic politically. Only during the war, when almost all younger male librarians had been drafted, was he allowed to resume direction of the popular library. Hofmann, who had been a Socialist, survived at Leipzig until 1937 when Carl Goerdeler, the mayor who had protected him, was replaced. Hofmann, too, was allowed to retain other positions. Both of these cases might be regarded as symbolic actions, evidence that the Nazis were asserting that the old leaders of the profession had been supplanted. In fact, both of these dismissals appear to have been the result of purely local circumstances. Other well-known directors of large city libraries who were removed included Gottlieb Fritz in Berlin, Eugen Sulz in Essen, Hans Ludwig Held in Munich (Ger. München), and Adolf Waas in Frankfurt/Main.[29]

That Germany was a federal rather than a unitary state imposed limits on the power of the central government. Not only did implementation of any policy require local cooperation, in the case of public libraries Gleichschaltung was exclusively a local responsibility, since public libraries were local institutions. This fact permitted local considerations to determine whether or not someone would be removed from a position, as they did in the cases of Ackerknecht, Schriewer, and Hofmann. Many removals were instigated not by government officials, but by the newly influential party groups such as the NS-Frauenschaft or the Hitler-Jugend (HJ).

One of the most interesting cases showing the primacy of local factors came from Rehau, a small town in Upper Franconia (Ger. Oberfranken) on the Czech border. The primary objective of the local Nazis was to remove the librarian, Friedrich Welscher, although other issues besides his political unfitness were raised. The library in question was a library of the Catholic Pressverein, the Catholic organization that delivered library service in Bavaria (Ger. Bayern), whose libraries often both styled themselves "public library" and acted as such. The director of the Rehau library was Hauptlehrer (master teacher) Welscher, a devout and organizationally minded Catholic who also led the local Catholic youth group.[30] The case foreshadows later, nationally coordinated assaults on Catholic libraries.

On April 25, 1933, Rudolf Wille, a teacher and member of the Sturmabteilung (SA), was put in charge of the purification of local libraries by the special commissioner for the district.[31] He and two other members of the SA visited the Pressverein library on July 1 and declared it closed in the name of the special commissioner, on the grounds that books had been found that opposed nazism, that exacerbated religious conflict, and were of un-German content. Welscher immediately protested; from the library's founding, a major objective had been to combat Marxism. As a Catholic library, although as one that was public in that it served all without respect to class, party, or faith, it naturally had many Catholic authors. A local Catholic official invoked the concordat, according to which purely cultural organizations were supposed to be left alone. Dr. Georg Reismüller, director of the Bavarian State Library, was called in and certified that Welscher was "alert to library technical things."

Reismüller's report went on to raise the fundamental issue of who was responsible for public library service. He argued that it was appropriate for the existing parish library to have writings of an improving and pastoral character, but that entertaining and instructive secular works belonged in a publically supported public library. The Bavarian Staatsministerium für Unterricht und Kultus (BSUK) adopted this position in a memorandum that defined its public library policy. Citing the Rehau experience as a cautionary tale, the memorandum to the administrations of Upper and Middle Franconia (Ger. Mittelfranken) declared that public libraries should not circulate books opposing national socialism. Nor was it acceptable that, in a place dominated by one religion (Rehau was overwhelmingly Protestant), "the public should be offered books primarily of the other religious denomination by the public library." Most significantly, and earlier than any other governmental agency, the Bavarian ministry asserted the important principle that in the National Socialist state the authority responsible for a local public library should be the local government, the body that bore the responsibility for the community's culture.

In the following spring a public library was established in Rehau, but in the meantime the party had brought more pressure to bear. Both Dr. Moll, head of the cultural division of the party for the Upper Franconia, Upper Palatinate (Ger. Oberpfalz), and Lower Bavaria (Ger. Niederbayern) region, and the local *Ortsgruppenleiter*, had written the ministry about the matter; both had urged the removal of Welscher, who was accused, among other things, of having "disturbed the peace of the teachers." In the end, only one-sided religious writings remained with the Pressverein. The remaining books, after being weeded of those inimical to the state, became the nucleus of the

48

new public library. Rudolf Wille was appointed librarian and made an effective one. In 1936 Schriewer commended the library, and the director of the provincial library administration in Bayreuth wrote Wille, "That it is today so clean and attractive in its collection and so technically well organized is in good part your work." Wille's work was sufficiently distinguished that he spoke at the conference of the Grenzbüchereidienst in 1936.

Although the mayor of Rehau, in a memorandum late in May, pictured what had happened there as a conflict between church and state, its principal significance was quite different. Rehau was, indeed, a defeat for the Catholic church, but it is more important as an example of the techniques by which the Nazis seized control of Germany. A combination of legal and extralegal forces, gross interference, and bullying intimidation were brought to bear on existing institutions. Existing personnel who proved uncooperative were replaced with more-flexible individuals, and, overnight, new priorities were adopted. The process of Gleichschaltung and the nazification of German government and society was an accumulation of many such small, local events.

Rehau typifies what took place on the local level; what happened to the VDV is typical of national, professional organizations. Founded in 1922, the association for public librarians had attempted to prevent the war between Alte and Neue Richtung from destroying it. Its constitution was designed to give equal representation to both parties, and strict neutrality was enjoined upon the chair. Both *BuB* and *HfB* were recognized as official journals. How many librarians were members is not known, although it cannot have been more than several hundred. Its importance lay not in its size, but in its role. Here was where the leaders of the profession came together; it spoke for the profession. It also, in the absence of appropriate governmental agencies, assumed some administrative responsibilities not usually the province of professional associations.

After the Machtergreifung the VDV assumed new importance. In 1933 Walter Hofmann rejoined the association, five years after resigning. Rehau and the many similar Rehaus laid the groundwork for a Nazi public librarianship, but direction had to come at the national level. In the first years an effort was made to mold the VDV to serve that purpose, but it did not succeed. It failed, not because the VDV resisted but because of limitations inherent in professional associations. Later, alternative administrative bodies were developed, and ultimately the VDV disappeared. Its demise was the result of a complex interaction of interagency rivalries, the need to destroy professional independence, and the decline of Wilhelm Schuster, its president.

In September the membership meeting of the association—originally scheduled for May—took place in Hanover, with 150 attending. Its theme was "Education to National Socialism," and the occasion was used both to inspire and instruct. On the first day both Schuster and Herrmann addressed the group on the inspirational topic of the public library and national socialism. The next day was more practical, as the speakers attempted to apply the new principals more specifically. The librarians were informed of the many changes that had taken place, such as the new responsibilities of the DZ, now converted into a professional institute associated with VDV. The librarians got the message. As one librarian attending reported in her summary of the event: "The German book is a weapon with which the fight for National Socialist educational goals must be fought."[32]

This meeting is in many ways more interesting for what it was not than for what it was. Obviously a preorganized propaganda event with the participants excluded from participation, it could have been the occasion on which public librarians brought their collective influence to bear on matters of professional concern. Instead, it displayed the embarrassing impotence of the VDV and the profession. Ackerknecht had foreseen this emasculation of the organization when he and Schuster were discussing the advisability of postponing the conference. Ackerknecht considered it quite out of the question that the VDV would be able to have any influence on events that were largely being decided at the local level.[33]

Ackerknecht was not quite so prescient in his conviction that by May everything would have been decided. In the fall of 1933 Schuster was negotiating with Hans Beyer from the Prussian Ministry of Culture and Heinz Wismann of the Reich Propaganda Ministry about the incorporation of the VDV as a professional organization within the newly created Reichsschrifttumskammer (RSK). The agreement that went into effect as of January 1, 1934, was both an administrative decision, making the VDV a constituent association of the RSK, and a statement about its future role; according to the RSK's statute, this umbrella organization was under the supervision of the Propaganda Ministry.[34]

Gradually, the VDV was deprived of vitality. In May 1934 it held its last conference, in Danzig. The following year it was announced that the VDV no longer existed independently, and in 1938 the steering committee voted to disband the organization. Its remnant survived as the Gruppe Büchereiwesen in the RSK. By this time the association had been reduced to a job placement service.

The Danzig conference was symptomatic of the organizational and political confusion that bedeviled the profession in 1934, just as its location in that strategic city symbolizes the permeation by nationalistic goals of social and economic life. In the bland report on the conference that appeared in the official journal, *Die Bücherei* (*DB*), little evidence of the disorder appears; only the announcement that Wilhelm Schuster was giving up *DB* hints that all was not as it was presented. The significant action was taking place behind the scenes. Ernst Saltzwedel, who had replaced Ackerknecht as head of the popular library at Stettin, wrote Ackerknecht that Schuster was being subjected to all kinds of opposition, fomented mainly by Herrmann. Rudolf Reuter sent Hofmann his account and interpretation of negotiations concerning the Institut für Leser- und Schrifttumskunde. Schuster had informed Reuter that he opposed any large role for the institute on the grounds that as Hofmann monopoly would inhibit the creative strengths of librarians.[35]

At the same time that the profession was being deprived of the organizational structure through which it could bring collective pressure, its means of communication were brought under control. In 1933 two professional public library journals existed, *Bücherei und Bildungspflege*, published by the Alte Richtung, and *Hefte für Büchereiwesen*, published by the Neue Richtung; both were recognized by the VDV as official journals of the association. Obviously, there was duplication, since few librarians could subscribe to both. But as Schuster concluded in an essay on rationalizing the profession: "Two association journals that are open without restriction to what is valuable, and yearly make a thick volume, are, as I said, certainly not too much, indeed it may be hoped they are sufficient to be able to contain our wisdom."[36] One of the first decisions taken under the new order was to eliminate this division of economic and intellectual resources and place the single journal under the editorship of a more cooperative librarian than either Ackerknecht or Hofmann. Herrmann delivered the news that *BuB* was to be closed down to Ackerknecht in the middle of May 1933, leaving him as his sole consolation that the journal would be permitted a dignified end. In the event, Ackerknecht was able to publish one last issue to accommodate already accepted manuscripts, but the last issue of his cherished journal was volume 13, number 5 for May 1933. *HfB* ceased about the same time but published fewer 1933 issues because it was running behind.[37]

In the issue of *BuB* in which Ackerknecht and Fritz took their journalistic leave, Schuster announced the new journal. It was to be a continuation of the two earlier journals, but most of all it was to be "an instrument of the National Socialist Volk in their self-fulfillment." Schuster was careful to point out in another announcement that the new journal was to serve all, even though it would be sponsored by the Prussian Landesstelle. The Prussian Landesstelle alone had the resources to support it. Schuster was equally careful to assert that the new journal was a continuation of *both BuB* and *HfB*.

Die Bücherei began with the January 1934 issue, three months later than the original plan had called for. Schuster edited it, after he failed to locate someone acceptable to all the necessary parties in Berlin. The issues followed a standard pattern—articles, news notes, book reviews, and applicable official decrees. There can be no doubt that *DB* fulfilled the needs of the profession. A memo from the director of the provincial library administration of Lippe explained its contribution from the point of view of the consumer. Dr. Wiegand described it as publishing all decrees from the RWEV and other official bodies that related to public librarianship. It had articles that explored the intellectual foundations and goals of the profession, and its book reviews were very useful. He commended it for including in the book reviews statements on whether a particular book was appropriate to the reading level of a peasant. The memo closed with a ringing endorsement: "It is clear that *Die Bücherei* is indispensable for every public library director, whether full-time or part-time."[38]

There were, of course, complaints, and they were sufficiently loud for Schriewer, the incoming editor, to mention them in the first issue

Die Bücherei

Zeitschrift der Reichsstelle für
volkstümliches Büchereiwesen

4. Jahrgang
Heft 3
März 1937

Verlag: Einkaufshaus für Büchereien GmbH., Leipzig C1, Königstr. 8

Cover, *Die Bücherei.*

of 1935. Walter Hofmann objected later that year that Schriewer had entombed *HfB* and was perpetuating *BuB*. Hofmann's opinion may well have been justified; certainly, Schriewer had been emphatic that he wanted to carry on the tradition of *BuB*, a tradition he saw as an emphasis on practice rather than theory. Schuster's plans had been equally pro-*BuB*; he stated that "it's not possible to publish a *new* journal. The position is such that every effort at a new journal will be sabotaged by those, to which among others Walter Hofmann belongs. The one possible way is to have the new periodical appear as a continuation of *Bücherei und Bildungspflege.*" Leipzig, however, had its revenge. In 1938 it was Schriewer's turn to complain that Fritz Heiligenstaedt, his successor as editor, had no working relationship with non-Leipzigers and had, moreover, not the least understanding of the profession, its history, or its accomplishments.[39]

DB had the usual problems of a professional journal. Although Dr. Wiegand got two copies for the Lippe Landesstelle, the journal had few subscribers. Out of eleven hundred members of the VDV in 1939, only 476 subscribed to *DB*. Directors of Beratungsstellen tended to subscribe, but not their assistants. Hamburg was unusual in that many of its branch heads had personal subscriptions, but then, three years before, its director, Dr. Albert Krebs, had applied pressure to achieve that result. Book reviews were a completely different category of problem. In 1937 Schriewer, still editor, sent a memo that pointed out that many contributions were in arrears and urged that the readers had a right to currency.[40]

Such vicissitudes aside, *DB* was all that could be desired in a National Socialist professional journal. It made public the decrees that gave librarians their instructions. It had the hortative speeches and the articles retailing practical experience that are so common in library journals. One can even find controversy, albeit controversy of the stripe in which Albert Krebs and Walter Hofmann squared off on the proper physical arrangements in a public library. Dissent is absent. Even so independent-minded an editor as Franz Schriewer, who held that the journal was the place for free conversation rather than directed expressions of opinion, qualified his position with the statement that in a multiplicity of opinion, the will of the state must prevail. The one article produced by the profession disagreeing with

Nazi policy was published not in *DB* but in *Die Tat*, a general journal for intellectuals.[41]

What happened to *BuB* and *HfB* is symbolic of the Gleichschaltung of public librarianship. Pre-Nazi institutions were adapted to new purposes or eliminated. By 1937 the process was complete. Public librarians had become Nazi public librarians, whether they were party members or not. Those gray, shadowy, and frequently changing figures who had tried to direct events could be well satisfied. They had used librarians against themselves, and now all was set for the accomplishment of Nazi objectives.

The profession had put up little resistance. Intellectually and emotionally weary from its long internecine warfare, like the rest of Germany hard hit by the depression, in 1933 the library profession had been in disarray. It had lacked the ideas, leaders, and institutions to resist the Nazi challenge. Most of all, it had lacked the will.

CHAPTER FOUR

The National Administrative Organization of Public Librarianship

WHEN HITLER came to power in January 1933 there was no authority in the Reich government responsible for public libraries. Such government involvement as there was took place at the local and provincial levels. From city to city and Land to Land the variation was considerable. In a state that claimed jurisdiction over every aspect of its citizens' lives, this neglect could not be allowed to continue. Aspirants to authority quickly presented themselves, and the ensuing struggle for power proved complex, nasty, and protracted. Who would control public libraries and how they would be managed were the critical questions between 1933 and 1937. On them were focused the energies of the profession's leaders; the answers would determine the nature of public libraries and affect their own futures.

The Nazi desire to impose rigorous censorship gave the state for the first time a strong motive to interest itself in public libraries. If the government was to be able to formulate national policy and then have it applied throughout the Reich, the creation of an administrative hierarchy was imperative. The censorship program was, therefore, both the stimulus for, and the result of, the establishment of an administrative organization, inaugurating a pattern of interaction between program and structure. As new demands were made of public libraries, the administrative framework would be strengthened and expanded.

The profession had an equally strong motive to involve the national government in public librarianship. Many librarians had long

56

wanted the central government to take a greater interest in public libraries because they saw it as a way of improving conditions. To them, a strong central government presence promised higher visibility for public libraries, more money, and smoother relations with local governments. It would regularize their position, converting public libraries from barely tolerated private charitable organizations to significant government agencies. Public libraries could become truly public.

On December 28, 1933, Bernhard Rust, the Prussian Minister für Wissenschaft, Kunst und Volksbildung (PMWKV) (scholarship, art, and adult education), issued the decree that was the first official definition of Nazi public librarianship. Erlaß U II R Nr. 750.1 was a truly revolutionary document; it declared the state's interest in public librarianship and inaugurated governmental regulation. The decree created a Prussian Landesstelle für volkstümliches Büchereiwesen (PLVB) with responsibility for the existing Prussian provincial library administrations and authority over them. In official terminology, the new Landesstelle was the "oversight body" on all questions of public librarianship. It was to publish the professional journal *Die Bücherei*, which would include all official decrees of the ministry. It would also be responsible for the certification of librarians.[1]

The limitation of the authority of both the decree and the Landesstelle to Prussia was significant, but in the end less than consequential. The modern German Reich had begun as a very loose federation of princely states. The Nazi regime accelerated its slow evolution toward centralization efficiently and brutally, officially by passing the January 1934 Law for the Reorganization of the Reich, less officially by often ignoring local rights and traditions that impeded the exercise of a single national authority. The establishment of national agencies for public librarianship was part of the larger pattern of the creation of a national state and the extension of central authority. At first, policy and organization had to be created on a province-by-province basis, a method that in fact had fewer drawbacks than would appear on the surface. As long as the Nazis controlled Prussia, they controlled two-thirds of the nation; they could also depend on the fact that the non-Prussian provinces would usually obediently follow the Prussian lead.[2] This was certainly apparent in librarianship. Within months, the non-Prussian provinces of Hesse and Thuringia (Ger. Hessen, Thüringen), Saxony and Baden had created Landesstellen for public librarianship. Within several years the remaining organizational unevenness had been eliminated; the Prussian Landesstelle became the Reichsstelle, and policy was formally made for the entire country.[3]

The landmark decree of December brought to an end ten months of negotiation, maneuvering, and intrigue. The instability and confusion of 1933 are almost beyond the imagination of anyone who has not experienced a revolution. In July 1933 one harassed librarian noted that there were no fewer than six organizations involved with public librarianship; he was understandably uncertain about his accountability to each.[4]

The establishment of a national order for public librarianship alone would have been demanding enough, but it was being determined within a political and governmental context of great uncertainty. After the Machtergreifung national socialism had to make the transition from party platform to governmental principles; the role of the party, the relation of state and party, and the nature and extent of state controls all had to be determined. Fluctuations and rivalries in the larger political environment increased the difficulty of reaching a settlement within librarianship.

As of January 1933 the national organizational structure of public librarianship consisted of two institutions librarians had created for themselves during the 1920s to fill the vacuum at the center—the VDV and the Deutsche Zentralstelle für volkstümliches Büchereiwesen. One of Walter Hofmann's many contributions to German librarianship, the DZ tried to do much of what a government agency would normally do. A 1931 memorandum described its goals as follows: to clarify the fundamental questions of librarianship; to educate the coming generation; to disseminate public library thought in Germany and abroad; and to prepare materials needed in running a public library. It included among its self-appointed tasks instruction and continuing education, the publication of professional literature, the dissemination of information, advertising about public libraries, the preparation of bibliographies and catalogs, and the collection of statistics.[5]

Another important body was the Prussian Ministerium für Wissenschaft, Kunst und Volksbildung, although it was a Prussian ministry and not a national one. During the 1920s, the ministry had taken an active interest in public library development. In the process of improving the condition of Prussian public libraries, it had created an administrative nucleus and a tradition of government activity in the largest part of the Reich. Both could readily be expanded.

The first act in the struggle over the administration of public librarianship began in March. Max Wieser, the librarian of Berlin-Spandau, played a leading role. Wieser was a member of the Nazi party, a true believer; he was also an aggressive and unbalanced personality. Within a week of the Machtergreifung he demanded that *BuB* publish a piece by Hitler on organization. At the same time he submitted a manuscript of his own on library collections, claiming that libraries were full of Marxist poison and that they had not bought German and nationalistically inclined authors. Ackerknecht found his claims "completely wild" and refused to publish the manuscript. Within a month, however, Ackerknecht was forced to print Wieser's "Aufruf an die Volksbibliothekare," a document that included many of these claims.[6]

On March 27 Wieser succeeded in getting himself named, as the representative of the profession, to the commission entrusted with the inspection of the collections of Berlin's libraries. The next day an attack originating in the Propaganda Ministry appeared in the Berlin newspapers, vilifying Gottlieb Fritz, head of the Berlin public libraries, and questioning the organization of public librarianship in Prussia. Wilhelm Schuster, already engaged in discussions with the PMWKV, hurried to Berlin to protect the interests of the profession in an obviously deteriorating situation. Negotiations between the Berlin city government and the PMWKV produced a revised version of the inspection commission, now named the Ausschuß zur Neuordnung der Berliner Stadt- und Volksbüchereien (Committee for the Reorganization of the Berlin City and Popular Libraries). In addition to Wieser, Hans Engelhardt and Wolfgang Herrmann, both also party members, were named to the new committee.[7]

For a brief period this committee was at the center of public library affairs, favored by its geographical location in the national capital and by the general disarray. Its energetic members not only carried through the purge of the collections of Berlin's public libraries, the purpose for which they had been appointed, but also concerned themselves with national library policy. They called a meeting of public librarians for April 21. Exactly who was present is uncertain, although Franz Schriewer was invited while Schuster was not. Wieser kept Schuster out for several weeks, claiming that he was half-Jewish, because his brother had brown eyes and black hair. The expanded group demanded Gleichschaltung of the VDV, amalgamation of the two professional journals into one, reorganization of the DZ as a professional institute of the VDV, and that the collections be "purified." Wieser's hand is apparent, but the suggestion about the journals had come from Schuster some years before. At this stage no one envisaged doing without the VDV, and Herrmann was appointed to its steering committee within a month, thus satisfying the demand for Gleichschaltung to some extent and creating a link between the two groups.[8]

Once the PMWKV had resisted the challenge from the Berlin group, the ministry intensified its negotiations with Schuster. Alternative models were considered. One arrangement used the VDV as the principal element. The VDV would have brought employer and employee together in a single body along the lines of a Fascist corporation. This plan was soon discarded, although the VDV continued to figure in the proposals and had various functions assigned to it at different stages.

By the end of May the outlines of the eventual solution were beginning to emerge. The report of a conversation in which Schuster, Wolfgang Herrmann, and Professor Ernst Bargheer from the Prussian Ministry of Culture participated makes it clear that they were agreed upon the main points. These men proposed that an advisory body for public libraries similar to that for scholarly libraries should be created in conjunction with (*neben*) the ministry. It would supervise the Gleichschaltung of public libraries in Prussia in cooperation with the appropriate officials. The Deutsche Zentralstelle would remain as a professional institute of the VDV, which was itself to continue as a professional organization, supplementing the new advisory body.[9]

As a first step in this direction, the PMWKV in July constituted the Beratender Ausschuß für volkstümliches Büchereiwesen, which functioned between the end of August and the publication of U II R Nr. 750.1. Schuster was its head and, during the fall of 1933, used its name as a letterhead for his letters and memoranda rather than that of the VDV, suggesting that he now perceived it as the premier public library institution. Its main purpose was to advise the PMWKV on public librarianship, a task that implied that the PMWKV had jurisdiction over public libraries. Because Schuster, chair of the VDV, also chaired the Beratender Ausschuß, it linked the VDV more closely to the PMWKV and increased the concentration of power in his hands.

Before the Beratender Ausschuß could begin functioning, however, yet another rival jeopardized the PMWKV's authority. A lengthy memorandum prepared by Karl Heinl of the Propaganda Ministry in June 1933 inaugurated the most serious territorial battle the PMWKV or its successor, the RWEV, would face; it was a contest that lasted with diminishing intensity until the onset of the war focused attention on other issues. The legislative order defining the role of the new Reichsministerium für Volksaufklärung und Propaganda gave it responsibility for "all activities that had an intellectual influence on the nation," a charge that inevitably brought it into conflict with existing ministries. Included in its purview were the book trade, film, radio, the press, theater, and propaganda. Heinl's fundamental argument was that public libraries were just as much an area of adult education in its broadest sense as these other areas were. Public libraries had little to do with the kind of school-based education that was the concern of the Ministry of Education. Heinl emphasized the explicitly political character of adult education, describing it as an inner Gleichschaltung, the conquest of men, counterpart to the external Gleichschaltung, the conquest of the state.[10]

The Propaganda Ministry put up a fight notable for its persistence and unpleasantness. Heinl's June memorandum on public librarianship attacked Schuster, a former National Liberal, accusing him of sympathy with Marxism, partly on the basis of his association, in professional organizations, with Marxists—one of whom was Walter Hofmann, of all people. Hofmann, a Socialist, was indeed a Marxist, but he could hardly be considered an intimate of Schuster. Schuster was also guilty of having favorably reviewed that Nazi bête noire, *All Quiet on the Western Front.* Later, another memorandum, reporting a conversation between representatives of the two ministries, used an off-the-cuff remark by an official of the Ministry of Education to strengthen the Propaganda Ministry's case. The Ministry of Education official had remarked that if public libraries were removed from their jurisdiction, the official in charge of them would not have anything to do. The Propaganda Ministry argued that this showed the Ministry of Education had no real interest in them.[11]

Although the organization of the Beratender Ausschuß had seemed to begin implementation of the PMWKV's integrated plan for public librarianship, events in the fall of 1933 altered the original design. The Propaganda Ministry tried to undermine the Prussian ministry's position by using its own newly created cultural agency, the Reichsschrifttumskammer, to claim the VDV. Negotiations between representatives of the Propaganda Ministry, the PMWKV, and Schuster eventually settled that the VDV would be placed in the RSK, although it turned out to be a hollow victory for the Propaganda Ministry. By the time this absorption took place in January 1934 the VDV had been left so little real responsibility by the December decree of the PMWKV that it could not be used as a power base.

The fall of 1933 was further complicated by Walter Hofmann, who chose to reenter the lists of public library politics in October with the distribution of a lengthy memorandum titled "Leitsätze, betreffend den Aufbau zentraler Organisationen im deutschen Volksbüchereiwesen" (Guiding principles concerning the establishment of central organizations in German public librarianship) that summarized his response to the changing situation. Hofmann had been waiting in the background for the right moment; he recognized 1933 as an opportunity and wanted Leipzig to be in the center. When he rejoined the VDV in May he served notice of his intentions. Hofmann may or may not have been guilty of trying to reestablish his "dictatorship," as Ackerknecht believed, but until his "Leitsätze" his efforts were making little impact. Schuster had succeeded in bypassing both Hofmann and the organizations that Hofmann was trying to use to improve his position, the DZ and Institut für Leser- und Schrifttumskunde. Nor had any of the adherents of the Leipzig Richtung done much better; the almost total absence of their names from the list of speakers at the Hanover conference of September 1933 was indicative. The "Leitsätze," combined with some well-chosen contacts in Berlin, forced Schuster to deal with him.[12]

Exactly what Hofmann and Schuster disagreed over is somewhat difficult to determine. Ostensibly, the main point of difference was the nature of the proposed central body. Schuster advocated an advisory body that would direct and lead librarianship. Hofmann emphasized the local ties of public librarianship in his "Leitsätze": "The work of the public library is closely intertwined with the intellectual, cultural, economic, and social realities of the place in which the individual library operates. The work of the individual library must therefore be to the highest degree indigenous." He affirmed the importance of a central professional institute that would "embody within itself the fundamental principles of both state and nation as well as complete professional expertise," but at the same time stressed that the central professional institute must give full recognition to the principle of indigenousness and rootedness in daily life. The organization must be kept separate from the professional political organization.[13]

These views could probably have been reconciled with Schuster's; they were, after all, agreed on many of the most important issues. In late October Schuster was describing his conception of a central agency for public libraries as having as its most important tasks transfer and mediation, leadership and stimulation. He did *not* want it to become a huge, overblown head with numerous officials and clerks. The real work on the library front took place in the individual library and was done by the practicing librarian.[14]

What impeded accommodation was less a matter of issues than it was one of style and habit. It was understandably difficult for Schuster to trust Hofmann, given Hofmann's talent for plotting and behind-the-scenes manipulation. It is significant that Hofmann found it necessary to write to Heiligenstaedt, one of his allies, denying that he was intriguing. Schuster had taken the precaution of remaining in close communication with Hofmann throughout 1933, but it was not true cooperation. It would have been difficult for Schuster, a man who was then director of the Hamburg library, one of the most important public libraries in Germany, not to mention chair of the VDV and of the Beratender Ausschuß, to accept Hofmann's assumption that he, Hofmann, had final approval on any arrangements. In fact, Schuster was making every effort to minimize Hofmann's influence. He refused, for example, to build on the DZ on the grounds that it cost too much in relation to the results and that, because it was narrowly based on Leipzig principles and practices, its results were of very limited applicability. The final organization of public librarianship embodies most of the DZ's goals without incorporating the DZ itself.[15]

Hofmann followed up his October "Leitsätze" with another memorandum in November, this one titled "Denkschrift zur gegenwärtigen Krise der deutschen Büchereipolitik" (Memorandum on the present crisis of German public library policy). In it he reprinted correspondence between himself and Schuster; its main thrust was to justify Hofmann. The memorandum's effect can only have been inflammatory. Hofmann concluded his tendentious self-exculpation with the provoking statement that the chief difference between Leipzig and the rest of public librarianship "lies in the quality of the Leipzig work."[16]

Although Hofmann attempted to influence the plans for a national public library administrative structure, his primary concern was what would happen to his Institut für Leser- und Schrifttumskunde. The institute had been founded as part of the Deutsche Zentralstelle, but by 1933 the paths of the two organizations had diverged considerably. The DZ had been taken over by the VDV; the institute remained very much a part of the Leipzig operation. Hofmann was the director of the institute and since withdrawing from professional politics in 1928 had devoted much of his energy to reading research, the institute's chief purpose.[17] It was, as Schuster wrote Hofmann in June 1933, very much "your agency and in great measure the expression and instrument of your creative personality." Schuster opposed the attachment of the institute either to the existing Deutsche Zentralstelle and thereby to the VDV or to the new central agency then being planned. Hofmann himself favored attachment only if the parent body in question did not become a clearinghouse for public librarianship and the original Zentralstelle with its close ties to Leipzig were recreated.[18] When it became clear that the existing Zentralstelle was going to survive only as a subsidiary of the VDV and that the new Prussian Landesstelle was going to take the form of a quasi-national advisory body, Hofmann was forced to examine other possibilities. The institute eventually found a home with the Reichsstelle zur Förderung des deutschen Schrifttums and continued to publish reading research and book reviews until 1937.

Yet another problem in the fall of 1933 was the question of a public

64

library law, an issue that was intertwined with whether Germany should have a national public library administration and, if so, what form it should take. A number of European countries had public library laws, but Germany did not. In 1919 Britain had passed a law that gave county councils the power to establish public libraries and removed limitations on the library taxation rate. The three Scandinavian countries had national library laws that were widely familiar to German librarians. Above all, they were conscious of the national library law in the neighboring country of Czechoslovakia, which required all communities of four hundred inhabitants to establish a library, mandated a minimum tax to support them, and placed them under control of the Ministry of Education. Thanks to this law, the Germans living on the Czech side of the border were far better served by public libraries than those who lived on the other side, within the Reich.[19]

A national law was desirable because it would affirm that public librarianship was a national priority, bring libraries to previously unserved communities, and establish a minimal acceptable level of service. On May 16, 1933, Wilhelm Schuster promised that national socialism would bring this much discussed and long-desired national library law to a successful conclusion. A month later he and an unlikely ally, Fritz Heiligenstaedt, were encouraging Ackerknecht to send his suggestions for a law. Ackerknecht had doubts that any advice he might have would be acceptable to the new order, but Heiligenstaedt pointed out that they did not wish to lose his knowledge and experience in this area.[20]

The draft law that Schuster eventually proposed in November established an advisory council for public librarianship that would operate directly on behalf of the ministry to which it was responsible. De facto, the Beratender Ausschuß was already doing this. Provincial public library administrations would carry out the public library work of the nation, and their directors, together with the members of the advisory council, would form a national advisory council for public libraries. Financial arrangements were left unspecified to avoid antagonizing the localities that would have to pay for the libraries; the draft of the law stated only that the provincial library administrations were to work to develop a building plan suited to the financial abilities of each district. The draft also provided a badly needed defi-

65

nition of public libraries; they were those libraries that worked exclusively in the spirit of the state cultural policy, with no additional goals, and were not in the service of a particular confession or viewpoint.[21]

Neither Schuster's draft nor any other became law, and it is clear that in 1933 librarians lost one of their best opportunities for one. They continued to urge a public library law, but U II R Nr. 750.1 deprived the matter of much of its urgency. The publication of the *Richtlinien* (guidelines) in 1937 put an end to their hopes. The Richtlinien did much of what a law would have done but, because they came as a ministerial decree, had less force.

With the decree of December 28 the PMWKV simultaneously preempted its rivals for control and determined the main outlines of national public library development for the future. One crucial task, however, remained to be accomplished: The Prussian Ministry of Education and the Prussian Landesstelle had to be converted to Reich institutions. Only then would the library system be truly national.

The first part was completed on May 1, 1934, when a decree from the Führer created the Reichsministerium für Wissenschaft, Erziehung und Volksbildung. It absorbed the PMWKV. For a while the new ministry was designated as the Reichs- und Preußisches Ministerium für Wissenschaft, Erziehung and Volksbildung; later the word *Prussian* was dropped. Adult education was assigned to it and, therefore, public librarianship. Bernhard Rust, Prussian minister of education, became Reich minister of education.[22]

The final step was the reorganization of the Prussian Landesstelle as the Reichsstelle für volkstümliches Büchereiwesen, a change that went into effect in September 1935. As early as January 1935 Dähnhardt was announcing publicly that the conversion of the Prussian Landesstelle to a Reichsstelle für volkstümliches Büchereiwesen was being planned. The "new" Reichsstelle would advise and facilitate the exchange of experience: "The Reichsstelle would further be commissioned to determine the important tasks and appropriate results of public librarianship, and coordinate and impose uniform principles." As examples of proper concerns, Dähnhardt gave space needs, technical care of books, and book selection. He promised territory conscious administrators that the existing provincial

Landesstellen would not change in function, although everyone recognized that the conversion was bound to mean even greater centralization.[23]

On the whole, librarians were reasonably satisfied with the settlement. When the PMWKV outmaneuvered the Propaganda Ministry to capture librarianship by enacting U II R Nr. 750.1, they regarded it as a victory for the principle that the public library is an educational institution. In retrospect, it is obvious that their relief was premature and their perceptions somewhat misguided. The two ministries were less different than they appeared. As presented in June 1933, the Propaganda Ministry's plans had been almost identical with what librarians urged: a library law; a central administrative body; a net of provincial library administrations; improved professional educational standards, and so on. And, as future decrees proved, the Ministry of Education's definition of education became almost identical with the explicitly political one of the Propaganda Ministry. Such a victory as there was, was a bureaucratic triumph rather than an assertion of principle.

The settlement did have positive features, though. The success of the PMWKV may not have preserved the educational purity of public libraries, but it did affirm the primacy of local government in public librarianship. The traditional decentralization of public librarianship was retained because the RV and RWEV worked through the provincial ministries of culture and education. The Propaganda Ministry's plans would have eliminated them and brought libraries under much more direct control. The system based on the RV and RWEV also secured the preeminence of professionalism. State control meant that library policy might be influenced by the party, but it would be made by individuals whose principal qualification was professional expertise. In several critical respects, therefore, the settlement of public librarianship indicates the limits of the Nazi transformation.

Wilhelm Schuster was the chief architect of the system. His original motive, as expressed to Hofmann in February, was to give public librarianship *Lebensraum*, by which he meant room to develop.[24] Most of his ideas he had long held; 1933 was an occasion and opportunity to implement them. Such adjustments as there were in his thinking were primarily a response to the threats implicit in the unsettled conditions. The one real exception to this was his willingness to sacrifice the VDV, an organization he had headed for some years.

The profession had reason to be grateful to him. The system he helped create did protect public librarianship from the worst excesses of local Nazi fanatics. It did involve the central government significantly in public library work, an institutional prerequisite for library development. It did unify and make possible rational growth. All these positive achievements, however, had their darker side, and that malevolence cannot be ignored. Efficiency and control came with no guarantee that they would be benign.

In later years Schuster confided to Rudolf Joerden that for him 1933 was, like 1914, a *Glanzpunkt*, or climax. The situation offered him great opportunity, but it also exacted a considerable price. In December 1933 he wrote to Ackerknecht that he had been in the nastiest fight of his life. He had been plastered with filth and was thoroughly disgusted with Herrmann. As long as he remained prominent, he was under almost constant attack.[25]

From time to time in the following years the issues of 1933 would reemerge. The settlement that put the Ministry of Education at the center of the system and created a professional institute subordinate to it did not eliminate all loose ends. To the end of the Nazi period, responsibility on some matters remained divided, and librarians were subjected to overlapping jurisdictions.

Nor did U II R Nr. 750.1 completely stifle the Propaganda Ministry. In 1934 the Propaganda Ministry attempted to use the Deutsche Städtetag, now renamed the Deutsche Gemeindetag, to further its interests. Albert Meyer-Lülmann, director of the Gemeindetag's Abteilung für Schul- und Bildungswesen, had been much affronted by the establishment of the Prussian Landesstelle in December 1933, which he saw as an attempt to undercut his own efforts to assure the influence of local communities on their public libraries. That Meyer-Lülmann had not been consulted by anyone from the PMWKV clearly did not help matters, even if the structure enacted in U II R Nr. 750.1 was actually much more in the interest of the communities he represented than one in which the Propaganda Ministry dominated would have been. Erwin Ackerknecht, who was in touch with both sides, summarized the issues as follows:

> It seems on the whole to me that the argument between Prussia and the Reich over jurisdiction lies in the foreground, and antag-

68

onism between an authoritarian state cultural policy and a cultural-political inclination to self-government on the part of the localities is in the background. . . . In my opinion it evades the question of whether in the totalitarian state a successful opposition by local self-governing bodies . . . is still possible. On the basis of the previously recognized arrangements of the Reich and Prussia it nonetheless seems to be the present state of affairs that the inclination to attach local self-administration to public librarianship is much stronger in the Prussian Ministry of Culture than it is in the Reich Ministry of Propaganda.[26]

In 1935 the RWEV again found itself fending off another Heinl memorandum, and as late as 1937 the Propaganda Ministry was still maintaining a division responsible for public libraries.

The irrepressible Walter Hofmann continued to reappear from time to time in the politics of public librarianship, despite his claim in 1934 that he was leaving the work of the revolution to a younger generation with a different style. At one point he tried to capitalize on the strength of the Leipzig party in southern Germany and the traditional dislike of the South for Prussia, to improve his position. Occasionally he would attempt to ingratiate himself with the ministry in Berlin. Not until his resignation as Leipzig's library director in early 1937 was he really out of the picture, and even then the Stettin group could not quite believe it.[27] Ackerknecht and his correspondents recorded rumors faithfully: August 1934, Hofmann's star in decline at the PMWKV; October 1936, Hofmann's intrigues have little effect on the ministry; January 1937, Hofmann triumphant (this was after a letter from Hofmann to Ackerknecht pluming himself on his closeness to Dähnhardt); February 1937, Hofmann defeated.[28] The vicissitudes reflected in Hofmann's own correspondence do not exactly match these rumors, but there is rise and decline. In May 1935 Rudolf Reuter, one of his most trusted lieutenants, was convinced that he could get the Hofmannian view of librarianship accepted in the new Reich; in June 1936 Hofmann thought himself being courted by the RWEV. The most significant document, however, is a letter from Dähnhardt in June 1935 in which Dähnhardt rebuked Hofmann sharply for inaccuracy and breach of confidence after Hofmann, in his usual way, had summarized a conversation between the two men and distributed it widely. Both words and tone show that

Hofmann was not held in any particular esteem at the RWEV, and by 1935 the RWEV was where power lay.[29]

Enabling legislation can only erect a framework, and the system decreed for public librarianship in 1933 and after had to be made to work. By the decree of December 28 the tasks of the Prussian Landesstelle, the central agency that was assumed to be the keystone of the new system, were defined as leadership, supervision, education, provision of professional services, and publication of the professional journal. This broad original mandate left considerable room for modification for the different directors, Schuster (1933–1935), Schriewer (1935–1937), and Heiligenstaedt (1937–1945), each of whom had his own priorities and his own style. The national library agency was also, like any governmental agency, subject to the normal fluctuations of events, as well as the special forces that kept all parts of the National Socialist state in almost continuous evolution. The Reichsstelle of 1945 was a far cry from what public library leaders had had in mind in 1933.

Wilhelm Schuster had designed the original Landesstelle. A memorandum of October 1933 set forth in some detail his views on its role. He saw its primary tasks as regulating professional activity by determining priorities, publishing guidelines for their implementation, apportioning professional work, making the results of professional work accessible, collecting statistics, and maintaining contacts with the central agencies of cultural organizations, the party, and adult education. Schuster also described the agency's director as one who should be a practicing library director, knowledgeable above all about rural librarianship. Such a director "must not only possess the full confidence of the state agencies, but also be able to *do* something."[30]

Measured against his own standards, Schuster's tenure as director of the Prussian Landesstelle für volkstümliches Büchereiwesen cannot be considered particularly successful. Aside from beginning publication of *Die Bücherei*, there is no evidence that he actually did anything with the newly created agency. His lack of achievement was not necessarily his fault; at the same time as he was getting the Landesstelle under way, Schuster was beginning a new job as the director of the Berlin public libraries. He was still enmeshed in the ongoing struggle between the Ministry of Education and the Ministry of Propaganda over who would have charge of public librarianship, a quarrel that dominated the 1934 Danzig conference of the VDV. Walter Hofmann continued to do what he could to make Schuster's life difficult. In these circumstances it is not surprising that Schuster came to feel more and more out of sympathy with people and events; he also recognized that his presence had become an obstacle to progress. In the spring of 1935 he resigned as director of the Landesstelle and wrote to Ackerknecht, "I hope that all will now run smoothly and that all efforts at disturbance from Leipzig can be easily put down."[31]

Schuster designed the system, but Franz Schriewer, who became the director of the Prussian Landesstelle in May 1935, was the one who made it work. He took over at a time when the RWEV was receptive to changes. Schriewer did not begin with any predetermined agenda. As he wrote to Ackerknecht shortly after becoming director, "Now I only hope that I am successful in moving the ship of German public librarianship that is presently sitting on the sand into deep water again. It's not my way to make great plans but to take hold where a breakthrough seems possible. I can't, therefore, give you any interesting news about what's going to happen in the near future." Schriewer was, however, an experienced administrator, the expert on rural librarianship Schuster had originally thought necessary for the position, and the change in leadership was immediately apparent. He regularized a great many procedures, such as the memoranda the Reichsstelle now issued and the collection of statistics. He drew up a model budget for the Beratungsstellen to follow. He began making visits to the provincial Beratungsstellen and addressed himself personally to such matters as the bookmobile in Pomerania (Ger. Pommern) and the progress of the Rehau library. Librarians responded by turning to him for advice, as when the Bayreuth Beratungsstelle asked him for suggestions on how to handle the difficult situation in the public library in the city of Bayreuth, where the director was never present and gave no direction.[32]

Schriewer took seriously the Reichsstelle's charge to provide guidance on technical matters. He obviously put much time and energy during his years as director into preparing material that would help the practicing librarian administer and serve more effectively. A par-

Statistik

Bücherei: _Friedrichsdorf_   Dostort: _Neustadt_   Jahr: 1936/37.

Name und Stand des Büchereileiters: _Hans Dreesen, Hauptlehrer_

Romane und Erzählungen	G	E	W	J	Summe
167	62	43	5	26	303
107	3	6	11	29	156
41	11	8	3	16	79
17			1	11	29
31	17	14	7	257	326
363	93	71	27	339	893

Model statistics. (Reproduced from Schriewer. *Das ländliche Volksbüchereiwesen*, 1937.)

tial list of his articles in *DB* during this period include "Basic Thoughts on Technique for a Village Library," an article that proposed forms to be used and explained statistical procedures; "Basic Questions in Cataloging;" and "The Cooperation of District, Locality, and Government Library Agency," which treated the establishment of new libraries and the arrangement of library contracts. His presence in this area was so overwhelming that at least one Beratungsstelle found it necessary to inquire if the arrangements outlined in his book *Technik der Dorfbücherei* were mandatory.[33]

Despite his many accomplishments, Schriewer chose to return to Frankfurt/Oder after less than two years as director of the Reichsstelle. One factor in his decision was his disappointment in the lack of progress of German public librarianship, but Schriewer had experienced other disappointments as well. Guidelines (the Richtlinien) were published in October 1937, a substitute for the library law for which Schriewer had hoped. Most important, however, was his fundamental difference of opinion with Dähnhardt over the function of the Reichsstelle. Dähnhardt saw it as a staff support agency for the ministry, delivering supplementary work, preparing for decisions but not itself making decisions. Schriewer wanted to be given some independence and the power to make decisions. As Schriewer explained to Ackerknecht, "Dähnhardt increasingly seeks to reduce the Reichsstelle to a purely routine operation, to underling's work. For that I am not the right man." The separation between administration and professional work had been blurred, and the ministry was taking over more and more of the latter.[34]

Personality conflicts contributed to Schriewer's difficulties. Doubts about Dähnhardt probably aggravated their professional differences, and Walter Hofmann haunted Schriewer just as he had Schuster. Hofmann's correspondence is sprinkled with uncomplimentary remarks about Schriewer, although when it came to the point of Schriewer's resignation, Hofmann decided that he was preferable to the alternatives. Hofmann piously declared "at no time have I worked for the fall of Schriewer," but others saw his actions in a different light.[35]

Schriewer was criticized for having failed to provide clear leadership and for too much concentration on details, but his resignation was deeply regretted by most knowledgeable librarians. Dietrich Vorwerk, director of the Thuringian Beratungsstelle, helped organize a petition to Dähnhardt that deplored Schriewer's departure and described him as "indispensable." Except for those most closely tied to Leipzig, it was signed by almost all the Beratungsstelle directors.[36]

In Fritz Heiligenstaedt, the former educator from Lower Saxony who succeeded Schriewer as director of the Reichsstelle, Dähnhardt finally found his man. The rumor in December 1936 was that Karl Taupitz, Leipzig-trained director of the Beratungsstelle of Saxony, would become director, but in January Heiligenstaedt's appointment was announced. Rudolf Joerden, then director of the library in Wiesbaden, greeted it with surprise and a marked lack of enthusiasm: "Heiligenstaedt! I really can't think that he as a full-time school principal will find the way to do anything. He is so unsympathetic a man that I can't imagine that he won't perpetrate many obvious offenses." Heiligenstaedt did not fulfil Joerden's predictions. As director he proved to be "ambitious, nimble, conciliatory." One former Beratungsstelle director spoke of his charm and his ability to make everyone like him. Ackerknecht, too, found him genuinely likable but also recognized that he was not the person to stir up difficulties.[37]

Professionally, Heiligenstaedt did little more than be agreeable. The general consensus is that he was a figurehead. In 1937 Joerden described him as a man of straw. In 1942 Ackerknecht wrote, "I have recently had an experience that shows me that in criticial situations Heiligenstaedt can't undertake anything determining if Dähnhardt doesn't want it and that isn't personally agreeable to him." In 1986 Dietrich Vorwerk described him as having had practically no power; no surviving correspondence contradicts this view. Most of Heiligenstaedt's letters request information to be forwarded to the RWEV or transmit decisions of the ministry to librarians. As director of the Reichsstelle für Volksbüchereiwesen, he was little more than Dähnhardt's errand boy, a bureaucrat confined to routine matters and without any power to act or, indeed, interest in acting on his own initiative.[38]

Although it took several years and several directors to work out what were to be the respective spheres of the Reichsstelle and the Ministry of Education, in the end all real power remained with the ministry, meaning, in this case, Heinz Dähnhardt. This locus of authority was never described or officially recognized in the decrees that shaped Nazi public librarianship. Even in the Richtlinien, which were intended to be both a codification of practice and a statement of standards, the role of the Ministry of Education was not mentioned. The closest thing to an official clarification of the relationship between RV and RWEV was an article by Dähnhardt on the Richtlinien that appeared in *DB*. He wrote, "The Reichsstelle für das Volksbüchereiwesen, as the directing professional body, stands over the provincial Beratungsstellen. It is a service agency, directly subordinate to the Reichsministerium für Wissenschaft, Erziehung und Volksbildung, whose director will be named by the Reich minister of education and whose activity will be conducted according to business orders granted by him."[39]

The lack of clear-cut channels of authority left librarians uncertain about where to turn for direction and what they could expect. In a 1935 consideration of the condition of German public librarianship, the director of the Munich Beratungsstelle urged that the Reichsstelle be reorganized; he saw its job as the tactical implementation of the strategy outlined in the ministerial decrees, which "cannot primarily come from the Reich ministry." Librarians would, like Ackerknecht, write to Heilingenstaedt for assistance with a problem, only to have him do no more than forward the matter to Dähnhardt for action.[40]

Ambiguity allowed Dähnhardt maximum flexibility in shaping the situation to suit his will, and a gradual trend toward the concentration of power in his hands is apparent. After Schriewer's departure, he became increasingly involved in day-to-day administrative problems, especially personnel decisions. He took over the intractable problem of the absentee Dr. Strobl, director of the Bayreuth public library, putting pressure on both the Bayreuth city administration and the Bavarian authorities, without success. He was responsible for the choice of Bernhard Rang as director of the Bielefeld Beratungsstelle and sometimes participated in the selection of individual local librarians, as at Paderborn and Konstanz.[41]

Often Dähnhardt acted as an intermediary. One facet of this role was to interpret the professional librarian's viewpoint to local government officials. In 1940, for example, he traveled to Konstanz, a town that had appointed as its librarian a local townsman's son without professional qualifications. The butcher's son did not perform to the satisfaction of the provincial library administrator, and Dähnhardt came "to settle differences." He also mediated between librarians. When a new Beratungsstelle was created at Bielefeld by removing two districts from the jurisdiction of the Hagen Beratungsstelle, Dähnhardt smoothed the ruffled feathers of Dr. Angermann, Hagen's director.[42]

One of Dähnhardt's most important functions was to stimulate local governments to act. His visit to Munich in 1938 produced a report that criticized in some detail the operations of the Munich Beratungsstelle. It had two fundamental problems: the area for which it was responsible was too large (it presided over the largest geographical area in the Reich); and local administrators in Bavaria had little understanding of what public libraries were all about, unlike their counterparts in Saxony, Thuringia, and many Prussian districts. The RWEV used this report to try to prod the Bavarian Staatsministerium für Unterricht and Kultus to action. A trip to Vienna three years later produced another such report, although this time Dähnhardt was clearly exercising more initiative and acting more independently with respect to local officials.[43]

Dähnhardt was very active in planning. In 1937, for example, he traveled to Hagen to consult with the provincial authorities of the province of Westphalia. He did his best to stimulate them to act, criticizing the province for the fact that most of the public libraries there existed only on paper, promising financial subsidies, and setting forth what needed to be done; for instance, the Kreise needed to subscribe to *Die Bücherei*. He also announced the somewhat sensitive transfer of authority over the Beratungsstelle from the *Oberpräsident* to the *Regierungspräsident*.[44]

It remains a significant question, of course, whether such activity resulted in any real progress or whether it was activity for activity's sake. Did the RWEV have any real power? In 1934 von Staa, *Ministerialdirektor* in the RWEV, informed a group of librarians that the RWEV could only forward requests for financial support to the education ministries of the provinces. Then they had to be handled by the appropriate local authorities.[45] Later Dähnhardt did obtain control over some funds that he was able to use to influence Beratungsstellen, but they were never substantial enough to have a major impact. Provincial and local authorities continued to provide the resources to implement programs, and they made the final decisions. Many provinces, especially in Bavaria, exhibited considerable independence, perhaps because they felt it necessary to tailor national policy to local conditions, perhaps merely to assert their independence of Berlin. National agencies, and that included both the Reichsstelle and the ministry, could pronounce, could suggest, and could attempt to lead, but their role remained essentially advisory rather than decisive. They influenced results but they did not dictate them.

The limitations under which the RWEV and the RV functioned should not obscure the very real accomplishment their existence represented. With the establishment of the RV and the assumption of responsibility for public libraries by the Reich Ministry of Education, the Nazi state made a significant contribution. The Nazis' motives may not have been pure, but they did create instruments that offered the means of developing national policies and programs.

Not only did the period between 1933 and the publication of the Richtlinien in 1937 see the establishment of these crucial elements in the administrative hierarchy, it also answered many important questions. The Ministry of Education, rather than the Ministry of Propaganda, would be responsible for public libraries; this was both an authoritative statement about the character of the public library and a pointed statement about the primacy of professional priorities over political. The Ministry of Education rather than the Reichsstelle would exercise the real power; this indicates the limits on professional independence. Walter Hofmann's influence would be limited; he would *not* be the power behind the throne. The sum of these answers help establish what was Nazi public library policy.

CHAPTER FIVE

Library Collections
and
Collection Policy

ALTHOUGH THE principal interest of the new regime in creating a national administrative body for public librarianship was to provide it with an agency through which it could control library collections, the removal of books from libraries had already been under way for some months when the December 28 decree established the Prussian Landesstelle. This circumstance led the PMWKV to expand U II R Nr. 750.1 to include regulations that attempted to bring some order to the numerous uncoordinated efforts at library censorship, so that it became as much a landmark in state supervision of library collections as it was in public library administration. It began the process in which libraries were integrated into the system of government censorship.

When fully developed, Nazi censorship encompassed all phases of the creation, publication, and dissemination of information and ideas; it oversaw authors, controlled the publishing industry, supervised the book trade, and controlled libraries.[1] As a system, it had its weaknesses, suffering from overbureaucratization and lack of clear boundaries between state and party organizations, but it did succeed in its primary objective. Once all books considered unsuitable by the Nazis, published before 1933, had been removed, effective prepublication controls prevented any others from reaching bookstores or libraries. The extremely limited range of choices left librarians little room to exercise judgment in their book selection.

Everyone knows that the heart of a library is its collection. It is the *sine qua non*; without it, there is no library, be the librarians helpful, the programs creative, or the building ever so stately. The collection and the library's social role are inseparable. With this perception the Nazis were in complete agreement. Like many Europeans, and now increasing numbers of Americans, they were convinced that reading can be dangerous. It has consequences: What people read shapes them and influences their behavior.[2] Before 1933 Nazis often singled out one or another book for attack as a subverter of German virtue. In some communities they brought pressure for books to be taken out of libraries. It was only to be expected, therefore, that once in power, the content of library collections would attract considerable attention. Within a month of the takeover the Nazi press was clamoring, "Control the public libraries and reading rooms!"[3]

Nazi interest in collections also had another side, one they considered "constructive"; they added books and journals as well as removed them. Nazism preferred a Volk that felt rather than thought, that abandoned reason for instinct, and that followed the Führer blindly, but its leaders were sufficiently in touch with the realities of human nature to be willing to substitute the more politically expedient and achievable goal of a Volk who thought acceptable thoughts, for a completely unthinking Volk. This realism created a function for libraries in the Nazi state. What the library had in its collections could be used to shape the attitudes and thoughts of the Volk. It was one more potential weapon in a program of thought control.

In the management of library collections, a definite progression from confusion to regimentation can be perceived. The year 1933 was unique, dramatic, and chaotic. It saw in public libraries the reversal of many well-established trends and policies and the beginning of the formation of new ones. It was the time of torchlight parades, bonfires of books, of blacklists, and of wholesale, uncoordinated purging of collections.[4] It was also, however, the time in which the foundation was laid for more-affirmative actions; the first lists of what should be in the good public library were published. In 1933 and 1934 the acquisitions process was organized on a national basis, first by the agreement of the VDV with the Börsenverein für den deutschen Buchhändler, then by a second, revised agreement and the creation of the Einkaufshaus (EKH, or Purchasing House) to centralize fulfillment for all public libraries. The 1935 purge of collections was assigned by the RWEV and carried out by the provincial Bera-

79

tungsstellen, a successful operation of the new administrative system. The remaining prewar years were years of adjustment, modification, and minor variation.

When the Nazis seized power in 1933, they had neither a cultural policy that could provide general guidance nor a specific collection policy for public libraries. What they did have were some strong antipathies and some equally strong preferences that would have to be primary considerations in future collection development. The library profession, on the other hand, had been arguing for decades over what its collection policy was, a discussion intimately tied to how the role of the library was defined. The content of library collections and, more particularly, the definition of a good book were the primary focus of differences between Alte and Neue Richtung. The Neue Richtung insisted that the book must serve as a transmitter of culture and applied this view rigorously. The Alte Richtung was more pragmatic and willing to allow books into collections because users wanted to read them. Ackerknecht had presented a vigorous argument that including works representing different political positions in the public library would contribute to a "healthy, modern, and stable state," but even Hofmann had called for variety in the collection at least once.[5]

German public librarians before the Machtergreifung thought of themselves as following principles of book selection that were "educational." Alte and Neue Richtung might dispute how completely the public library was to be an educational, as opposed to a recreational, institution, but they agreed that its *raison d'être* was education. A visiting German librarian trying to explain German methods to British librarians asserted that in practice a middle course between the two Richtungen was followed. "The general opinion is that the task of public libraries is education through popular scientific literature, and educational entertainment, not mere entertainment, through fiction." German librarians felt that it was their job to raise the cultural and educational level of readers by increasing their store of useful knowledge and improving their taste; they differed over how authoritarian they should be in guiding individual readers. Circulation policies enforced their convictions. Readers were generally permitted to borrow only a limited number of novels each month, and in some places even nonfiction had similar restrictions.[6]

Book selection was geared toward the same ends; librarians displayed no trace of self-doubt about the superior virtues of their middle-class values. Lists of books removed during the various purges indicate that the collections of German public libraries, especially those in such major cities as Hamburg, were repositories of high culture and included the best of Western thought and literature. In place of detective novels, "written for pure sensation," public libraries offered adventure writers such as Jack London, R. L. Stevenson, and Joseph Conrad. The eternally popular Karl May was unacceptable because his stories were based on nothing but imagination; he had not seen one of the countries in which his novels were set. Librarians refused to permit the sweet, simplistic novels written for women and girls by such authors as Hedwig Courths-Mahler to pollute their shelves, regardless of the fact that they were so much in demand. These novels depicted a wrong and sentimental view of life. Imaginative biography, such as Lytton Strachey's *Elizabeth and Essex* or Emil Ludwig's *Napoleon*, was dismissed as undesirable and misleading. Even major literary figures such as Giraudoux, Galsworthy, and Thomas Mann might have works excluded from public libraries if they were not up to the librarian's standard.[7]

Nazism had its own, somewhat different ideas. To be rejected were all expressions of political views that differed from national socialism, most importantly Marxism and pacifism but also extending to defenses of democracy. "Liberal democracy" was a term of condemnation and contempt after the Machtergreifung. Any writings by or about Jews (except for attacks on them) were noxious, possibly attempted subversions of the good German Volk. Anything that might damage or debase the Volk was unacceptable. Librarians should add works that supported Nazi truths and values, by which were meant the basic texts of nazism, beginning with *Mein Kampf,* the philosophical precursors of the Nazis such as Paul de Lagarde and Moeller van den Bruck, racial theorists of the proper persuasion, and those that advocated militarism and nationalism either explicitly or by example. Nordic sagas and legends, tales of heroism and loyalty, and regional novels were highly desirable. Nazi libraries promoted *Blut und Boden* (blood and soil) novels, a literary form that combined an emphasis on racial purity and family with an almost mystical reverence for land and landscape.[8]

These different but not necessarily incompatible views of librarianship and nazism had somehow to be integrated, a process that took place in the course of the first years of the new regime. The assumption of librarians that there ought to be standards facilitated the integration; a few key changes in definitions effected most of what was needed. It helped that librarians found it easy to subscribe to the elimination of what harmed and debased the Volk, a vague, all-encompassing principle many probably believed they were already following.

Nazis and librarians shared a common hostility to *Schmutz und Schund* (dirt and trash), a category all its own. Librarians had long been leaders in the fight against the mass-produced trash that was sold at every newsstand. The 1926 law to protect youth from this intellectual rubbish of an urbanized, industrialized society had had little effect. Cheap magazines, dime novels, pornography, and publications that, while not technically pornography, were definitely of very dubious taste abounded. The Nazis were able to use this shared abomination as a selling point for far more broadly based censorship. In the early days some librarians welcomed the Nazi revolution because it appeared to be an opportunity to replace the license of Weimar that had produced such politically and culturally offensive publications with healthier and "better" material.[9]

Although policy usually shows progression, Nazi collection policy stabilized early. All essential elements were present in 1933, even if they were not phrased as smoothly as this 1939 statement of book selection priorities—"to waken the life of the Volk where it slumbers, to purify it where it is decadent, and to secure it where it is under assault." The most important groups that were not supposed to be in collections had been identified well before the takeover: Marxist, pacifist, and Jewish writings. Special categories varied with the exigencies of the moment; in 1934 all traces of those purged in the June 30 upheaval were ordered expunged, and in 1938 all publications on the sensitive theme of the South Tirol (It. Alto Adige) were to be removed from public view in anticipation of the Führer's meeting with the Duce. The early lists of recommended books likewise made clear the types of materials to be added.

A talk presented at a meeting of local librarians in October 1933 by the director of the Beratungsstelle for Westphalia, Dr. Rudolf Angermann, and later distributed to the *Landräte* of the province is a good example of a librarian's attempt to apply Nazi imperatives to collection policy.[10] The national revolution required that collections remove everything "that could in some way be a hindrance to the full realization of the National Socialist state." The *Schwarze Listen* (literally, blacklists), prepared in Berlin, enumerating Marxist, pacifist, and Jewish writings, were to serve as guides for removal. For material not covered by lists the following practical principles were to apply: Everything that endangered the interest of the state, that undermined the sense of the volkish community, was anti-Christian, was asphalt literature, or was written by authors who behaved inimically to the Nazi state was to be removed. (Angermann omitted one category for removal that had been stated at the September meeting of the VDV: "those books of a mentality which lacked proper seriousness.")[11]

The new, properly nazified library was to display above all the character of masculinity, by which Angermann meant the heroic, the vigorous, and the rational. It was to emphasize Nazi writing; that is, concern for Germanness, for the Volk, for racial thought, for military valor, for unity of thought and feeling, and for practical works. Strict standards of quality were to be applied, especially in fiction.

According to Angermann—a Leipzig adherent—in everything, the new state was promoting the recognition of principles of achievement and quality without compromise. German writers and poets were therefore to be emphasized more than previously. The library was to orient itself to youth, to give preference to the needs of those sixteen to twenty-five, and to strengthen young adult services. The internationalism of the public library was to be reduced.

Angermann's proactive suggestions retained their validity throughout the Nazi years, as did his description of the unacceptable. The negative aspects, however, were without question dominant in Nazi collection policy, despite Angermann's assertion to the contrary, and they were refined further after 1933. An analysis of the 1938 list of unwanted books published by the Reichsschrifttumskammer has eighteen categories of indictment. Mind-numbing in their relentless detail, they indicate a great deal about the Nazi state's antagonisms and fears, its fundamental paranoia. The categories of material to be expelled include: all German-language Marxist literature; all writing directed against nazism from abroad; all German-language writing from foreign powers on questions that touch the German national interest according to national socialism (e.g., the Sudeten German question); writing from a Christian point of view that opposes national socialism or the claims of the totalitarian state; publications of the Haus Ludendorff; all writings of a pacifist-liberal character; German writings in which the basic values of the Nazi outlook were undermined or misrepresented; writing that criticized the legal foundations of the Nazi state; writings of the traitors Ernst Röhm and Otto Strasser; reactionary writings; writings that are inconvenient on grounds of foreign policy; writings that could lead to an impairment of the military security and defensive strength of Germany; writings that appear to weaken the strength of the Volk (birth control advocate Margaret Sanger was given as an example); the destructive asphalt literature of the civilized literati, pornographic writing; writing by quacks or of an occult nature; Nazi *Kitsch* or what countered nazism; and anything on the history or present problems of Jews and Judaism.[12]

Intended for local government officials with little enough understanding of library problems, Angermann's presentation is straightforward and uncomplicated. Walter Hofmann's writings and actions are probably a better indication of the difficulty librarians faced in accommodating their collection values to nazism. In March 1933 he prepared a draft statement on the collections of the Leipzig library that rejected the idea of "parity" in cultural work, or cultural relativism. Instead, Hofmann argued that the library should be more concerned with the spiritual growth of the German Volk. After invoking Moeller van den Bruck and Lagarde, he went on to state that he was convinced that the extirpation of, for example, Marxism in a mechanical way would lead to the (unhealthy) repression of disorders in the mental circulation of the Volk and therefore fail in its purpose. Hofmann used figures showing how little Marxist and pacifist literature was read, as opposed to *Mein Kampf,* to imply that purges were unnecessary. He concluded with a most un-Hofmannlike practical argument:

> For working-class readers, the fact that the public library has literature of their outlook is a guarantee that the library does not seek their intellectual rape. If this literature were removed, the workers would lose confidence in the public library. They would, as under

the Socialist law, consequently avoid the public library, they would be compelled to use the purely Marxist workers' libraries and, even if it were forbidden, would secretly pass this literature from hand to hand. In any case, the extraordinary success the public library has had in attracting the working class to non-Marxist literature would be called into question if the Marxist literature were simply removed from the public library.[13]

This statement remained in draft form, however, and Hofmann's publications from this early period of nazism were far more compliant with the new order. His introduction to the 1933 Richtlinien that guided the *Säuberung* (purging) of the Leipzig collections acknowledged the realities of the contemporary political situation and the new primacy of the political. His 1934 book provided a more theoretical justification of censorship; the purpose of literary policy was "to free the true conscience of the nation from the grasp of pseudoforms and to secure its free operation." Hofmann cited his own earlier writings frequently, trying to show that his views were compatible with national socialism. With such statements as his 1922 pronouncement that only authentic, legitimate works belonged in the library or his 1923 comment that the public library's biggest problem was the lack of a point of view, this was not difficult. But to present himself as a prototypical Nazi required that other, equally Hofmannian, pronouncements be ignored. In 1913 Hofmann had, for example, declared that all important viewpoints should be in the public library.[14]

Boese describes Hofmann's behavior as a balancing act typical of the times. Hofmann did accept the censorship of collections; he even strengthened the theoretical case for it. On the other hand, he also defended some banned authors, such as Joyce, and successfully challenged the authority of the provincial Beratungsstelle over Leipzig's collection. His comment to Reuter in May 1933 that there was nothing much to say about the Leipzig situation except that the purge had been carried out does not suggest a particularly pleased man.[15]

In most situations, articulation of policy precedes execution; that is, after all, a principle of good management. In Nazi Germany, statement of collection policies lagged behind action, and the removal of books from libraries acquired a dynamic of its own. Librarians were forced to produce plans and policies or run the risk of having them imposed upon them. Many of their actions in 1933, therefore, are reactive, an attempt to guide forces that might otherwise overwhelm them. It is this loss of influence and the terrible insecurity of the early months of 1933 that underlie the comment of Rudolf Reuter, librarian of Cologne, to Walter Hofmann, in July 1933, after Reuter had first been responsible for the supervision of the Säuberung, then for new acquisitions, all the while participating in discussions of the entire public library program: "I hope that the greatest dangers for the further progress of public libraries as educational institutions has been turned aside."[16]

Nazi attacks on library collections began even before January 1933. A very interesting series of events in 1931 and 1932 in Rostock, a city on the Baltic, appears to have been almost a pilot project for the nazification of public libraries. Located in Mecklenburg-Schwerin, a province in which the Nazis would be taken into the government in the course of 1932, Rostock was a promising testing ground. On the city assembly the Nazis, when counted together with their allies the German Nationalists, were in a clear majority.

The affair began on March 2, 1931, when the German Nationalist group in the city assembly demanded that Erich Maria Remarque's *All Quiet on the Western Front* be removed from the Rostock public library. Considered pacifist, *All Quiet on the Western Front* was much disliked by conservatives for its realistic portrayal of the horrors of war. In addition, the Nationalists called for the general prohibition of all books that degraded the old German army and "falsified" German history; the immediate removal on moral grounds of Jaroslav Hašek's *Good Soldier Schweik;* a change in ordering procedures so that new acquisitions would be reviewed not only by the librarian but also by the Kuratorium, an oversight board of some twelve members; and demanded that books taken over from unions be returned. Later in the month, in an obvious attempt to rid themselves of the man who had been the director of the public library since its founding in 1919, Metelmann, they urged that the part-time director be replaced by a full-time one.

On April 22, 1931, the Kuratorium voted on the proposals of the German Nationalists. It unanimously (in a vote that included

86

Metelmann!) approved the prohibition against books denigrating the German army and those that falsified German history, split seven to four with one abstention on *Good Soldier Schweik*, and rejected the proposal to alter the book selection policy to include a review by the Kuratorium. Metelmann was not, however, prepared to withdraw *Good Soldier Schweik* from the collection; it was listed in the printed catalogs and readers would therefore continue to request it. Nor was he willing to share the responsibility for book selection.

This vote did not conclude the affair, and Metelmann's situation became even more uncomfortable. In June 1931 he threatened to resign. At this point the representative of the NSDAP on the Kuratorium, a man named Volgmann who later became the Nazi mayor, voted for the replacement of Metelmann by a full-time director. In December the position was advertised, but at the end of January Metelmann withdrew his resignation. On February 1 the city council passed the following resolution:

> In the city library a group of books inimical to volkishness have been found in the postwar years that are not compatible with the goal of a public library, which is to make available to the population, especially to youth, valuable literature of a German viewpoint. In order to remove these books, a committee, independent of the public library committee, will be constituted, which, together with the responsible officials and the director, will carry out an inspection of the materials. The committee will consist of three representatives of the city assembly and three professionals.

Metelmann did his best to resist this political invasion of the library. He transmitted documents from Erwin Ackerknecht that showed that a judicious acquisitions policy had been followed and that volkish works were present in sufficient quantity. On February 12, 1932, Ackerknecht himself wrote directly to the mayor, urging that acquisitions policy not be subjected to political influence. Wilhelm Schuster, then director of the Hamburger Öffentliche Bücherhallen, also counseled continuing adherence to politically impartial book selection.

Nothing had much effect. When the Rostock city council decided on February 16 that it was inappropriate to create a committee to review the library's collection, the city assembly reiterated its February 1 decision. The council then reversed its earlier support of Metelmann, and on April 25, 1932, Walter Butzow was selected as the new, full-time director.[17]

Although the Rostock newspapers carried accounts of these events, they were not generally known throughout the profession. Ackerknecht, who was deeply concerned that "the moral basis of politically impartial education was called in question," supported Metelmann forcefully. He saw events in Rostock as essentially Nazi-inspired and recognized the threat the Nazis posed to adult education. At the height of Metelmann's difficulties in February 1932, Ackerknecht consulted Schuster and Beer, his co-editors of *Bücherei und Bildungspflege*, about publishing an account of the affair in the journal, but nothing ever appeared on the subject.[18]

The Machtergreifung made it possible for the Nazis to expand their scale of operations from a local to a national level. Within days of January 30 it was obvious that library collections were going to be used as an index of the success of the Nazi revolution. Various groups addressed the matter: agencies and departments of the national government; local government officials; the librarians themselves; and a variety of political and social organizations of concerned citizens. By December 1933 no fewer than twenty-one organizations had issued a total of one thousand prohibitions of books.[19] Eventually, an orderly system of control emerged out of this confusion, tied to the administrative hierarchy in which the Beratungsstelle was the pivotal feature, and to the structure of local government.

The first move to reduce library collections to the new order was the *Reichspräsident*'s Emergency Decree of February 4, 1933, that declared, "Publications of unsuitable content, which endanger public security or order, can be confiscated by the police and withdrawn." The order should have come as no surprise. The 1930 attempt of the Nazi delegation to the Reichstag to introduce a Gesetz zum Schutz der Nation (Law for the Protection of the Nation), which included such concepts as "cultural treason" and "treason against the Volk" and promoted Rosenberg's Kampfbund für Deutsche Kultur (Militant League for German Culture), had announced Nazi intentions unmistakably. In 1932 the *Völkischer Beobachter* had published a list of "decadent" authors who could expect to be banned in the event of a Nazi takeover. On the strength of this presidential decree, some local officials and local police began removing books from public libraries. The police commissioner of Dessau has to have been one of the most eager; on February 5 he ordered the removal of Communist and pacifist works from the city library.[20]

The first pronouncement of the library profession on the subject came shortly after the election of March 5 that consolidated the Nazi seizure of power. By this time events were already well under way and librarians were having to respond to them. The "Erklärung und Aufruf des Verbandes Deutscher Volksbibliothekare" (Explanation and call of the Association of German Public Librarians) welcomed the new era with an aggressive enthusiasm:

> The time, in which adult education is constantly hard pressed and attacked by philosophies and parties that seek to destroy the unity of German culture and its great and proud accomplishments in the service of its goals and to transfer the pluralism of the political state into the cultural arena, is gone. Therefore the theories of the autonomy of education and of positive neutrality, which until now offered the public library protection from attacks on the national and provincial levels by the changing party governments from province to province and city to city, also fall. Today, however, we no longer need this protection and are free in our efforts to attain a concentration on the true and building cultural system, to lay stress on a continuity from the deepest sources of German blood and spirit, and from there push through to the *Volksgemeinschaft* in the new German state.

The "Aufruf" went on to outline the new tasks of librarians. It was not enough to rid themselves of the products of the literati and of asphalt literature, which would, in any case, probably not be numerous in view of librarians' long opposition to such material. "More important and more difficult than the sanitizing is the reconstruction of the public libraries, centering on the new tasks and the new educational objectives." The "Aufruf" was signed by Wilhelm Schuster and Wolfgang Herrmann; Max Wieser attached a clarification.[21]

Herrmann's essay in the widely distributed *Börsenblatt für den deutschen Buchhandel* on May 16, 1933, discussing the principles of sanitizing, was also part of the profession's response. Herrmann began with Mussolini's dictum: "Book and rifle—that is my order," a statement he interpreted to mean that the cultural-political goal of the public library of making the nation spiritually fighting-fit lay in the total mobilization of the Germans with the help of native writing. "The first step toward this goal is the effort, spontaneously intro-duced in all places, to concentrate the resources and book collections of public libraries on what is important." He then quoted from a memorandum issued by the PMWKV: "The fight is directed against those publications that destroy our forms of art and life—that is, against asphalt literature that is overwhelmingly written for the urban man, in order to reinforce his lack of connection with the environ-ment, to the Volk, and to society and completely to uproot him. It is the literature of intellectual nihilism." Not coincidentally, the prin-cipal creators of asphalt literature were Jewish.[22]

An important part of the article was the list of books and authors that Herrmann intended for use as a general guide to those in charge of sanitizing collections. Most on the list were pacifist or Marxist. Jewish and urban-oriented writers such as Döblin and John Dos Pas-sos were generously represented. Herrmann believed that whether all items on it could be removed depended on the extent to which new acquisitions could fill the gaps, but the temper of the times encour-aged librarians to thoroughness. As Ackerknecht wrote to a col-league, "In doubtful cases obviously it is advisable to put aside too much than too little."[23]

By the time Herrmann's article appeared in mid-May all local government was in the hands of the Nazis, and the momentum of the movement to control libraries had accelerated dramatically. Public libraries were being subjected to both externally and internally gen-erated pressures. Police in many areas were inspecting collections on the basis of the February 4 presidential decree. Patriotic groups such as Kampffront Schwarz-Weiss-Rot of Duisburg were making angry noises. City officials were ordering that all unacceptable material be withdrawn. The official in charge of public libraries in Stettin made known his wish to have removed from the collection "the broadest possible range of instructive and belletristic literature of Marxist or pacifist tendency." Book burning began May 8.[24]

The Hamburger Öffentliche Bücherhallen offered the profession a model of how to proceed with the Säuberung. Headed by Wilhelm Schuster, president of the VDV, the library could be sure that its ac-tions would be closely observed. It organized early. At the branch heads' meeting of March 18, 1933, Schuster discussed principles of book selection based on a circular of March 9. The political upheaval of the March 5 election demanded the removal from the book collection of works detrimental to the new will of the nation. A review of the collection would take place, and, after its completion, a list of those books to be removed would be sent to all branches. Cards for these books were to be taken out of catalogs but were to be retained. If readers asked for these books, they were to be told that they had been withdrawn.[25]

Few public libraries proceeded as systematically as Hamburg. The experience of Durlach, a very small town just outside of Karlsruhe, is probably more typical. On April 14, 1933, the mayor of Durlach wrote to Joseph Letzelter, the librarian, asking that the library collection be inspected. Those books "no longer suitable for a German public library in view of the spiritual direction that has come into force through the national revival" were to be removed. Letzelter responded a month later that he was carrying out a check of the collection, but that he would be grateful for a copy of the list he had heard the Zentralstelle had prepared. By the end of June Letzelter was able to announce that he had complied with the March decree of the PMWKV[26] against destructive works, although a July newspaper story informed readers that they must return their books so that the library could reopen as soon as possible after a review of the collection.[27]

Concurrently with these actions organized either by the libraries themselves or by city administrators, planning was progressing for what would be Nazi Germany's most famous literary event, the burning of thousands of "un-German" books. Books by Germany's most respected contemporary authors—Thomas Mann was only the best known—were taken from libraries, bookstores, and private collections and consigned to the fire in imitation of Luther's famous burning of the papal bulls. The literary world has few dramas that can compare: flames against a dark night from a ring of torches surrounding the victims, inspiring oratory, the chanting of aroused participants, and, finally—the focus and culmination—a gigantic funeral pyre of the intellect.

The book burnings were intended to look like a spontaneous repudiation of all that was spiritually unhealthy, by an outraged youth.

In fact, they had nothing to do with chance, spontaneity, or impulse. Two weeks before they took place, the *New York Times* was running stories about protests made by various groups against the planned burnings. Probably under the inspiration of the newly created Ministerium für Volksaufklärung und Propaganda (Ministry for Popular Enlightenment and Propaganda) and its head, Joseph Goebbels, the Deutsche Studentenschaft first proposed the burning in a memorandum of April 8. Students were to remove from public libraries "those dirty and trashy works of Jewish-inspired destructive thought." On April 12 the "12 Thesen wider den undeutschen Geist" (Twelve theses against the un-German spirit) were to be posted; the press was to be sent articles for publication and talks presented on the radio. Between April 26 and May 10 the "destructive" writings would be collected, public libraries purified, and the material brought to a central location. The books would be burned on May 10 at 6:00 P.M., after a torchlight parade and a speech of a "positive" character. Positive in their sense meant contrasting the class struggle and materialism with the volkish society and an idealistic attitude to life, or decadence and moral decay with race and tradition in family and state.[28]

The twelve theses, an obvious evocation of the Ninety-five Theses Martin Luther tacked on the church door at Wittenberg, proclaimed the group's demands. Kurt Herwarth Ball, author of the first article distributed by the news service of the Deutsche Studentenschaft, described them in these terms: "Twelve times the strong will of the young race: German! Twelve times the ancient, strong, native cry, as if from the blood: German!" Although intended for publicity and couched in extravagant language, his summary accurately conveys the sense and spirit of the theses. The first asserted the fundamental theory: "Language and literature root themselves in the Volk. The German Volk therefore bears the responsibility for ensuring that its language and literature be a pure and unfalsified expression of its volkishness." After execrating the Jew, the seventh and central thesis drew the following logical conclusions:

We therefore demand from the censor
- That Jewish works appear in Hebrew; if they appear in German, they are to be considered translations
- The sharpest intervention against the misuse of German writing

- That German writing only be at the disposal of Germans
- That the un-German spirit be ejected from public libraries[29]

Most cities followed the prescribed plan; the only student group to refuse was that at the University of Tübingen in Württemberg.[30]

Göttingen can serve as a typical example of the occasion. On April 12 the "12 Thesen" appeared. At the end of the month the Deutsche Studentenschaft received a copy of the first Schwarze Liste of seventy-one un-German titles and printed it in the *Göttingen Tageblatt*. Distributed by the Verband Deutscher Volksbibliothekare, this list had been prepared by Wolfgang Herrmann to assist those responsible for sanitizing libraries; it was very similar to the list published as part of his May article. The student groups, which included the Deutsche Studentenschaft's rival, the Nazi Deutscher Studentenbund, then checked it against their own book collections, those of their acquaintances, the Göttingen booksellers, and the public library.[31]

The ceremony on the night of May 10 was well reported by the Göttingen newspapers. The spectacle began with a lecture in the Auditorium Maximum of the university. After introductory remarks by the rector, Privatdozent Dr. Gerhard Fricke exhorted the students to carry the national revolution into the creative realm. As the national organizers suggested, Fricke took a positive tone, "It [the symbolic act of burning] will remain valueless and unfruitful without a renewed and ever-wakeful will to affirmation, to responsible construction, without a vow of fierce and tireless spirits, to want something new. We await the new and we believe in the future." The students then paraded with torches through the central city to the newly renamed Adolf-Hitler-Platz, where the student leader, Heinz Wolff, spoke briefly, using a part of the suggested invocation. The books were then set afire.

These well-coordinated performances were planned as drama, to make a statement, to attract attention, and they succeeded. It is hard to convey the depth of the outraged reaction. Erich Kästner, one of the authors whose books were burned, has left a moving account of the Berlin action, which he observed in person. Oskar Maria Graf, an author whose works were not on the Schwarze Liste, protested vigorously because his had *not* been burned! In the United States groups

93

marched, and Helen Keller sent a cablegram to German students pointing out that burning books did not kill ideas.[32]

Symbolism suffused the entire extravaganza, and there is little doubt that symbolic considerations were the primary motivation. Most books withdrawn from circulation were taken from collections by librarians following routine procedures and were placed, quite unspectacularly, in locked rooms. Book burning was mainly designed as an act by which the past and its false values were rejected, secondarily to give students practice in taking the offensive against their professors. It became a sacrament prerequisite to establishing a National Socialist society. After the Anschluß, a book burning on the German model took place in Salzburg.

Not only was the impact of the book burnings intended to be symbolic,[33] the proceedings themselves were rife with symbolism. Fire, for example, has been associated with purification rites. Use of the term *auto da fé* linked the book burnings with such historic conflagrations as Savonarola's Burning of the Vanities, many of which were expressions of religious zeal. The Hauptamt für Aufklärung und Werbung of the Deutsche Studentenschaft heightened the sense of religious ritual with the phrases it recommended to the student speaker. Intoned with proper rhythm, they are more than slightly reminiscent of the litany.

In the various professional and nonprofessional, official and unofficial efforts to manage library collections, lists of books played a prominent role. The earliest official lists were the Schwarze Listen. Originally prepared by the Berlin public library for internal use, then taken over by the Zentralstelle für das deutsche Bibliothekswesen, they rapidly acquired wide influence when they were distributed by the VDV to librarians. The transfer of responsibility for preparing them from the Zentralstelle to a special committee of the Propaganda Ministry and the Interior Ministry guaranteed an even greater impact.[34]

Police in the different Länder had their own lists of proscribed books, the content of which varied drastically from Land to Land. Before October 1, 1935, the Prussian Gestapo had banned all the writings of only thirty-three authors; in Bavaria 360 writers were completely banned. The Berlin Gestapo did not get around to pro-

94

hibiting that object of National Socialist hatred, *All Quiet on the Western Front,* until November 1933.[35]

After 1935 all preparation of unacceptable books was the responsibility of the Reichsschrifttumskammer. Several editions of their list, the *Liste des schädlichen und unerwünschten Schrifttums,* appeared. A definitive catalog was published as of December 31, 1938, and was kept up to date with annual supplements. The year 1938 also saw a list of Jewish authors. Recipients of these lists included provincial officials, police, the postal service, the army district libraries, university library directors, and the SA.[36]

Although the various authorities who promulgated and enforced these lists of banned books sought to present them as directed against such unhealthy writings as pornography, trash, and asphalt literature, in fact such material was only a small proportion of books banned. A statistical analysis of the first Reichsschrifttumskammer list of 1935 showed that of the individual titles banned 23 percent were Marxist, 11 anti-Nazi, 33 pornography, and 33 percent miscellany. In 1938 the figures were Marxism, 27 percent, anti-Nazi, 11; and pornograpy, 21; miscellaneous had grown to 41 percent.[37]

The full-scale book lists were supplemented from time to time by decrees banning individual titles or authors. In July 1935 the Prussian Landesstelle ordered that books on the foreign legion, spying, and wars of the future would not circulate "because of difficult questions." Earlier in the month coffee-table books were declared unsuitable for libraries.[38]

These individual decrees are among the best illustrations of the inconsistent and arbitrary nature of the system. A 1941 decree announced that the works of Graf Luckner, author of the much read *Seeteufel,* were once again to be allowed to circulate, thanks to the personal intervention of Adolf Hitler. War accentuated the inherent caprice. When the formerly esteemed, admirably Nordic author Sigrid Undset criticized the German army after the invasion of her homeland, Norway, her books were ordered removed. Although concern for ideas had created far-reaching censorship, decisions, especially in later years, often had little to do with the content of a work.[39]

Libraries sometimes were inconvenienced by the operations of a censorship system that was not infallible. The works of Eugen

Dühring, an early activist in the Nazi movement, were mistakenly included on one list of banned books. An interesting case involved the writer Manfred Hausmann. The problem for the librarian of Gütersloh arose when Edwin Erich Dwinger, an author prominent in Nazi literary circles, could not participate in a literary evening in Gütersloh in 1934 and was replaced by Hausmann. Hausmann's appearance at this NS-Kulturgemeinschaft–sponsored event produced requests for his books at the public library. But his books had been ordered removed. The Beratungsstelle was able to advise the puzzled librarian only that such inconsistencies could occur. Hausmann had been judged by the Kampfbund as "partially obscene and excessively erotic."[40]

The system of control did not leave librarians much room for judgment. Angermann's 1933 address on the purge and reconstruction of the public library collection made the significant point that the Schwarze Listen did not absolve librarians of responsibility. The individual librarian "cannot hide himself behind them." In practice, however, librarians followed lists slavishly; when they deviated from them, it was to exceed their requirements. One provincial library administration banned Mommsen's *History of Rome.* Hanover was so eager to comply with the new regime's wishes that it removed books and authors to which no one had yet objected—Bret Harte, John Galsworthy, Knut Hamsun, and Selma Lagerlöf. Quite incomprehensibly, the memoirs of the still-living, still-in-office President von Hindenburg and the Hochlandsmärchen (highland tales) of Ludwig Ganghofer, a *Heimat* writer other libraries were working hard to get enough of, were also included in this purge. The limits of professional competence had become so restricted by 1936 that Walter Hofmann pleaded with Dähnhardt for librarians to be allowed more latitude. If the public library were to exist and work, it could not give up selection, and selection was not possible without the exercise of critical judgment.[41]

From time to time librarians would try to change or modify a decision. The librarian of Saarbrücken hoped to obtain permission to continue to use the *Lexikon für Theologie und Kirche* and Pauly-Wissowa, the definitive reference source on the classical world. The *Lexikon* had been banned because it was a "religious work," and after 1934 public libraries were no longer supposed to include polemical religious works, "polemical" being defined as anything lacking a Nazi tinge. Could he not continue to refer to them? They were not available to the public. In contrast, Dr. Betty Schladebach of the Lippe Beratungsstelle attempted to get a book still deemed permissible, banned. She was concerned that in *Monika fährt nach Madagaskar*, Monika, Germany's Nancy Drew, and her father stayed with Sally Mendel, a Jew. Even though Sally was portrayed unfavorably, Schladebach found the book unacceptable.[42]

Librarians had the principal responsibility for implementing official decrees and satisfying the demands of other responsible bodies relating to collections, but various governmental and party officials supervised and verified their compliance. Police inspected libraries to ensure that librarians were enforcing the rules. After fifty years, a branch librarian in Duisburg could still recall vividly the occasion when the Gestapo found an anthology in her library with a story in it by a Jewish author. Only the assurances of the library director that this was inadvertent, an oversight, and that the librarian was both loyal and obedient, saved her from punishment.[43]

The organization of public libraries into a hierarchical system that covered the entire country made it easier to carry out decisions. The RWEV would ban a book, the RV disseminate that decision to the Beratungsstellen. They would in turn inform the libraries in their jursidiction, and the libraries would remove the books from the shelves. Reporting action taken moved in the opposite direction, although sometimes the Beratungsstellen informed provincial officials or communicated with the RWEV directly, rather than going through the RV. It was to achieve this kind of fully integrated chain of command that the Prussian Landesstelle had been converted to the Reichsstelle für volkstümliches Büchereiwesen, and the Prussian Ministerium für Wissenschaft, Kunst und Volksbildung to the Reichsministerium für Wissenschaft, Erziehung und Volksbildung in 1935. The director of the Beratungsstelle in Braunschweig testified to the success of the change when he wrote that since the Prussian Landesstelle had become the Reichsstelle, it was scarcely possible for any Beratungsstelle to remain apart from "energetic participation" in the new establishment of public librarianship in the Reich.[44]

The 1935 Säuberung was the first major activity undertaken by the new administrative system, and it was this purge that removed the majority of titles taken from libraries during the Nazi period. On August 14, 1935, the RWEV published an order, calling for no more, really, than the execution of the December 28, 1933, decree. All Marxist, pacifist, and, especially, Jewish works were to be removed. A companion order from the RV supplemented it, requiring that entries for withdrawn books in card catalogs and lists also be eliminated. Conspicuously absent is a call for the removal of Schund and Kitsch, the cultural Säuberung Rudolf Angermann had urged several months earlier to accomplish in the cultural realm what had already been achieved in the political. The RWEV call is, in fact, an admission that the purges of 1933 had not fulfilled their purpose; they had been more style than substance.[45]

Correspondence in the records of the Beratungsstellen for Westphalia and Lippe shows that in well-run provinces the system did operate as intended and could be very effective. Angermann in Hagen reported to the Regierungspräsident on October 3, 1935, that the Säuberung had been completed; in all, 224 catalogs had been checked and an average of 0.5 percent of the existing collections removed. The 1936/37 annual report of Dr. Wiegand, Angermann's counterpart in Detmold, does not give figures but describes the Säuberung as having been a major area of activity and very time-consuming. Certainly, if Beratungsstelle directors had to deal with too many argumentative officials, such as the mayor of Barntrup who tried to persuade Wiegand that Thomas Mann's *Buddenbrooks* "did not belong to the books forbidden by the police and had no destructive content," his use of "time-consuming" was an understatement.[46] An occasional difficulty might arise if the authority appealed to for a decision were unfamiliar with the book. Given that libraries were full of elderly fiction and obscure authors, this must have been a not infrequent problem.

The 1935 Säuberung was not uniformly thorough in all provinces. A 1936 report of the Bavarian Ministerium für Unterricht und Kultus to the RWEV acknowledged that all unsuitable books had not been taken out of the collections. Legal difficulties impeded the Beratungsstelle in Munich from exercising the right of oversight, and incomplete development of Bavarian police law made it especially important for the Beratungsstelle to be able to proceed. Suggestive of widespread shortcomings is the 1937 RWEV decree requiring that a

1935 memorandum from the RSK on unwanted books again be circulated to designated libraries.[47]

These procedures contrast sharply with those for the *Leih-büchereien*, or subscription libraries. Where the censorship of the public libraries was supervised by the individual provincial Beratungsstellen, the purges of the collections of the Leihbüchereien were handled centrally. Each individual Leihbücherei would send its catalog to Berlin, to the RSK. Karl Heinl, who was responsible for the project, reported that by March 1935, 5,445 Leihbüchereien of the estimated fifty-two hundred had sent their book lists, and that 3,853 had been checked. Much of this disparity in procedure must be attributed to organizational differences. The Leihbüchereien had been enrolled in the RSK from the beginning. The public libraries, on the other hand, were the responsibility of the RWEV and at least technically part of local government. It was public librarians, not libraries, that were members of the RSK.[48]

The extent and impact of the purges varied considerably. As of 1938, 27.7 percent of Berlin's collection had been acquired since 1933, 22.7 of Hamburg's, 27.2 of Essen's, and 25.4 percent of Leipzig's. The figures for Munich, Breslau, Dortmund, and Frankfurt/Main were 40.9, 72.2, 9.4, and 34.4 percent. For each city, between 1933 and 1938 the following volumes remain unaccounted: Berlin, 190,332; Essen, 142,176; Leipzig, 27,603; Munich, 149,612; Breslau, 80,571; Dortmund, 3,386; and Frankfurt/Main, 41,704. Only at Hamburg do the gains outnumber the losses. Some of the books removed would have been weeded because of their age and dilapidation, but the majority of these huge totals, as, for example, at Essen, where 69 percent of the 1934 collection was no longer there in 1938, or at Munich, where the same figure was 76 percent, have to be attributed to the rigorous censorship.[49]

A consistent pattern is apparent when libraries in large cities are contrasted with those in small towns and villages. Between 1933 and 1935, the years of greatest censorship activity, Hamburg withdrew 24 percent of its collection; Leipzig, 11; and Breslau, approximately 10 percent. Gütersloh, a town in Westphalia of 25,879 people (Hamburg, Leipzig, Breslau, and Frankfurt were all over 500,000) removed 360 books, or 6 percent, of its collection. Villages lost even less. In 1933 the VDV had claimed that in some rural districts of Pomerania and Bavaria only 0.1–1.4 percent needed to be weeded. The 0.5 percent of the libraries supervised by the Westphalian Beratungsstelle corroborate that this was a realistic estimate.[50]

The essentially antiurban orientation of the Säuberungen is also obvious when the reading patterns of users are examined. Of the most frequently read books in the large cities of Leipzig, Hanover, Düsseldorf, and Stettin for 1930, 65 percent were removed by the Nazis; the four small towns of Aumund (Hanover), Belgard (Pomerania), Bunzlau (Silesia [Ger. Schlesien]), and Nördlingen (Thuringia) lost only 9 percent of their most frequently read books of 1930.[51]

This variation was, of course, the result of the variation in collections, which in turn reflected divergent collection policies. A large-city library would have a substantial working-class readership, for which the Marxist writings and the novels set in cities, known to their detractors as asphalt literature, would be bought. If a town were like Freiburg, whose library had for the fifteen months preceding April 1933 emphasized "recognized authors of a nationalistic inclination" and completely ignored Socialist and Communist works, naturally there would be little to weed. Village libraries, which served peasant communities, were full of Heimat novels and nondescript nonfiction.[52]

The figures available for the purges can, in the end, only give an impression and need to be viewed with caution. Often they included books withdrawn for such unexceptionable professional reasons as dilapidation or outdatedness. Boese has also suggested that librarians used this opportunity as a screen to carry out their own objectives, removing the light, perhaps trashy books, as Angermann urged, and accomplishing a cultural Säuberung as well as a political one.[53]

The removal of unwanted books was the most dramatic and spectacular aspect of Nazi collection policy, but it was not its totality. Collection development also had a positive side, the addition of books that would inculcate and reinforce the new regime's values. Early calls to purify libraries or explanations of the Säuberung carefully paired the concept of purging with that of reconstruction, as in "Aufruf": "More important and more difficult than the purge is the

100

rebuilding of public libraries, their focusing on their new tasks and the new ideal of education."[54]

Just as each year brought increased organization and tighter control over unwanted books, each year brought more systematization and uniformity to book selection and procurement. The network of Beratungsstellen was essential to achieving this result. The Beratungsstellen provided professional services to the small libraries; they evaluated collections, reviewed new publications, recommended selections, and placed orders. They linked the policy-making agencies with those that actually served the public.

Beratungsstellen spent much time examining the catalogs of the small public libraries in their jurisdiction and scrutinizing their requests. These reviewing procedures had originally been developed to improve the small libraries and had been the major responsibility of the Beratungsstellen before 1933; the main effect of Nazi changes was greatly to increase the scale and to introduce political considerations. The earlier concern for quality and the educational role of the library remained, however, and much advice was directed to those issues. In 1931 the Beratungsstelle in Westphalia discouraged the library in Halle/Westphalia from purchasing Remarque's new book, *Der Weg zurück*, because the director considered that it was sentimental and weaker than his first book. The responses of the Beratungsstelle for Lippe when it lectured the librarian of Bösingfeld in 1938 on filling up his collection with purely entertaining works such as Ganghofer's stories, or the Bayreuth Beratungsstelle that came down hard on the director of the library in Hof for ordering four Karl May titles, are in the same tradition.[55]

Beratungsstellen increased the influence their supervisory activity gave them by reviewing books. Because only the larger libraries usually subscribed to *Die Bücherei*, the principal national book-reviewing medium, the Beratungsstelle was essential in widening the journal's impact by passing on its judgments. Local book reviewing depended on how energetic and organized the Beratungsstelle was. Hamburg, where branch librarians met regularly to discuss new books, was a model, but, although technically a Beratungsstelle, it was functioning as a large, urban public library system rather than a typical Beratungsstelle. Usually reviews were written, prepared by

101

junior staff. Characteristically they summarized the content of a book in some detail, gave attention to the point of view, tried to predict its probable effect, and recommended the groups for which it was suitable. Neither the instructions that survive from the Hamburger Öffentliche Bücherhallen nor sample reviews take notice of Nazi political values as such, although they are present in subtle ways, as when a review recommends Felix Timmermans's novel *Bauernpsalm* because of the "nourishment" and "health" the reader experiences. All book reviews were expected to "make clear the particular political function" of each book.[56]

Beratungsstellen created two kinds of book lists to be used by smaller libraries in selection. The first was the kind prepared by every library, a list of titles on a particular topic that might interest a user. The Beratungsstelle at Hanover, a large, active organization that provided leadership to the other Beratungsstellen in Lower Saxony, had published a list of Nazi books in its journal within a few months of the Nazi takeover. The second was a type that became increasingly common as the system became more organized, a list of titles to which libraries were limited in their selections. The Detmold Beratungsstelle published such a list, titles culled from nationally produced lists and then examined by the Detmold staff for suitability to conditions in Lippe.[57]

Most lists of recommended titles were prepared at the national level and were substantial efforts. Counterparts to the blacklists, these "white lists" identified works libraries either should add to their collections or were acceptable for them to add. The highest priority, obviously, was Nazi and Nazi-oriented books. In 1933 the only list of Nazi writings generally available was Wolfgang Herrmann's list, "Der neue Nationalismus und seine Literatur," which had been published in *BuB* the preceding year and was not really satisfactory. Not only had it not been designed for the purpose of establishing guidelines of collection development, Herrmann had committed the unforgivable sin of describing *Mein Kampf* as not containing "a single intellectually original or theoretically fully realized idea." His observation dogged Herrmann until his death and was an obvious drawback to wide distribution.[58] The gap was, however, quickly filled by library and literary organizations at all levels.

By 1934 the Reichsstelle zur Förderung des Schrifttums list, *Die ersten hundert Bücher für nationalsozialistische Büchereien* (The first hundred books for National Socialist public libraries), was in its seventh edition. After 1935 specialized subject lists such as "Politik und Weltanschauung" (Policy and worldview) and "Kultur und Natur" (Culture and nature) proliferated. There were also elaborate catalogs intended to represent core collections for all types of public libraries, ranging from village to hospital libraries, that included all subject areas.[59]

Die ersten hundert Bücher is especially interesting because it defined a minimum standard for a Nazi public library. The categories in which libraries were supposed to expand their collections were national socialism, race and Volk, the war and postwar period, and literature. On the list were the books of the Nazi leaders, Hitler, Goering, Goebbels, and the inevitable Rosenberg; the authors who had provided national socialism's intellectual foundations, such as Houston Stewart Chamberlain and Paul de Lagarde; and an assortment of novels. This last group included Kitsch that inculcated Nazi values by example: Werner Beumelberg's *Sperrfeuer um Deutschland*, Dwinger's *Zwischen Weiss und Rot*, and *Hitler Junge Quex*. The memoirs of President von Hindenburg, then still living, were included, although they were not listed in the far more extensive *Reichsliste für kleinere städtische Büchereien* that appeared in 1939, after his death.[60]

Once the titles to be ordered had been determined, they needed to be acquired. In this area, too, the Nazi period saw notably increased centralization, primarily because of the Einkaufshaus. In 1933 a public library could order through its Beratungsstelle. With the definition of the role of Beratungsstellen in 1934, those libraries were then required to order through their Beratungsstelle, if they had one. The Beratungsstellen were in turn expected to place orders with the EKH, a fulfillment center created in 1934.

These changes in the procurement procedures of libraries had major consequences for the book trade. Local book dealers did not welcome centralization and both individually and through their association, the Börsenverein für den deutschen Buchhändler, attempted to oppose the new system. The statement, announcing the founding of the EKH, that the EKH would be "an intermediary between libraries and the book dealers," was a major concession. What it meant in practice was that Beratungsstellen placed orders with local book dealers, thus leaving their profits unaffected. There was also some room for local variation. Two other agreements regulated discounts. The first was negotiated by Schuster in 1934 on behalf of the VDV. The second, two years later, came as a decree from the RWEV. It reflected the changes brought by the enhanced responsibilities of the Beratungsstellen and the growing numbers of small libraries. Coincidentally, it illustrates the considerable power of the government in library affairs and the diminished role of the professional association.[61]

After an initial period in which its inability to deliver what had been promised threatened its survival, the EKH became a vital part of public librarianship. In 1936 complaints were so frequent that the director of the RV requested the Beratungsstellen to enumerate their problems in writing. Six months later the RV distributed guidelines for dealing with the EKH that improved the situation, but delays remained endemic. At its best, the EKH offered libraries popular books ready to go on the shelf, a convenient source of library supplies, and centralized ordering and accounting. Practicing librarians especially appreciated the library bindings in which all books could be obtained. As the EKH solved the worst of its operational problems, it was able to take on new tasks. Working with individual Beratungsstellen, it developed standardized block collections that made possible a rapid increase of the number of small libraries during the height of the Nazi expansion program. It tied book ordering to the *Reichslisten,* both simplifying procedures and guaranteeing greater uniformity.

The paucity of library catalogs does not permit detailed analysis, but the scattered lists surviving indicate that collections were of high quality within the established political limits. They did invariably contain the basic Nazi texts and Nazi novels—when in doubt about what to order, a librarian would simply get another copy of *Mein Kampf* or the *Völkischer Beobachter*—but they also included an impressive array of the best of Western culture. Not until all writings of enemy nationals were banned after the outbreak of war did they become really parochial. A 1936 list of titles to be added to the library of the town of Tirschenreuth, a small town of forty-five thousand on the Czech border in the depths of the Upper Palatinate, included *Oliver*

Twist, St. Francis of Assisi's *Sonnenlied, Gulliver's Travels, The Hunchback of Notre Dame,* Henry Ford's *My Life and Work,* and books by Edith Wharton, Jack London, H. Rider Haggard, Oscar Wilde, Guy de Maupassant, Sir Walter Scott, Emile Zola, Henry Sienkiwicz, Leo Tolstoy, and Feodor Dostoevsky, as well as many works by the ever-popular Ganghofer and all of Goethe's writings.[62]

Lists of books withdrawn in the purges also attest to the breadth of German public libraries until Nazi restrictions were imposed. Included in the titles removed from the Hamburger Öffentliche Bücherhallen in March 1933 were works by numerous Marxist writers, theoreticians as well as Russian revolutionaries. There were anti-Nazi and anti-Fascist works, which, when coupled with the library's statement in 1933 that it did not need to add pro-Nazi titles because it had been buying them all along, are evidence of a collection of range and depth.[63]

To appreciate the centrality of collection development in Nazi public library policy, a document prepared by the Hamburger Öffentliche Bücherhallen in 1935, summarizing the adaptation of the library to the principles and requirements of national socialism, is helpful. First on its list of accomplishments, and the foundation of all other activity, was the removal of unsuitable books and the establishment of procedures for regular oversight. This was followed by the eradication of all traces of these books from catalogs. The library had added "to a great extent" Nazi novels and books in the categories of race, militarism, the joys of work, agriculture and the land, and German history. It had reorganized its nonfiction into Nazi-approved groupings and revised its subject catalog "from a Nazi viewpoint." Topics of Nazi interest were promoted by book lists, exhibits, and through readers' advising. The youth section was expanded and revitalized, naturally from a Nazi point of view. The library also cooperated with such groups as the Hitler-Jugend and school classes, preparing reading lists and small specialized collections for them and offering tours. Some small libraries were organized for those serving their year on the land or doing another type of labor service. As one of the best-organized and best-funded libraries, Hamburg was obviously able to do more than most public libraries, and its operations show the system at its optimal.[64]

Just as the collection was the focus of Nazi library activity, it was also the focus of opposition to Nazi library policy. To some extent the importance of the collection made this focus inevitable, but the disagreeable character of collection policy in contrast to more-welcome changes in other areas also contributed. Not that there was much opposition, and such opposition as there was tended to take the form of veiled recalcitrance rather than outright challenge. Wieser's question in the "Aufruf"—"Do you believe, colleagues, you must still fight further against the spirit of the new age?"—suggests resistance to Nazi plans and actions, a resistance he attempted to discourage by pointing out that it would be at the expense of them and their work. Few librarians were as courageous as Joseph Letzelter of Durlach, who wrote to the town's mayor, "Although I have been a warm supporter of the National Socialist movement for many years, in this matter I am personally of the opinion that these applicable principles will be all too conscientiously employed. All areas of human knowledge and of art ought in my opinion to remain international." Letzelter then compared reading to the radio broadcasting of music that since January 30 had continued to offer Tschaikowsky, Donizetti, and Gounod. On a very limited basis, some librarians would circulate the banned books from the storage rooms in which the books had been placed to people they could trust. One librarian who trained during the war years remembers the director of the library in which she served her apprenticeship taking the trainees to the locked room of banned books and telling them, "Here is German literature. Read it."[65] For the most part, however, librarians cooperated, their degree of reluctance undisclosed.

The attitude of Wilhelm Schuster was common. A self-described "practical" man, Schuster, who in 1929 had advocated a book selection policy above party lines and in 1931 supported Metelmann in Rostock, believed it was in the interest of German librarianship to accept limitations. As he put it in May 1933, "it will not be too long until we can separate the wheat from the chaff." He, like Rudolf Reuter of Cologne, clearly hoped to preserve public libraries through compromise.[66]

Public indignation, to the extent that it existed, was no more effective than resistance from members of the profession. The *New York Times* described the Berlin crowd as unenthusiastic about the book burnings, but this lack of enthusiasm did not translate into a challenge to the action. A student group at the University of Berlin answered the "12 Thesen" with twelve theses of its own. Among its more polite assertions were that anti-Semitic students were liars and cowards. The dissidents pointed out that the Jews were a royal people at a time when the ancestors of the anti-Semites were at best warthogs in the Teutoburger Marsh.[67]

A more subtle measure of public response is circulation figures. By all the evidence available, people simply stopped using public libraries. Cities as far apart and as different as Kiel, Hanover, and Lingen show that circulation declined steadily from 1932/33[68] and did not begin increasing again until 1937/38. The drop at Kiel between 1932 and 1935 was 21 percent; at Hanover between 1932 and 1936, an even sharper 42 percent; and at Lingen between 1930 and 1935, 45 percent. Ackerknecht wrote of readers staying away in droves. At the time librarians argued that this decline was the result of people returning to work and therefore having less leisure for reading, but it was so precipitate, and the figures are so much lower than those of the full-employment years of the 1920s, that increased employment can have been only part of the story.[69]

This marked reader response is a measure of the success of Nazi efforts. The regime had made the collection the centerpiece of their library policy and had achieved their goals. By 1935 public libraries had been thoroughly nazified: They inculcated Nazi values and offered a reader no opportunity to acquire inconvenient ideas. Libraries immediately adjusted to every shift in the political wind. They were thus able to serve Nazi purposes in a way they had not been able to in 1933, yet this improved utility had at the same time cost them some of their institutional effectiveness.

The radical purge of public library collections remains the best-known fact about Nazi public libraries, familiar well beyond professional circles. Its notoriety is deserved, even though the reshaping of collections to inculcate the values of national socialism may have been even more pernicious in the long run. By their willing participation, librarians committed what Lotte Bergtel-Schleif has called "spiritual suicide."[70] Librarians were, as she pointed out, the ones who, with their own hands, removed the books from library shelves.

107

Proud of their humanism, they found themselves enforcing the principle that "the protection of the humanistic worldview belongs to the [unacceptable] bourgeois opposition."[71]

Librarians had long practiced guidance, but what took place between 1933 and 1945 was so different in degree that it changed the character of public libraries. They might have used the new conditions to accomplish some of their own cultural objectives, but it was at a very heavy price. The act of censorship was the truest indication of the Gleichschaltung of the profession.

CHAPTER SIX

The Provincial
Beratungsstellen

ALTHOUGH THE National Socialist state developed a top level of an administrative hierarchy for public libraries, the most important institution in the hierarchy remained the provincial library agency. Variously known as a Landesstelle (provincial authority), Beratungsstelle (advisory authority), Volksbüchereistelle (public library authority), or, if in a border area, Grenzbüchereistelle (border library authority), the provincial library agency was the agency that bore primary responsibility for the implementation of Nazi public library policy. (In this book Beratungsstelle is used as a generic label.) Located between the policy-making institutions and the front line of library service, it was called upon to interpret, apply, advise, and supervise. Preliminary guidelines (Richtlinien) on the establishment and activity of Beratungsstellen were published in 1934 by the Preußische Landesstelle. Refined and expanded, they were given definitive form in 1937 and enacted as an RWEV decree.[1]

At the time the Nazis took over, there were twenty-four Beratungsstellen in Germany. The oldest was that of Westphalia, its office located at Hagen. It had been founded in 1909 "so that public libraries may be appropriately planned, administered, and developed." The period after World War I saw fairly rapid growth in the numbers of Beratungsstellen, especially in the border areas, as other administrative districts and provinces followed suit; the Beratungsstellen of Allenstein, Flensburg, Cologne, and Kaiserslautern all date from this time. By 1933 most of the major provinces and Prussian administrative districts had a Beratungsstelle, although there remained many areas without such an agency. The administrative net had some very large holes; no systematic national plan had guided its development.[2]

Beratungsstellen were, as the director of the Munich Beratungsstelle remarked in 1935, "completely different." They varied tremendously in size, from Munich, responsible for an area of almost twenty-nine thousand square miles, 7,337 different localities, and 6,694,000 people, to Braunschweig, which had approximately one-fifteenth Munich's responsibilities, fourteen hundred square miles, 446 localities, and 512,000 inhabitants. Hanover acted as a kind of supra-Beratungsstelle for the other Beratungsstellen of Lower Saxony. Generally concerned with rural librarianship, a few Beratungsstellen were really a large-city system under a different name, while others dealt with districts that lacked any significant population center. According to Wilhelm Schuster, if the large-city systems were excluded, the average German Beratungsstelle was responsible for 1.3 million inhabitants. This situation compared most unfavorably with Denmark, where each rural Beratungsstelle was responsible for only eighty-nine thousand. Most German Beratungsstellen were attached to a public library and run by its director as a supplementary task, but a few were part of a provincial library or operated independently.[3]

It had long been recognized that Beratungsstellen were institutions that filled, or could be made to fill, an essential place in a national administrative hierarchy for public librarianship, and 1933 offered the opportunity to put this into effect. Schuster described in some detail the current status of Beratungsstellen in two memoranda on the subject in October 1933, one on rural Beratungsstellen, the other on Beratungsstellen in cities of over twenty thousand. He made a case for their extension, laid out some necessary conditions, and then defined their tasks. Schuster declared that if the state wanted to control the great possibilities offered by public librarianship for the intellectual creation of the Volk; assure consistent development throughout Germany without curtailing the initiative and cultural independence of the localities; guarantee a regular, professional, and rational use of available public monies; and ensure the strengthening of cultural defenses, then Beratungsstellen must be correspondingly organized. To achieve these goals, it was necessary to do several things: assign the Beratungsstelle to a politically reliable, completely professionally prepared and experienced librarian; attach the Beratungsstelle to an efficient public library; incorporate the Beratungsstelle into the administrative network of the state; invest Beratungsstelle directors with the necessary authority over all public libraries in their jurisdiction; and provide sufficient financial support.[4]

Schuster's memorandum proposing that rural Beratungsstellen be reorganized as the foundation of a national library policy identified the fundamental administrative problem of public librarianship from the point of view of the National Socialist state: It was the localities who were the supporters of public libraries, *not* the national government. This fact limited the effectiveness of the Reichsstelle für Volksbüchereiwesen and the RWEV, and created even more difficulties on the provincial level, where a Beratungsstelle director was often in the position of trying to persuade, prod, or coerce a reluctant town council or rural district into putting out the money to establish and properly maintain a public library. Throughout the Nazi period there was a critical separation of authority and responsibility; on the one hand were the library-focused institutions—RWEV, Reichsstelle, Beratungsstellen, and individual library—on the other, the governments supporting each tier of these institutions. Accountability ran not vertically, as administrative theory prescribes, but horizontally, creating an inevitable schizophrenia within the system and making innumerable problems for individual librarians. They were answerable to different parties, who only rarely agreed on priorities.

The ministerial decree of December 28, 1933, charged Prussian Beratungsstellen with the task of insuring that all libraries in their area "worked in the spirit of national socialism," a broad directive that could be interpreted as general jurisdiction. Provinces without Beratungsstellen were urged to create them, and new establishments followed in rapid succession. The year 1934 saw the foundation of Beratungsstellen at Dresden, Königsberg, Halle, Bremen, and Stadthagen; 1935 brought Wiesbaden, Bayreuth, Dessau, and Detmold; and 1936 added Erfurt, Aachen, and Freiburg. By the late 1930s a new Beratungsstelle usually did not mean that a previously unserved district or province was acquiring a library administration, but that a large area was being divided in the interests of improved service.[5]

The circumstances under which each new Beratungsstelle was established varied tremendously. Sometimes it was routine, passing almost unnoticed in the flow of day-to-day provincial administration. This appears to have been the case at Bremen where a memorandum simply announced the establishment of a Beratungsstelle to which all public libraries would be responsible. The establishment of the Beratungsstelle involved little more than giving the director of the Bremen Stadtbücherei a few new reports to write. The Bremen statement of purpose echoed the Prussian decree of the previous December; the new Beratungsstelle was to see that "all public libraries in the jurisdiction of the Bremen area would work in the spirit of the National Socialist state." Other creations were equally smooth, especially when they were really not entirely new creations, but the redirecting or renaming of an existing operation, or when they did not require major expenditure. At Detmold in Lippe the province created a Landesstelle that was given formal responsibility for many things the Landesbibliothek had already been doing, and the director of the Landesbibliothek was appointed to head it.[6]

Absence of strife was not, of course, always the case. In those instances where there was no obvious individual or organization to take the lead, where local officials needed to be educated about the role of public libraries, or where money was in even shorter supply than usual, discussion was apt to be long and contentious. The prehistories of many Beratungsstellen display considerable acrimony and competition between individuals or other parties; the compromises required to allow establishment often influenced the future direction of the Beratungsstelle and what it was able to accomplish.

Bayreuth is a particularly interesting case because the establishment of the Beratungsstelle was the occasion for the expression of a host of rivalries, some peculiar to the Nazi state, others of long-standing origin. In 1933 Bavaria had two Beratungsstellen for a province that covered more than twenty-nine thousand square miles and included such dispersed and diverse territories as Upper and Lower Bavaria; Swabia (Ger. Schwaben); Upper, Middle, and Lower Franconia; the Upper Palatinate and the Palatinate on the Rhine (Ger. Rheinland-Pfalz). One Beratungsstelle was in Kaiserslautern and served the Rhenish Palatinate; until July 1933 it was headed by A. Trumm, a Social Democrat and an adherent of Walter Hofmann.

112

Trumm was replaced by Willy Pfeiffer, a man whose library experience had begun only in May 1933, but whose political credentials included a claim that he had tried to join the party in 1928 when working for an import firm in the United States.[7] The other Bavarian Beratungsstelle was in Munich and responsible for the remaining 28,998 square miles. Its limited resources and overextended responsibilities made any conspicuous presence in the outlying areas impossible.

The initiative for the establishment of a Beratungsstelle in the "Bayerische Ostmark," a Nazi term for that part of Bavaria that lay along the Czech border and included Upper Franconia, the Upper Palatinate, and Lower Bavaria, was largely local. Probably the idea came from local party officials in Bayreuth and was then taken up by Hans Schemm, the *Gauleiter* of the Bayerische Ostmark and Bavarian minister of culture, although the stimulus may have operated in the opposite direction. But whatever its genesis, the project was primarily a party endeavor and neither professional librarians nor the educational establishment was involved in any significant way.

An early move was to call a conference of the leaders of south German librarianship for July 7, 1934. Dr. Moll, the director of the Kulturpolitische Abteilung of the Nazi party in the Bayerische Ostmark, began his report to the RWEV on the conference with the statement that the Gau Bayerische Ostmark was in the process of building its important border public librarianship. The conference had been held in Stuttgart and had addressed the problems of public librarianship in southern Germany. It had been attended by the director of the Stuttgart public libraries, an official from the Württemberg Ministry of Culture, the directors of the Beratungsstellen of the Rhenish Palatinate and Hesse, assorted librarians and cultural officials from Baden, the Saarland, and Bavaria, and by Walter Hofmann. One of the miscellaneous cultural officials was Josef Wutz, a secondary school teacher from Bayreuth and business manager of the Grenzlandamt of the Gau Bayerische Ostmark, who would emerge as the prime mover to establish a Beratungsstelle in Bayreuth and who eventually became its first director. Conspicuous for their absence from this conference were Dr. Anton Fischer, director of the Munich Beratungsstelle, and Dr. Ernst Boepple, the official in the Bavarian Ministry of Culture responsible for public libraries, both of whom had been invited to attend. Moll made it clear that all that had taken place had done so "with the express agreement" of the Gauleiter, Minister of Education Schemm.[8]

The meeting with Reich Minister of Education Bernhard Rust that Moll hoped would be the next step did not take place. Instead, Gauleiter Schemm was able to bring about a visit in November 1934 from the director of the Grenzbüchereidienst in Berlin, Wilhelm Scheffen, and its secretary, Franz Schriewer, then at Frankfurt/Oder. They met with Moll, Wutz, and Peter Langendorf, Walter Hofmann's assistant from Leipzig; this time the director of the Munich Beratungsstelle was present. Although Wutz later described this meeting as having recommended that a governmental Beratungsstelle directly responsible to the minister of culture and with special, far-reaching powers be established in the Bayerische Ostmark, his statement was only partially true. The report makes clear that, while the group agreed on such general pieties as the necessity of taking public librarianship in the Bayerische Ostmark in hand as soon as possible, it differed over two important specifics: whether the new Grenzbüchereiberatungsstelle should be governmental or nongovernmental, and who should be the director. The sides formed along geographical lines; those from the Bayreuth Gauleitung argued that the Grenzbüchereiberatungsstelle must remain in its hands. Scheffen, Schriewer, and Fischer countered that existing financial resources could be used only by a governmental organization and stressed that both Dr. Boepple and Dähnhardt supported this view.[9]

After this November meeting Wutz prepared a memorandum that became the essential justification for the creation of the new Beratungsstelle in Bayreuth. He argued that the Bayerische Ostmark was neglected, and that the area had not received any fructification from Munich after the National Socialist revolution. The Beratungsstelle in Munich was responsible for too large an area. In addition, it suffered in Wutz's eyes the additional disadvantage of being of a scholarly type, not appropriate for furthering public librarianship. The public libraries in the Bayerische Ostmark were without an internal relationship to the Munich Beratungsstelle. Although his initial point about the overextension of the Munich Beratungsstelle really made the case and summarized the problem, Wutz went on to pile detail upon detail: The training of library personnel was not adequate; book selection was not politically satisfactory; and the large libraries of the area, in towns such as Amberg, Passau, Regensburg, and Hof, were not getting attention.[10]

In January 1935 Schemm announced formally that he intended to establish a Grenzbüchereiberatungsstelle, directly subordinate to his ministry, that would be responsible for public librarianship in Upper Franconia, the Upper Palatinate, and Lower Bavaria. This was, however, an announcement rather than a decree, even though Schemm's death in an automobile accident in March of that year sanctified it. It was, moreover, a statement of future intention rather than present formation. As an interim measure, Schemm entrusted the Gauvolks-büchereistelle of the Bund Deutscher Osten—in other words, Wutz—with the organization of public librarianship in the Bayerische Ostmark. Schemm may have adopted this temporary solution to give the Bayreuth party a chance to strengthen their position, to get available money out of Scheffen, or, as appears on the surface, to get things under way while he negotiated with other ministries for a budget.[11]

Wutz tried to carry out his charge, but with Schemm's death the project languished. On December 18, 1935, Wutz was pressing (his letter had "urgent" typed at the head) for some decision; the Grenzlandamt in Bayreuth was about to move out of its rooms, and the Grenzbüchereistelle would lose most of the furniture. Finally, on December 21 a ministerial decree brought the Bayreuth Beratungs-stelle into official existence. Such details as a budgetary allocation and whether it would be administratively located directly under the ministry were left to be worked out.[12]

The establishment of the Bayreuth Beratungsstelle was especially turbulent because a number of conflicts were played out simultaneously. The first was that between Bayreuth and Munich. It is perfectly obvious that south German librarianship in general suffered from an inferiority complex; Moll began his report of the July 1934 conference with a reference to it. Even more striking is the sense of inferiority of provincial Bayreuth vis-à-vis the capital city of Munich. Resentments surfaced frequently, especially in Wutz's writings; at one point he declared emphatically that the Bayerische Ostmark was no "colonial district" but had a proud cultural heritage of its own.[13]

Another conflict was that between the party and the state, a struggle that often seemed to be a contest between party officials and those professionally concerned with education and libraries. The fundamental point of disagreement at the November 1934 planning session was over whether party or state should control the proposed Beratungsstelle. After a compromise on that issue was reached and the Beratungsstelle established, the question became: Should it be answerable only to the ministry or, like the Munich Beratungsstelle, supervised by the Bavarian State Library? Wutz argued that the German public library was political and therefore could not be properly directed by a scholarly institution.[14]

A third subject of dispute was the role of Leipzig; that is, how large Walter Hofmann, his ideas and minions, should loom. In general, the Leipzig Richtung dominated in southern Germany and Austria, but the Bayerische Ostmark seems to have been a positive hotbed of Hofmannism. At this period Hofmann was particularly close to Moll; his *Die deutsche Volksbücherei* was published by the Gau press. Hofmann or one of his subordinates attended the important planning sessions, and at one time his son was considered a candidate for the Beratungsstelle's directorship. Wutz was a convinced Leipzig advocate. From the beginning he wrote strongly worded justifications for adopting the Leipzig model. The director of the Bayerische Staatsbibliothek, on the other hand, argued that both Hofmann's previous views—that is, he had been a Socialist—and the one-sidedness of his library policies made them unacceptable in the Bayerische Ostmark.[15] Scheffen, an important source of financial support, found the Bayreuthers' insistence on following the Leipzig model ill-advised and irritating; in his opinion the needs of the Bayerische Ostmark and the practical necessities should take precedence over rivalries.[16]

Personal animosities complicated the situation, many centering on Wutz. Ambition is a quality that motivates many individuals who go on to make important contributions, but Wutz combined his with a penchant for intrigue. One librarian in the Munich Beratungsstelle, who found him so unpalatable that she did her best to avoid being in his presence, described Wutz as a party member who played everyone against each other. He made fun of Fischer, the head of the Munich Beratungsstelle, and denied Scheffen any redeeming features, this at a time when the three of them were visiting in Munich to negotiate with the Staatsbibliothek and ministry over the not-quite-realized Beratungsstelle's future. On his home front Wutz appears to have disposed successfully of a rival, Dr. Müller, the director of the Bayreuth library and original favorite for the directorship of the new Beratungsstelle. He also survived antagonizing a powerful local official.[17]

The establishment of the Beratungsstelle for Baden bears many resemblances to the Bayreuth situation, although it was not quite as convoluted. Here, too, the initiative was largely local; indeed, the work of one person. Philipp Harden-Rauch, the director of the Freiburg public library, decided he wanted to be the director of a Beratungsstelle. He mounted an active campaign; the city archives of Freiburg have many letters written to an uncomprehending mayor. Eventually, Harden-Rauch managed to persuade the mayor and local party that a Beratungsstelle should be established, that Freiburg should be its site, and that he should be the director.[18]

This accomplishment required overcoming a number of obstacles. Although "encouraged" as a Beratungsstelle-less province by the various ministries to establish one, Baden authorities remained fundamentally indifferent. Freiburg, a town of only 99,122 at the last official census, had to be exempted from the 100,000 minimum population requirement for a Beratungsstelle city. Another point needed to be stretched to permit Harden-Rauch, a man from the book trade without the requisite formal education, to be named director.[19]

Whatever his academic deficiencies, Harden-Rauch was an extraordinarily successful tactician. He managed to call into question the suitability of the Landesbibliothek in Karlsruhe as the site for a Beratungsstelle, despite the fact that it was already more or less operating one; to cast doubt upon how well run the public libraries were in Freiburg's chief rivals, Mannheim and Karlsruhe; and to convince the mayor of Freiburg that if the less than optimally qualified Walter Hofmann—not to mention Euringer (Essen), Jacobi (Mannheim), Held (Munich), and Jennewein (Stuttgart)—could run a public library, so could he. He involved the local party organization in an effective way. Appointed the professional advisor to the local party's Commission for the Fight against Dirt and Trash, he used this position to get himself appointed Gau commissioner for public librarianship, charged with responsibility for creating a *governmental* Beratungsstelle. In fact, the party did not really have the authority to make such an appointment, but in the absence of any interest from the provincial government, the Gau Schulungsamt assumed authority and exercised it. A year later, in 1936, the Baden Ministry of Culture roused itself and created a Beratungsstelle, "an instrument of public law," confirming the party's action. Harden-Rauch remained the director of the reconstructed organization.[20]

The openings of two later Beratungsstellen, Nuremberg and Bielefeld, illustrate how the situation changed in the course of the Third Reich, especially with respect to the role of the RWEV. Totally absent from the picture in the Baden and Bayreuth cases, it played a prominent role at Nuremberg and Bielefeld. Discussion about a possible Beratungsstelle for Franconia (Ger. Franken) began in 1938 at the suggestion of Dähnhardt, who was also the architect of the Bielefeld Beratungsstelle. After finding out on a visit in 1941 that Bielefeld was opening a new library, he decided to establish a separate Beratungsstelle for the administrative district of Minden, then a part of the Hagen Beratungsstelle's territory. Dähnhardt turned the Nuremberg project over to Dr. Boepple in the Bavarian Ministry of Culture. In Bielefeld, he enlisted the librarian of Bielefeld, Bernhard Rang, who produced a memorandum that echoes Wutz's arguments advocating the Bayreuth Beratungsstelle. The Hagen Beratungsstelle had too large an area; Minden, a strongly Catholic district, needed more-careful oversight than it could give; Minden was different from southern Westphalia; Bielefeld was centrally located; there were commercial as well as cultural questions.[21]

Neither the Westphalian administration nor Angermann, from whose jurisdiction the territory of the new Bielefeld Beratungsstelle was being removed, offered much resistance. Angermann indeed expressed some pique that the promising young librarian he had sponsored for a middle-level administrative position had so quickly become his equal, but relations between the two librarians became overly polite rather than hostile. Dähnhardt remained close to the planning, a measure made easier because Westphalia was Prussian territory, and smoothed Angermann's ruffled feathers. A decree of the RWEV on August 26, 1941, empowered the Regierungspräsident of Minden to establish the new Beratungsstelle, and in November, Dähnhardt, Rang, and Angermann met in Berlin to work out the details of the separation and to discuss the budget. Bielefeld was

118

functioning independently as a Beratungsstelle by the beginning of the new year.[22]

Progress in Bavaria was slower. The Bavarian Ministry of Culture was not sufficiently in touch with the public library situation to make recommendations when Dähnhardt first raised the issue, and consulted the Munich Beratungsstelle. The Beratungsstelle's director, Hermann Sauter, made it clear that he would welcome the creation of a Beratungsstelle for Franconia, *if* it did not mean that the already straitened resources of the Munich Beratungsstelle would be reduced. In comparing the relative merits of Würzburg and Nuremberg as possible sites, he strongly recommended Nuremberg. Würzburg was directed by a woman, and a female Beratungsstelle director seemed to him "less suitable" than a male. As plans went forward, the local party organization became involved. Franz Kafitz, a teacher, became their candidate for director and eventually received the appointment. He was a devoted party member, devout to the point of being uncomfortable that the Beratungsstelle's quarters were in a house owned by a Jew. Not an especially competent director, he had the additional disability of being subject to army service. His call-up by the Wehrmacht in August 1939 postponed the establishment of the Nuremberg Beratungsstelle until after he was wounded and discharged in 1941.[23]

In three out of four of these cases, the man chosen to head the new Beratungsstelle might be considered a "new" man. All of them involved the creation of a Beratungsstelle where there had been no existing operation upon which to build and where there was no obvious library or librarian to head it. The choices made indicate the diminished dominance of the establishment within the profession.

A job that required knowledge, tact, and energy, the position of Beratungsstelle director was crucial. When questioned on its qualifications in 1935, Dähnhardt replied that "professional inclination and political reliability" were prerequisites. More-specific criteria were prescribed in the Richtlinien of 1934 and those of 1937. For convenience, the 1934 Richtlinien urged that the Beratungsstelle be attached to a major public library. The library's director could then also serve as the Beratungsstelle's director, guaranteeing a professionally knowledgeable person. The 1937 Richtlinien gave somewhat more detailed standards; they took into account the administrative revisions implemented since 1934, as well as other changes in conditions. By 1937, for example, directors of Beratungsstellen were no longer uniformly part-time; some were Beratungsstelle directors and nothing but Beratungsstelle directors. In an attempt to curb the tendency to value political activity over professional, the 1937 Richtlinien spelled out that the Beratungsstelle director was to be knowledgeable about questions of public librarianship and capable of organizing and planning. The Reich minister of education also felt it necessary to assert his right and responsibility to name directors.[24]

In his book on Beratungsstellen Franz Schriewer considered the question of the director in detail. His perspective was completely different from that of the official regulations, influenced more by his many years as a Beratungsstelle director than by his experience in Berlin. Schriewer held that Beratungsstelle work was a distinctive form of librarianship and required distinctive capabilities. Administrative ability was traditionally emphasized, but he also called for "an unlimited will to work and an almost unlimited ability to work." The director had to have a deep conviction of the importance of the job. Those who were dominated by a love for literature and did not possess the urge to push forward would not have the strength to overcome the opposition still to be encountered in public librarianship. Schriewer stressed that directors of Beratungsstellen needed to be able to plan and organize, but, because they did not perform their work in a quiet cell, they also had to be skilled in speaking, presenting, and interacting. In other words, they needed to have communication skills.[25]

Perfection being in short supply in the human race, compromise was often required, nor did the profession necessarily have the last word. To judge by the cases of Wutz, Pfeiffer, and Kafitz, political reliability was of greater importance than professional qualification during the Nazi period. Another director, of the Braunschweig Beratungsstelle, was described as "an enthusiastic adherent of the National Socialist state" who did not welcome questions about his professional preparation. Preeminence of political considerations, however, was not invariable. When Wolfgang van der Briele retired as director of the Beratungsstelle of the Düsseldorf district in the Rhine province, he was succeeded not by the obvious choice, the director of the Düsseldorf library, but by the eminently qualified Carl

Jansen, librarian of Essen. The Düsseldorf director was a party member, but he had not been professionally educated and there had been controversy about his appointment as librarian.[26]

Another kind of compromise is represented by the Württemberg Beratungsstelle. There the director was Dr. Franz Cuhorst, a local politician, but the managing director was Alfred Jennewein, the head of the Stuttgart public libraries. Similarly, professional and technical staff could compensate for a director's deficiencies. Each Beratungsstelle was supposed to have at least one professional librarian, a position almost invariably filled by a woman, and one clerk. In some Beratungsstellen it is quite clear that the librarian actually ran the operation.

Besides regulating what kind of director the Beratungsstelle was supposed to have, the Richtlinien of 1937 attempted to regulate its administrative relationships, especially those with the RWEV. They affirmed that the Beratungsstellen were under the ministries of education in the respective provinces, but at the same time directed many aspects of their activities. The authority of the RWEV was particularly apparent in controlling the budget, once money had been appropriated by the province. The Richtlinien also provided for an advisory council, composed of government functionaries, party officials, and officers of publicly recognized organizations concerned with public libraries. Such a council might have brought yet further administrative complexity, but no provincial library agency seems to have made any effort to implement this provision.[27]

In addition to establishing organizational and personnel rules, the Richtlinien defined the duties of the Beratungsstellen. Both sets of Richtlinien were very similar, although in this instance the 1934 Richtlinien are more detailed than the later ones, a reversal of the usual pattern that probably occurred because by 1937 many activities had become common practices. As stated in the Richtlinien, the Beratungsstellen were responsible for planning and development; providing technical assistance to small libraries in acquisition, cataloging, and binding; maintaining a central catalog of all the libraries' collections; selecting and training librarians; collecting statistics; and preparing annual reports. And to this already overwhelming list must also be added public relations, a task so taken for granted that it was not mentioned.[28]

121

Just how overwhelming the job could be is clear in a statement that the director of the Düsseldorf Beratungsstelle prepared in 1937 to support a request for additional personnel. Extracting from his annual report, van der Briele listed the following accomplishments: seventy-five letters to and from the Grenzbüchereidienst and book orders for new libraries on special Grenzbüchereidienst forms; checking the proposed acquisitions of eighty-two libraries, and a total of about three hundred letters in and out to them; two continuing education workshops; four issues of the *Westdeutsche Blätter für Büchereiberatung* prepared and published; twelve full and eight half days spent visiting libraries by the director and eight full and five half days by the librarian; correspondence and consultation with local officials about the establishment of new libraries, then ordering and preparing books for those new libraries; memoranda to mayors and local officials and to the large libraries in the system. Van der Briele dwelt with particular emphasis on the paperwork. In addition to the business correspondence he had already noted, he mentioned correspondence with publishers, distributing questionnaires, and preparing eighteen separate reports for provincial administrators, the Reichsstelle, and the RWEV. One price of the organization and systematization of public librarianship was obviously a sea of paper.[29]

Until after the 1935 "Säuberung nach der Säuberung," Beratungsstellen seem to have focused most of their attention on complying with censorship guidelines and on collection development. As procedures were created and most work with the collection reduced to following prepared lists, this activity diminished in quantity and significance. The Beratungsstellen must have welcomed this abatement because 1936 and 1937 were the years in which plans were being developed for an ambitious expansion program. The goal adopted was "for every school village a public library," and since every village of five hundred or more was supposed to have a school, this meant hundreds of new libraries; an institution that had developed primarily in an urban setting was being exported to the countryside. Beratungsstelle directors spent much time trying to persuade local officials to spend money on public libraries. Gradually, much of this aspect of their work was also reduced to routine and forms. Several Beratungsstellen developed standard contracts to be signed by the mayor or other responsible official of a village that had

122

agreed to establish a library. Spending formulae and standardized collections were worked out.

Sometimes a Beratungsstelle could go too far in its efforts to expedite and to maximize the numbers it could claim. The controversy over the activity of the Graf Buchhandlung of Augsburg, a book dealer, in Bavaria is one particularly complex and telling example of slipshod practice and illustrates many of the difficulties that hampered Beratungsstelle work. As the expansion program got under way, the Munich Beratungsstelle, responsible for so much territory, contracted with Graf Buchhandlung to deliver book collections to the newly established libraries. Hanns Graf was a party member, one of the "old fighters," who before 1933 had created a Nazi library in Gau Schwaben. After the Machtergreifung his business had expanded and he had devised a clever arrangement whereby small towns and villages could purchase a library collection for themselves on the installment plan. They would make a small deposit, Graf would deliver the collection, and the town would have the use of it while paying off what it owed Graf.[30]

The controversy between Graf and the Beratungsstelle is obscured by an avalanche of detail. Once it surfaced in 1938, claims, counterclaims, reproaches, and charges flew thick and fast. The Beratungsstelle accused Graf of ignoring its requirements and of delays; Graf argued that he was supported by party officials in the Gau and that the agreement had been, not for any specific time unit, but "as soon as possible."

Although the hostility of the two parties generated much invective, the basic issues were more serious than the denunciations indicate. The episode illustrates some of the fundamental problems of Nazi public librarianship. The Munich Beratungsstelle was being called upon to carry out greatly increased responsibilities with inadequate staff, virtually forcing it to compromise its standards. In a confrontation with an individual who had the strong support of the local party, it was almost powerless. Only with the help of the RV, which lodged a complaint with the Börsenverein, was Graf eventually curbed, and even then, loyal party member Franz Kafitz, director of the Nuremberg Beratungsstelle, went on to avail himself of the book dealer's services. Graf's call to army service finally "solved" the problem.[31]

The reform of the book collections and the program to create new public libraries began as extraordinary projects, designed to put a National Socialist stamp on public librarianship. Commonplace tasks, such as supervision of the libraries in their charge, were at least as important in the work of the Beratungsstellen, even if they were less fashionable. That the RV found it necessary in 1938 to remind the Beratungsstellen not to neglect their relations with the individual library directors in the press of technical and organizational work suggests that these relations were indeed being slighted under pressure to satisfy new demands. A major aspect of supervision was related to collection control, but supervision extended well beyond, to encompass every area of the libraries' activities. Adequate oversight of the collection could be achieved at a remove; libraries submitted lists of present holdings and proposed purchases that were reviewed by the Beratungsstelle staff. Required annual reports checked activity and progress, and occasional on-site visits provided additional evidence. The responsible Beratungsstelle librarians were expert at sniffing out poor librarianship. Library directors must have trembled when Betty Schladebach of the Lippe Beratungsstelle announced her arrival. Her reports note dust, books lying on their sides on shelves, and improperly constructed furniture, as well as such faults as inadequate circulation, improperly kept statistics, and a poor attitude. Reports at the Bayreuth Beratungsstelle are equally penetrating but less inclined to dwell upon each transgression. It is clear from her reports that Ingeborg Bruns took less pleasure in policing and treated her visits more as an opportunity to encourage and communicate.[32]

The Beratungsstelle's task of supervision was made somewhat easier by its role in selecting librarians. Local officials might propose a candidate, candidates might propose themselves, but the consent of the Beratungsstelle was necessary. Smaller Beratungsstellen could sometimes know the individuals concerned, but those with large areas had to rely more on local recommendations. Usually, it was enough for these predominantly part-time librarians to be teachers; problems were most likely to arise when no suitable teacher was available or willing to take on the library in addition to his or her regular job. The Bielefeld Beratungsstelle was forced to settle for the uneducated but enthusiastic local saddler in the village of Kirchborchen when no more-appropriate candidate could be found.[33] The political reliability of the prospective librarian might be verified either by the Beratungsstelle, as in Saxony, or by the local party, as in Lippe.[34]

Another responsibility of the Beratungsstellen was to provide the small libraries with certain kinds of technical assistance, as in preparing catalog cards. This was an area of activity so ordinary that it surfaces only in annual reports of Beratungsstellen or when there was some particular problem. In 1937 the head of the Braunschweig Beratungsstelle pleaded with the Braunschweig Ministry of Education for a typewriter for the Beratungsstelle. The Beratungsstelle staff had thus far used the typewriter of the Braunschweig library, but now the number of catalog cards was so greatly increased that it was no longer possible.[35] How necessary the technical expertise of Beratungstelle staff was can be judged by the village librarian who wanted to know how soon he could cover the newly printed call number. The Lippe Beratungsstelle tartly replied: "When it's dry," emphasized by three exclamation points.[36]

Because only the library directors in the largest towns had any kind of professional preparation, Beratungsstellen often conducted educational conferences or workshops (*Tagungen*). Ideally, each Beratungsstelle would hold at least one of these a year, and the part-time library directors would attend at least every third year. These workshops usually instructed the library directors in proper circulation techniques and how to collect and present statistics. Bayreuth was able to offer a deluxe version in 1937 when Wutz persuaded Dähnhardt to address such a group and got the south German writer Rothacker to read from his works.[37]

The scope and quantity of these activities obviously required the prodigious "will to work" called for by Schriewer. Throughout the period, demands on the Beratungsstellen were steadily increasing. With a sufficient and dedicated staff the job could be accomplished, but the professional staff of most Beratungsstellen usually consisted only of a director, who was frequently part-time, and one librarian. The size of the supporting staff varied more. Although one clerk was all too common, the larger Beratungsstellen and those in the border areas that could receive subsidies from the Grenzbüchereidienst might have three, four, or more technical staff.

When the job of the Beratungsstellen became too great, as it did in the late 1930s, the choice was made to create yet another layer of administration rather than to enlarge and strengthen the staff of the Beratungsstellen. The office of *Kreisbüchereipfleger* (district library curator) is first mentioned in the Richtlinien of 1937. "If the development of public librarianship goes forward in a district, then a Kreisbüchereipfleger can be appointed for the relief of the provincial library authority director." Kreisbüchereipfleger were supposed to be professionally trained librarians; their most important tasks included advising the Kreis administration on planning and finances, identifying and recruiting library directors, and advising the Beratungsstelle directors on conditions in their districts. In fact, this plan never made much progress. After the war began, several Beratungsstelle directors did try to appoint Kreisbüchereipfleger, only to encounter considerable difficulties as most of the desirable candidates were drafted.[38]

To verify that the Beratungsstellen were carrying out their responsibilities, they filed annual reports with their provincial ministries and with the RV. It is clear, however, that the real supervision came from the RWEV. There are countless letters in the records of various Beratungsstellen from Dähnhardt, querying how money is being spent, progress on a particular project, or a personnel decision. The provincial ministry was likely to become actively involved only when a problem arose. Dähnhardt's visits also include some that were quite clearly intended as inspections.

His report on a trip to Munich in 1938 shows how closely the Beratungsstellen were scrutinized after the new system was fully operational. As part of his visit, he accompanied the director on an inspection trip of libraries, finding the existing libraries generally satisfactory, although he deplored the fact that the Munich district had only 250 libraries instead of the sixteen hundred it should. Dähnhardt was able to comment on the prospects in the different regions of Bavaria, and on the cooperation to be expected from local party and government officials. His suggestions were numerous and specific: The Munich Beratungsstelle needed to begin to print its newsletter rather than mimeograph it; it should improve its relations with library directors and pay particular attention to its training conferences and workshops; the director and Beratungsstelle librarian should increase the number of visits they made to libraries; more space was required for the technical work—a bindery was especially necessary; a fourth Bavarian Beratungsstelle for Franconia was essential; more work with local officials needed to be done, some of it by provincial authorities, to lay the groundwork for the necessary expansion of public librarianship in Bavaria. Dähnhardt made no suggestions as to where the money for this was to come. Not surprisingly, Dähnhardt's report prompted responses both from Sauter, the director of the Munich Beratungsstelle, and from the provincial officials.[39]

This episode in Munich, informative in its own right, can also serve as a typical example of Nazi Beratungsstelle work. There is evidence of overly ambitious undertakings begun with inadequate resources. The difficult division of authority is clear: The RWEV held accountable what was an institution of local government. Even the "missing" element, the omnipresence of politics, is typical. Although Nazi ideology informed and influenced every action and decision, it usually remained implicit rather than explicit, a backdrop to the busy professional activity.

Beratungsstellen often found themselves caught uncomfortably between competing forces and institutions, but their location in the middle was their raison d'être. They served as the intermediary between national and provincial authorities, between provincial and local officials. They provided technical assistance and brought a measure of professionalism to the tiniest libraries in their jurisdiction. Nazi public librarianship depended on them. Their success as an institution and their collective accomplishments brought into being a distinctively National Socialist public librarianship.

CHAPTER SEVEN

The Library

Development

Program

THE MOTIVE underlying the creation of a national administrative structure for public librarianship had been concern for the collection, but by the time that structure was fully realized, collection controls were firmly in place and collections thoroughly purged. That accomplishment left the new organization free to direct most of its attention to building new libraries. With many towns lacking public libraries and the countryside almost completely unserved, the need for more libraries had been obvious long before 1933. Opening new libraries would also further priorities of the regime that had little to do with libraries: Expand the presence of the state in an area of community life; accumulate impressive statistical evidence of the achievement of a specific task; and offer an alternative to the Catholic libraries that provided so much of the library service in rural areas. Now, the administrative capacity existed to plan and to implement on a national basis.

In 1934 Germany had 824 libraries in towns of over five thousand people and 8,670 in towns of under five thousand, a total of 9,494 public libraries. By 1940 that number had grown to 13,236, an increase of 40 percent within six years. The National Socialist regime was understandably proud of this achievement, and Dähnhardt, Heiligenstaedt, and the provincial library directors frequently boasted of it in public addresses. The raw figures, however, conceal as much as they reveal. Like so many Nazi claims, they cannot be taken at face value.[1]

Library service was, for example, very unevenly distributed

throughout the country. Looking at the country as a whole in 1933/34, it is apparent that the disadvantage of which southern German librarians complained was, with some exceptions, true. Bavaria and Baden offered library service to only 40 percent of their inhabitants in 1934. On the other hand, in Oldenburg, an unquestionably northern province, only 40 percent of the population had access to a public library, while Württemberg with 62 percent was one of the better-served provinces. The best and worst were Saxony and Lippe where the figures were 84 and 27 percent, respectively. The Prussian statistic of 64 percent compares favorably with most of the other provinces, but even within Prussia there were variations. East Prussia with 34 percent, Grenzmark Posen-Westprussia with 33, and Hanover with 37 percent of the population served were the provinces at the low end; Westphalia had 51 and Schleswig-Holstein 52 percent.

Even after the development program of the late 1930s greatly improved the availability of library service, serious inequities remained. Baden, which had been poorly served in 1934, added four new libraries in 1937/38, 151 in 1938/39, and 297 in 1939/40. By 1940, 735,551 Badeners had a public library in their community, but that still meant that only 61 percent of the population of Baden had library service. Thuringia, which had started from a 1934 base of 60 percent, had increased its service in those years to close to 100 percent.

As of 1940, the building program still had some distance to go to reach its goal of a library in every community of over five hundred. It did increase the number of libraries to 13,236, but Franz Schriewer had estimated that almost twenty-five thousand communities should have a library.[2] Some of these communities had formerly been served by *Wanderbüchereien,* an arrangement that could mean either a bookmobile or a traveling collection deposited for a few months in the local school. Wanderbüchereien were quickly eliminated after the Machtergreifung, however, because only a permanent collection, regardless of its size, with a regular attendant was considered capable of providing the educational guidance that was the goal of National Socialist librarianship. Such permanent collections were also easier to control.

The cost of this expansion was RM 2,748,913 for the three years of greatest activity, 1937/38 to 1939/40. Of that total, RM 1,280,538 (47%) was provided by the communities, RM 579,474 (21%) by the

Kreise, and RM 888,900 (32%) by the Beratungsstellen.[3] These figures, like other national figures, conceal wide variation from year to year and from province to province (see Table 7.1).

By 1940 spending on libraries as a whole had increased dramatically. In 1933/34 a total of RM 8,560,612, or RM 0.19 per individual served, was being spent. It became RM 11,484,885 and RM 0.28 per individual served in 1937/38, percentage increases of thirty-four and forty-seven. And, although no comprehensive statistics are available for the remaining years, it is obvious from the records of different Beratungsstellen that the improvement continued during the first few years of the war.

Much of this considerable increase can be attributed to the local government law of 1935. In this law communities were charged with the administration of "all public activities insofar as they are not otherwise specifically assigned by law to other agencies or are not by law taken over by other agencies," a general assignment that made public libraries their legal responsibility. It was this clause that gave teeth to the many exhortations from Dähnhardt or Beratungsstelle directors; communities no longer had the option of ignoring libraries. The change was a milestone in the development of German public libraries and probably the most significant contribution the Nazi regime made in this area.[4] Little attention or concern was given to improving library service in cities. Hamburg, for example, proposed an extensive expansion but was able to open only one new branch before the war, although the system did absorb the libraries of the surrounding districts of Altona, Wandsbek, and Harburg. Hanover, where the need had been greater, did slightly better, but not much.[5]

The new libraries were located primarily in villages, as was consonant with the regime's values. Of the libraries opened between 1937 and 1940, the years in which the development program was concentrated, a total of 2,844 were in rural communities and 167 in communities that can be designated cities; this is a ratio of seventeen to one. That the average population of the community with a new library was only 1,088 shows the rural orientation in another way, as do the records of the individual Beratungsstellen, which demonstrate that the thrust of the development program was in the countryside. But an average population of 1,088 also means that many considerably larger communities, too, were acquiring public libraries at this

Table 7.1 Sources of Library Funding in Selected Provinces (Percentages)

	Gemeinde	Kreis	Beratungsstelle
Baden			
1937/38	43	0	56
1938/39	67	5	28
1939/40	60	0.5	39
Bavaria			
1937/38	41	28	31
1938/39	42	28	30
1939/40	36	58	7
E. Prussia			
1937/38	16	16	71
1938/39	11	36	53
1939/40	35	19	42
Thuringia			
1937/38	40	31	29
1938/39	58	21	21
1939/40	48	26	26
Westphalia			
1937/38	80	13	7
1938/39	72	17	12
1939/40	70	20	11

time. As late as 1939, forty-eight of the 273 cities of over ten thousand did not have independent, publicly supported libraries, cities that included Braunschweig, Aachen, Mainz, Bonn, Regensburg, Bamberg, and Jena.

Most of the new libraries were very small. The Richtlinien of 1937 had mandated collections of at least two hundred volumes for communities of five hundred, five hundred volumes for communities of a thousand, fifteen hundred for communities of five thousand, and two to four thousand volumes for those of ten to twenty thousand inhabitants.[6] Unfortunately, the actual libraries only rarely met these standards. In 1937/38 the average size of a new library was 192 books, and in 1939/40, 213 books. The Beratungsstelle in Minden was regularly opening libraries with 150 volumes, and one library in Braunschweig had only thirty-four volumes when it opened in 1937. Franz Schriewer, a librarian with extensive experience in rural li-

A typical village library collection. (Reproduced from Schriewer. *Das ländliche Volksbüchereiwesen*, 1937.)

brarianship, had even higher standards. His minimal requirements for satisfactory ratings were, for communities of under five hundred, seventy-eight volumes per hundred inhabitants; for those of five hundred to a thousand, thirty-seven volumes per hundred inhabitants; for one to two thousand, thirty-five volumes per hundred inhabitants; and for two to five thousand, thirty-four volumes per hundred inhabitants.[7]

How far the new libraries fell short of the Richtlinien standards is even clearer when the standards are translated into volumes per inhabitant. The Richtlinien mandated 0.4 books per inhabitant in villages of five hundred, 0.5 for villages of a thousand, and 0.2 for towns of ten to twenty thousand. The actual collections had 0.13 books per inhabitant in 1937/38 for the Reich as a whole, 0.15 in 1938/39, and 0.17 in 1939/40. This represents, of course, a steady improvement, although the geographical inequity persisted. For newly established libraries in Prussia the number of books was consistently higher than the national average—0.14 in 1937/38, 0.17 in 1938/39, and 0.18 in 1939/40.

Despite the vast improvement in quantity, German public libraries remained inadequate by their own standards of quality.[8] A contemporary analysis of the libraries in Thuringia, one of the better-off provinces, concluded that only 142 out of a total of 385 libraries, or 36 percent, were "satisfactory," a term the report defined in relation to size. Because the Thuringian figures were grouped by size of the community, it is clear that the larger the community, the more likely it was to have a good library. This correlation between quality and size generally held true for the nation as a whole, although it was not invariable. Large-city libraries show great disparity. The 1935/36 statistics on Ruhr libraries (see Table 7.2) indicate how different libraries[9] could be, even in towns with shared social values and similar economic resources. When the four large-city libraries considered the best public libraries in Germany—those of Berlin, Hamburg, Leipzig, and Essen—are compared with some of the poorest, even greater differences are apparent (see Table 7.3).

It is clear that, even after the gains of the 1930s, German libraries remained much smaller and less well-funded than comparable U.S. libraries. With only a few exceptions, German collections were just a

Table 7.2 Characteristics of Libraries in the Ruhr, 1935/36

Town	Inhabitants	Volumes	Vols/Inhab.	Readers	Readers/Pop. (Percentage)
Düsseldorf	511,137	104,233	.20	23,622	4.5
Duisburg	440,083	107,463	.24	6,080	1.3
Essen	662,343	215,027	.32	20,417	3.0
Krefeld	167,632	39,680	.23	3,471	2.0
Mühlheim	135,000	31,791	.24	3,714	2.7
Remscheid	101,500	30,000	.29	3,438	3.3
Solingen	140,202	45,000	.32	4,346	3.1
Wuppertal	410,594	154,228	.37	9,544	2.3

fraction of the size of those in the United States, as was the per capita expenditure. German spending did show very large percentage increases between 1934 and 1938, but so did U.S. spending (see Table 7.4).

The German gains that occurred during this period, the increases in the number of libraries and in the level of financial support, were achieved because more money was available for public purposes as wages and salaries were not allowed to increase. Not that a share of this money was easy to obtain. Numerous congenitally tightfisted local officials had to be persuaded to loosen purse strings. City librarians and Beratungsstelle directors begged, reasoned, and chided, mayors and other local officials pleaded poverty and procrastinated, provincial officials were enlisted to put pressure on their local colleagues.

Some cities could acquire a library with little exertion, simply by taking over an existing society library. This happened frequently as the principles of tax support and public control of libraries were adopted. In at least twelve of the twenty-five towns with a population over twenty thousand that had a private but no publicly supported library in 1934, the libraries had been transferred to their cities by 1938. Often, however, such a change marked an increase in responsibility for the city government rather than the assumption of a totally new obligation, because most of the twenty-five societies had received some grant support from the town government as private institutions.

The transfer could be done either with or without difficulty. In Oldenburg the Verein Lese- und Bücherhalle conveyed its library to

Table 7.3 Major German Cities: Comparative Statistics

City		Population[a]	Volumes Acquisition 1937/38	Vols./ Inhabitant 1937/38	Acquisition	Circulation	Readers	Percentage Young Adults	Rdrs./Pop.	Total Spent (in Reichsmarks)	Amt./Cap. of Pop. (in Reichsmarks)
Berlin	1933/34	4,236,414	840,332	.20	250,000	2,939,100	132,057	31	3.3	242,349	.22
	1937/38	4,332,242	900,000	.20		2,225,450	100,101		2.3	394,943	.23
Hamburg	1933/34	1,125,025	158,881	.14	49,766	796,422	36,602	26	3.1	1,689,758	.40
	1937/38	1,682,220	219,257	.13		843,459	39,362		2.3	2,116,980	.49
Essen	1933/34	654,538	204,386	.31	55,730	497,799	20,484	19	3.1	357,100	.55
	1937/38	659,871	117,940	.18		387,660	17,520		2.6	387,000	.59
Leipzig	1933/34	712,475	106,671	.15	26,952	318,823	24,791	30	3.5	279,785	.39
	1937/38	701,606	106,000	.15		303,087	20,314		2.8	317,744	.45
Munich	1933/34	734,785	197,912	.27	33,434	359,008	10,293	NA	1.4	352,555	.48
	1937/38	828,235	81,734	.10		222,470	107,584		12.9	268,735	.32
Breslau	1933/34	625,219	97,313	.16	43,484	544,613	13,761	20	2.2	257,057	.41
	1937/38	615,006	60,226	.10		236,279	11,740		1.9	257,415[b]	.41
Dortmund	1933/34	540,480	50,265	.09	4,981	108,235	3,877	14	.7	30,300	.06
	1937/38	537,000	51,860	.10		65,342	2,150		.4	20,790	.04
Frankfurt/M	1933/34	555,071	106,405	.19	34,028	341,826	17,167	33	3.1	218,791	.39
	1937/38	546,649	98,729	.18		281,639	13,807		2.5	244,097	.45

Notes: a. Population figures are from the 1933 and 1939 censuses.
  b. 1936/37.

Table 7.4 Comparative Statistics for

		Population[a]	Volumes	Circulation	Percentage of Change	Borrowers as percent of population
Berlin	1933/34	4,236,416	840,332	2,939,100	−24	3.1
	1937/38		900,000	2,225,450		2.3
Chicago	1933/34	3,376,438	1,578,589	10,992,812	18.5	
	1937/38		1,718,867			
Hamburg	1933/34	1,125,025	158,881	796,422	+6	3.3
	1937/38		219,257	843,459		2.3
Los Angeles	1933/34	1,238,048	1,443,479	13,033,939	−19	31.4
(city)	1937/38		1,559,516	10,524,990		30.3
Leipzig	1933/34	712,475	106,671	318,823	−5	3.5
	1937/38		106,000	303,087		2.8
Milwaukee	1933/34	725,263	956,474	5,407,781	−24	21.2
	1937/38		943,559	4,117,844		19.7
Hanover	1933/34	438,922	183,736	239,781	+4	2.0
	1937/38		207,300	249,422		23.3
Birmingham	1933/34	399,713	241,123	1,498,064	−23	24.1
Ala.	1937/38		222,893	1,153,329		22.5
Würzburg	1933/34	100,937	13,840	50,577	+6	2.9
	1937/38		21,000	53,589		3.9
El Paso, Tex.	1933/34	102,421	46,828	248,567	−11	13.2
	1937/38		59,549	221,977		13.3
Göttingen	1933/34	47,026	10,929	30,302	+9	2.7
	1937/38		11,426	33,115		4.0
Montclair,	1933/34	42,017	88,577	415,007	+4	48.2
N.J.	1937/38		148,403	432,898		54.6
Gütersloh	1933/34	25,879	5,233	7,671	−22	2.5
	1937/38		4,383	5,700		3.0
Bangor, Me.	1933/34	28,794	168,439	378,448	+3	66.0
	1937/38		195,726	389,785		62.1

Sources: Germany, Statistisches Reichsamt, *Die deutschen Volksbüchereien nach Ländern, Provinzen und Gemeinden.* The 1934 statistics for U.S. libraries are from "General and Salary Statistics—Public Libraries Serving More Than 200,000 Population," pp. 200–203; "General and Salary Statistics—Public Libraries Serving 100,000 to 199,999 Population," pp. 204–207; "General and Salary Statistics—Public Libraries Serving 35,000 to 99,999 Population," pp. 208–10; and "General and Salary Statistics—Public Libraries Serving 10,000 to 34,999 Population," pp. 211–13, all in *Bulletin of the American Library Association* 29 (April 1935). The 1938 statistics are from "General and Salary Statistics—Public Libraries Serving More Than 200,000 Population," pp. 279–83; "General and Salary Statistics—Public Libraries Serving 100,000 to 199,999 Population," pp. 284–288; "General and Salary Statistics—Public

Percentage of Change	Circulation per borrower	Budget[b]	Percentage of Gain	Expenditure per capita	Percentage of Gain
−26	22.32	402,167	+25	0.09	+23
	21.42	503,814		0.12	
	17.60	1,271,678	+56	0.35	+71
		1,988,726		0.60	
−30	21.76	57,674	+63	0.05	+5
		93,996		0.08	
−4	33.7	997,199	+4	0.81	+4
	28.09	1,036,877		0.84	
−20	12.86	66,588	+14	0.09	+15
	14.92	75,623		0.11	
−7	33.7	388,015	+21	0.53	+23
	28.76	470,713		0.65	
+1,065	27.53	47,172	+32	0.11	+33
	2.44	62,207		0.14	
−7	15.57	90,019	+39	0.22	+40
	12.84	125,192		0.31	
+34	17.27	3,868	+114	0.04	+50
	13.49	8,266		0.08	
+1	18.43	26,009	+34	0.25	+36
	16.20	34,786		0.34	
+48	23.58	1,942	+57	0.04	+59
	17.56	3,057		0.07	
+13	20.49	63,933	+34	1.52	+34
	18.87	85,813		2.04	
+20	11.82	244	+10	0.01	+100
	6.91	491		0.02	
−6	19.94	58,236	+10	2.02	+10
	21.83	63,817		2.22	

Libraries Serving 35,000 to 99,999 Population," pp. 290–93; and "General and Salary Statistics—Public Libraries Serving 10,000 to 34,999 Population," pp. 294–97, all in *Bulletin of the American Library Association* 33 (April 1939).

Notes: a. U.S. population figures are from the 1930 census; German, from the 1933 census. The 1933 census figures reported in *Der Grosse Brockhaus: Ergänzungsband* (Leipzig: F. A. Brockhaus, 1935), pp. 207–23, are somewhat larger but seem to be corrections rather than a deliberate attempt to misrepresent. The population of Berlin, for example, is given as 4,242,501 rather than 4,236,416; Göttingen is 47,149 rather than 47,026.

b. All figures are in U.S. dollars; the Reichsmark was valued at $0.238.

the city on April 1, 1934; the provincial government agreed to provide a room and to pay for a librarian. (The librarian earned RM 1,835.25 a year in 1934.) The city contributed RM 2,000 a year. In contrast, Braunschweig had to be urged repeatedly. Even though the Beratungsstelle was headed by the director of the Braunschweig public library, his library continued to be a private society. In 1940 Heiligenstaedt inquired into this situation yet again, and Dähnhardt made one of his hortatory visits, but the city government responded that war taxes were too great to permit them to consider taking over the library until after the war. In 1941 the city reconsidered its position and gave in; where the pretransfer subsidy to the Verein Volkslesehalle had been RM 25,000, the Braunschweig library now cost the city RM 100,000. Neu Ulm's problem was different. The city took over a library that had begun as a regimental library with a collection suited to officers' military interests. In July 1936 it was disbanded, and all its books given to more-scholarly collections. Nazi educational material, young adult books, and writings on the question of Germans abroad became the nucleus of the reconstructed Neu Ulm library. The Munich Beratungsstelle had to monitor the situation closely for several years.[10]

More frequently a community had to start from scratch. Few small rural communities had any kind of library at all that could serve as a nucleus. If they did have a library, it was probably a Borromäus Verein library and those, as property of the Catholic church, could not be transferred, nor would they have offered an acceptably secular collection.

Schriewer outlined how the process of establishing a community library should proceed ideally. First, the way had to be prepared. People had to be convinced that a library was something other than outdated, worn-out books left over from a bookmobile. They had to be disabused of the idea that little reading went on in rural areas. A tentative collection would be developed by the Beratungsstelle, and then the local education officer would prepare a list of those communities he thought were ready to fulfil the necessary conditions. Conversations would take place with the mayors and school officials of the designated communities to determine whether they would take a collection from the Beratungsstelle and then follow through on their own. The Beratungsstelle would deliver a collection of one hundred

138

volumes; the community would put up RM 100 for a cabinet and agree to a continuing subsidy of 15 Pfennigs per capita a year. This was how it had happened in Papitz, a small village in Brandenburg within the area of the Frankfurt/Oder Beratungsstelle.[11]

Schriewer was well aware of how unusual it was for things to proceed as smoothly as they had in Papitz. He opened his section on the founding and securing of libraries in *Die staatlichen Volksbüchereistellen* with a long passage on problems. Present practices had to be stopped. Instead of random openings that owed their existence to the whim of an individual or to chance, the founding of a library had to be planned to have the cooperation and involvement of local administrators. No more libraries in communities of under five hundred people should be started. Continuity and security had to be primary considerations. A happy optimism was not enough to guarantee the survival of what had been started. Schriewer was most explicit: "The promises of communities are of little use here."[12]

Schriewer proposed several improvements in existing practice. He placed great emphasis on the involvement of the Kreis. As he saw it, rural public librarianship "stands and falls with the participation of the Kreis." As long as there was no library law, only the Kreis could assure effective development. Although the community would remain the principal library supporter, the Kreis should take the lead in establishing new libraries and offer administrative support. The Richtlinien of 1937, which Schriewer had a large hand in framing, incorporated this idea in a diluted form. Minister of Education Rust declared, "As a rule the community should be responsible for the costs of establishing and the continuing support of libraries. I expect of the Kreis that they will support communities, especially those that are small and weak, with grants and add corresponding subsidies to their budgets."[13]

To protect the library against loss of interest, Schriewer recommended a contract, to be signed by Kreis, Gemeinde, and provincial Beratungsstelle. This contract would set forth the responsibilities each party was assuming. Schriewer was well aware that inadequately supported collections could not afford the new acquisitions that would keep readers returning. He printed sample contracts both in his 1936 *Die Bücherei* article and in his *Das ländliche Volksbüchereiwesen*.[14]

Above all, Schriewer relied on the groundwork that had been done as the best guarantee of the future: "The later response depends on this preparatory work." Only with preparation would the proper cooperation of the various forces take place; it could not be accomplished post facto by administrative tinkering. First and foremost, the Landrat had to understand clearly what lay in the future and what his task would be. He had to be personally convinced. It would be good if the provincial administrators could be brought to declare their support for the establishment of libraries so that the proposals of the Beratungsstelle directors would no longer have such a personal character. Before any serious conversations took place, the mayor should be won over. The future librarian should be enlisted. At the first negotiation all interested parties should be present. There, the Beratungsstelle director was to discuss planned arrangements, explaining such technical operations as the catalog. The Landrat should also speak and inquire separately of each community whether each agreed to the terms. "If financing has already been found, the preparation thoroughly done, the choice of community rightly determined, then the game is won."[15]

The contrast between Schriewer's tone of near surprise at how well things went in his model village of Papitz and the long pages he devoted to handling difficulties reveal indirectly but unmistakably how unusual it was to establish a library without a struggle. The experience of the Bayreuth Beratungsstelle in Tirschenreuth, a town of about fifty-five hundred in the Upper Palatinate on the Czech border, was far more typical. At the end of 1934 Josef Wutz visited Tirschenreuth on behalf of the Bund Deutscher Osten, the organization that had made itself responsible for librarianship in the Bayerische Ostmark.[16] His letter followed in February 1935, informing the director of the existing, unacceptable library in Tirschenreuth that regulations had finally been formulated for public librarianship in the Bayerische Ostmark. Wutz wrote again a month later, to complain about how poor the rooms were; the newly created Gau Beratungsstelle of which he was director could not give any subsidies until better rooms were rented. In July he pressed the mayor to come to the opening of the new library in Waldsassen, a showpiece of Nazi librarianship in the Bayerische Ostmark, so that he could see the difference between what a modern library should look like and the library in Tirschenreuth. He wrote to the Bezirksamt in August; the Beratungsstelle wanted to support the library "to the utmost," but they had to do something about the rooms.

A year later the library director was writing to the Beratungsstelle, trying to persuade Wutz that the present rooms would be adequate if they were frequently aired. The assistance of the Beratungsstelle was desperately needed. Wutz did not accept these arguments, and finally, in October 1936, Tirschenreuth's mayor announced with pride that a new room had been found. In January 1937 the mayor begged the Beratungsstelle: "I now request that, as in Waldsassen and Markt Redwitz, our library be built into an attractive border library and further steps immediately be taken." The next month the mayor promised eighteen Pfennigs per capita per year, a generous amount when compared with the five or ten Pfennigs usual in the Bayerische Ostmark, although it could not be the full amount that year. The mayor hoped that the Beratungsstelle would understand that weak communities had an especially important task, and that its support did not depend on the community's ability to pay.

Then, in May 1937, Wutz visited Tirschenreuth again. A thoroughgoing indictment, his subsequent report destroyed the pleasant fantasies of the mayor. The room of which he was so proud was not good; the book collection was in a dreary condition; the number of readers was too small; the resources of the library were too limited; Lehrer Zintl was an unsuitable director who failed to understand the educational task of the National Socialist library and thought it enough to give readers what they wanted. Wutz concluded sanctimoniously, "It is necessary to say that it is not responsible to give public resources to an institution that only gives out entertainment. Spending money is only appropriate when the public library is established as a responsible institution in the frame of the National Socialist educational task." Only when Tirschenreuth followed his suggestions would it get RM 900 worth of books.

Three months later Wutz had had no response to his report and wrote again to Tirschenreuth, reminding the mayor that efforts to get Tirschenreuth a new library had been under way since February 1935. That October Tirschenreuth reaffirmed its promise to provide a rent of RM 1,000 for a room, but a year later there was still no new library. What the town considered an adequate room for a library, the

Beratungsstelle found lacking. Tirschenreuth had not lived up to its other financial commitments to a public library, and Wutz reminded the mayor of the existing library's failings.

Wutz's strong letter of November 4, 1938, finally brought results. In December the mayor plaintively replied that of course the town was maintaining its library in accordance with the Bavarian Richtlinien. He promised special attention to the acquisition of Nazi writings, one of Wutz's requirements. Eventually, the librarian whom Wutz recommended replaced the inadequate Zintl, and Tirschenreuth ceased to receive Wutz's personal supervision. It reported regularly to the Beratungsstelle, provoking no special comment.

Although the Beratungsstelle had to negotiate community by community, some provincewide preliminary work could be done. The director of the Braunschweig Beratungsstelle sent a mimeographed memorandum as a follow-up to a questionnaire to mayors about the availability of a public library. In it he reminded those mayors still without a library that the national government had decreed that each school village was to have a library. He advised them to speak with local party officials and the schoolmaster, informed them of the probable cost and the help that could be expected from the Beratungsstelle, and enclosed a copy of instructions on how to found a library.[17]

Wutz promulgated his own set of Richtlinien for the Bayerische Ostmark a year before either the national Richtlinien of 1937 or the Bavarian Richtlinien. After quoting various ministerial pieties on the virtues of a public library, he described what the responsibilities of the community were and what communities could expect from the Beratungsstelle. He set minimum per capita subsidies from the communities. His Richtlinien were modeled on the earlier "Grundsätze für den Aufbau des ländlichen Volksbüchereiwesens" for the province of Hanover, which had been widely circulated throughout the country. The Hanover "Grundsätze," however, had the advantage of being the statement of the provincial Oberpräsident rather than of an individual Beratungsstelle director.[18]

Obviously, support from provincial leaders strengthened the hand of a Beratungsstelle director. Local officials were much more likely to respond to exhortations from their provincial superiors than they were to those from someone outside the hierarchy of authority. The

Office of the Reichsstatthalter in Hesse urged Kreis officials and the mayors of the larger towns to support libraries. As a follow-up to the Richtlinien of 1937, the Regierungspräsident of Minden was persuaded to issue a proclamation similar to, but less formally disseminated than, the Hanoverian "Grundsätze."[19]

By 1937 planning had been systematized. Each individual library was treated as one unit in a comprehensive development design for the entire province, which in turn was a constituent element in a national project. A methodical, relentless persistence was most apparent in the border areas and in parts of the country where the Catholic church was strong, but all Beratungsstellen were expected to have a long-term plan.

Dähnhardt described the organization of public libraries as having achieved "technical precision,"[20] and it is easy to believe that when one sees the long, orderly lists of Gemeinden, organized by Kreis, in so many Beratungsstelle archives. Librarians would target communities of special importance and those that seemed to offer greater probability of success. As time went on, they standardized the process of development, from negotiation to contract to basic collection. Thanks to such procedures, they were able to accelerate the pace of library development.

In addition to working with provincial authorities to develop public libraries, the RWEV attempted to cooperate with other groups that might conceivably have an interest in public libraries. One of the most coordinated of such efforts was that with the Reichsnährstand, a body that, like most of the institutions responsible for public libraries, was more or less outside the chain of government authority. The Reichsnährstand symbolized the Boden of the Blut and Boden precept. Officially responsible for food production, its scope extended to all areas of rural life. Early in 1937 the RV announced in a memorandum that the Reichsnährstand had decided not to establish its own libraries but would instead encourage the creation of village libraries. A year later a memorandum from the RWEV confirmed the understanding and described examples of cooperation that had taken place. One of the most common was the organization of a model library by a Beratungsstelle for an agricultural exhibition. For its part, the Reichsnährstand carried publicity for public libraries in its various media, including radio programs in Wiesbaden and Königsberg/

143

Prussia. Rust encouraged Beratungsstelle directors to add a representative of the Landesgemeinschaft to the advisory bodies created in the Richtlinien. During the war a formal agreement was signed between the Reichsnährstand and the RV, extending the cooperation between the two organizations to joint preparation of lists of recommended titles for village libraries.[21]

Regardless of such formal agreements and ministerial encouragement, activity with the Reichsnährstand had little impact on the rural library program. Reichsnährstand officials regarded the establishment of libraries as the concern of the library authorities and contributed little more than pious endorsements and some free advertising.[22] The central figures in library development remained the Beratungsstellen, provincial officials, and local community leaders.

The library building program was in many ways typical of Nazi endeavors and can be compared with such projects as the *Autobahn* program or the plan to establish elite schools to train the next generation of Nazi leaders. A new bureaucracy was formed, much money and effort expended, and physical objects constructed that could betoken accomplishment. By almost any standards it was a considerable success. The program undeniably brought library service to many. It had acquired so much momentum that only wartime shortages brought it to a halt about 1943. Rural library service was, however, put on a different basis after 1945 in West Germany. Many of the new village libraries were closed, bookmobiles reintroduced, and central libraries established. This reverse not only points up the fundamentally different assumptions of public librarianship of the postwar period, it also inevitably calls in question the soundness of the Nazi approach.

CHAPTER EIGHT

The Library

and Its

Readers

ALTHOUGH INCREASING the number of libraries often seemed to become an end in itself, Nazi library dogma clearly recognized that the importance of a library transcends physical reality. Libraries were important, not for what they were, but for what they made possible. They did not exist for librarians or for government officials but for their patrons. The ultimate raison d'être of the Nazi public library was to influence the reader to be a better German, measured, of course, by National Socialist standards. That required more than a building or books sitting on shelves.

Context cannot, of course, be completely discounted. Readers were influenced by their physical environment and an unattractive library was not an effective lure. The library of Hülsenbusch, a typical village library, does not sound very inviting: "In a tiny area for teaching materials stood a cupboard with some one hundred books. They had uniformly stiff, dark brown calico bindings and, well ordered and well cared for, made a depressingly monotonous impression."[1] Pictures of libraries taken during the 1930s show rooms that are sometimes light, sometimes dark, but furniture, books, and people are always arranged with painful neatness.

Nor was the atmosphere of most libraries particularly welcoming. Readers were expected to obey strict regulations. Berlin-Schöneberg's were told to avoid:

READING IN BED OR WHILE EATING
WRITING IN BOOKS OR ILLUSTRATING THEM
TURNING DOWN THE CORNER OF A PAGE
TURNING THE PAGE WITH A WET FINGER
LEAVING BOOKS OPEN AND UNPROTECTED

HOLDING A BOOK BY ITS COVER OR SETTING IT ON ITS EDGE

DAMAGING THE BACK OF A BOOK BY OPENING IT WITH TOO MUCH
FORCE

LAYING OPEN BOOKS FACE DOWN, OR PILING THEM UPON EACH
OTHER WHEN OPEN, OR USING THEM AS A WRITING PAD

REMOVING ENDPAPERS OR PICTURES

RETURNING BOOKS *WITHOUT A WRAPPER*

FORGETTING THESE RULES

They were then given a shorter list of things they were to do.[2]

The size and scope of an individual library's collection also influenced its readers' perceptions of service. If a library did not have a certain book, it was irrelevant whether it had been removed or simply never bought; the user could not read it. Inevitably, when judged on this basis, the quality of library service was better in larger libraries, if only because readers were offered more variety and could pursue interests in greater depth. Fundamental inequality between urban and rural library service remained intractable.

The validity of these considerations does not, however, change the fact that Nazi public librarianship put a new emphasis on library use, just as it brought money and resolution to the creation of a national administrative system and to the building of new libraries. Public libraries of all sizes had been essentially passive; when potential readers sought them out, they would be served, but no attempt was made to engage their interest. Now, active rather than passive was the order of the day. New vigor and energy animated all aspects of library activity. Programs were developed to bring new readers into the library and to keep their interest once they were there.

Who these readers for the most part were, can be stated only in general terms. The detailed statistics on the profession that were so common thirty years previously had become the exception and are only occasionally available. Emphasis on the folk community militated against drawing invidious distinctions and would have accelerated the decline already under way. Some major trends can nonetheless be perceived: With a few exceptions, the number of readers was decreasing during the 1930s, both in absolute numbers and as a percentage of the population; and the numbers and percentages of younger readers were increasing[3] (see Table 7.3).

To an American, one of the most striking characteristics of the

Mobile library service for the suburbs, Frankfurt/Main.
(Reproduced from *Die Bücherei.*)

German public library is that such a small proportion of the population was registered as readers. Compared to U.S. patterns, few Germans took advantage of their public libraries. This lower use, while justifying to some extent the proportionally smaller library collections of German libraries, would also have been more difficult to raise without larger and better collections (see Table 7.4).

Much of the comparatively low use reflects different social patterns. Because the German upper and middle classes had a tradition of buying books, German public libraries had an inescapable association with being unable to afford one's own. Political and social cleavages had encouraged the working class to found its own libraries, leaving other public libraries by implication the libraries for the less independent-thinking members of the lower classes. Nazi closing of Socialist libraries probably did not change fundamental perceptions, even if it reduced a potential reader's alternatives.[4]

Some low use can also be attributed to the prevalence of fees, although fees cannot explain the decrease in readers at a time when prosperity was increasing. Public support did not imply access without charge. Fees were charged by all public libraries, and no contradiction between their continuation and the desire to increase readership was perceived. Elimination of reader fees and charges was not even desired. In 1934 Wilhelm Schuster described access without charge as "a doubtful blessing." A small charge was seen as a means of protecting the serious reader from a flood of readers in search of superficial entertainment. Schuster compared books to cigarettes and the cinema; the state did not provide those commodities free, either.[5]

Few aspects of library use escaped charge. First, readers paid a monthly or annual registration fee that usually entitled them to take out several books per month. If it did not, or if they exceeded the monthly limit, there was a per volume circulation charge. Replacement of a reader's card was another possible expense, and, like almost all libraries, German public libraries had fines and charges for damage.

The library fee may have been ubiquitous, but it did lie in the power of libraries to reduce or waive it in special circumstances. During the depression some large cities made concessions to the unemployed; during the war soldiers were often exempted. Most common was providing free library service to the HJ, either by depositing block collections in their facilities or by issuing them library cards without charge on presentation of proof of membership. Such arrangements were usually part of the terms of the agreements between library authorities and HJ provincial organizations.

These agreements contributed to the most noticeable change in the character of public library readership brought by the Nazi years: growing numbers of young readers. Nazism venerated youth, and public libraries addressed themselves to attracting more children and young adults. Libraries exclusively for youth were opened. By 1937/38 almost every town of over 100,000 had at least one youth library, and Berlin had twelve. Two national youth libraries were created, the Reichsjugendbücherei (National Youth Library) and the Dietrich Eckart Library. The Reichsjugendbücherei was founded as a scholarly library, to preserve youth books and enhance appreciation for their role in transmitting culture; the Dietrich Eckart Library was the model library of the Nationalsozialstische Lehrerbund (National Socialist Teachers Association). Towns too small to have a special youth library augmented the youth materials in their collections. The new attention produced results, and the percentages of young readers all over the country increased dramatically. In 1936, 15.9 percent of Hamburg's readers were young adults or children, and in Berlin in 1938, 46.6 percent were under eighteen. The percentage of young readers in Hof, a town of 48,567 in the Upper Palatinate, rose from 3.1 percent in 1936 to 17.6 in 1943.[6]

Although the situation was changing, the readership of urban public libraries remained predominantly adult and male until the war began. In Kiel in 1935/36, for example, 81 percent of the library's readers were adult and 61 percent were male. The readers of Freiburg im Breisgau in the same year were 77 percent adult and 58 percent male. The reports of librarians took for granted that most readers would be adult males; male readers outnumbered females in every age group, including the young adult group.[7]

Rural readers were also predominantly adult and male during this period. Schriewer considered a ratio of two males to one female typical. The part-time librarians who staffed the small libraries in the villages did not share their professional colleagues' obsession and affection for statistics, but when they did collect them, they usually distinguished between male and female. In the assorted villages in the

Upper Palatinate, Franconia, and Lower Bavaria that reported to the Bayreuth Beratungsstelle, male readers continued to outnumber females until the war was well under way.[8]

Social values and the higher levels of education of males contributed to the preponderance of male readers, but another factor is also at work here. In some cases the adult male reader was really a "family reader"; the father would register and pay the fee at the library and then charge out books for the entire family. This practice was most unpopular with librarians because it prevented them from advising the individual who was actually going to read the book, but there was no way they could stop it.

The middle-class character of readers is more debatable and could only be resolved with more-extensive statistics, not to mention a clear definition of middle class. If one includes those with private incomes, the academically educated, higher- and middle-level civil servants, artists, teachers, technicians, engineers, students at gymnasia and universities, and independent small businessmen, then 42 percent of male readers at Kiel and 51 percent at Freiburg were "middle class." This motley assortment fails to indicate that the petite rather than the haute bourgeoisie were in the majority. It also does not show that the largest single group of readers often was that of educated workers, a group that shared many values and problems with lower-middle-class white-collar workers.[9]

Librarians worked hard to avoid identification of the library with the middle class. Emphasis on the concept of Volksgemeinschaft rather than class divisions helped minimize the problem in theory, although it did not disappear in practice. Schriewer argued that "the readership of the library must be a picture of the Volksgemeinschaft." Striving for this ideal, librarians established branches in working-class districts of towns, as in Saarbrücken, where the readers in the main library were evenly divided between the middle and working classes, but those in the two branches were predominantly working class. They opened libraries in industrial communities, co-ordinating them with factories.[10]

Library use also reflected the most infamous aspect of the Nazi regime. After Kristallnacht in 1938 Jews were prohibited from using all institutions of German culture and confined to their own separate facilities. This ruling included libraries.[11]

150

Most librarians considered readers' advising their most important professional task, since this was the point at which reader and book were actually brought together. It had been a major point of dissension between Alte and Neue Richtung, although their disagreement was not over the act of advising itself but over more-fundamental principles. At the point of giving advice to a reader, Hofmann's elitist definition of culture and conviction that the librarian was there to educate and improve the patron obviously became important. In fact, Hofmann's pronouncements on readers' advising per se are unexceptionable. He advised librarians to put themselves in the position of readers and warned them that if they tried to influence a reader, it would lead to nonuse of the library. Yet at the same time he advocated an organization and practices that forced the reader to consult the librarian and assigned the librarian the functions of educating and improving taste. Much of the Alte Richtung's distaste for Hofmann's views on readers' advising in the end had less to do with their content than with their autocratic, didactic tone. They could counter only by urging a less formal approach.[12]

Perhaps because it was so obvious that the advice given to readers had to embody the principles of the library, or perhaps because they recognized the essential truth of Hofmann's warning that attempts to influence readers against their will drove them away, librarians made little effort to develop any specifically Nazi approach to it. Schriewer's very detailed book on rural librarianship provides no guidance on the subject. In his pamphlet on librarianship in the village and small town, Karl Taupitz, director of the Beratungsstelle in Saxony, said only that public library work was National Socialist leadership of men: "The librarian, whether full-time or part-time, should help the Volksgemeinschaft create and maintain itself through his library work."[13]

Almost all writing on advising is of a similar opacity. Wilhelm Schuster described it as an art and "no mechanical transaction." A training session of the Hagen Beratungsstelle described the process in straightforward if obvious terms: "The advising librarian is the mediator between man and book. Men of all professional classes and all ages come with their diverse wants to the library. It is there for everyone and should be able to fill every reading need—if it is not too specialized or professional—in the right way. Out of this demand they

151

perceive the great and important task that the library and library director have to accomplish." Suggestions of how to do it were usually as vague as Hofmann's instruction that librarians put themselves in the place of the reader. Schuster counseled cultivation of humane understanding. When suggestions were more specific, they were not particularly helpful. The Hagen librarian developed an elaborate classification scheme by point of view: men, women, boys, girls; simply written, written with more difficulty; exciting books for action-oriented men, contemplative books for thoughtful men; realistic books, books of fantasy; books set in the mountains, books set on the plains. The possible dichotomies were endless.[14]

No set of precepts could avoid the fundamental fact that good advising depended on knowledge of the collection and understanding of people. Each encounter was individual and distinctive. Ultimately, librarians had to develop their own styles and techniques to suit their own personalities and the environments in which they worked. Advising was an important activity in the Nazi public library, but how it was actually performed depended on how the librarian interpreted the goals of the library.

Political considerations and the omnipresent police state unfortunately often turned readers' advising into a sham. Lotte Bergtel-Schleif emphasized the absence of trust between librarians and patrons that marked the period after 1933. Readers did not dare tell librarians what they really wanted to read if their preferences diverged from what was acceptable in the new Germany. Librarians had to recommend books they knew full well were not of interest to the reader, and readers did not have the option of rejecting them. Librarians could also exercise a considerable amount of control simply by stating that a book was out, if a reader requested a book of which the librarian did not approve.[15]

Physical arrangements reinforced readers' advising. By clearly separating circulation area from service area, the counter (*Schalter*) advocated by Leipzig adherents fostered their own view of the librarian as educator, as an authority figure. A different kind of counter (*Theke*) could change space relationships and encourage greater self-sufficiency of the reader, minimizing the educational role of the librarian.[16]

152

Ernst-Abbe Library and Reading Room, Jena. Circulation desk.
(Reproduced from *Die Bücherei*.)

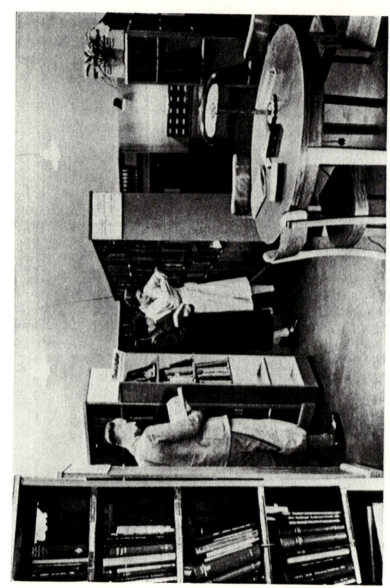

Open stacks in Neustadt branch library, Hamburg. (Reproduced from *Die Bücherei*.)

Open stacks, the ultimate in reader self-help, were rarely to be found. Hamburg took the lead in experimenting with them and promoting their spread. Alfred Krebs, the controversial director of the Hamburger Öffentliche Bücherhallen, gave a lecture on open stacks at the 1936 Würzburg meeting of librarians in which he insisted on treating it strictly as a practical question. The great theoretician Walter Hofmann, chief defender and advocate of the Schalter, found the idea distasteful and Krebs himself intolerable. Krebs had not endeared himself by suggesting that open stacks were perhaps more appropriate for the obstinate Germans of Lower Saxony than they were for the more easily led people of central Germany. After the meeting Hofmann dashed off an angry letter to the RV, claiming that Krebs had accused the pro-Schalter group of having "limited minds." What he had actually said was that the librarian dispensing advice stood in danger of being unable to find a synthesis between his own taste and education and political importance; instead of advising, he would intellectually rape.[17]

By 1940 four of Hamburg's eight libraries were completely open stack, and in three of the remaining ones adult nonfiction and young adult materials had been opened while adult fiction remained closed. Statistics confirmed the success of the new system; both circulation and registration of readers rose. Other northern libraries began to imitate Hamburg. Bremen opened its first open stack branch in 1939, and in 1942 *DB* reported that Glucksburg in Schleswig had converted its library to open stacks.[18]

Rudolf Joerden, director of the Hamburger Öffentliche Bücherhallen from 1938 to 1970, felt that, had it not been for the war, many other libraries would have quickly adopted the new arrangement.[19] Instead, the conversion of German libraries to open stacks was largely a postwar phenomenon, an existing inclination intensified by strong Anglo-American influence. Joerden is doubtless correct, but the whole concept of open stacks that, as one report put it, allow "the widest room for individual readers to exercise their own initiative" was antithetical to the fundamental concept of Nazi librarianship. The purpose of the Nazi library was to promote a specific, predetermined set of ideas, not to enhance individualism. A controlled collection would, as Krebs assured his listeners, limit the scope within which individual initiative could be exercised, but the

155

whole notion of individualism was anathema in Nazi Germany. An advisor would serve as yet another means of restraint on what people read and was thus a natural element in the Nazi public library.

During the Nazi period what library users read underwent some change. In all the cities for which any kind of comparison of different periods is possible, the reading of belles lettres—a category that, except for small groups of poetry and drama, was synonymous with fiction—declined markedly (see Table 8.1). The size of the community affected how much fiction was read. The larger the town, the less fiction. Schriewer estimated that readers in rural areas read 10 to 20 percent more fiction than did those in large cities, a characteristic he attributed to the preference of the simple rural reader for experiencing the world through fantasy. Young adult reading, on the other hand, was increasing. These figures reflect Nazi policy, which was hostile to many of the most popular forms of entertaining reading, such as romances and detective novels, and venerated youth.[20]

Another factor in the increase of nonfiction circulation was the attitude of librarians. Bergtel-Schleif has described a "flight to nonfiction" by librarians.[21] The predominantly value-free character of nonfiction made it both a safe refuge and a form of passive resistance. Librarians could avoid advocacy of a Nazi viewpoint and protect themselves from recommending something that might turn out to be dangerous. This behavior has much in common with that of scholars who turned from research on political history to such apolitical topics as Roman coins, or of writers who sought escape in inner migration.

The distribution of reader interest within nonfiction also changed. Most striking were the dramatically increased interest in history and the somewhat less dramatic decrease of interest in law and political science. Many categories remained stable, such as local history, art, and music. Some showed growth in one library and a reduction in another, as did geography, which increased at Hamburg and Lingen, remained unchanged at Kiel, and decreased at Hanover. The categories most read in several geographically dispersed libraries during the 1930s are shown in Table 8.2.

Many libraries created a separate category for National Socialist writing to enhance its importance and increase circulation. At Freiburg the most frequently read books in this section were, according to the director, Hitler's writings, Rosenberg's, and books on racial

Table 8.1 Distribution of Reading, by Fiction,
Nonfiction, and Youth (Percentages)

Berlin		1933/34	1937/38
Belles lettres		50	41
Nonfiction		34	33
Youth		16	26
Hamburg		1933/34	1936/37
Belles lettres		65	59
Nonfiction		29	33
Youth		6	8
Kiel	1928/29	1933/34	1936/37
Belles lettres	71	59	59
Nonfiction	29	41	41
Hanover	1932/33	1933/34	1937/38
Belles lettres	64	61	57
Nonfiction	36	39	43
Lingen	1927/28	1933/34	1937/38
Belles lettres	97	81	77
Nonfiction	3	16	15
Youth	–	3	4

questions and the peasantry. Given the nature of *Mein Kampf* and *Mythus des 20. Jahrhunderts*, it is difficult to believe.

The absence of statistics on who and what were read in fiction make any conclusions in this area tentative. But if librarians were, as most librarians do, buying the books most in demand, then Zoberlein, Wehner, Luckner, Dwinger, Beumelburg, Berens-Totenohl, and Lons were the most popular authors.[22] Hans Grimm's ponderous, doctrinaire 1923 novel *Volk ohne Raum* achieved a mass readership it never had had in the 1920s. In addition, library readers displayed a strong interest in regional writers that national lists do not usually include. Writers in Plattdeutsch were much read in Hamburg, and Anzengruber and Dörfler in the South. Hansjakob enjoyed an enduring popularity in his native Black Forest area, and librarians in Bavaria seemed unable to get enough Ganghofer titles to satisfy demand.

What library reading patterns during the Third Reich do not indicate is what people wanted to read but could not. After the thoroughgoing censorship, many books that readers would have requested and

Table 8.2 Distribution of Nonfiction Reading

Freiburg (1935/36)	Hamburg (1936/37)	Kiel (1936/37)
World war	Geography, travel	Biography
Geography	History	Geography
National socialism	Natural science, health	History
Biography	Technology	Technology
	Biography	Natural science

Hanover (1937/38)	Lingen (1937/38)	Saarbrücken (1936/37)
Biography	World war	Travel
Geography	Travel	History
History	Biography	War memoirs
Medicine, natural science	History	National socialism
Art	Law, political science	Geography

Sources: Generallandesarchiv, Karlsruhe, 235/6799, Freiburg, "Jahresbericht 1935/36 der Städtischen Volksbücherei Freiburg im Breisgau"; Stadtarchiv, Saarbrücken, G. 6418, "Statistik der Stadtbücherei Saarbrücken vom Rechnungsjahr 1936." (Sources for the Hamburg, Kiel, Hanover, and Lingen information are given in note 20 to Chapter 8.)

read with pleasure simply were no longer in their public libraries. Three of the fourteen most popular authors in the Freiburg public library in 1932/33 were banned: Alice Behrend; Thomas Mann; and Franz Werfel. Nor were the writers who were unavailable forgotten. As soon as the war ended in 1945 there was a heavy demand for many of the books that had been placed on blacklists. One librarian then in her teens remembers the excitement of at last being able to read writers of whom she had only heard.[23]

During the 1930s library circulation declined and did not begin to rise until the war began. The contraction of circulation (see Table 7.4) was general throughout the country, although there were a few exceptions to this trend. Comparing figures for 1933/34 and 1937/38 in the ten largest German cities, all of which had populations of over 500,000, ten cities of between 100,000 and 150,000, and ten small towns of just over twenty thousand shows that the decrease was greatest in the large cities. Eight of the ten towns of over 500,000 experienced a decline in circulation during these years, as did six of the ten medium-sized cities, but six of the ten small towns increased rather than decreased their circulation, and one remained stable.

Explanations of this fact can only be speculation. Contemporary librarians avoided the subject entirely, commenting only when circulation rose. It is tempting to seek causes in the changes in public libraries, to say that the Nazi public library was not meeting the needs of the population, and readers were expressing their opinions by staying away. Such interpretations would be more convincing were it not that circulation in libraries in the United States was also declining at this time. Having risen during the depression, it began to decrease about 1934 in libraries of all sizes of cities, and that can hardly be attributed to ruthless censorship or propagandistic goals. U.S. librarians, too, were silent about this decline—it can be discovered only by careful inspection of statistical tables—but one commented in 1938 with some irony that at least the fall indicated a no-depression year.[24] This librarian believed that people were using libraries less because they had more money available for other amusements and travel. She may well be correct. Both in Germany and the United States the library was encountering strong competition as a provider of entertainment from radio and films, both of which grew considerably in this period. Other alternative consumers of time, present in Germany but not in the United States, were the organized activities required of people in party organizations such as the HJ, and the spectacles provided by the state that demanded or attracted mass participation.

Not all librarians viewed the decline of circulation as a bad thing. The Essen Public library publicized its decrease in a poster headed "Die Gesundung" (becoming healthy). Making a virtue of necessity, the poster hailed the shrinking circulation and reduced number of library users between 1933 and 1937 as evidence of subsidence of the dread disease of *Vielleserei* (voracious reading). Vielleserei was one of Walter Hofmann's bêtes noires; his antipathy was based on the belief that if a reader was reading many books, said reader was likely to be reading entertaining books rather than becoming educated.[25]

Most librarians were less concerned with Vielleserei and more interested in having the library fulfil its educational goals, an impossible task if readers refused to use the library. Quite apart from that, the desirability of increasing library use has been an important element in the librarian's faith since public libraries first began. During the Third Reich, librarians responded actively and aggressively. They expanded the range of library activities and labored to make them

159

Readers using card catalog, Berlin-Steglitz.
(Courtesy, Amerika-Gedenkbibliothek.)

better known. Publicity became an important library enterprise. Librarians did not experiment with any particularly innovative ideas, but they did implement existing ones with enthusiasm. New vitality infused the public library.

For many years Erwin Ackerknecht had been writing on how to enliven public libraries and make them more useful, and much of what was done in the 1930s closely resembles his suggestions. One 1917 essay had been addressed to the question of how to attract a broad circle of users, especially nonreaders. Ackerknecht emphasized the importance of advertising and recommended both advertisements in newspapers and well-distributed posters. Conveying a sense of invitation and welcome was essential, and Ackerknecht discussed the architecture of the building and its interior design in these terms, as well as such practical matters as the physical location of the library and the hours it was open. He pioneered activities that became commonplace in public libraries during the 1930s. He urged evening entertainments as a way to acquaint people with the library. Lectures and musical performances were a part of his thinking. He advocated separate collections and comfortable reading rooms for children and those interested in music.[26]

One of the most common activities sponsored by a library was the *Dichterlesung*, an author reading from his work. New, appropriately National Socialist goals gave these evenings a suitably political slant. As one librarian put it, instead of piquing the interest of the literary gourmet, the objective of the Dichterlesung was now to free German literature from its traditional confines and cliques and make it the possession of the entire Volk. Planning and presentation were the responsibility of the Nazi cultural organizations, and some of the most prominent writers of the Third Reich participated. Like most such supplementary library activities, Dichterlesungen were more frequent in large cities, but even some very small towns held them occasionally.[27]

Exhibits were another frequent tactic used to entice people into the library. The 1936 Spandau exhibit on youth and the library was typical and shows both the style of exhibits and how they became occasions for political persuasion. The exhibit's title was "Peasant and Soldier," and it celebrated the official rejection of the last limitations imposed by the Treaty of Versailles on the armed forces and the

161

Library exhibit: 200,000 Sudeten Germans too many. (Reproduced from *Die Bücherei*.)

rebuilding of the German army. The Führer was featured prominently; at the entrance he was pictured eye to eye with Walter Darré, the *Reichsbauernführer* (national peasant leader). Every effort was made to identify Hitler with the past glories of German arms and to portray him as a modern version of Frederick the Great. Recommended books, such as those published by the Blut and Boden Verlag, were displayed, and numerous book lists on such topics as "Blut und Boden," "Rassenkunde und Rassenpflege" (racial knowledge and care), and books suitable for boys and girls were available free of charge.[28]

Book lists had long been used by libraries to draw attention to a subject or take advantage of an existing trend. Their number increased during the 1930s. Some of the topics on which the Freiburg library prepared book lists were the literature of the new nationalism and national socialism (1933), mother and child (1935), bolshevism (1936), National Socialist writing, and the German destiny. For the occasion of the Führer's fiftieth birthday the Institut für Leser- und Schrifttumskunde prepared one titled "The Führer in One Hundred Books" for the RV. Heiligenstaedt announced its availability in a memorandum and proclaimed in underlined words, "I recommend to the libraries and Beratungsstellen the broadest distribution of this list!" It was to be given free of charge. At the Hamburg Public Library this particular book list gave rise to two memoranda; the director reminded the staff that if the books requested were not available, the central library could arrange an exchange. For Book Week in 1934 the city library and Beratungsstelle at Hagen brought out a list of books suitable for gifts.[29]

Well-organized libraries regularly published lists of their new acquisitions, and occasionally a Beratungsstelle would adapt this promotional device to its own circumstances. Lippe put together a "Second Selected List from the Library Authority for the Province of Lippe" that was tied to book procurement in the small local libraries of the district. Most of the titles were culled from the new Reichslisten, but, in an interesting example of independence, the Beratungsstelle made it clear that they could recommend these books from their own examination.[30]

Book Week became an annual extravaganza. Public libraries participated with other literary institutions to create a spectacle that grew

163

bigger and more elaborate every year. The ostensible purpose of Book Week was to celebrate the book and culture, but the Goebbels ministry took control and infused it with politics. Sometimes the occasion had a specific theme; in 1937 it was named "Week of the German Book" and in 1938 it marked the incorporation of Austria into the Reich with the title "Greater German Book Week." In 1941 it was "War Book Week." Usually there was little unity. Book Week 1935 featured a publicity pamphlet, "Book and Volk," with words of wisdom from the Führer and other Nazi leaders, seventeen book lists, posters blazoning the slogan "The book—a sword of the spirit," public prize givings, a publicity film, and seventy-eight different radio programs.[31]

As the building program got under way, openings of new libraries became a prominent feature of Book Week. Dähnhardt announced during the 1937 Book Week that 730 new libraries were being opened. Thirty of them were in one district of the Palatinate alone. Each opening was used as a publicity opportunity, with speeches by the mayor, the new librarian, and Beratungsstelle director. Beratungsstelle directors were busy during Book Week.[32]

Book Week in Lippe in 1938 was typical. Local Detmold book dealers organized a joint exhibit of books. The Beratungsstelle entertained numerous visitors. A special archive was opened; there were exhibits. In cooperation with the HJ, a special exhibit for youth was created and book lists developed. The Kreis educational officer spoke at the annual meeting of the mayors of Kreis Detmold, which was scheduled for that week, on the virtues of libraries; and the Beratungsstelle director spoke to the majors of Kreis Lemgo. The high point was the dedication of two new libraries in large villages.[33]

Book Week was the most elaborate publicity undertaking, but libraries devoted considerable effort to all kinds of publicity. They prepared stories to be placed in newspapers. Posters were put up. In an effort to increase the number of its users the Freiburg library posted notices in the streetcars. The library of Greiz had a float in the May Day parade of 1934, and the city libraries of Düsseldorf had a model library at the 1937 national exhibit on "Working Volk."[34]

To encourage use, programs might also focus on a special group rather than being aimed at the public at large. The group had, of course, to be carefully chosen to be compatible with the goals and values of the state. In 1935 Dähnhardt sharply rejected the idea of any special library service for the Wends, a small Slavic-speaking enclave in Brandenburg, left behind in the great push of the German peoples to the East in the early Middle Ages. The concept of Volksgemeinschaft did not include a concern for minority rights.[35]

There was some attention to the special interests and needs of factory employees, but from the point of view of libraries the most important special interest group was youth.[36] The two national libraries took the lead and developed model programs. Both offered extensive lectures, discussions, and exhibits aimed at young people. Some exhibits attracted as many as six thousand visitors. The Reichsjugendbücherei sponsored poetry readings; Baldur von Schirach, head of the HJ, was one of the featured poets.

Both youth libraries reached beyond their immediate communities with other programs. The Reichsjugendbücherei took an important part in censorship, printing lists of both banned and recommended books. Beginning in 1934 the Dietrich Eckart Library distributed copies of every book it cataloged to ten school libraries in border areas. It also sponsored nationwide essay contests for youth on themes such as "The Greater German Reich."[37]

Some young adult work was done through schools. Several decrees from Minister of Education Rust, whose jurisdiction included both schools and public libraries, mandated cooperation between the two, and in 1937 the Beratungsstellen were given formal responsibility for school libraries. Franz Schriewer wrote about the work of the Frankfurt/Oder Beratungsstelle with youth in the schools, but few libraries or Beratungsstellen did much in this area. The tours of the library for school classes and the posters distributed for display in schools by the Hamburger Öffentliche Bücherhallen were more than most libraries offered.[38]

Most youth work was done in cooperation with the HJ. The two organizations were natural partners. The public library had always been an educational institution outside the hierarchy of formal education. As the Nazi state evolved, the role of the HJ changed from that of the neglected junior branch of the party to an important instrument for the political socialization of future citizens. The 1935 Law

165

Young readers, Breslau. (Reproduced from *Die Bücherei*.)

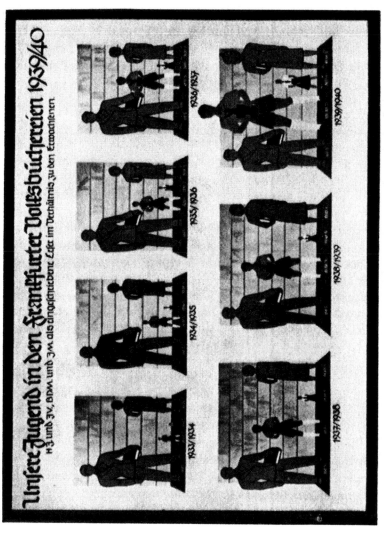

Graph showing growth in young readers, Frankfurt/Main.
(Reproduced from *Die Bücherei*.)

for German Youth decreed that the whole of German youth was organized in the HJ; in other words, all young people between ten and eighteen were supposed to join. "The whole of German youth is to be educated, outside the parental home and school, in the Hitler Youth physically, intellectually and morally in the spirit of National Socialism for service to the nation and community." The HJ could thus, at least in theory, offer the public library access to the entire population of young adults; the public library offered the HJ much needed support for its activities.[39]

Work with the HJ began on an ad hoc basis; individual HJ leaders would contact a library or the Beratungsstelle. In the early years, efforts apparently were made to confine relations to an institution-to-institution basis. Readers' cards in Hamburg, for instance, were issued to members through the group leader. Only in 1937 could members get their cards directly from the library by showing the HJ membership cards.[40]

Efforts became increasingly systematic, especially after the Youth Law of 1936. Many Beratungsstellen concluded agreements with their provincial youth authorities. A typical agreement, concluded early in 1937 and covering the provinces of Westphalia, Lippe, and Schaumburg-Lippe, provided that the three Beratungsstellen and the HJ leadership would jointly prepare a list of youth books and magazines to be made available in public libraries. Local Heimat literature was to be featured. The HJ was to encourage active library use by its members, and the public library was to attempt to satisfy the reading needs of the group by appropriate acquisitions. To obtain the additional financing necessary, their leader was to encourage localities to increase public library appropriations. A similar national agreement later in 1937 supplemented these provincial agreements; it established the important principle that the HJ was to use public libraries whenever possible rather than establishing their own.[41]

Cooperation with the HJ took a variety of forms. One of the most frequent was the joint preparation of reading lists. The Beratungsstelle of Lippe, for example, prepared a list of Heimat literature for the HJ summer school of Horste in 1937. Many reading lists were tied to the *Heimabend,* originally simple weekly meetings but gradually evolving into a carefully coordinated educational series with ra-

168

dio broadcasts and discussions on a set theme. Each member was supposed to have prepared beforehand by reading books from the lists of recommended titles. Libraries often placed small collections at the disposal of local HJ groups, sometimes to support a particular course, sometimes simply for general recreation. The Beratungsstelle of the Saar made such a collection available to the HJ camp in Scheid, as well as for weekend courses.[42]

However desirable and encouraged by national leaders, the extent of cooperation between any library and the HJ depended on the enthusiasm of the local youth leader for reading and the enthusiasm of the librarian. Schneidemühl, directed by Richard Kock, was considered a model. It pioneered the practices of group loans and participation in HJ lectures and developed formal guidelines for the selection of books especially for them. In Schneidemühl, HJ members accounted for 55.8 percent of the library's readership and 51.9 percent of its loans.[43]

Work with the HJ was important not only because of increased use of the library by young adults; it also demonstrated library cooperation with a party organization. During the Nazi period public libraries were under pressure to find ways to serve the party. The cooperation of library and HJ satisfied this requirement and benefited both.

The pressure to work with the party had its roots in practical and political considerations. Until the takeover, party cells had had their own libraries, but in a state where the distinctions between party and government were blurred, such libraries seemed an unnecessary diversion of resources. Librarians consistently opposed them. Taupitz acknowledged in a 1934 article that not all public libraries had an appropriately National Socialist spirit, but by 1936 he was arguing that the public library must see as its primary duty being the trustee of the party in literary education. The public library, like the party, was a political organization but was dedicated to developing character and deepening knowledge, while the mission of the party was shaping the worldview. Some party officials, such as the Gau educational director of the Palatinate, urged that the collections of party libraries be transferred to public libraries. Others preferred to maintain their independence. Schemm, who was both a party and a government official, agreed that public libraries could serve the party effectively but was careful to leave room for party libraries where public libraries did not exist or were inadequate.[44]

No official national directive ever resolved the relationship. The Richtlinien of 1937 referred to "sympathetic cooperation between public library and party," but for the most part relations were determined on an ad hoc basis. Although the Bayerische Ostmark was one of the few areas where the Gauleiter officially discouraged public libraries, many party libraries were quietly turned over to the local public library. In fact, public librarians had little to fear from the competition of party libraries; on a list of party libraries in Franconia the largest collection had twenty-five volumes. Recognizing that the public library was also the party library was more important for symbolic reasons than for real, and recognition of public libraries as officially the library of the HJ was a major psychological victory.[45]

Despite the absence of real competition, public libraries worked energetically to prove their utility to the party. In the late 1930s Beratungsstelle annual reports regularly included a section on how they were cooperating with the party. Between 1937 and 1939 the Braunschweig Beratungsstelle reported placing placards in the local HJ quarters and those of the NS-Gemeinschaft Kraft durch Freude, making the library available at a reduced rate to several groups, and providing a tour of the library for participants in the local party leadership conference. Munich in 1937/38 prepared new basic book lists for Gau library officials, issued a proclamation on creating suitable community libraries jointly with provincial agricultural authorities and the Beratungsstelle at Bayreuth, and helped reorganize local Deutsche Arbeitsfront (DAF) union libraries. The Lippe Beratungsstelle prepared a book list for the HJ and made a list of the Heimat literature of Lippe available at a nearby HJ summer camp. It relinquished responsibility for the union libraries of the NS-Gemeinschaft Kraft durch Freude to the local party adult education authority.[46]

At the same time that the threat from the party libraries was gradually receding, public libraries were also eliminating an old enemy, the subscription lending libraries, or Leihbüchereien. Regarded as purveying the worst in literature and pandering to the lowest in human nature, Leihbüchereien had been an object of librarians' hostility, envy, and contempt for many years.[47] The usual Leihbücherei was a very small collection of books, often run as an adjunct to a newspaper or tobacconist's shop. They were frankly commercial enterprises and offered the popular literature the public craved and for which it was willing to pay. The collections featured endless rows of popular romances of the ilk of Hedwig Courths-Mahler and detective novels of Edgar Wallace style, but it was not unknown for them to contain works by such authors as Zola, Balzac, and Strindberg.[48] Although they obviously did not share the exalted educational pretensions of public libraries, Leihbüchereien were neither the threat to public morality nor the danger to the intellect they were portrayed to be. They were meeting a demand public libraries refused to satisfy.

It was the existence of the Leihbüchereien outside the channels of control rather than their offense against the puritanical values of national socialism that made the new state their enemy. By degrees they were subjected to the same rules of censorship as the public libraries, hampered by restrictions prohibiting the proprietor of a lending library from engaging in any additional business or commerce, and deprived of their independence by being incorporated into the RSK. They were even expected to contain National Socialist works. In some provinces, such as Thuringia, they were placed under the jurisdiction of the Beratungsstelle. In 1937 the RSK decreed that no new Leihbüchereien were to be opened, and the wartime shortages of books and paper finished them.[49]

Victory over the Leihbüchereien was a significant step in asserting the public library's claim to be the sole purveyor of library service to the community. Strengthening its external position went hand in hand with internal improvements that helped transform the public library into a vigorous, modern institution. During the 1930s public libraries ceased to be small, rather dreary places, used only by a few devotees. To become the library envisioned in National Socialist library theory, they were forced to become more active and aggressive. The new focus on the reader was necessary if they were to accomplish their political tasks and essential to modernization.

CHAPTER NINE

Librarians
and
Their Jobs

URING THE Third Reich public librarians made important strides toward consolidating their profession. They asserted the individuality and importance of their craft, distancing themselves further from academic librarians. They defined their values and expanded their control over their sphere of activity. Reluctant municipal and provincial officials learned what they were and were forced to hire them. Public librarianship communicates a new sense of vitality and purpose after 1933.

Reflecting and contributing to this improved morale, the number of public librarians grew considerably. As of 1937 there were approximately seven hundred public librarians, about two-thirds of them female. Library school attendance was rising. Where the 1935 yearbook of public libraries listed fifty-five candidates, it gave 302 in the spring of 1940 and 520 in the fall of 1941.[1] Although it hardly became a major profession, public librarianship undeniably became a more substantial presence.

At the same time, the Nazi era had many negative effects on public librarians. Some trends, such as increased cynicism and greater secretiveness, they shared with the general population. Ackerknecht's correspondence silently testifies to the many broken friendships. Other negative consequences were more specific to the profession. It is clear from postwar comments that librarians knew they were not doing a good job by their own professional standards, impressive statistics notwithstanding. Many librarians lost faith in the value of what they were doing. The idealism that is an inherent part of professionalism disappeared in the environment of national socialism. Intellectual isolation prevailed. Where formerly public librarians had looked to other countries, especially Scandinavia, Great Britain, and the

172

United States, who were the pioneers in this area, now they were expected to draw their inspiration solely from German roots.

Most professional librarians were located in large-city libraries. The twenty-eight largest cities, all with a population of approximately 200,000 or more, employed 480 or two-thirds of the professional librarians, not including their directors.[2] Berlin alone had 188. This physical concentration in urban areas was a reality that ran counter to Nazi idolization of rural and peasant life. Official interest might focus on rural librarianship, but the profession remained primarily urban. An inherent contradiction thus lay at the heart of public librarianship.

The official concentration on rural areas is reflected in *DB*, which published very little on urban librarianship, except for the occasional news note or an article on a specific aspect of service in an area of high priority; for example, youth work. One rare exception is a 1936 article by Karl Tauptiz titled "Die Bücherei in der Großstadt" (The public library in the large city).[3] Taupitz was the head of the Dresden public library, but he was also the head of the Beratungsstelle for Saxony and his heart was definitely in rural librarianship. His most important publication was *Das Büchereiwesen in Dorf und Kleinstadt* (Librarianship in the village and small town). The village library was his model, and the city library was a library only to the extent it conformed to that pattern. When it did not, it was to be criticized. His article clearly conveys prevailing attitudes and indirectly shows some of the difficulties under which urban librarians labored.

For Taupitz the great task of the public library, whether rural or urban, was to maintain the Volksgemeinschaft. But by its very nature the urban public library was at a disadvantage in this effort. It was impersonal in a situation that called for closeness to the Volk. The lingering class divisions in cities made the library's task more difficult, and the unemployed complicated things still further. Taupitz criticized the reading rooms that were so characteristic of large-city libraries. U.S. models had inspired them, and they needed to be adapted to German conditions. They should serve a different function and be planned with the help of the party to contribute to political education. He found offensive and life-threatening the pride of the large-city library, which he perceived as holding itself professionally and intellectually aloof.

Criticism such as Taupitz's and the official disdain for large cities cannot have helped the outlook of urban librarians. The accommodation between rural and urban librarianship was uneasy, and during the Nazi period the moral advantage lay with those in the countryside. Most city librarians, however, would have found their jobs considerably more appealing than those of their rural counterparts. Their libraries were large enough to offer a variety of specialized services, their libraries pioneered the new ideas such as young adult work, and their programs had the greatest range. City librarians did not work in professional isolation. Encouraged and often subsidized by their libraries, they were more likely to be professionally active, attend conferences, and subscribe to the professional journal. The nature of a library system required regular staff meetings and internal memoranda. Much nonprofessional social interaction was also built into their situation. The Hamburger Öffentliche Bücherhallen, for example, had monthly programs for staff and hosted an annual picnic.

But if they had the advantages of greater mass and organization, city librarians suffered concomitant disadvantages. They were easier to control. The Hamburg librarians, for example, had their monthly staff evening canceled in February 1939 so that they could listen to a speech by Goebbels. They were required to be present at Sunday lectures and library outings. When they failed to attend a memorial service in 1943 in sufficient numbers, they received a wrathful memorandum from Dr. Krebs, their former director, then in the city's cultural administration.[4]

In addition to its primarily urban composition, public librarianship also labored under the disadvantage of being predominantly female. Nazism was a man's ideology, allowing women only their traditional roles of homemaker and mother. Theoretically, it had no place for the professional woman, and a female profession could have little status.[5]

In 1937 Elisabeth Propach, the director of studies at the Berlin library school, estimated that two-thirds of librarians were women. In fact, Propach seems to have understated the case, perhaps to present a more positive image for the profession. In 1935, 710 of the 934 members of the VDV, or 76 percent, were women. Rarely were they married. And the profession was becoming more female. Of the fifty-five library school students listed in 1935, only 20 percent were male. By

1940, a year that still included the normal admissions from the pre-war year 1939, that number had fallen still further, to 18 percent. Although Walter Hofmann had called for an increase in the number of men in the profession in 1934, they simply had not materialized.[6]

Women were considered to be especially suitable for librarianship. It was a profession in which they practiced two—helping and educating—of the three traditional activities of women, the *helfen, heilen und erziehen* (to help, heal, and educate) triad. Hofmann saw librarianship as having tasks of a caring kind, both in the material and intellectual-spiritual sense. His wife, Elise Hofmann-Bosse, had stated this position in more detail in a 1927 article. In her opinion women displayed strongly the appropriate personal-spiritual characteristics. It was a part of feminine nature that women had the pliability of spirit and the elasticity to understand the different spiritual needs of people. When women's higher relationship to life was enhanced by education, they made the best readers' advisors. A successful administrator and a power in her own right in the Leipzig movement, Hofmann-Bosse was enough of a feminist to point out also that while librarianship called for a certain business acumen, usually considered a masculine attribute, women were competently administering many middle-sized libraries.

The arguments of Lilli Volbehr, the head of Branch G in Hamburg, were similar. In a 1934 article, Volbehr tried to show that, although in a Nazi society women belonged at the stove, they were needed in librarianship. And not only were they needed, their work conformed to Nazi specifications for women's activities in all aspects except location. She argued that women brought different and special abilities to the profession, and that cooperation between men and women was necessary to fulfil the new National Socialist goals.[7]

Men who did enter the profession could expect to occupy the leading positions. Hofmann asserted that public librarianship was neither a masculine nor a feminine profession; there was room for both. Men had the task of laying the foundation and of leadership, women of maintaining internal cohesion and carrying out the routine tasks of administration. Certainly this division of labor was characteristic until the war sent most men into the army. In 1940 all the Beratungsstellen were directed by men, except for one in which the position was empty. Men monopolized the positions of head librarian in the public libraries of large cities. The librarians and technical assistants, on the other hand, were with rare exceptions female. It was extremely unusual for a woman to have any major administrative responsibility.[8]

The advantage that men had because society accepted them as the natural leaders was enhanced by the educational patterns within the profession. Of the ninety-three members of the VDV who held the doctorate in 1935, only twelve, or 13 percent, were women. By the Nazi period, although a university education alone was no longer sufficient, it still conferred a decided advantage on the individual who could present it. At least it could if the individual were male. None of the twelve university-educated women held a major administrative post in 1935, although some of them undoubtedly ran things behind a male front. Dr. Betty Schladebach of the Lippe Beratungsstelle, for example, was obviously indispensable, and Dr. Maria Steinhoff, director of studies at the Cologne library school, received the credit for keeping it going.[9]

The social origins of librarians, especially of the females, were relentlessly middle class. Volbehr, born in 1890, explained that while at the turn of the century the sons of the upper middle class would become officers and merchants and the sons of the lower middle class would become lower-level civil servants or business employees, only careers as telephone operators, shop assistants, or domestic employees were open to their sisters. These opportunities had little appeal for girls with a good education, who therefore flocked to such professions as teaching or librarianship that offered them a more challenging alternative.[10]

Lists from the Berlin school in the late 1920s certainly confirm Volbehr's analysis of the situation. The students about to make a visit to Stettin in May 1925 as part of their library school studies were the offspring of two engineers, two lawyers, two university professors, a tax administrator, a gymnasium teacher, merchant, postal administrator, chemist, city official, nursery owner, city tax supervisor, ministry official, director of a lycée, and mayor. One engineer's daughter had been born in Ossining, New York. A similar group five years later had fathers who included three merchants, two retired military officers, two lawyers, two library directors (one was Gottlieb Fritz), five educational administrators, two provincial inspectors, a city ad-

176

ministrator, raw-silk importer, professor, ministry official, school administrator, nobleman, minister, provincial surveyor, government inspector, master baker, administrator, banker, blast furnace director, surveying administrator, deputy headmaster, engineer, sanitary administrator, and one of unknown profession. Occasionally the daughter of a member of the gentry or nobility would become a librarian. The group of Berlin students who visited Stettin in the spring of 1929 included one *Freifrau* (baroness) who, the director of studies reported with a wry smile, had to have a single room because "she can only sleep alone." The 1935 list of VDV members included this sensitive Freifrau, then employed in the Brunnenstrasse branch in Berlin, an imperial knight, at least one librarian who could use the high-status "zu" in her surname, and a sprinkling of lesser "von's."[11]

To these women their profession was important not only because it was a means of earning a living, but as a calling. Volbehr's 1934 article expresses eloquently the fear that the establishment of a Nazi regime with its aggressively masculine ideology brought to them. As it turned out, such concern was unnecessary. Far from the profession's being closed to women, their numbers increased both absolutely and relatively. Although male librarians expected that Machtergreifung would enhance their chances of professional advancement, there is little evidence that this occurred. Men continued to occupy the positions of leadership, but this did not represent a change. At lower levels, some men may even have been replaced by women, who had the attraction that they commanded lower salaries.[12] As in many other professions, the employment of women was both necessary and desirable for the community, and the Nazi regime was forced to accept this social and economic reality, however unwillingly.[13]

The tasks of the professional librarians in the public libraries of Nazi Germany were similar to what they had been in Weimar Germany, or what they are in present public libraries, because the common purpose of bringing book and reader together imposes a degree of uniformity. Certain things must be done for that task to be accomplished. The book (or other format) must be selected, ordered, cataloged, and put on the shelf. The book must then be recommended by a librarian who is sufficiently familiar with both its contents and the prospective reader to identify a good match. Records of its circulation must be kept and its return noted. Readers may have complaints of one kind or another that have to be dealt with. There are housekeeping tasks; bindings need to be repaired and the library's quarters maintained. Clerks and assistants must be supervised. Librarians usually summarize these functions as acquisition, cataloging, and classification; readers' advising; circulation; and management. How many of these any one librarian does depends on the size of the library and the amount of specialization within it, and on whether the library is part of a system that provides some of these services.

Contemporary writings describe these tasks in various ways. In 1927 Elise Hofmann-Bosse divided the tasks of the librarian into two categories, the craft-technical and the personal-intellectual. In the first she placed writing, ordering, accounting, organization, and maintaining order. The second included interaction with people, intimacy with books, judgment of books and people, and the bringing together (*In-Beziehung-Setzen*) of books and men. Somewhere between the two lay work with the alphabetic author catalog, bibliographic knowledge, and thought for bibliographic precision, as well as the ability to master the grammatical and logical rules with which the individual bibliographic entity is supposed to be grasped. Dähnhardt was briefer on the subject of the librarian's job; he described circulation and readers' advising, book reviewing, and cataloging as the three principal responsibilities. Schuster waxed poetic: "He [the librarian] is a middleman between reader and book. He protects the intellectual inheritance of the Volk, provides him with help for his daily works and needs insofar as it can be found in writing, and directs his thought and his will to the goals of the future."[14]

Although it is not especially informative about how librarians actually spent their time, Schuster's description at least suggests the political dimension of public librarianship. After 1933 politics was ubiquitous and unavoidable in the performance of one's job. In book selection, National Socialist goals took precedence over reader preferences. Public librarians evaluated books in accord with Nazi standards and guided readers to becoming better members of the Volksgemeinschaft and better subjects of a Nazi state. They designed programs to implement Nazi priorities, and their circulation statistics show a desire to placate Nazi sensibilities. Management reflected

178

such Nazi principles as the cult of the leader, and anti-Semitic personnel regulations were enforced.

Even cataloging and classification were given a Nazi direction. Most libraries quickly produced special book lists on National Socialist topics such as the world war or race and genealogy, or satisfied the need to conform with a guide to national socialism as a whole. As time passed, however, librarians began to take a more comprehensive and sophisticated approach. By the fall of 1935 the Hamburg library had introduced the following new book groups into its classification scheme: Germans on the border and in other countries; national socialism; leading German personalities; Heimat and folklore; and race. Schriewer proposed a complete rethinking of the basis of cataloging. His theory was hardly revolutionary: The purpose of organizing books is to facilitate their location. The principles of cataloging, therefore, need to match the thought patterns of readers. Because national socialism was penetrating more and more areas of life, the principles of cataloging needed to reflect this new reality. A librarian from the border town of Schneidemühl echoes this idea but approaches it from the other direction. "They [book lists] should with their groups and subgroups link the ideas and wishes of readers to books in which Volk and state in all their relations are represented." Gradually the thought patterns of the readers would become entrenched in the direction indicated by the categories, and their political education furthered.[15]

Another routine activity that could take on a peculiarly Nazi coloration was the area of readers' complaints. Most complaints of the period were of the kind that could have happened in any library anywhere, as when the librarian of the Hamburger Öffentliche Bücherhallen had to deal with an angry patron denied access to toilets that were for staff use only and another who claimed that the branch had shut, before its posted closing time, when he was trying to return books. Unique to the period was a complaint from a reader who had been given as wrapping for his books a foreign newspaper with anti-Nazi cartoons. His complaint came through the Gau office, and the matter was resolved by not giving out foreign newspapers as wrapping.[16]

The perception that the job of the public librarian required both intellectual and social abilities determined the kind of person sought as a recruit to the profession. In 1925 Ackerknecht described the *Seelsorgertyp* (soul-caring type) as the ideal librarian, "who wants nothing except to serve with the book," and recognizes that not all readers could achieve the heights of culture in a generation. In Karl Bayer's opinion, fulfilling the librarian's responsibility required individuals with the proper inclination and maturity, who had thought about man's being and had developed values, and who had also had the kind of experience that could not be taught in books. Schriewer's discussion of the librarian's qualifications is the most detailed. He saw the librarian's job as requiring three characteristics: a proper relation to the book, by which he meant a proper understanding of its role in the life of the Volk and of his role as teacher; a distinct appreciation of order; and exactitude in administrative details.[17]

Prerequisites for admission to library education programs are less vague and abstract. In 1934 Walter Hofmann prepared a position paper on the continuation of the Leipzig library school and as part of it he went into considerable detail about what kind of students it should admit. The public librarian had to have "a good head, a good lively knowledge, and a sure instinct for value." To Hofmann, a self-educated man from the working class, it was irrelevant in what field they had been educated or even, indeed, if they had been formally educated. Librarians needed to have an involvement with the real world. The students must be at least twenty-two years old. The *Handbuch der deutschen Volksbüchereien* was even more specific. It advised applicants that they were required to present a handwritten résumé; photograph; guarantee of Aryan ancestry; school-leaving certificate or certificate of other educational or vocational training; statement of party membership or participation in one of its organizations, such as the HJ; police certificate of good conduct; health certificate; and work permit.[18]

References written for public librarians evaluated job candidates in the categories of literary knowledge, technical skills, judgment, and personality. Dietrich Vorwerk was recommended as "an industrious and quick worker with an outstanding appreciation of order. Organization-administrative tasks were his specialty." When Rang was selected as the librarian of Bielefeld, the mayor proudly informed the Regierungspräsident that he was a doctor in literature, had passed the examination for public librarian, and was a cell leader in the Nazi party.[19]

Political reliability had, in fact, become a professional prerequisite. This unavoidable reality was only rarely mentioned by librarians, but it was not, as the list of evidence required for admission to library school shows, something they could ignore. Within six months of the Nazi takeover, ordinances decreed that librarians had to be "professionally educated, personally suitable, and politically reliable." "Politically reliable" was typographically emphasized. This decree, however, merely codified what was already in practice; politically unreliable librarians had been losing their jobs for some months.[20]

One important means of enforcing political conformity was denunciation, the reporting of one citizen by another to the authorities for behavior defined as undesirable by the state. This process set child against parent, student against teacher, colleague against colleague, and friend against friend. The undesirable behavior for which one could be reported in Nazi Germany covered a wide range, at one time encompassing fare dodging on the Berlin subway, unsafe driving, and, during the war, black marketing, but the most significant was political. People could never be sure when the most casual remark or a momentary expression of annoyance might be reported and bring the weight of the state upon their heads. Denunciation was so often a weapon to settle personal scores that the authorities themselves became skeptical, but it remained a threat, greatly increasing the insecurity of all.[21]

That denunciation was not an idle threat in the world of Nazi public librarianship is demonstrated by the records of several cases found in the correspondence of libraries and library organizations. One took place in Mannheim, where the director, Elisabeth Jacobi, was denounced by a local book dealer. Philipp Harden-Rauch, director of the Baden Beratungsstelle and a rival of Jacobi's, provided what he considered corroborative evidence to the Baden Ministry of Culture, which was investigating the charge. Because Jacobi had published a list of new acquisitions in the period before the takeover that included both a number of books later banned under Nazi rule and a section on the new Russia, he described her as a "single-minded Communist." A more impartial observer might have noted that the list also contained a section of Heimat literature. The list, in fact, demonstrates only that she had an interest in the wider world (e.g., a book on the Australian outback) and believed in making available books on modern life. Jacobi was permitted to answer the charges against her but lost her job by the end of the year. The authorities did not accept her argument that she had selected books that corresponded to the social structure of Mannheim. They were not impressed by the fact that the library contained the works of the forerunners of nazism, a generous selection of Nazi Kitsch novels, owned the many publications of leading Nazis, and had had *Mein Kampf* in the biography section since 1931.[22]

In Hamburg the director of the public library, Dr. Albert Krebs, was denounced in 1937 to the Gau educational authority for matters concerning the Goering collection and the library's social evenings. Krebs was incensed to be held accountable for something that he felt had nothing to do with the party and strongly suspected that a disaffected employee was at the bottom of the affair. The incident may have contributed to his replacement as library director within the year, but there is no evidence that it did any lasting damage, since he moved into the city cultural administration.[23]

A third case occurred in Saarbrücken, where the director, Dr. Walther Koch, was accused both by a patron and a library employee of un-Nazi and unprofessional behavior. They claimed that Koch had been a Socialist, a fact well known to staff and citizenry, and that he feared that his past would haunt him in the new regime. Koch's writings, even those that precede the return of the Saar to Germany in 1935, hardly reveal this but rather have a strongly nationalistic and volkish cast. The specific complaint of the patron, an *Altkämpfer* and a member of the SA, was that Koch was adding books to the collection that did not correspond to the National Socialist view. The patron had recently chosen a book on the Empress Elizabeth of Austria that actually praised Heinrich Heine, a Jew. When he had spoken to the librarian on duty, she had said that Koch had personally added the book to the collection. The library employee, on the other hand, discussed how Koch's nervousness about his past affected his professional behavior. The employee had reached the point where he was no longer willing to work under Koch.[24]

Although Jacobi lost her job as a result of the denunciation, none of the three situations was life-threatening. All of them are typical of the phenomenon of denunciation, which was as much economically inspired as it was politically. The denouncer was often rewarded with the job of the person denounced. The Mannheim book dealer, for example, probably shared the common perception that libraries were the competitors of book dealers, and the two library employees involved in the Hamburg and Saarbrücken cases may well have hoped for advancement, if not to replace their directors. Denunciation was primarily a practice of the middle class, a group whose ethos emphasized the importance of the individual's getting ahead.

To balance this picture of self-service and dog eat dog, there is at least one documented case in which a librarian did *not* report another librarian, whom she knew to be less than enthusiastic about nazism. In October 1944 Gertrud Baruch, the supervising librarian in the Bayreuth Beratungsstelle, reported, after an inspection of the Feilitzsch village library, "Herr Reidel is an intelligent, well-read man. The public library is in good hands with him." Although she regretted his lack of faith in statistics, she commended him for sending them in anyway. In the fall of 1945 she agreed to his request to remain in charge of the Feilitzsch library. Yes, she had noted in her short visit there that he did not share the values of the finally past time.[25]

In the world of public librarianship, denunciation seems to have been more important *in posse* (as a potential threat) rather than *in esse*. Two librarians who worked under the system both felt that denunciation was rare in libraries; professional solidarity kept problems within the profession. It remained as a threat, however, exerting strong pressure to conform to prescribed behavior.[26]

In the circumstances it is remarkable that anything occurred other than eager compliance with whatever was the latest policy. Librarians were no more noted as a group than any other profession for resistance to the Nazi regime, but they did practice some. A very few members of the profession were members of the organized resistance movement. One such was Lotte Bergtel-Schleif, a librarian who was a member of the Communist party. More usually librarians' resistance was part of their professional activity. It took the form of personal, unrecorded acts that were less a matter of outright defiance than of the degree of cooperation. Some circulated banned books privately to those they trusted. At least one librarian encouraged the library school students in training under his direction to read the banned books in his custody. There were also numerous instances, many of

183

them doubtless unconscious, in which a librarian selected a book for the collection that was less propagandistic than an alternative or recommended a title to a reader that was less doctrinaire or completely free of doctrine.[27]

Another kind of resistance was in the profession's behavior toward Jewish colleagues. One librarian who came into the profession late in the period stated that Aryan public librarians did their best to protect their Jewish colleagues. Although all Jewish librarians ultimately lost their jobs, and most of them their lives, her statement does have validity if the case of Hedda Guradze is in any way typical. Guradze was a librarian in the Hamburger Öffentliche Bücherhallen who continued working until 1937, long after decrees expelling Jews from municipal jobs had come into effect. Nor was her presence there accidental. The library administration, then under the direction of the Altkämpfer Dr. Krebs, had made a special case for her. Gradually her position changed from that of a regular, full-time librarian to a part-time, casual employee before she was finally dismissed, but the ineffectiveness of the library's efforts does not change the fact that everything possible to delay her expulsion had been done.[28]

How one evaluates the worth and significance of public librarians' resistance to, and cooperation with, the Nazi regime depends upon one's view of the role of the public library and upon personal values. The question of librarians' guilt or moral rectitude is a microcosm of the larger question of national guilt. One possible position is apology: Librarians could not see what the Nazi regime would become; library leaders hoped to save libraries from the worst by moderating Nazi attitudes; librarians did not really do anything very bad; and so on in this vein. At the opposite extreme is condemnation. In an article written in 1947 Lotte Bergtel-Schleif identified the three possible responses to the Nazi regime as waiting it out, passive resistance, and illegal opposition. For the first two she had little but contempt. Acts of passive resistance she dismissed as a way of appeasing the individual's conscience but devoid of political impact. Only active opposition had value.[29]

For those of us who are of another generation or in another country, who have not been faced with the difficult choices of German librarians in the 1930s, it seems most appropriate to confine ourselves to asking whether or not the librarians betrayed their own professional ethics. In making more-specific, personal judgments, a certain caution is advisable. No one, after all, has appointed us judge and jury. Yet at the same time something more than situational ethics or the virtue of tolerance seems called for if we are to learn from the experience.

Unfortunately, the answer to the question of whether librarians as a group betrayed their professional ethics must be yes, they did. No formal statement of what those ethics were existed, but there was a general consensus on some fundamental principles. Librarians regarded their profession as a humanistic one, a profession that valued the individual. They clearly felt that their collections should contain a wide range of opinions and open to their readers a wider world in every sense, and practiced this principle; otherwise there would not have been so many books to remove during the Säuberung. Lotte Bergtel-Schleif raised the question of whether the public library had fulfilled its function, a function she defined as the mediator between the most valuable intellectual creations of German and international thought on the one hand and the creative strengths of the Volk, or had it, like other cultural institutions, betrayed it. She concluded emphatically: "We have betrayed it! This fact must be recognized in its full, uncomfortable truth. We have failed, because we, like the greater part of our intellectual leaders, stood aside from the political-social life of our Volk and from the rest of the world."[30] Although the words are strong, they do not seem too strong.

Having said that, however, it is well to recall that there were many librarians who grieved over the fate of their profession. For most it was a matter of the degree of their cooperation and whether their personal integrity required them to draw the line. Several librarians, men such as Rudolf Joerden and Franz Schriewer, accepted less than outstanding careers rather than become more deeply involved. Many of those who survived 1945 lived with a knowledge of guilt. The vast majority of librarians seem to have done no more and no less than most Germans—conformed to the extent necessary for economic and social survival, refrained from conforming when they thought they could get away with it. As a group, librarians were not enthusiastic Nazi supporters.

Political acceptability may have been a prerequisite for a library position, but it was not the only requirement. Once the first flurry of dismissals and installation of a few individuals as library directors to reward them for their ardent support of the NSDAP during its struggles had passed, the importance of the proper professional training was reasserted. As part of a general effort to restrain the excesses of party members anxious to reap the spoils of success, the Prussian Ministerium für Wissenschaft, Kunst und Volksbildung issued a memorandum to the Regierungspräsidenten urging them to appoint "only trained professional public librarians." Although this memo was more the result of the need to control a revolution that threatened to get out of hand than it was a defense of public librarianship's integrity, it set limits on the value of political orthodoxy in public librarianship. Political acceptability was necessary, but professional preparation was corequisite.[31]

Formal preparation specifically for public librarians had begun with the founding of the Deutsche Volksbüchereischule by Walter Hofmann in 1914 in Leipzig, marking a major advance over the occasional in-library courses that were all that had previously been available. Two years later the Zentrale für Volksbüchereien offered courses in Berlin under Paul Ladewig's direction, an Alte Richtung alternative to the Leipzig school. The Berlin courses were suspended during the disastrous inflationary period, but the school had revived within a few years. Periodically other short-lived training courses were organized at major public libraries such as those in Essen and Breslau, and many future leaders prepared by doing an apprenticeship with Ackerknecht at Stettin. A formally organized Stettin school existed briefly from 1932 to 1934, but for most of the Nazi years there were only three schools: those at Berlin; Leipzig; and Cologne, the last founded by Hofmann adherents in 1928. A school at Stuttgart admitted its first class in 1941 but had barely gotten under way before its program was broken off, along with those of the other schools, because of the worsening war conditions.[32]

Like the rest of the profession, these schools were "gleichgeschaltet" by the new regime. Gottlieb Fritz, who had restored the Berlin school after the inflationary period, was forced out of its directorship by an exceptionally vicious campaign and died soon after. Wilhelm Schuster replaced him as director of the school, as he did as director of the Berlin public library. The faculty was changed; in the early Nazi period Wolfgang Herrmann, hero of the first round of censorship, and Max Wieser, author of the supplement to the "Aufruf," were prominent in instruction in the public library area. Leipzig underwent a somewhat less drastic transformation. Elise Hofmann-Bosse was forced out as director on the technicality that it was a second position and therefore no longer permitted, but Walter Hofmann remained titular director. Its faculty was replaced. Only at Cologne did the personnel and administration remain fundamentally intact, a result purchased at the price of their conversion to national socialism.[33]

Study in library schools normally took one and one-half years, with an additional one and one-half years of supervised practical experience. Walter Hofmann's essay "Die Ausbildung für den volksbibliothekarischen Beruf" (Education for the profession of public librarian) argued that both theory and practice were necessary, but it was a view that all public librarians already shared. The 1935 *Handbuch der deutschen Volksbüchereien* explained that in the first semester the student was at school, with some work in the local library. The second semester was devoted to classroom instruction, the third and fourth spent in a large-city public library, the fifth at a Beratungsstelle, and the sixth and last back at the school. In 1938, in an effort to increase the number of public librarians quickly, the RWEV reduced the period of training to two years, cutting both time spent in libraries and time in the classroom.[34]

What went on in the classroom was much modified after the takeover, and the content changed to reflect Nazi ideas and values. A comparison of the curriculum of the Berlin school in 1930 with that of 1935 shows how thoroughgoing the change was. In 1930 the subjects covered were general adult education, public librarianship, public library administration, readers, and literature, which included sections both on foreign literature and on socialism. These broad topics were subdivided further: library administration, for example, covered an introduction to, and practical exercises in, all technical work; organization of work in the public library; care of the collection; buildings; practical work in the Berlin public library; cataloging according to the Prussian instruction; library handwriting; children and youth librarianship; music libraries; and lectures. In 1935 the subjects of instruction were listed as National Socialist teaching about Volk and state, principles of adult education in the National Socialist state, the history of public libraries and adult education,

187

nonfiction, fiction and belles lettres, principles of literary care and criticism, children and youth librarianship, administration of public libraries, cataloging, teaching of subject knowledge and general scholarship, bibliography, care of books and the book trade, and library handwriting.[35] Similar changes took place at the other library schools.

These general categories do not, however, make clear the full extent of the penetration of the curriculum by national socialism or, indeed, its narrowness. When the content of the courses of literature is examined, it shows that of the approximately one hundred required titles almost all were by German authors. Two in the nature and animals section were from acceptably Nordic lands. Twenty-six titles were from classical German literature and there were four titles by Kolbenhayer, three by Hans Grimm, and others by assorted novelists favored by the Nazis. The Nazi orientation was ever clearer in the selection of historical novels, novels about the peasant life, and in the section on Germans outside the Reich. The hundred titles included no poetry or drama, natural science, technology, sociology, psychology, economics, or law, unless it happened to creep in through biography. *Mein Kampf* was given the premier place on the list of nonfiction.[36] With good reason librarians considered that those who had been educated during the Third Reich were less well prepared than their predecessors or than they ought to be.

How to handle the political aspects of professional socialization, which is another way of saying how to inculcate political conformity, caused library schools continual problems. Were they teaching nazism or were they teaching public librarianship? Hofmann infinitely preferred to leave the matter of instruction on the *Rassenfrage* (race question) to the party; in 1935 he stated that, with only two exceptions, the male Leipzig students had been schooled in national socialism by the SA and the women by the Nazi student organization, thus making explicitly political instruction superfluous. In 1938 Schuster was saying that the current Berlin students had grown up as Nazis. He cautioned that exaggeration and tirades earned their mocking response, "Aha, also a Nazi!"[37]

By the beginning of the Nazi period, education for public librarianship had made important advances in separating itself from education for academic librarianship. The VDV had adopted guidelines in 1922 emphasizing the importance of differentiation, and the 1930 Prussian order regulating library education accepted this principle, although the same testing authority was charged with examining both. Until then, examination—which Schuster described as a torture for both examinee and examiner, but necessary—had been done by the individual schools. The establishment of a separate examination board for public librarians came in 1938 and carried the separation a step further. One of the last remaining vestiges of the original combination of preparation for public librarianship and the middle ranks of academic librarianship disappeared when theoretical instruction for academic librarians was removed from the Berlin school, the only school that had prepared both types of librarians.[38]

The regulation of education and of testing were prerogatives of the individual Länder, but the Nazi period brought greater standardization and uniformity. As with so many other matters, Prussia usually took the lead and the other Länder followed. The 1938 order regulating public library education was first applied to Prussia, then extended to the entire Reich. A series of national guidelines for the practical experience in libraries followed.

Until a Prussian examination was established in 1930, students from Cologne had taken the exam for Saxony to certify their competence. In general, there seems to have been a good deal of reciprocity. One holder of a Leipzig diploma worked in Stuttgart, capital of Württemberg; Berlin graduates worked in Bavaria and Saxony; both Berlin and Leipzig graduates were to be found in Flensburg and Breslau; and there was even one lonely Leipzig graduate in Berlin. Vienna was eager to obtain the services of a Berlin-trained librarian.[39]

An entrance to the profession, other than through a library school followed by an examination, was created in 1938. The shortage of librarians had persuaded the RWEV to establish this alternative route. Individuals could obtain certification by passing a special test alone, if they could present the other required credential of a *Reifezeugnis* (school-leaving certificate) and satisfy the criteria of political and social acceptability. This option was aimed mainly at the technical assistants in libraries, who were regarded as a potential pool because they had practical library experience. At about the same time, month-long workshops were also being offered. Many of these were intended to certify the librarians of the newly incorporated territories of Austria and the Sudetenland and later the Baltic lands.[40]

The RWEV tried to impose some sort of order on the placement of new librarians. As the economic situation improved and the surplus of librarians became a shortage, the ministry attempted to coordinate available new librarians with empty positions. On several occasions they wrote to the Beratungsstellen asking them to list their unfilled jobs. Some matching was also done through the public librarians' section of the RSK, the rump of the VDV, and positions were regularly advertised in *DB*.[41]

One educational issue that remained unresolved by the Nazi regime was that of the proper preparation for the higher levels of public librarianship. This matter had been the subject of heated debate in the 1920s, with proposals and counterproposals flying thick and fast. Heinl's comprehensive position paper on public librarianship had included a recommendation to establish a special school to train library leaders. His proposal remained unique and idiosyncratic, however; usually the question was debated in terms of whether or not a university degree was necessary. Because the question was not settled affirmatively by ministerial decree, officially no more than the regular education for a public librarian was required. Unofficially it was another matter. Almost all directors of major public libraries had the university degree, as did most of the Beratungsstelle directors. In fact, in most cases the university education was a substitute for the librarian's diploma, although most of those in this position had spent substantial time as volunteers in a large public library after their university studies. Schriewer, Schuster, and Joerden all fall into this category. A few of the younger librarians had both the university education and the librarian's diploma.[42]

Training was one characteristic that set professional librarians apart from a large group of individuals who were also librarians, the *nebenamtlich* library directors. A *Nebenamt* is a subsidiary office, and most of these library directors were already practicing another profession when appointed to serve part-time in the village library. Although Heiligenstaedt claimed that there was an essential difference between the full-time, professional librarian and the part-time nebenamtlich librarian, the only real difference seems to have been one of the size of library in which they worked. Nebenamtlich directors were used in communities too small to pay for more than a few hours of library service a week. They did not do all the tasks a librarian was expected to be able to perform, but they did do the most important, readers' advising.[43] The Beratungsstelle ordered, cataloged, and, increasingly, selected books for them.

Because public librarianship considered itself a form of adult education, the preferred nebenamtlich library director was the local teacher. In 1936 Dähnhardt stated that in almost all villages and hamlets the local teacher was the local librarian, but Heiligenstaedt was not so sanguine. He warned that too often the position of village librarian was regarded as a means of relieving financial necessity in the middle class. Nor was it enough to appoint someone who liked to read. Local officials ignored the importance of an understanding of education and appointed annuity recipients, retired local officials, or broken-down teachers.[44]

As the new libraries established under the development program began opening, Beratungsstellen, which approved the choices of the local officials, had to spend considerable time finding appropriate librarians. The Detmold Beratungsstelle sent the mayors in its jurisdiction a memorandum that pointed out that while in many cases teachers had been found suitable, librarians did not always need to come from that profession. The ability of librarians to serve effectively depended on their personality, and, next to the good knowledge of books, the inclination to the work was most important. Lists from Beratungsstellen show that teachers were almost always the librarians, although there were exceptions. Beratungsstellen were sometimes grateful to settle for a librarian who had only some of the desirable characteristics. The report on the saddler who had served at Kirchborchen's library since it opened in 1943—he was not the Hagen Beratungsstelle's first choice—read, "The library is in good hands, even if the intellectual care that is important to the Volksbüchereistelle would be welcome in him." Frau Karges, who kept the library in a suburb of Weiden, was considered adequate for wartime, but it would be quite different in peace; she helped readers willingly, even outside of official hours, but had little literary knowledge. By 1943, with so many men in the army, teachers' wives, NS-Volkswohlfahrt-sisters, and leaders of the Bund Deutscher Mädel were considered suitable.[45]

191

For these individuals unfamiliar with librarianship some sort of training was essential. They needed to be able to make independent decisions and to apply principles. Heiligenstaedt would have liked teacher-training courses to include a general introduction to the principles of adult education, but in reality the preparation of part-time librarians was up to the Beratungsstellen, who presented regular workshops as part of their activities. That offered by the Bielefeld Beratungsstelle in 1943 was typical. It included a general overview and predominantly inspirational introduction, discussed cooperation between the Beratungsstelle and the library directors, taught the preparation of library statistics (an eternal problem), gave some information on technical work such as the care of books, and allowed for an exchange of experiences. Although their responsibility for continuing education was written into the Richtlinien, the RWEV was constantly nagging the Beratungsstellen on this subject.[46]

Continuing education for professional librarians the RWEV considered important but not as critical as that for the nebenamtlich librarians. Continuing education institutes for librarians, similar to retreats, were organized in 1936 and 1937, one at Burg Rothenfels on the Main, another near Gleiwitz in Silesia, and a third on Schauinsland near Freiburg im Breisgau. They combined recreational and educational elements. For somewhat more traditional week-long institutes held in May 1937 and in September 1937, the Hamburger Öffentliche Bücherhallen reserved fifteen places for its staff.[47]

By the time the war began, public librarianship had greatly improved its position. A growing sense of worth, increased numbers of librarians and applicants, abundant educational opportunities, numerous available positions, and progress in the status of women in practice if not theory interacted to produce good morale. Librarians' sense of professional well-being was tempered by fears of political dangers and regret for the narrowly restrictive collection policies, but most librarians accommodated themselves successfully to the situation. Librarianship offered women a profession in which they could use their intellectual and organizational talents, and men a career in which they could expect to become leaders. Despite the many restrictions, the individual librarian enjoyed considerable independence.

192

German librarians congratulated themselves that they were better off than their Russian colleagues.[48] National socialism gave at least as much as it took away, although the gains and losses were in different categories.

CHAPTER TEN

Public Librarianship
and the
Catholic Church

IN 1933 CATHOLIC libraries were an important element in German public librarianship. Often the only library in a community, they had an importance beyond their local parishes. They were one manifestation of the Catholicism that had created Catholic trade unions, Catholic gymnastics societies, Catholic youth groups, and the Center party. Although these institutions were intended to preserve Christian values in an increasingly secular world by protecting the faithful from contamination, at the same time they represented a compromise of the church with the modern world. From the Nazi point of view, they were unwelcome evidence of the pluralism of German society and competitors with a worldview that demanded total commitment. In a series of decrees that imposed ever-harsher restrictions on their activities, by 1945 the Nazi regime reduced the Catholic libraries to mere shadows of the effective institutions they had been in 1933.

In 1931 a newspaper report in *Germania*, the Center party newspaper, declared that in the eighty-six-year history of the German public library movement, Catholic library work had "grown to be the strongest branch on the tree." Its author was indulging in only slight journalistic hyperbole. A 1934 statistical report on public libraries shows that the two Catholic library organizations, the Borromäus Verein and the Pressverein, had a total of 4,880 libraries with 5,124,277 volumes and had lent 10,393,587 volumes during the 1933/34 reporting year. At the same date there were 15,407 public libraries. They had slightly more than 10 million volumes and a circulation of just over 21 million, a total achieved by including the holdings and loans of 5,931 Wanderbüchereien. Catholic libraries were, therefore, providing roughly one-third of the library service in the Reich. Their accomplishments are even more impressive when they are compared with those of the Protestant libraries, which had almost as many libraries but only one-third the active readers.

The situation varied considerably from province to province, with Catholic libraries obviously concentrated in Catholic-dominated areas. In 1934 Westphalia had 608 Borromäus libraries and 261 public libraries; in Bavaria there were 961 Catholic libraries to 690 public libraries. In several other provinces the imbalance was even greater, with Catholic libraries providing almost all the library service available. The Rhineland (Ger. Rheinland) had 1,189 Borromäus Verein libraries to sixty-seven public libraries; Baden, 491 Borromäus Verein libraries and forty-seven public. Rudolf Reuter, director of the Cologne Beratungsstelle, was not exaggerating when he said that the Catholic library organizations had a virtual monopoly on public library service in the South and West. Catholic librarianship was also very strong in Upper Silesia. In 1929 its leaders had seized control of the Beratungsstelle in Beuthen.[1]

Catholic libraries were not rich but accomplished a great deal for what they spent. In the 1933/34 fiscal year the Borromäus Verein had a budget of RM 1,410,387 and the Bavarian Pressverein RM 121,004, a total RM 1,531,391 expenditure. This compared with RM 152,290 for the Protestant libraries and RM 8,650,612 for the public libraries. Their money came from a variety of sources. Like public libraries, Catholic libraries had membership fees, and small charges were made for each book borrowed. Some money came from the church; each year a Sunday was designated Borromäus Sunday and the collection on that day dedicated to library work.

Catholic libraries also received subsidies from provincial and local governments. Before 1933 local governments in many areas had chosen to support a confessional library rather than establish one of their own, a policy that officials encouraged. At a 1930 meeting on public librarianship in the Bavarian border regions, Dr. Fischer, director of the Munich Beratungsstelle, had recommended that district officials contact the appropriate confessional group if a district needed a public library. Only if it failed to act would an independent

195

library be encouraged. As late as January 1934 a Württemberg Landrat hoped to provide "public" library service by supplementing the resources of the Catholic parish library and working with it.[2]

For 1933/34 the income of the Borromäus Verein was derived from a number of sources (see Table 10.1). The contribution of governments was a mere 2.3 percent of the society's income, even if it had, in Reichsmarks, increased over the preceding year. Clearly, arrangements of the kind proposed in Bavaria were greatly to the financial advantage of local governments.[3]

The principles of Catholic librarianship were somewhat different from those of secular public libraries. Catholic libraries in Weimar Germany acknowledged no obligation to make available the range of political and religious opinions. Instead, their collections emphasized Catholic values and, as Catholic librarians argued when confronted with the first wave of censorship in 1933, excluded Marxism, socialism, and all Schmutz und Schund. In many respects they were out of the cultural mainstream and lacked intellectual strength, although they were not the worthless lending libraries painted by Nazi propaganda. One Franciscan-sponsored popular library did rejoice in more than sixty Courths-Mahler titles and fifty Karl Mays, but it was atypical. The lists of the holdings of Catholic libraries were usually filled with unexceptionable books that had little attraction then and are now totally forgotten. One Catholic librarian was convinced that people who wanted to spend their free time reading were going, not to Catholic libraries, but to the modern lending libraries.[4]

Initially, Catholic librarianship welcomed the Nazi takeover with enthusiasm, at least outwardly. In May 1933 Dr. Johannes Braun, director of the Borromäus Verein, issued a confidential memorandum that began, "It should be understood that the Borromäus Verein greets the principles of the present regime in the cultural area joyfully, especially those of literature." He then announced optimistically that there was no reason to change the Verein's work in any way. Implying that its cultural objectives were the same as those of nazism, he reminded his readers that the Verein had always fought against destructive forces. Borromäus Verein libraries had only books that supported the Volk, national writing, and works that served civic education. Braun's final sentence was: "We rejoice in the help that we

Table 10.1 Sources of Funding
for Borromäus Verein, 1933/34

Church funds	RM 217,213.86
Church collections	93,196.91
Provincial governments	3,528.79
Kreis governments	4,949.71
Local governments	23,059.64
Private donations	47,856.88
Miscellaneous income	999,346.70

Source: Borromäus Verein, Bonn, Verein vom heiligen
Karl Borromäus, *Jahresbericht 1933*, p. 13.

will now receive from the government in the fight against Schund
and Schmutz." Five months later, in October 1933, he was telling the
participants in that year's educational institute that the new policies
of adult education stood on a Christian foundation.[5]

Within a year that early optimism had disappeared. Events had
made it clear to the speakers at the 1934 institute that, with a free
Catholic press eliminated, books were of much greater importance.[6]
They saw an enhanced role for the Borromäus Verein in the care of
souls and in religious and church life. While the exclusivity of Catholic culture and spirituality were asserted, at the same time there was
a tentative reaching out. Several speakers stressed *Christian* humanism and the *Christian* man rather than limiting themselves to Catholic versions. Refusing to allow the National Socialists to appropriate
the concept of the Volk, one speaker referred to the Borromäus
Verein's responsibility for the spiritual life of the Volk.[7]

During the early months of 1933 Adolf Hitler had been cultivating
good relations with the church. An ex-Catholic, he had a healthy respect for its strength, and in 1933 he was trying to avoid rousing its
opposition. In March he issued a policy statement that described the
two Christian confessions as the most important factors in the preservation of national culture. He spoke of the common interest of church
and Nazi state in opposing a materialistic worldview and creating a
genuine national community. He expressed his wish to improve relations with the papacy and concluded piously, "The rights of the
churches will not be restricted, nor will their relationship to the state

be changed." In April Hitler met with delegates from the Roman Catholic conference in Berlin, declared his belief in the power and importance of Christianity, and identified himself as a Catholic.[8]

The concordat followed in July. It was intended by Hitler as a temporary expedient to neutralize the church during the crucial period when he was dismantling the Center party and dissolving the free press; the church saw the concordat as a legal guarantee of its rights. It formed the basis of the church's relationship with the Nazi state during the Third Reich, although it proved ultimately to be of little protection. The regime violated almost all its provisions, in both letter and spirit, and its existence compromised the church's moral authority. For Catholic libraries, Article 31 was crucial: "The property and activities of those Catholic organizations and associations whose aims are purely religious, cultural, or charitable and which, therefore, are under the authority of the hierarchy, will be protected."[9]

No sooner was the concordat concluded than the Nazi state began a long drawn-out assault on Catholic libraries. Whether there was a systematic, articulated plan at this early stage, designed to strangle the Catholic libraries, is doubtful, but a memorandum from Wilhelm Schuster in October sketched what would eventually be the main thrust of state policy. Schuster described the dangerous strength of the Borromäus Verein in certain provinces and attributed to it a diabolical plan to masquerade as a public institution. To counter the threat the Verein posed, he urged the establishment of a strong and energetic public librarianship. He did *not* call for the destruction of the Catholic libraries. The memorandum had the immediate effect of bringing about withdrawal of official recognition of the Borromäus Verein library education program, which Schuster had identified as the "crowning" of Catholic librarianship. Its influence can also be detected in the important December 28 decree from the Prussian Ministry of Education, which included a definition of public library and assigned responsibility for nonreligious writings in Catholic libraries to the government Beratungsstellen. Both these provisions hit Catholic libraries hard and submitting to them would dominate the next few years of German Catholic librarianship. They were a major factor in the drastic about-face of Catholic library leaders.[10]

The December 28, 1933, decree, U II R Nr. 750.1, defined public library as follows:

Only those libraries that view their work as a public function in the spirit of the National Socialist renewal of society and acknowledge the oversight of the state in all fundamental literary questions are to be considered public libraries in the sense of this decree. Popular libraries that do not fulfil these conditions and depend partially or wholly on guidelines other than those of the state in building their collections are not public libraries and therefore may not employ that designation.[11]

This definition was a much needed clarification. In 1933 Catholic libraries called themselves public libraries, functioned as public libraries, and, most important, were perceived as public libraries. Local government officials were often confused about just what constituted a public library. When the Hagen Beratungsstelle sent a form memorandum to the communities in its jurisdiction inquiring whether or not they had a public library, many mayors proudly responded yes. A great deal of correspondence was necessary, with much quoting of the U II R Nr. 750.1 definition, before they could be brought to recognize that they had a Borromäus Verein library, but not one that could any longer qualify as a public library. Bavarian officials had the same problem.[12]

Once the designation "public library" was officially defined, the next step was to get Catholic libraries to change their names. According to U II R Nr. 750.1, libraries that failed to conform to its definition were no longer permitted to call themselves public libraries, but it took two years to translate this assertion into action. On August 23, 1935, Dr. Braun issued a memorandum informing the Borromäus Verein libraries that whereas they were formerly "Catholic public libraries of the Borromäus Verein," they must now call themselves *Pfarrbüchereien* (parish libraries) to comply with a Reich ministry decree of the previous month, RWEV Vd 2087.[13] At first, mayors verified that libraries had changed their signs, but in 1936 the Gestapo assumed responsibility. Stamps were more difficult than signs to control, and a sharp reminder to some libraries was necessary.[14]

This name change is one more example of the Nazi emphasis on symbols, but depriving Catholic libraries of the name "public libraries" and forcing them to call themselves parish libraries had more than symbolic significance. The change underlined that Catholic libraries were no longer eligible for public subsidies. They had continued to receive public money in 1934, as well as other financial benefits, such as free heat and light, but that now stopped. Where before they had been identified with the community, now they were tied to a specific church and congregation.[15]

Some Catholic officials tried to make a virtue of the ruling. At the 1936 conference in Augsburg of the Sanktmichaelsbund—the renamed Pressverein—the provincial secretary pointed out that although people did not like the new name of Pfarrbücherei, it had its good side. Relations between public, lending, and parish libraries were clearer.[16]

In the threatening atmosphere of which the enforced name change was one symptom, the organizational position of the Borromäus Verein assumed new importance. Director Braun worked hard in this early period to find some arrangement that would protect the society. In April 1933 the Catholic conference held in Berlin had called for Catholic organizations to be tied more closely to the episcopate, and in the following month, the same month in which he had written so glowingly of what the new state offered Catholic librarianship, Braun echoed that call with respect to libraries. He looked to the bishops to shield Catholic libraries from the dangers of a prospective library law. Such a law, he feared, would not recognize their work as being independent of, but having equal validity with, that of the public libraries. The annual report of 1933 announced that the bishop of Cologne, Dr. Joseph Schulte, already the society's protector, had been chosen first chair, and Dr. Wilhelm Stockums, the assistant bishop whom Bishop Schulte had appointed archepiscopal commissioner for libraries, had become the second chair of the Borromäus Verein's board of trustees.[17]

Another avenue Braun explored was the possibility of incorporation into the Reichsschrifttumskammer. In January 1934 he wrote to the president of the RSK, requesting admission for the Borromäus Verein collectively and for its libraries individually. His request was immediately rejected on the grounds that the Borromäus Verein was not a professional organization in the sense of the RSK's charter. Braun continued to pursue this scheme for several years, although he was not entirely convinced of its benefits.[18]

By 1936, however, incorporation was no longer a realistic plan, and the possibility of anything that would strengthen the Borromäus

200

Verein was dead. The July 1935 decree relating to Catholic libraries had withdrawn recognition of the Borromäus Verein as the Beratungsstelle for Catholic libraries, and plans to weaken it further were being discussed. Ironically, the Borromäus Verein was finally admitted into the RSK in January 1940, just in time for the most damaging attack on Catholic libraries.

The cancellation of the Borromäus Verein's status as Beratungsstelle in 1935 had little real impact, since its independence was already so circumscribed. By U II R Nr. 750.1, the government Beratungsstellen already had been given responsibility for making sure that "all libraries work in the spirit of national socialism." All libraries were required to submit lists of their holdings to the Beratungsstellen by January 15, 1934. All, in this case, included the confessional libraries, although their holdings in religious literature were specifically exempted. The Bavarian decree of December 19, 1933, V 58852, imposed the same principles on Bavarian confessional libraries, although it did not specify how they were to be enforced.[19]

The arrangements for supervision of the nonreligious literature in confessional libraries varied from province to province; they also changed over time. For example, in Bavaria, where U II R Nr. 750.1 did not apply until May 1934, the confessional libraries submitted their catalogs to the Gemeinde or to the library director of a public library, if a public library existed. After that date Bavarian confessional libraries, like other confessional libraries, submitted lists of their holdings to the Beratungsstellen, but it was by decree of the Bavarian Ministry of Culture. The Gestapo steadily increased its participation in verification.[20]

Failure to mandate clear national arrangements caused some confusion. How much autonomy the Borromäus Verein retained was not defined nor was the precise relationship of confessional libraries to the governmental Beratungsstellen. In December 1935 Franz Schriewer, as director of the Reichsstelle, was informing Reich Minister of Education Rust of the problems in the Rhenish Palatinate, where Catholic librarians were refusing to submit book lists on request to the Beratungsstelle in Speyer. The librarians contended that they were responsible to the state-recognized Buchberatungs- und Beschaffungsstelle (Book Advisory and Acquisitions Organization) of the Borromäus Verein in Bonn. Early in 1937 A. Cardinal Bertram, archbishop of Breslau, sought advice about what rights the Beratungsstelle at Gleiwitz had over the confessional libraries in his diocese, which was Prussian territory. The Borromäus Verein administration in Bonn had failed to clarify whether under U II R Nr. 750.1 "a request by the government Beratungsstelle for specific information about a parish library of the Borromäus Verein derived from a general right of supervision and should be granted on the church's side, or not."[21]

The main purpose of U II R Nr. 750.1 was to establish an organizational structure capable of carrying out an orderly purge in public libraries of materials proscribed by the Nazis, but in relation to the Catholic libraries, censorship appears to have been more a means than an end in itself. The right to oversee Catholic library collections was asserted not to rid Catholic libraries of noxious books, but to assert a right of supervision. Catholic libraries simply did not have the Marxist, pacifist, and Socialist books that were the target of the first wave of censorship, and everyone knew this. Wolfgang van der Briele, director of the Düsseldorf Beratungsstelle, in whose territory the Borromäus Verein Central in Bonn was located, wrote to Director Braun in 1934: "I can be sure from my own experience that writings unsuitable on political grounds are hardly to be found in the libraries of the Borromäus Verein and that, in my opinion, review will therefore be a formality." Cardinal Bertram of Breslau was incensed when the Beratungsstelle of Upper Silesia, alone among the Beratungsstellen, demanded that the books of Jewish authors Romain Rolland and Hermann Muckermann be removed. His anger was untempered by his recognition that Catholic libraries rarely held these authors. Statistics from the Detmold Beratungsstelle confirm impressionistic opinions; after examining 224 catalogs, 180 of which were from nonpublic libraries, in the 1935 wave of censorship, only 0.5 percent of the existing collections had to be removed. This was, as the Beratungsstelle director noted, "a happily small number."[22]

Although censorship of Catholic libraries was more symbolic than real, achieving even the symbolic level posed particular problems for the Beratungsstellen. Authors such as Rolland and Muckermann were indeed rare; instead, collections were full of writers known only within Catholic circles. Braun feared that many Beratungsstelle directors would not recognize that those authors could contribute to the national educational task. Anton Fischer, director of the Munich Beratungsstelle, shared Braun's opinion that they were unknown, but his fears were of a different character. Fischer declared: "A general list of books to be removed from the collections of secular literature in confessional libraries, as has been proposed by the district office of Aibling, can scarcely achieve its purpose properly, because, from experience, the confessional libraries of both denominations carry rather often books of more or less hole-in-the-corner publishers, which even in good bibliographic undertakings are difficult to discover." Because no one knew them, such books, "which often contradict the spirit of National Socialist educational work," would be overlooked and remain in libraries.[23]

Chronologically speaking, the next limitation imposed on Catholic libraries came when circulation of books from Borromäus Verein libraries was restricted to society members on January 1, 1935. To become a member of the parish library an individual now had to be a parishioner and pay the annual membership fee. It was recognized that this regulation would hit especially hard the poor and unemployed who were often allowed to borrow books without becoming members. Such readers formed quite a large proportion of Borromäus Verein users; according to one report, in 1934 the Borromäus Verein libraries had 361,465 nonmember readers. Borromäus officials regretted this change—a special supplement to the Osnabrück diocesan newsletter denied that the Borromäus Verein was trying to strengthen itself—but they made it clear to member libraries that noncompliance might endanger their survival.[24]

A real effort was made to convert the newly excluded readers into properly certified readers. The following stratagem was employed: Of each 10 Pfennig lending fee, 5 would go to the parish library as a lending fee and 5 Pfennigs would be credited to the reader's membership fee. When the reader had borrowed enough books, he would be a full-fledged member.[25]

Some priests broke the spirit, if not the letter, of the new rule by lending books without charge from their own collections. Catholic leaders contended that since such private lending did not involve circulation for a fee from a parish library, the priests did not have to follow regulations. This practice greatly irritated authorities, as did the membership by installment plan ruse: They rightly viewed them as nothing but an attempt to circumvent library regulations.[26]

The authorities who imposed the limitation to use by members on the Borromäus Verein and Sanktmichaelsbund can hardly have been pleased that it helped strengthen the Catholic library organizations. During the Nazi years membership of the Borromäus Verein libraries grew steadily. Many nonmember readers obviously became members (see Table 10.2). Only after the war began and all nonreligious writings were withdrawn from Catholic libraries did membership decline. Even in 1945, however, the Borromäus Verein could claim approximately 222,000 members, a figure well above its 1933 level.[27]

This level of membership was maintained in the face of yet another prohibition, even more harmful than previous restrictions. On August 14, 1940, Reich Minister of Education Rust issued regulation Vb 1545 (b), which required Borromäus Verein libraries to withdraw from circulation all titles in the *Reichsliste für kleinere städtische Büchereien* and all books that served only to entertain without addressing religious questions, such as detective stories, adventure tales, and young adult materials. They were given until January 1, 1941, to comply. Rust's basic argument was that in lending "worldly" materials, Catholic libraries were exceeding their accepted role as a charitable-religious organization. The resulting competition with public libraries, moreover, was unacceptable and endangered public order.[28]

The Borromäus Verein tried to protest the new ruling. On October 5, Director Braun wrote to Minister of Education Rust denying that lending nonreligious books detracted from the goal of the society. He quoted the statement of purpose of the Borromäus Verein: "The society pursues the task of disseminating good books in the service of the Catholic church, which cannot only be to bring religious writings above reproach to the Volk, but that also has the duty, in the interest of their religious-moral behavior, to advise its members on their education in good reading and to protect them from danger in this area." This goal had been unchanged since its formulation in 1900. No one objected when the Borromäus Verein was registered as a society in 1935 or when it was accepted into the RSK in January 1940. Why was it now unacceptable seven months later? Braun argued that the charge of unsuitable behavior was undeserved, since, as they had

Table 10.2 Growth in Membership of
Borromäus Verein Libraries

1933	187,865
1934	unavailable
1935	263,500
1936	287,966
1937	327,996
1938	331,473
1939	366,399

Source: Borromäus Verein, Bonn, "Gesamt-Bor-romäus-Verein Mitglieder, 1905–1925 [sic]."
Note: This report gives the 366,399 figure for 1939 used here; another report, "Vereine und Mitglieder 1939," gives 329,647.

been compelled to be, the Borromäus Verein libraries were not public libraries or even true parish libraries, but society libraries.

He concluded with his own reproof; the Catholic population would be very bitter if a century-old Catholic organization that had made good books available at home and among Germans abroad, and had fought bad and demoralizing literature, were, in the middle of a burdensome war, "to be subjected to such prejudiced principles, [not] less so since a legal basis for them is lacking." Braun's letter was followed by one from Assistant Bishop Stockums, but the civil authorities were immovable. On October 26, 1940, Dr. Stockums was informed by a representative of Dr. Goebbels that "unfortunately" no possibility existed of changing the regulation or of revoking it.[29] Braun made one more effort to change the order by traveling to Berlin, but the decision to eliminate secular literature from Catholic libraries was truly closed. He was allowed to speak only with Dähnhardt and Heiligenstaedt. He was curtly informed by them: "Only Catholic writing; belles lettres in the service of the care of souls goes too far." They wanted no lists and told him the decisions would be made in the libraries on "strict principles." "Strict" was used more than once in the conversation.[30]

Bavaria had experimented with limiting Catholic libraries to religious writing in 1933, although it had later reconsidered. A November 1933 memorandum from Dr. Reismüller, the head of the Bavarian State Library, proposed that the "profane collections" of

Catholic libraries be placed in public libraries. BSUK V 58852, the basic Bavarian library decree, was somewhat less clear on the subject. It stated that one-sided religious writing belonged in parish libraries, and entertaining and instructive books in public libraries. This is hardly the same as the unequivocal prohibition of RWEV Vb 1545 (b), nor is it as direct as Reismüller's proposal, but it was often interpreted by local officials to be a prohibition. There were a number of cases in which a Pressverein library was summarily "cleansed" of its secular literature and that secular literature "donated" to the local public library. The BSUK regretted that the Pressverein libraries preferred to transfer their collections to the parishes, but it was forced to accept their decision. In May 1934, under pressure from the church, the ministry issued a clarification that stated that it was not necessary for the libraries of the Catholic Pressverein to deposit their worldly books in the public libraries. The memorandum was distributed to all concerned church organizations, ministries, and local officials.[31]

What happened at Kraiburg, a village on the Inn in Upper Bavaria, was typical of the Bavarian episode. The books in the Catholic library were confiscated in January 1934. When the parish protested, it was told by the Bezirk office that having such books in a parish library did not serve the general welfare. The diocesan office then protested to the BSUK, but this objection, too, was in vain. Not until April 1935 did the village government finally agree to return the library to the parish, and when it did so, it churlishly pointed out that it was keeping all books acquired since January 1934.[32]

No retraction occurred with Vb 1545 (b). At a secret meeting in Berlin in October 1940, Beratungsstelle directors in Catholic areas expressed reservations about the effect it would have on the Catholic population. Hitler himself decreed that provocative actions aimed against the church were to be avoided, but the purging from Catholic collections of nonreligious writings was carried out expeditiously and without amelioration. Braun's letter reporting the Borromäus Verein's compliance with the decree indicated cases in which forty to sixty books remained out of two thousand, seven from an original one thousand, and four of 607. In the hasty and indifferent inspections supervised by the Gestapo, religious writing was indiscriminately categorized as unacceptable under Vb 1545 (b), labeled, and removed from the library's control. Only occasionally was an individual library able to protect its collection successfully. Maria vom guten Rat in Frankfurt/Main-Niederrad was one such exception. There the staff, by working through the night underlining such words as *God, church, priest,* and *prayer,* managed to limit the purge to the specified items. Braun considered that the action could hardly be described as a purging, when it was in reality an extermination of Catholic librarianship. After Vb 1545 (b)'s enforcement, many Catholic libraries simply gave up and closed.[33]

Braun had sought to prevent the wholesale invasion of Catholic libraries by the Gestapo, who had been given responsibility for overseeing the purge. He had persuaded Dähnhardt and Heiligenstaedt to agree that lists of books to be removed would be prepared, the books taken to the local deanery, and there inspected by the Gestapo. The Gestapo failed to abide by the agreement. Instead, police went directly to the individual libraries, maximizing the disruption of operations and demoralizing priests and parishioners. Braun did, however, succeed in asserting the principle that the books remained the property of the Borromäus Verein and that they should be kept in its custody, even though he angered Dähnhardt by informing the Borromäus Verein libraries about the agreement and antagonized the Cologne Gestapo over the matter. As it turned out, that principle was also ignored, but it was on an occasional basis rather than a systematic one. In Baden the books from Catholic libraries might be given to the public libraries, but such a "donation" was exceptional.[34]

From time to time during the war years the matter of nonreligious writings in Catholic libraries would resurface. In 1942 the local police in Egern in Upper Bavaria became anxious because the priest was holding a "so-called" early mass at 6:30 A.M. To enter the room in which it was held, parishioners had to pass a row of sealed cupboards that contained the books of the former parish library, now closed. The police feared that they would notice the confiscation of the library and become unnecessarily excited. In 1944 the archbishop of Cologne offered the secular books owned by the Borromäus Verein for the use of the troops, but his offer was rejected.[35]

Concurrently with its efforts to cripple Catholic libraries, the Reich Ministry of Education encouraged the development of public libraries to create an alternative to Catholic libraries. The numbers alone

207

show that competition from the Catholic libraries was keen. Even worse would have been the fact that in some areas party members themselves actually used them. As late as 1938 the Kreis literary officer in Weiden, a town in the Upper Palatinate, was deploring the use of the local Catholic library not only by the Volk, but by members of the party. He considered that sufficient reason to urge the establishment of a public library.[36]

Although Catholic library activity was a major concern throughout the 1930s, no explicit declaration of war existed until RWEV Vb 1546 (b) of June 18, 1938. That decree declared: "The erection and maintenance of efficient community libraries is the method through which the confessional opposition in the area of public literary activity can be fought most effectively and with lasting success." Vb 1545 (b) was even more emphatic. After ordering the limitation of Catholic libraries to religious literature, it reminded local officials of their responsibility to establish a public library, the fulfillment of which had been made even more necessary by the newly created gap in many communities accustomed to library service.[37]

By the time the policy of building public libraries to counteract Catholic libraries was officially published,[38] it had already been in force for some time. A report of a conversation between Dähnhardt and local officials on his trip to Westphalia in November 1937 discusses a concerted plan to offset Catholic libraries in the area, a locality in which they were very strong, by building more public libraries. The Beratungstelle at Düsseldorf, responsible for another area with numerous Catholic libraries, also planned new libraries with an eye to Borromäus Verein activity well before 1938.[39]

Philip Harden-Rauch, director of the Freiburg Beratungstelle, mounted what was almost a crusade against Catholic libraries in Baden. As early as 1935 he was trying to impose restraints on the Borromäus Verein libraries in his district above and beyond the national restrictions. Local Richtlinien stated that "confessional libraries shall continue to exist in addition to public libraries as long as the need for them continues," and "we do not expect cultural-political work in the sense of national socialism from the confessional libraries." The church protested both statements, the first on the grounds that it implied a coming closing when the need ceased to exist, the second because the church felt that insofar as the worldview of national socialism was a positive Christian one—as the regime claimed it was—church libraries were working in the National Socialist sense.[40]

In his dealings with local officials, Harden-Rauch frequently used the argument that it was necessary to counter the strength of the Borromäus Verein. In July 1935 he wrote to the mayor of Freiburg that a branch in Stuhlingen was important because, "on the one hand, a very strong confessional library is available, and, on the other, the residents of this area fear the long way to the Münsterplatz to fetch a book." In 1936 he was urging a branch in Herdern on the grounds that the Borromäus Verein was so strong, and in 1937 it was Littenweiler, Zahringen, Betzenhausen-Lehen, and Haslach that badly needed public libraries because all had strong Borromäus Verein libraries.[41]

Harden-Rauch exaggerated for the sake of his proposals, but there is no doubt that the Borromäus Verein was strong in Baden and, even more important, that it was increasing that strength. Harden-Rauch wrote to the Gauschulungsamt in February 1938 that the Borromäus Verein had twenty times as many libraries in Baden as there were public and that it had grown from 430 libraries in 1935 to nine hundred in 1937, spending RM 200,000 in the preceding year alone. Borromäus Verein statistics show an increase from 697 libraries to 745 over the same period, growth that was hardly as Harden-Rauch pictured it, but still serious enough from a Nazi point of view. The new policy of Vb 1546 (b) could not have been more compatible with Harden-Rauch's practice, and public libraries were established at a still more rapid rate in Baden after 1938. At the secret October 1940 meeting that followed the publication of Vb 1545 (b) Baden was praised and its success held up for emulation; if Baden could do it, so could other provinces.[42]

Baden achieved its distinction because of a particularly committed and active Beratungstelle director. Some localities were singled out by the RWEV for special treatment in the contest with Catholic libraries because of their real or symbolic importance. Aachen was one such case. Located on the Belgian border, in an area that had been fought over for centuries, Aachen was part of the Düsseldorf Beratungsstelle's territory. Although it had a population of 162,774 in 1933, it lacked a public library.

Progress toward a public library began with an anti–Borromäus Verein campaign by the private lending libraries of the town. In October 1934 Paul Walz, the local officer of the lending library association, protested to its parent organization, the RSK, about the opening of a Borromäus Verein library on the Kaisersplatz; the Borromäus Verein library had audaciously announced its charges and hours on a poster one meter high! A month later another member of the local group reported to Walz about a sermon that had included discussion of libraries; Walz passed it on to higher authorities. Supposedly, the priest in question said that Alfred Rosenberg, author of *Mythus des 20. Jahrhunderts*, was a Jew, and that the church's prohibition against the book was so far-reaching that anyone who owned, read, or lent the book could be excommunicated. The priest also set out the advantageous lending terms of the Borromäus Verein from the pulpit and stated that Dr. Goebbels was a great friend of the Borromäus Verein libraries. Two years later, Walz presented a detailed report to the RSK on how the Borromäus Verein had damaged the private lending libraries, decried their unhealthy influence on the public, and concluded with a moving plea for help.[43]

Rather than relieving the lending libraries, however, the authorities chose to open a public library in Aachen and make it the headquarters of a new Beratungsstelle for the areas that bordered the Netherlands. On July 1, 1936, the public library was formally established, under the direction of Bernhard Schlagheck, who came to Aachen after five years experience in the Saarland. Schlagheck expressed all the right sentiments for a Nazi public librarian. In a 1936 article in *DB* he described the task of the public library in a medium-sized town as "to work for the intellectual-spiritual formation of men in the sense of national socialism's worldview through the spread of worthwhile writing." The librarian should be the steward of the party. The RWEV took a special interest in the Aachen project, and subsidies were received from the Grenzbüchereidienst. The year after the library opened the Grenzbüchereidienst held its annual conference in Aachen.[44]

An even more conspicuous example of the anti-Catholic motivation of Nazi public library policy was Paderborn. Because Paderborn was considerably smaller than Aachen (only 37,272 people in the 1933 census), its lack of a public library was less serious in real terms. But, although small, Paderborn was the seat of one of the greatest and most ancient bishoprics in Germany, and had been elevated to the status of an archbishopric in 1930. Local leaders, the Beratungsstelle, and ministry officials all saw the establishment of a public library as an opportunity to challenge the church on its own ground. Paderborn's public library was intended to be not only a model but an enduring assertion of state supremacy.

In terms of Catholic librarianship, Paderborn was one of the most successful areas. With a total of 672 Borromäus Verein libraries in 1936, it was in the same elite class as the bishoprics Freiburg, Cologne, and Trier. The general impression of Catholic librarianship in the diocese was one of health and growth, and the cathedral city of Paderborn was the headquarters. The city had eight Catholic parish libraries in 1936 with a total of 691 members, up from 668 members the previous year. In the diocese the number of library societies increased from 631 to 690 between 1933 and 1939, members rose from 23,076 to 40,152, and collections grew from 25,633 volumes to 29,611, in spite of the considerable losses to the various censorship programs. Only circulation dropped, from 1,267,840 to 1,187,274, a decrease of 6.3 percent and consistent with the general decline in library circulation.[45]

The decision to make Paderborn a special case was taken by the Regierungspräsident in Minden, probably at the urging of the director of the Hagen Beratungsstelle, Rudolf Angermann. In March 1937 Dr. Kratky, an official in the Regierungspräsident's office, wrote to the Landrat of Paderborn, telling him about the state subsidies available to help establish public libraries. Kratky made his intention clear: "I would welcome it if a public library based on a National Socialist foundation could be established as a counterweight to the confessional libraries in Paderborn." The Landrat replied that the Kreis was not in a position to put up the required matching funds, but the mayor responded to a similar suggestion with greater interest. The mayor's plan to use money already appropriated for an HJ library was not acceptable, however, and the plan languished.[46]

A year later the Landrat of Paderborn reopened the matter and wrote to the Regierungspräsident in Minden. He reminded him that

211

strong church libraries existed but that Paderborn had only a library recently established by the DAF, a library that was, in any case, insufficient for the needs of the city. Finally, working through the Beratungsstelle and the RV, the city obtained the final RM 7,000 it needed from the RWEV. The Kreis put up RM 5,000; the city contributed RM 10,000. The mayor's request had used the usual theme: In view of the strength of Catholic libraries, a public library based on National Socialist principles was essential . . . The grant was dated January 27, 1939, and by September 1939 the city had hired a full-time professional librarian with the important Nazi credential of having joined the party in 1926. The library opened on October 27, 1940.[47]

Although Aachen and Paderborn were important in their own right and were particularly important as showpieces and evidence of the regime's determination to offset the success of Catholic librarianship, the primary thrust of the anti-Catholic building program was actually in the countryside. Limiting Catholic collections to religious writing in 1940 and the subsequent closing of many Catholic libraries speeded up the tempo of founding new libraries. Development plans became more explicitly directed against the church and against Catholic libraries. On November 11, 1940, the director of the Düsseldorf Beratungsstelle filed a four-year plan for the ninety-two communities under three thousand people and forty over three thousand in his district that still lacked public libraries. Because the area was so overwhelmingly Catholic, all designated communities had a population more than 50 percent Catholic and most had had strong Catholic parish libraries. The director's reports of new foundations in the next two years identified with a red cross communities in which Catholic libraries had previously existed. A major reason to split the territory of the Minden Beratungsstelle and create a new Beratungsstelle at Bielefeld was to oppose Catholic efforts more successfully. Development plans from the new Beratungsstelle show the same targeting of Catholic communities as those of Düsseldorf.[48]

Whether it was worth the effort may be questioned. In Kreis Paderborn the new libraries had achieved only small collections, readership, and circulations by 1944 (see Table 10.3). The most positive sign was that these tiny libraries were attracting more users.

Table 10.3   Kreis Paderborn Libraries, 1944

Date opened	Community	Population	Readers	Collection	Loans	Catholic readers, 1936
December 1942	Alfen	724	11	193	75	23
February 1944	Altenbeken	2,700	184	426	1,047	45
1942	Dahl	704	35	215	314	–
1943	Dorenhagen	767	46	101	323	–
1942	Kirchborchen	1,670	92	248	1,840	18
1942	Nordborchen	1,036	53	201	296	28

Sources: Borromäus Verein, Bonn, "Jahresübersicht des Borromäus-Vereins in der Erzdiözese Paderborn für 1936"; Nordrhein-Westfälisches Staatsarchiv, Detmold, D 14 Nr. 146a, 1943/44.

Nordborchen, for example, had increased its membership from twenty-two to fifty-three and its loans from 190 to 296 over the preceding year, and Dahl had grown from fourteen readers to thirty-five and from eighty-eight loans to 314. It is also encouraging that, even in a time of severe wartime shortages of books, the collections grew, a circumstance that would help avoid reader boredom with static collections. And, quite apart from any real accomplishments, these libraries did achieve the policy objective of creating alternative library service to the Catholic.

Changing the names of Catholic libraries, restricting their use, and eviscerating their collections were the main points of Catholic library policy, but they alone do not exhaust the totality of anti-Catholic action or convey the full measure of hostility. On many occasions the policies were enforced in as mean-spirited and brutal a manner as possible. Priests had to return again and again to a local police station on some library-related problem, when the business could have been accomplished in one visit. Books were removed from a collection without regard for what they were. One priest and his coworker in the Saarland were imprisoned and sent to a concentration camp for their library work. On the local level a Kafkaesque aura pervades much of the enforcement of Catholic library policy.[49]

There were many additional ways in which Catholic libraries were harassed and impeded, beyond the major rulings. Among the many instances: School and public libraries were being encouraged to co-operate; Catholic libraries were specifically eliminated from participating. Catholic workshops and institutes were attended by Beratungsstelle directors or policed by the Gestapo. Teachers were told they could no longer serve as part-time librarians in confessional libraries. Confessional libraries were forced to pay the turnover tax, from which public libraries were exempted, on the grounds that they were very similar to lending libraries. In those areas of Bavaria in which there was also a competing lending library, they were required to limit their opening to business hours and prohibited from circulating books after 7:00 P.M. or on Sunday. Austrian parish libraries, once Austria was incorporated into the Reich, were not permitted to have more than 380 books. The Borromäus Verein Central in Bonn was a favorite target of indignities; in 1942 it was raided by the Gestapo, seeking in vain for forbidden books.[50]

The Börsenverein, a constituent organization of the RSK, also contributed to the problems of Catholic libraries, doubtless at official instigation. After 1933 donations were permitted only at the retail price. In 1934 the lending libraries, another RSK group, made difficulties over the Börsenverein contract about nonmember readers. Contractual relations remained generally uncertain throughout the period.[51]

Occasionally Catholic libraries benefited from local variations in the way rules were applied. The Nazi regime could not instantly erase the population's, including local officials', ingrained deference to the church, nor could they obliterate the many years in which church institutions had filled important social and economic needs in the community. At the May membership meeting in 1940 Braun reported on the effect of Vb 1545 (b), the single most important anti-Catholic decree, on a diocese-by-diocese basis: Cologne, all entertaining literature removed; Aachen, a few libraries closed and their books sold, otherwise postponed; Trier, 175 (of a total of 736) libraries had had all entertaining literature removed; Speyer, most libraries closed; Freiburg, inspection in progress, thirty-four libraries closed on account of forbidden books, thirteen libraries had closed themselves; Hildesheim (city), nothing had happened; Paderborn, very little action; Berlin, in the city, only the small library of St. Clemens inspected, in Potsdam and Stettin districts only random checks; Mainz, mainly nothing happened; Breslau, only in two Kreise.[52]

Anti-Catholicism was a major element in Nazi library policy. Manifestations of it appeared at regular intervals, sometimes coordinated with attacks on the church, sometimes independently. By 1943 what had been an effective network of Catholic libraries in 1933 was in disarray, its collections decimated, its activities restricted at every turn, and many libraries closed. Although there had been no comprehensive plan to destroy Catholic librarianship in 1933, the sum of the individual restrictions amounted to a highly effective attack. There might just as well have been a plan. Yet, in spite of all the regime's efforts, Catholic libraries survived. In an ironic postscript to the development program that hostility to them had inspired, after the war Catholic libraries took over the collections of many of the small, new public libraries as they were closed.

> *It will remain as long as the sun—as long as the sun rises and sets: that is, as long as the ages of time shall roll, the church of God—the true body of Christ on earth—will not disappear.*
>
> —St. Augustine.

CHAPTER ELEVEN

Defending German Culture:
Public Libraries on the
Borders of the Reich and Across

I N 1933 THE MAP of Europe was a mosaic of ethnic groups. French, Germans, Danes, Poles, and Czechs, not to mention Slovaks, Slovenes, Croats, Romanians, Walloons, Italians, Dutch, and scores of other groups, strewed the landscape; a large clump here, a small enclave there, a patchwork that was the outcome of more than a thousand years of population movements. Activated by economic, religious, and political concerns, sometimes fleeing for their lives in front of alien armies, the peoples of Europe had intermingled to produce an intricate tangle of ethnic identities.[1]

When the peacemakers of 1919 had adopted national self-determination as a principle, they had initially hoped to sort out this confusion and draw a neat map on which territory and ethnicity were coterminous. Circumstances prevented them from applying the principle of self-determination uniformly, circumstances such as wartime promises, economic and strategic considerations, and the reality that many areas were ethnic mixtures. The treaties of Versailles and St. Germain therefore brought into existence nation-states that included substantial minorities, while at the same time they left many ethnic groups without states of their own.

As far as the Germans were concerned, the settlement of 1919 was most unsatisfactory in the relations it established between territory and ethnicity. Put together by those who had defeated Germany, it stripped the nation of lands that had been German for centuries. It created a Reich with relatively few non-Germans, but at the same time excluded millions of Germans from that Reich. Two important

216

groups of Germans left out were those of the Sudetenland and those of Poland, important both because they were numerous and because they lived in territory contiguous to the Reich. The millions of Germans in Austria, who had wanted to be incorporated into the German Reich, were forced to establish a republic of their own. Substantial German minorities in Romania, Yugoslavia, and on the Volga were ignored, except for the protection granted them by treaties guaranteeing minority rights. Only the Germans of the Saar were granted a solution the Reich considered acceptable; they were to determine by a plebiscite in 1935 to which nation they wished to belong.

Because European ethnicity was largely defined by language, public librarianship had an important role to play in ethnic rivalry. As hostility increased with the rise of competing nationalisms in the course of the nineteenth century, controversies over language-related issues, such as schools and the use or nonuse of a language for official business, became common. Culture and politics coalesced. Different groups began to found libraries to reinforce other educational efforts; by providing good reading in a given language, the library was sustaining and supporting the identity of the language group.

Such work was an integral part of German public librarianship. Franz Schriewer, a man identified with this kind of library work by virtue of his long experience in the border province of Schleswig, included it when he characterized librarianship:

> In political life we distinguish in our speech and in the treatment of problems between domestic and foreign policy, and we rightly give foreign policy the dominant position. So, too, in the same way German cultural and library work has a double face, a domestic and a foreign policy. Considered from a domestic point of view, library work means that the question of the relationships of Volk, state, economy, and society take precedence. From a foreign policy perspective the questions of the relationships of the national culture to the foreign culture and the rising national will to life dominate.[2]

The Grenzbüchereidienst was the single most important institutional embodiment of this culturally militant aspect of German librarianship. It was both a product of, and a belligerent in, European ethnic hostilities. Organized in August 1919, the Grenzbüchereidienst was a direct response to the signing of the Treaty of Versailles six weeks previously. The Deutsche Schutzbund für die Grenz- und Auslandsdeutschen (German Protective Organization for Germans Living on the Borders and Abroad) called the first meeting and the introductory remarks of the representative of the Verein für das Deutschtum im Ausland (VDA, or Society for Germans Abroad) immediately defined the goals of the new group. He pointed out "the great importance of immediately supplying the separated districts and those in which plebiscites will be held with books and reading materials, and the national importance of this question." In more detail he specified, "it matters that these districts be provided immediately with good German books and periodicals to strengthen their spirits and to support and consolidate the strength of their activity for our national goals."[3]

This statement of purpose continued to express the fundamental objectives of the Grenzbüchereidienst until its dissolution in 1945. Obviously, its aims harmonized with those of nazism, and the Machtergreifung neither threatened it nor required redefinition. For the Grenzbüchereidienst the events of 1933 were an affirmation; at most, one could claim that national socialism had clarified its goals.[4]

Although the goals of the Grenzbüchereidienst did not change with the Nazi revolution, the language in which they were expressed became more hostile and militaristic after the takeover. In 1930 its director spoke of the maintenance of the German character of the border areas as not only a question of political legality, but also as the highest task of the cultural life of the Volk. In 1938 he talked about the importance libraries on the border had in the battle to support the Volk and referred to them as outposts of education of the political will. Reports after 1933 abound in such words as *fight, resistance, front line, armed,* and *defeat.*

The maps in its post-1933 reports also expressed the aggressive spirit of the Grenzbüchereidienst. The map accompanying the proceedings of the Bayreuth conference of 1936 visually included the Sudetenland within the Reich by shading both sides of the border uniformly. In the report on the Aachen conference a year later a map shows the retreat of the German language in the Netherlands from its high-water mark in the seventeenth century.[5]

Almost every year the Grenzbüchereidienst held an annual conference. These were carefully planned events that fulfilled a variety of functions—continuing education for librarians, inspiration, and propaganda. Library school groups might attend, combining recreation with an extension of their professional political education. The sites chosen for these meetings were often the scene of the Reich's latest political triumph or of an especially successful border library program: 1935, Silesia; 1936, Bayreuth; 1937, Aachen; 1938, Schneidemühl; 1939, Klagenfurt. The conferences featured welcoming addresses by local dignitaries, brief sermons by leading library officials, and then speeches and reports on border library work, usually emphasizing the local area. Not only did the Beratungsstelle directors speak, but occasionally a librarian on the line would talk about work in the village library. Library-oriented sightseeing tours were a part of them.

Within the Reich the Grenzbüchereidienst also engaged in education work about the cultural situation on the borders. It prepared book lists for use in libraries, arranged lectures, and printed speeches. Occasionally, it would organize an exhibition. As a section of the 1933 exhibit of the Bund Deutscher Osten in Berlin the Grenzbüchereidienst presented an East German library, complete with book cabinet and books, that was accounted a great success.

The first, and really only, director of the Grenzbüchereidienst was Wilhelm Scheffen. Scheffen became a kind of éminence grise of German librarianship during the Nazi period, dispensing money, wielding—or at least attempting to wield—influence outside the hierarchical structure being established for public librarianship, and intriguing constantly. He was a former army officer, a Rhinelander who had served in the Prussian army. During World War I he had organized a committee to provide the armed forces with reading material within the Verein zur Verbreitung der guter volkstümlicher Schriften (Society for the Dissemination of Good Volkish Writing), a rather conservative cultural organization best known for its opposition to Schund literature. By the war's end Scheffen had established close relations with the Börsenverein der deutschen Buchhändler, had made his committee a division of the Red Cross, and was acting under commission of the War Ministry.[6]

Although the Grenzbüchereidienst was responsible for implementing public policies, it was a private organization, a *Treuhänder* (trustee). In 1933 Schriewer urged that it be taken over by the state, but it remained private and outside the RWEV-RV-Beratungsstelle chain. Its monies did, however, come from the Reich Ministry of the Interior. A spokesman for the ministry explained this cooperation in 1938: "We have done this [given money for public library work] because here is an area of endeavor in which the interests of the state and private initiative match. Not only the work of the state is accomplished here, but here are also laid the foundations for a free adult education." Like so much of the financing associated with German resistance to the Versailles Treaty, the funds given to the Grenzbüchereidienst were not accounted for through regular channels. From the Grenzbüchereidienst's own reports, it is clear that, even if it did not become a public body, the organization received considerably increased appropriations after 1933 (see Table 11.1).[7] Some additional support came directly from publishers, who were encouraged to donate books to this righteous cause. Most of the Grenzbüchereidienst's largesse was, in fact, distributed in the form of books rather than money.

Because the Grenzbüchereidienst received its funding from the Reich Ministry of the Interior, it was restricted to operation within the Reich; other agencies concerned themselves with the library needs of Germans and German-speaking groups in other countries.[8] The presence of German minorities in close proximity across the border, however, obviously posed a constant temptation, and, occasionally, client Beratungstellen would violate this restriction in spirit if not in deed. In its annual report for 1934/35 the Baden Beratungsstelle included a map with highly suggestive arrows emanating from German towns and pointing into French territory. Cleves (Ger. Kleve) pleaded for money for its library because it needed to impress the frequent Dutch visitors. The Grenzbüchereidienst itself did not attempt to extend its activities. Ackerknecht, who neither liked nor trusted Scheffen, grudgingly acknowledged that he knew of only one instance in which Scheffen had illegally gone outside the borders of the Reich.[9]

Its character as a quasi-governmental agency imposed other constraints upon the Grenzbüchereidienst. It had to be both secular and apolitical. But this neutrality did not remove it from, or elevate it above, the confessional and party divisions that flourished in public

Table 11.1 Appropriations to the Grenzbüchereidienst

	Volumes	Value (Books and Binding) (in Reichsmarks)		Volumes	Value (Books and Binding) (in Reichsmarks)
1924	10,768	60,708	1933	39,702	179,079
1925	25,055	89,559	1934	56,947	216,471
1926	43,041	175,636	1935	45,475	216,772
1927	33,706	160,065	1936	45,749	174,009
1928	46,375	195,060	1937	59,300	225,329
1929	40,419	195,376	1938	84,338	400,305
1930	51,166	244,199	1939	143,938	644,854
1931	34,854	147,684	1940	140,728	650,368
1932	29,835	141,588	1941	271,250	1,329,552

Sources: These figures are collected from the service's annual reports (Grenzbüchereidienst 1933, etc.) published by the Grenzbüchereidienst in Berlin in 1934, 1935, 1937, 1938, and 1941, for the years 1933, 1934, 1936, 1937, 1940, and 1941, respectively.

librarianship in the border areas; the Grenzbüchereidienst during the 1920s was merely one more competitor. Elimination of Catholic and Socialist organizations after the Machtergreifung left it and its values without opposition.

The arena in which the Grenzbüchereidienst concentrated its efforts was the East. The stakes were high, the situation politically and culturally fluid, and the people considered vulnerable to propaganda because of their poverty. There, public libraries could have the greatest impact. In 1919 the Reich Ministry of the Interior directed that funds be divided as follows: two-eighths for Posen, two-eighths for West Prussia (Ger. Westpreußen), one-eighth for Upper Silesia, one-eighth for East Prussia (Ger. Ostpreußen), and one-eighth each for Schleswig and the entire western border area. This emphasis continued throughout the Grenzbüchereidienst's life, although during the Nazi period the organization expanded its activities in other areas. Book distribution figures for 1936 and 1939 demonstrate clearly that the East remained the focus of the Grenzbüchereidienst.[10]

The eastern border of the Reich extended, as Heiligenstaedt pointed out at the Grenzbücherei conference of 1938 in Schneidemühl, 1,930 kilometers from the Baltic to the Dreivölkerecke (Three Peoples' Corner) at Mährisch-Ostrau (Cz. Ostrava), a dis-

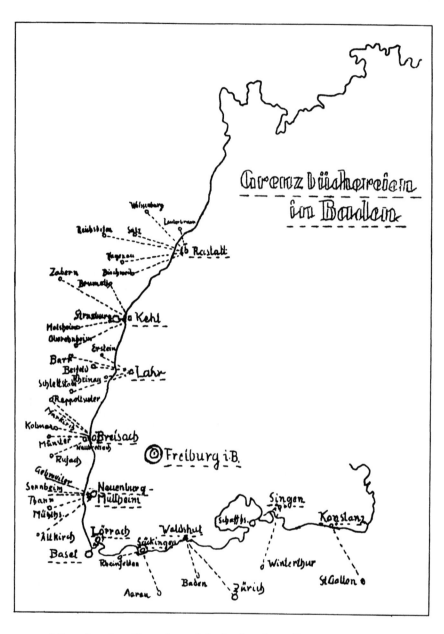

Map showing French and Swiss border villages targeted by
Freiburg Beratungsstelle. (Reproduced from *Aufbauplan
für das Volksbüchereiwesen in Baden* [1935],
courtesy of Generallandesarchiv, Karlsruhe.)

tance equal to that from Berlin to Naples.[11] The border provinces included East Prussia, Posen, West Prussia, and Upper and Lower Silesia (Ger. Niederschlesien). These provinces were homogeneous only when viewed from Berlin; their problems may have been parallel, but they were of considerably different economic, social, religious, and ethnic composition. These were provinces that contained both the great latifundia of the East Elbian Junkers and the poverty-stricken smallholdings of the forest areas of Upper Silesia. A few areas had begun industrializing; there were towns with a German commercial class. The provinces had mixtures of Germans with Poles and other Slavs in varying proportions; religious affiliations were likewise multifarious. A traveler from the United States at the end of the 1920s described it: "Now we set out into a countryside that is so unlike the familiar homelike, tidy, and flower-strewn Germany. This vast area is somehow strongly suggestive of Poland and despite protests to the contrary has been markedly influenced by it. I can sense and smell and see it everywhere. Among other things it is unkempt and positively unclean, both of which are decidedly un-German. Everything in sight seems in need of repair, worn out, and knocked to pieces."[12]

What united these eastern provinces was the perception, shared by residents and nonresident Germans alike, that they were culturally and politically in danger. It is almost impossible to convey the strength and obsessive quality of the German paranoia with regard to the East, a reaction not without some justification. Germany was bordered on all sides by countries whose friendship was dubious, and on the east by, usually, antagonism. East Prussia was an island in a Slavic sea. Even more disquieting was the memory of the fighting that had taken place along the German-Polish border in 1921, when the Poles had attempted to take advantage of German weakness and seize Upper Silesia. For their part, the Poles could not forget German efforts in the nineteenth century to colonize these areas and to buy out and expel Poles. They treated German minorities in Poland accordingly, and the level of hostility was understandably high. Numerous propaganda works such as *Polen greift an!* harrowed German sensibilities still more.[13]

A mixture of defensiveness and arrogance pervaded German cultural work in the East. Librarians frequently expressed the idea that this was rightfully a land of *German* culture; the Germans had

been there first. They portrayed their activity as a response to dia-
bolic Polish propaganda. They preached the superiority of German
culture. Who could the brutish, ignorant Poles present to compare
with Goethe?[14]

Cultural hostilities in the East had a history dating back into the
nineteenth century. There had been private reading societies, and in
1897 the first library organization in any border area was established
in Oppeln (Pol. Opole), a major provincial town in Upper Silesia. By
1903 this group had sixty-eight libraries in fixed locations, containing sixty-four thousand volumes with twenty thousand readers. In
that year Karl Kaisig founded the Verband Oberschlesischer Volksbüchereien (Organization of Upper Silesian Public Libraries), the
first provincewide organizations of public libraries in a German
province. Encouraged and subsidized by provincial authorities, the
Verband grew to 180 public libraries in fixed locations, 400,000 volumes, twelve hundred traveling collections, and some 140,000 readers at the beginning of the 1920s. In other border areas, where the
challenge from Polish cultural organizations was not as great, development came somewhat later, largely in the post–World War I period. The Beratungsstellen of Frankfurt/Oder, founded in 1919,
Königsberg, founded 1922, and Schneidemühl, founded 1923,
played an important part in that growth.[15]

Figures for 1933/34, before Nazi programs had any real effect,
show that the eastern provinces were relatively well provided for in
terms of libraries, despite their poverty. With the exception of Lower
Silesia, they were distinguished by unusually high numbers of active
readers (see Table 11.2). If Wilhelm Scheffen is to be believed, and
the evidence is in his favor, this relatively healthy situation was in
large part a result of Grenzbüchereidienst work during the late
1920s. He shows the number of libraries increasing 7.5 times between 1925 and 1933 in the Grenzmark (Posen and West Prussia),
the number of volumes per reader increasing tenfold in the same period, the readers per hundred inhabitants by a factor of seven, and the
loans per hundred inhabitants by eight times. For the eastern part of
Pomerania, that part considered border, between 1927 and 1933 the
number of libraries doubled, the volumes per hundred inhabitants
grew 2.5 times, readers per hundred inhabitants increased almost
threefold, and loans per hundred inhabitants almost doubled. East

Table 11.2 Libraries in the Eastern Provinces, 1933/34

	Number of Libraries	Number of Volumes	Active Readers/ 100 inhabitants	Vols./ Reader	Circ./ Reader	RM/ Inhabitant
			Towns over 5,000 Population			
E. Prussia	34	208,098	3.21	8.1	16.2	0.26
Pomerania	42	254,120	3.12	10.0	22.8	0.19
Grenzmark	10	29,995	5.34	8.1	22.6	0.14
L. Silesia	41	253,803	2.65	7.1	29.2	0.29
U. Silesia	20	152,747	3.58	6.8	20.9	0.26
German average			2.68	8.7	21.4	0.25
			Towns under 5,000 Population			
E. Prussia	221	60,885	5.56	4.3	7.5	0.02
Pomerania	904	139,632	5.16	5.1	6.0	0.05
Grenzmark	258	80,846	8.12	6.0	6.6	0.03
L. Silesia	186	59,458	2.66	8.2	9.1	0.02
U. Silesia	246	44,309	6.13	3.0	6.3	0.03
German average			4.49	6.6	7.1	0.03

Source: Germany, Statistisches Reichsmat, *Die deutschen Volksbüchereien nach Ländern, Provinzen und Gemeinden 1933/34* (Berlin: Ver lag für Sozialpolitik, Wirtschaft und Statistik in Berlin, 1935), pp. 8–9.

Prussia, during the even shorter period between 1929 and 1933—a time, moreover, of economic depression—multiplied its libraries by 2.5 times, increased the number of volumes per hundred readers by 1.5 times, raised the number of readers per hundred inhabitants by 1.6 times, and increased the number of loans per hundred inhabitants by almost 1.5 times.[16]

Growth during the Nazi period was even more dramatic, and the impact of increased appropriations was visible as early as 1935. In that year East Prussia opened forty-five new libraries; Pomerania, thirty-eight; the Grenzmark, fourteen; Lower Silesia, thirty-six; and Upper Silesia, forty-two. East Prussia established sixty-seven new libraries in 1937/38, eighty-two in 1938/39, and thirty-nine in 1939/40. For Pomerania the figures were thirty-one new libraries in 1937/38, fifty-six in 1938/39, and thirty-four in 1939/40. The Grenzmark Posen–West Prussia founded eight new libraries in 1937/38. Joined together in the administrative reorganization of 1938, the two Silesias had ninety-five new libraries in 1937/38, 150 in 1938/39, and seventy-five in 1939/40. This sustained growth, particularly strong in the most threatened province of Silesia, demonstrates the clear commitment of the Nazi state to strengthening the eastern border areas in every possible way.[17]

Concentration tends to foster a sense that the object of concentration is special, and librarians in the eastern areas certainly felt that their work was different from that of other German librarians. Franz Schriewer, who as librarian of Frankfurt/Oder had responsibility for part of the eastern border district, wrote an article on the public library of the East in which he tried to indicate just how it was unlike the public library in the core areas of the Reich. Schriewer's points boil down to a single thesis: Public library work in the East was different because the class structure was so different. True, the greater distances influenced operations, but it was the essentially agricultural and feudal character of the area that set it apart. It lacked the self-conscious peasantry typical of other German agricultural districts where the smallholding was the dominant form of land organization. It lacked a self-reliant middle class. Schriewer politely refrained from stating that the East was backward, less advanced, or undeveloped, but in comparison to the rest of Germany, it was.[18]

The economic and social backwardness of the East translated into low levels of education and a librarianship imposed from above, rather than one demanded and created by readers and potential library users. These same conditions could also, however, be an advantage. Schriewer emphasized the unpretentiousness of the East and that librarians could be closer to the Volk. The task was large, but so were the opportunities, and, when the librarian succeeded, the rewards were considerable.

Librarians in the East commonly described the reading level of the population as below the German average. Because so many who lived in the East were bilingual or, as they put it, of "mixed language," their command over German was not as reliable as if they had spoken only German. Librarians frequently, therefore, found themselves depending on light novels and books with pictures, types of literature they would normally have ignored. Readers in the East could not understand the Heimat novels of other areas, and, even more serious, it was difficult to get them to read the basic writings of national socialism. These same complaints were heard from librarians working in other rural areas, but they do seem to have been particularly true on the eastern border. Schriewer, with extensive experience in Schleswig, found the East considerably less advanced. An unemployed librarian from the Saar, who volunteered for work in Upper Silesia, commented after spending several months analyzing collections that they were exceptionally filled with the shallowest novels.[19]

The Nazi years brought other changes to eastern public libraries besides money and growth. Two new Beratungsstellen were created, at Görlitz (Upper Silesia) and Insterburg (East Prussia), and the Beratungstelle in Beuthen was moved to Gleiwitz and reorganized. A comprehensive development plan was drafted. Signs of a network concept are visible; public libraries of Kreis capitals such as Flatow in Pomerania became *Stutzpunktbüchereien* (supporting point libraries). There was some experimenting with increased cooperation with school libraries, as in Frankfurt/Oder. As in the rest of the Reich, collections were purged and traveling collections eliminated. Local governments were persuaded to increase their expenditures on public libraries.

After the East, the border area that loomed largest in the perception of the Grenzbüchereidienst and other Germans was the West, and especially the Saar. Much less money and other resources were available for the West, but the political and cultural stakes were at least as high. In the Rhineland pro-French sentiment had been strong for centuries. A fairly significant separatist movement had existed there in the 1920s. The Saar was scheduled for a plebiscite in 1935 that would decide its future allegiance.

The Saarland, as such, was a creation of the Versailles Treaty. For the first time an area whose constituent parts had belonged to different principalities and nations was given political unity. Rich in resources, it had both mines, largely owned by absentee French businessmen, and prosperous farms. Its coal reserves were vast. The population was German-speaking, a mix of peasants, miners, and foundry workers. It was predominantly Roman Catholic, but there were substantial numbers of Protestants. The coming plebiscite endowed it with great psychological value, which, combined with the inherent strategic and economic importance it possessed, made the winning of that election crucial.[20]

German library service in the Saar began in the 1920s. Shortly after World War I several of the larger towns, such as St. Ingbert and Saarbrücken, began adult education societies that as part of their activity maintained a library. In other towns there were factory libraries, and Saarlouis had a city-maintained library. In 1924 a public library was opened at Saarbrücken that was intended to serve as a kind of central provincial library. A professional librarian was appointed to direct it.[21]

The creation of the Verband der Volksbüchereien des Saargebietes (Society of the Public Libraries of the Saar District) in 1927 marked another important advance; now a unified approach in the province was possible. Its director, Adolf Waas, made an immediate impact when he began bookmobile service, then a novel form of librarianship. In less than a year the bookmobile was serving thirty-four communities that would otherwise have had no library service. The region continued to depend heavily on this form of service until more fixed-location libraries began to be created in 1934.[22]

Because part of the Saar remained in the Rhenish Palatinate, which in turn was part of Bavaria, the Beratungsstellen in Kaiserslautern and Speyer were involved with its public libraries. They contributed indispensable organization and planning. Funds were channeled through the BSUK; the Reich Ministry for Occupied Territories regularly put money for cultural purposes at the disposal of the Beratungsstellen. (It should be noted that public libraries received approximately one-quarter the allocation for the orchestra).[23]

The desire to defend German culture motivated all border library work, and if librarians in the East had been defensive vis-à-vis Polish culture, with how much more reason did those in the West feel threatened by French. French culture, a culture that had been the European model for centuries, a culture that had set standards in philosophy and literature, offered new political forms, given words to the language, and dictated fashion, could hardly be dismissed as primitive. Hostility to French culture during this period was so great that teachers and writers were officially urged to use good German equivalents for such unwelcome foreign invaders as *marschieren* and *probieren.* In the Saar as in the East, cultural work could not be purely cultural; inevitably library work had political implications. The highly politicized nature of librarianship in the Saar and its militancy were expressed by Walther Koch, librarian at Saarbrücken. He spoke of a "cultural front" and described libraries as "the weapon of Germanhood." "Propaganda" he firmly rejected; work that was developing the natural tendencies of a Saar that was German by nature was not propaganda. His statement that, "where fortresses and weapons are lacking, there the lasting strengthening of volkish ways of thinking and the sense of volkish belonging is a living rampart against a threatening foreign penetration" conveys the underlying principle, not only of library work in the Saar, but of all border library work.[24]

Although attention to public librarianship increased in the Saar somewhat in 1931—the year of Polish threats in Upper Silesia, the abortive Austro-German customs union, and the banking crisis—the main thrust came in 1934, immediately preceding the plebiscite. In that year the headline of the Grenzbüchereidienst's annual report blazoned, "The Saar is German!" and the Saar dominated its work. The Grenzbüchereidienst saw its task as two-pronged: to develop libraries in the Saar, which it did with money and books; and to inform Germans who did not live on the border about the Saar, accomplished by encouraging border librarians to lecture and by publishing special reports and a book on the subject.[25]

The annual report of the Saarbrücken public library for that year contains two attachments that shed light on how the process worked on the local level. In February 1934 Otto Keller, a teacher in the local school in Jägersfreude, a suburb of Saarbrücken, went to Koch. Keller painted a grim picture. Jägersfreude, a community with many miners, was a stronghold of French propaganda. Only a Borromäus Verein library existed, and it was unequal to such an important mission. Where books that would reveal the execrable nature of separatism and unmask traitors were needed, the Borromäus library offered trashy novels. Koch agreed immediately to supply Jägersfreude with books. Lehrer Keller began distributing books to the students in his class to take home to their parents, aiming first at children whose fathers wavered between the two sides, or who opposed the pro-German front. Keller claimed success and cited a miner who, unsolicited, had written to him announcing his conversion to unification with Germany after reading the novel *Der Jüngling in Feuerofen* that dealt with separatism.[26]

The plebiscite resulted in the return of the Saar to Germany, and the Jägersfreude branch turned itself to the business of informing the eager populace about national socialism. A Beratungsstelle was established immediately in Saarbrücken, and public librarianship in the Saar coordinated with that of the Reich. Work in the Saar continued to receive extra attention and money. Plans for 1935 called for the creation of a German-French *Grenzgürtel* (border girdle) of public libraries about six kilometers deep. The concept was not new; plans for new libraries in 1931 indicated distance from the border, and it is clear that establishing libraries close to the border was a high priority.[27] What was new was the speed and efficiency with which plans became reality. The Saar shows the same pattern of growth as the rest of Germany. In 1933/34 it had nine libraries in towns of over five thousand people and nine in communities of under five thousand; 38.9 percent of the population was served. In the first year after the plebiscite, 1935/36, fifteen new libraries were added; in 1937/38, another seventeen; fifteen in 1938/39; and one in 1939/40.[28]

The eastern border and the Saar received the most attention and money, but the Grenzbüchereidienst was also concerned with the other borders. In the North, Schleswig was an object of early interest and developed one of the most successful border library programs. Economic and social conditions were different from those in other border areas, but that is, of course, equally true when viewed from any border's perspective.[29] More significant, its cultural conditions provided a fertile ground for libraries. The peasantry was more modern, relatively sophisticated, and well educated. Comparing Schleswig with Posen, Schriewer attributed the greater success of library work in Schleswig to the fact that in Posen the book was a cultural *Neuland* (new territory). Schleswig readers read two volumes each where eastern readers read an average of only half a book. In Schleswig alone did German culture abut on another culture that was both advanced and Germanic. It benefited from the example set by the pioneering Scandinavians in adult education. The Wohlfahrts- und Schulverein (Charity and School Society) in Flensburg was responsible for the Zentrale für Nordmarkbüchereien, an administrative arrangement to which Schriewer attributed great advantages in flexibility for library work. By 1925 the Zentrale had outfitted 125 libraries, 115 of them village libraries, mostly of between three and five hundred volumes, but some of as many as seven or eight hundred. In 1937/38 it was responsible for twenty-two city libraries and 239 village libraries, of which twenty-seven were new that year. In 1939/40 thirteen new libraries were established, bringing the total to 309 active libraries. Obviously, Schleswig was relatively well provided with libraries by 1933, if the years of the great building program added so few new ones.[30]

Grenzbüchereidienst work along the western border remained minimal until work in the East was firmly established. But in the mid-1930s that area began to attract greater interest, benefited by its proximity to the Saar. Its growth also reflected the increased organization and strength of public librarianship in the West. Grenzbüchereidienst cooperation, after all, depended on the existence of something with which to cooperate; most of the many eastern Beratungsstellen, it should be remembered, had been established to facilitate border work. The Catholic Rhineland was particularly weak in public libraries because Borromäus libraries had served as a substitute. Many of the major towns, towns that would normally have been potential sites for a Beratungsstelle, did not have a public library. Aachen, Mainz, and Bonn were frequently cited for their lack of a public library. In 1933 only Cologne and Kaiserslautern among the Beratungsstellen could be considered to serve western border

231

areas. The subsidies for public libraries in Baden from the Grenzbüchereidienst were a direct result of the establishment of a Beratungsstelle for that province and the appointment of an energetic director.

The West was also less obviously culturally endangered than other areas. As Rudolf Reuter, director of the Beratungsstelle in Cologne, pointed out, the West was a border area, but it was also part of the German core: How much of what was counted "German" culture had been created there! With its many archives, museums, orchestras, and libraries, it could hardly be considered culturally deprived, even if it were lacking public libraries. Only after the Nazi takeover sharpened hostility to France did the threat from French culture loom larger in official perceptions. The effect of increased interest and funding shows in the statistics. All western border districts show substantial growth during the 1930s. By the end of the decade the major towns all had public libraries, and new Beratungsstellen had been established in Aachen and Freiburg; Beratungsstellen in Trier and Koblenz were added by 1942.[31]

Another border area that had been neglected by the Grenzbüchereidienst until the 1930s was the southeastern border of Bavaria with Czechoslovakia. Lacking the compensating cultural richness of the Rhineland, it shared its lamentable deficiency of a strong public library foundation. Much of the available library service was provided by the Borromäus Verein. The administrative structure was woefully inadequate. Although the Upper Palatinate and Bavarian Forest were part of the Munich Beratungsstelle's jurisdiction, they were too distant for the already overworked Beratungsstelle to give them much attention.

The Machtergreifung changed the public library situation dramatically in this area, now renamed the Bayerische Ostmark. The party took a serious interest in public libraries here. Eventually, a Beratungsstelle was founded in Bayreuth, and energetic Lehrer Wutz set about building a network of libraries. The Grenzbüchereidienst began making substantial contributions. The area was deemed of sufficient importance and enough of a showpiece for the annual Grenzbücherei conference to be held there in 1936.[32]

One strong motivation for establishing public libraries in the Bayerische Ostmark was the knowledge that Germans on the other side of the border in Czechoslovakia were much better served. Thanks to the Czech library law of 1919, every community of four hundred or more was required to support a public library. A specific sum per capita was set by law. The figures for 1938 of libraries in a Reich that included the Sudetenland demonstrate the success of the Czech law; where the pre-1938 Reich had 9,765 libraries, the Sudetenland alone had 2,840. Their collections did not include writings from a National Socialist viewpoint, since Czechoslovakia had outlawed some of the most dangerous, but adding them was a far easier task than beginning libraries from scratch would have been.[33]

The Sudeten Germans were one of the largest and most cohesive of the German minority groups outside the Reich. *Auslandsdeutsche* (foreign-country Germans), sometimes known as *Volksdeutsche* (racial Germans), came in many different varieties: citizens of a predominantly German country other than Germany, such as Austria or Switzerland; Reich Germans traveling or living abroad; German-speaking minorities who had been Reich citizens until the borders were redrawn in 1919, such as many of the Germans in Poland; German-speaking groups that represented the farthest extension of the German push to the East in the early Middle Ages, left behind when the Slavs began pressing westward—for example, the Germans of the Volga; and groups that had been invited by the reigning monarch to settle in an area that needed their economic skills, such as the Swabians of the Danube. The Reich preferred to ignore the recent German emigrants who had settled in countries such as the United States; it considered them Germans, although few of them thought of themselves that way.

These very different groups could not have been more economically, socially, and culturally disparate. Some were peasants, others belonged primarily to the urban commercial or industrial bourgeoisie, and a few to the landowning aristocracy. The Germans of Poland labored under severe economic and political disabilities; the Germans of Czechoslovakia had considerable economic and political power. The dominant culture in which they lived created varied responses; the Germans in English-speaking lands, for example, were usually absorbed and lost their identity as a separate group.

Library service was correspondingly dissimilar. With the exception of Czechoslovakia where there were both a library law and a

233

geographically solid block of German communities, libraries for Auslandsdeutsche tended to be privately supported, extremely poor, and small islands of Germandom in a sea of something else. The health of German popular librarianship depended upon the ability of the local German community to support it, the existence of leadership to create and keep it going, and the attitude of the country in which it was located.

In 1939 the Deutsche Gemeindetag estimated that there were approximately four thousand of these Auslandsdeutsche popular libraries. An undated preliminary statistical report of the early 1930s analyzed the situation on a country-by-country basis that makes obvious their heterogeneity. Bulgaria was friendly to Germans, but other foreign-language organizations worked against them. In Burgas, a town on the Black Sea with a population of forty thousand of whom seventy were Germans, there was a German Club with sixty members and a Leihbücherei of 250 volumes. Separation from the Reich had brought no changes to Danzig, where public libraries were in a relatively healthy condition. The best developed libraries in Yugoslavia were in the Banat, with about thirty libraries, one of them with over one thousand volumes, and the Batschka, with over twenty-five libraries, one of more than two thousand volumes. The report considered the Auslandsdeutsche libraries of Poland better organized than in any other country. Most libraries in that country were affiliated either with the Verband deutscher Büchereien (Organization of German Libraries) in Posen that covered Posen, Pomerelle, and the former Russian districts, or the Verband deutscher Volksbüchereien in Polen (Organization of German Popular Libraries in Poland) for the Polish part of Upper Silesia, Eastern Silesia, and Galicia. The Verband deutscher Katholiker (Organization of German Catholics), Christliche Gerwerkschaften (Christian Unions), Deutschnational Handlungsgehilfenverband (German National Commercial Assistants Organization), and the Bund für Arbeiterbildung (Society for Worker Education) each maintained several libraries, and there was also an assortment of confessional popular libraries, reader circles, and school libraries that could be considered German. The report made clear the strength of public librarianship in Czechoslovakia. As of 1928, 3,230 German municipal libraries in Czechoslovakia with a total of some 1,446,978 volumes existed; only

239 German-speaking communities in Czechoslovakia lacked a public library at that time. The report did not include the numerous popular libraries, less closely linked to the Reich, in countries such as the United States, Argentina, Brazil, or China, which served expatriate communities.[34]

Although the numbers are superficially impressive, the quality of Auslandsdeutsche libraries was for the most part pitiful. They were tiny and their collections usually verged on the antique. The representative of the Deutsche Gemeindetag commented in 1939 that little had been done to modernize them since 1914. Heinz Roscher, director of the central agency maintained by the Foreign Office for public libraries abroad, dismissed them in a 1934 *DB* article as rich in Kitsch. He criticized them for disseminating such un-German authors as Feuchtwanger, Remarque, and Heinrich Mann that the more advanced Reich Germans had "learned to reject." Indeed, the collections seem to have deserved criticism, if not the criticism they received. They did lack current publications; the library in El Dorado, Argentina, was unusual in that it had *Volk ohne Raum*, *Sperrfeuer um Deutschland*, and *Armee hinter Stacheldraht*. They were strong in Kitsch and in authors unknown to modern librarians. Even the works of great German classical authors that might be expected to be the foundation of such collections were rare.[35]

One of the greatest sources of weakness was the lack of an organizational foundation. With the exception of the two major societies in Poland and central library agencies in Latvia and Estonia, any kind of coordinating framework was lacking. These libraries badly needed something comparable to Beratungsstellen that could provide professional advice, centralized services for book ordering and cataloging, and liaison. Karl Koberg in Leitmeritz (Cz. Litoměřice), Czechoslovakia, founded the Deutsche Volksbüchereigenossenschaft (German Popular Library Society) in the hope that it could provide such services, but it did not become a significant force. Koberg then tried to obtain these services first through Hofmann at Leipzig and, when that failed, through Ackerknecht at Stettin. The Sudeten German librarians did develop a professional association and publish a journal, meeting at least some of their needs.[36]

Most of the Auslandsdeutsche librarians, however, did not have a sufficient mass to create viable institutions on their own. Expecting the political authorities of the country to do it for them was hopeless; few of these countries had such institutions for the majority population, let alone being willing to establish and support them for minorities. Instead, the Auslandsdeutsche looked to the Reich for different kinds of library support, as they did in other activities. The Ackerknecht correspondence is full of letters from librarians in Czechoslovakia, Poland, and the Baltic republics seeking advice and help. Several organizations were responsible for giving help: the Deutsche Auslands Institut in Stuttgart, the Zentralstelle für Deutsche Auslandsbüchereien (Central Authority for German Foreign Libraries) renamed the Mittelstelle für deutsches Auslandsbüchereiwesen (Agency for German Foreign Librarianship), and an Abteilung für Auslandsbüchereien und Volksbildung (Division for Foreign Librarianship and Adult Education) in the VDA. The Borromäus Verein regularly rendered assistance as part of its program, and some other groups, such as the Deutsche Dichter Gedächtnis Stiftung (German Writers' Memorial Foundation) and the Gesellschaft für Volksbildung (Society for Adult Education), were involved to a lesser extent.[37]

Most help came in the form of book donations. The Deutsche Auslands Institut regularly sent packages of books, donated by publishers to them, in a program that bore some similarities to the Grenzbüchereidienst. Some idea of the scope can be obtained from the seventy-seven book packages distributed in the second quarter of 1936 that contained 557 books. The Borromäus Verein, too, sent book donations. A report in 1938 shows that it sent books to Africa, to Buenos Aires and Patagonia in Argentina, to an assortment of Belgian libraries and priests, to La Paz and Potosí in Bolivia, and so on through the alphabet to conclude with Riverdale, New York, Washington, D.C., and Zacatecotoca-Analoc, which it mistakenly thought was also located in the United States. Korea and Guatemala were two of the more exotic countries; Romania had a particularly large number of places receiving books.[38]

The Reich also provided other forms of support and assistance, especially in the area of training. Both the Borromäus Verein and the VDA offered courses for Auslandsdeutsche librarians. The Borromäus training usually took the form of a six-week study tour, while the VDA held short institutes. The 1932 VDA institute was held in

Flensburg and lasted from Friday, July 10, through Saturday, July 18. It featured a welcoming address by the director of the VDA, Hans Steinacher, and presentations by Schuster, Schriewer, and some of the Schleswig librarians. It covered the whole of librarianship, beginning with a theoretical introduction and proceeding through cataloging, book selection, binding, readers' advising, children and youth services, to conclude with an address by Schuster on professional literature as a means of continuing education. The participants were taken to several libraries. One librarian from Latvia who attended the 1934 VDA institute praised it: "We were very inspired by Schuster and Schriewer; they complemented each other very well in their lectures and both understood how to find a contact with us." Some Auslandsdeutsche librarians went through the regular German preparation at one of the library schools or spent a year working at one of the large public libraries. Ackerknecht had a steady stream of such librarians at Stettin.[39]

Although most Auslandsdeutsche libraries were less explicitly and less self-consciously political than the border popular libraries, they shared a common founding principle: the defense of German culture. Because of their geographical location, librarians' assertions were less emphatic, but the idea was the same. Some Auslandsdeutsche libraries, on the other hand, were at least as blatantly political as the border libraries. This was particularly true in Poland, which both Germans and Poles treated as a cultural battlefield, shaping their policies accordingly. There the mere existence of a German institution was regarded as an act of aggression. Librarians labored under difficulties during this period, labeled the time of the Polish terror. One acquaintance of Ackerknecht was refused permission to visit the Reich and had his mail opened. Because of this open hostility, German popular libraries in Poland probably received the most assistance from the Reich. One Sudeten German librarian complained that "unfortunately the Reich has less than a hundredth of the interest in we 3.5 million [Sudeten Germans] as it has for the half million Germans in Poland."[40]

The belligerence that marked librarianship in Poland was unusual. The Machtergreifung, however, radically changed the context in which Auslandsdeutsche libraries operated. Nazism asserted the unity and superiority of the German Volk; political aggression inspired cultural aggression. Even if German minorities simply wished to keep themselves informed about current trends, reading about national socialism had to be viewed with suspicion by Poles or Czechs or any non-Nazi government. A 1935 report on German popular libraries in Latvia makes clear the dilemma of Auslandsdeutsche, caught between hostile governments and their interest in the Reich.

> The formation of the book collection in Latvia, as in almost all other Auslandsdeutsche districts, has been made much more difficult by the hostile behavior of the dominant people to the National Socialist Reich. While the Germans of the entire world feel themselves more a part of the German people than ever before in history, while they wish more burningly than ever before to participate in the turn of destiny in the German Reich, almost everywhere they are cut off by governmental actions from the tie. The public distribution of National Socialist writing through the central library agency [in Latvia] would endanger the entire German educational system by endangering library work. Even if it is not to be expected that a distancing between Reich and German minorities is to be accomplished by such principles, it is still the obvious task to seek books that will lead to an understanding of the National Socialist revolution.[41]

As the German troops swarmed over Europe in 1939 and 1940, Auslandsdeutsche librarianship in the newly occupied territories underwent a radical transformation. No longer were they barely tolerated private societies, serving an unwelcome minority. As the territory in which they were located was incorporated into Hitler's greater German Reich, they became a part of the public librarianship of the Reich.

Librarianship reflected official policy, and in the early war years the new territories were treated as colonies to be developed, as well as land to be exploited. Librarianship, however, offers only limited opportunities for exploitation, and the excesses and illegality that characterized the treatment of subject countries, especially in the East, are not apparent. Librarians confined themselves to establishing libraries. New Beratungsstellen were quickly organized on the foundation of former Auslandsdeutsche popular libraries. The librarian of the Posen library described this progress: "They created a tradition on which the National Socialist Reich can thankfully and proudly build." By April 1942 there were Beratungsstellen for Danzig–West Prussia, Posen, Hohensalza, the Generalgouvernement, and the Sudetenland. In the West a Beratungsstelle was established for Alsace-Lorraine. Librarians came from Germany to support this development; the director of the Beratungsstelle of Schaumburg-Lippe spent several years in the East. Resources were made available, and show libraries opened in such major cities as Posen and Prague. The 1941 Grenzbüchereidienst report shows substantial numbers of books being given to these newly acquired areas.[42]

The Germans had no shortage of grandiose plans for their new territories. A 1940 *Völkischer Beobachter* article on public librarianship from Strasbourg to Łódź reported that in the foreseeable future 2,924 new libraries with almost a million volumes would be opened. What is more astonishing is that a country engaged in a world war actually managed to do this. At a conference in Posen in November 1943, the high-water mark of German librarianship in the East, Heiligenstaedt announced that at the beginning of the war there had been fourteen thousand public libraries in the Reich. Now there were twenty-two thousand. Some of these eight thousand new libraries undoubtedly were added by conquest rather than creation, but in the East alone seventeen hundred had been begun since April 1942. Shortly thereafter the military situation rendered public libraries in this area irrelevant.[43]

Austrian libraries were treated somewhat differently, because Austria's accession to the Reich was regarded as a reunification rather than a conquest. Six new Beratungsstellen were immediately established, but they reported to the Austrian Ministry of Instruction. To judge from the correspondence and lack thereof in ministry files, Austrian public librarianship retained a considerable measure of independence. The collections were purified, but few other Nazi programs had much impact. By 1940 only twenty-one new libraries had been added to the 432 ones existing at the Anschluß. Austrian border libraries did begin to receive assistance from the Grenzbüchereidienst.[44]

The politically militant aspect of German public librarianship represented by the Grenzbüchereidienst and the organizations to assist Auslandsdeutsche public libraries disappeared with the Third

Reich. The Grenzbüchereidienst was dissolved in 1945, and the Auslandsdeutsche ceased to exist as German minorities fled or were expelled from their ancient homelands in Eastern Europe. A spirit of cooperation gradually replaced nationalism in the West and was imposed in the East by the theory of Communist solidarity.

Although the Nazi state practiced cultural warfare, exacerbating an already dangerously unstable situation, there is nothing inherently evil about the idea of the defense of culture, as long as that defense remains in the cultural realm and is not politicized. In the postwar years Schriewer, returned to his position in Flensburg, spoke on this theme on several occasions. Reflecting on pre-1933 border library work, he defined its goal as having been to produce not a political or politicized Schleswiger, but a German-inclined man to whom could be applied Goethe's words: "He does not allow himself to be robbed of his own thoughts. What the crowd believes in is easy to believe." With feeling, Schriewer argued that border work could not be advanced if it were tied to party policy, state policy, or border policy. From experience he could testify that if political symbols are overused, educational work sinks to propaganda. Cultural and educational work that is politicized is based on hidden inferiority and compensates by overstating. The emphasis of border work had to be on the moral and not the aesthetic.[45]

German border libraries and work with the Auslandsdeutsche were very much of a time and place. A manifestation of European nationalism, they reached their extreme under the Nazis. As with so many other institutions and programs of the Weimar period, the National Socialist state had taken them over, imbued them with new aggression and virulence, and used them for its own purposes. There had been a political element present before, but under nazism these libraries were almost nothing but political. The cultural aspect was subordinated until it almost disappeared.

CHAPTER TWELVE

The War
Years

THE WAR that would eventually bring the Thousand-Year Reich to an end began on September 1, 1939. Before it ended, it involved more countries, more men under arms, and cost more than any previous war in history. Because of the disruption of societies and the breakdown of governments, the number of killed and wounded has never been known; all that can be stated with certainty is that it was more than ever before. Millions of noncombatants were caught up, and whole groups of people, such as the Jews, exterminated. Property losses were so enormous that estimates use such terms as *astronomical* rather than figures.

World War II created the concept of total war; not only did the flower of youth go marching off, as it always had, but thanks to air power, blockades, and economic warfare, the whole population was at war. The war blurred the distinction between soldier and civilian, and the idea of the "home front" expressed the total involvement found in all the major warring countries.

As far as public librarianship was concerned, the effects of the war created similar problems in all enemy countries, whether Allied or Axis: drafting of personnel; air raids in which books and libraries were destroyed; the need for new programs to supply soldiers and those left behind with good reading; and an overwhelming paper shortage. To German public librarianship it also brought new lists of books to be removed from libraries. As in other areas of governance, the war intensified the specifically Nazi direction of librarianship. It removed normal restraints, enabling government to become more authoritarian. At the same time, however, it placed insuperable obstacles in the way of accomplishing Nazi goals, as resources disappeared and disorganization increased.

Although the ultimate impact would be enormous—we are still living with its consequences—World War II began almost quietly and on a small scale. In February 1940, as seen from a German public library, it looked as if the war were already over. In a textbook campaign completed in less than a month, Germany had invaded and conquered Poland. Armies were now resting quietly in barracks. Public librarians who had been drafted for the Polish campaign were being demobilized. At this early stage librarians carried on business as usual. If anything, the war was treated as an opportunity to impose more-stringent restrictions on the Catholics and to develop even more grandiose building plans.

In Germany the outbreak of war changed the rhetoric of public discourse only slightly, aside from introducing conveniently identifiable enemies. While World War II brought Britain and the United States unaccustomed slogans and campaigns directed at the citizen, such exhortation had been an integral part of the National Socialist modus operandi. Emphasis on the common good was fundamental Nazi doctrine; "Gemeinnutz vor Eigennutz" had been proclaimed for years. The concept of the Volk needed only be modified to that of "Volk at war" or "Volk under siege." In public librarianship the content of homilies changed very little.

The Reichsstelle and RWEV took the lead in providing public librarianship with attitudinal guidance, indicative of their enhanced and growing role in the profession. No longer was it an individual library leader writing a hortatory article for *DB* or making an encouraging speech, but Heiligenstaedt and Dähnhardt setting standards in their official capacity. The first example was RWEV Vb 2249/39, dated September 12, 1939. It had come to the attention of the Reichsstelle that a number of libraries had been closed in cases where it was not necessary. Deploring this overreaction to the outbreak of war, the ministry exhorted librarians to reopen immediately and to restore normal hours of service. Librarians were reminded of the importance of libraries.[1]

Beratungsstellen obediently passed the message down to the communities. A memorandum from the Lippe Beratungsstelle to librarians, Kreis officials, Landräte, and mayors stressed the importance of books and instructed officials to appoint a substitute if the librarian was called to the army, to maintain the level of book acquisition, and to carry through plans for new libraries. The director's encouragement to local officials to continue funding for library programs shows a fine appreciation of his audience; it did not take long for local governments to begin complaining that library allocations could not be sustained in wartime.[2]

In 1943 the success of Allied air raids and the growing difficulties gave rise to another major pronouncement from the RWEV. This statement emphasized the needs and problems of public librarianship in districts designated to receive evacuees from heavily bombed areas, but all provincial education ministers and Beratungsstelle directors were obviously intended to take it to heart. They were again reminded that the task of the librarian is even more important in wartime. They were urged to appoint an appropriate person as library director if the library had lost its director to the army and were exhorted to see that libraries were kept open adequate hours. Books were to be procured from the local book trade if necessary, and Beratungsstelle directors were to provide short introductory courses for the newly appointed librarians.[3]

The transmission of the content of this pronouncement by the Beratungsstellen to the libraries in their jurisdictions gives a hint that public librarianship was beginning to be affected by the regionalization of opinion that took place in the later stages of the war. Where formerly Beratungsstelle directors had customarily simply repeated the contents of a ministerial decree without comment, this statement was summarized and interpreted. Dr. Wiegand of Lippe, for example, wrote a strong paragraph on the place of the book in German culture. The Ministry of Education in Baden flatly disagreed with the Reich ministry's instructions. In its opinion the areas receiving refugees could not be expected to provide more resources for libraries; additional support would have to come from the Reich.[4]

With the situation becoming more critical day by day, a decree on public librarianship's place in a total war was published in October 1944. A policy originally formulated by Goebbels in January 1943, total war required the use of all resources—economic, military, human, and psychological. As applied to public librarianship, total war closed the library schools at Berlin, Cologne, and Stuttgart in October 1944; Leipzig remained open until the end of the Easter 1945 term. Female candidates were to be redeployed to armaments production or other war-related tasks. Libraries were told to carry on only essential tasks, those directly related to circulation and readers' advising. Beratungsstellen were to continue their collection activities but to cease planning new libraries.[5]

In addition to these three major pronouncements, a steady succession of less-pointed memoranda punctuated the war years; no opportunity was lost to urge librarians on. Reports of increased circulation were the occasion to remind librarians of the importance of their contribution to the war effort. A death in battle called forth praise for librarianship as well as of the individual.

Probably the most revealing documents on the progress of the war, however, and of its real impact on librarians are the reports of the Reichsstelle, especially its annual reports. The elimination of the Verband Deutscher Volksbibliothekare left the Reichsstelle the logical preserver of professional solidarity. This was a responsibility the Reichsstelle appears to have accepted gladly, and its wartime messages and reports often have the character of alumni newsletters. A memorandum of October 1939 listed public librarians drafted and gave their addresses for those who wished to keep in touch. At intervals the list was updated, and occasional accounts of the army from soldier-librarians were published. Later a casualty list was added. By 1941 Heiligenstaedt was publishing an annual message, which he used to celebrate the accomplishments of public librarianship and to establish the officially correct attitudes to the war. His 1940/41 statement, for example, began "with deepest gratitude to the Führer and our army" and spoke of the library activity that was carried on within "the secured and protected borders of the Reich." The message for 1942 was especially hortatory; Heiligenstaedt quoted the old proverb "Where there's a will, there's a way." In 1943, after the Allied landings in North Africa, he spoke of "this phase of the war" and described the book as "the truest and most reliable helper of the member of the Volk." His last message came just before Christmas 1944. Its tone was reflective, even resigned. Looking at the loss of libraries on the eastern borders, to which so much effort had been devoted, he asked whether all the work had been in vain. He may have answered with an unhesitating *nein*, but the question had been posed, and lingered. Heiligenstaedt concluded with thanks to the numerous librarians (in the feminine gender) and technical staff who continued working selflessly for the common good.[6]

Given the notable lack of realism in the top echelons of government and the well-known refusal to admit that Allied efforts were increasingly successful, it is surprising to encounter genuine and publicly expressed understanding on the Reichsstelle and RWEV level of the difficulties the war was creating for librarians. Both Heiligenstaedt and Dähnhardt seem to have realized that, with the best will in the world, librarians simply could not fulfill goals. Their exhortations were frequently tempered with plain speaking. The December 1943 announcement that the Einkaufshaus had been destroyed also informed Beratungsstellen that they could not count on book deliveries from publishers, most of whom were, like the EKH, located in Leipzig. In July 1944 a memorandum urged that, even if reduced personnel did not permit much activity, efforts be made to place publicity in local newspapers. The "Total War" memorandum sacrificed the statistics beloved of German librarians.[7]

The first major change introduced by war was yet another round of censorship. In a memorandum delicately titled "Adjustment of Public Libraries to the Political Situation," Heiligenstaedt advised librarians three weeks after the war began that "writings about England and France are to be checked to determine whether the books contain what encourages the strength to carry on and the will to victory on the German side by their posing of questions and method of treatment." Soviet literature was to be handled with kid gloves. "In the circulation of material about Russia and Russian relations, great reluctance is to be practiced insofar as they are disagreeable to the Soviet regime." A later memorandum clarified this somewhat obscure language; anti-Bolshevist literature was not to be circulated.[8]

Although the basic premise was that books written by authors of enemy countries were dangerous, there were so many exceptions and qualifications to that principle that wartime censorship was even more complex than that of the 1930s. Writers considered "classical" were allowed to remain on the shelves. Carlyle, for example, qualified as a classical English author—that his biography of Frederick the

Great was adulatory cannot have hurt his cause—but T. H. Lawrence and Galsworthy did not. Differentiation was also made between fiction and nonfiction, and between translations, which were not acceptable, and the work in the original language, which could be kept because fewer people could read it. As late as May 1942 books by Lord Jellicoe, hero of the Battle of Jutland; Basil Liddell-Hart, the British military historian; J. E. Neale, the historian of Elizabethan England; and Harold Nicolson, diplomat, writer, and Bloomsbury intellectual, were allowed to remain on public library shelves.[9]

Because Britons and North Americans shared a common language, an author's nationality was sometimes unclear. One of the more absurd episodes involved that highly political work, Alan Evans's *Reindeer Trek*, a naturalistic novel of Eskimo and Lapp life. It had somehow been blacklisted but was rehabilitated once it was demonstrated that the author was American, not English. Presumably, once the United States entered the war, *Reindeer Trek* was again *liber non gratus*.[10]

Russian writers and works about Russia were even more problematical; throughout the Nazi years librarians had to treat any Russian writer with extreme caution. Marxist and pro-Soviet writings had been among the first books to be removed from German public libraries after the Machtergreifung, and many books recommended during the Nazi period portrayed the fight against Russia and communism. The German-Russian Non-Aggression Pact brought an about-face in library policy. Although the regime did not go so far as to restore Marxist writers to collections, anti-Soviet material could no longer be circulated. This restriction was in turn lifted after Germany attacked the Soviet Union in 1941, and anti-Soviet material was restored to circulation. Classical writers escaped censorship at first, but after 1941 they, too, were included in a general ban on all Russian writers. Even the cards for Russian books were removed from catalogs at that point. The ministry did reconsider the status of the great Russian novelists, and five months later Tolstoy, Dostoevsky, Gogol, and Pushkin were back in circulation. It is easy to understand, however, that in these conditions prudent librarians sought clarification from someone with more authority.[11]

In addition to these broad categories, some writers and subjects were singled out for special treatment. Early in the war, books dealing with codes and ciphers were limited to circulation to officials; presumably the regime feared that amateur spies would be obtaining useful guidance from their local public libraries. The books of Sigrid Undset, a formerly honored Nordic author, were ordered removed after she had the poor taste to object to the German invasion of her native Norway. Albert Schweitzer, however, received a special dispensation; his theology was permitted to circulate.[12]

Wartime censorship was implemented in the same way as the censorship of the late 1930s. Rules were issued at the ministerial level and distributed to the Beratungsstellen. Beratungsstellen then informed the libraries under their jurisdiction. At times, other party or government offices might get involved, as in Bavaria in 1944, when the Gau literary officer of Kreis Miesbach tried to interfere in the library of Miesbach. An appeal or an interpretation might also be necessary, but these cases went to the RWEV.[13]

Just as earlier censorship was accompanied by efforts to make appropriately Nazi books available, wartime collection policy also included books to acquire. Libraries were told that they were "to assure the widest dissemination of newly published books that explain the intentions of our enemies and that portray the course of the war and our own war aims." Some subjects received special notice. In July 1939, just before the outbreak of war, the Reichsstelle ordered that thirteen books about Poland, the Polish Corridor, and the German minority in Poland immediately be procured and put in public libraries. In 1943 libraries were urged to pay particular attention to "the Jewish question." Such classic anti-Semitic novels as Freytag's *Soll und Haben* and Raabe's *Der Hungerpastor* were cited. With the advantage of hindsight, a clear connection with Nazi intentions is not hard to detect.[14]

Telling libraries to acquire books was easier said than done. The availability or shortage of books dominated public librarianship during the war years. All the countries at war experienced paper shortages; printing during the war was customarily done on poor-quality paper, in small type face, and with very narrow margins. Nowhere, however, was the book trade so disrupted as in Germany.

German libraries began to experience problems almost immediately. The Einkaufshaus had hardly conquered the worst of its previous difficulties when the war began and erased its gains. Within

247

months Beratungsstellen were complaining about the delays in book deliveries, complaints that would only increase in frequency and escalate in intensity as the war proceeded. By the end of 1940 the RV was soliciting reports on the problems the Beratungsstellen were experiencing. As the Bavarian Ministry of Culture was quick to point out, the EKH's failure made it difficult to overcome political Catholicism. Delays in EKH deliveries in turn postponed scheduled openings of new libraries.[15]

Before the first year of the war was over the pattern was established. A letter from Förster of the EKH in response to the complaints of the Lippe Beratungsstelle made the situation clear; the roots of the problems lay outside the control of the EKH. As an example, Förster cited the enormous increase in orders received by the EKH since the war's beginning; the Luftwaffe alone was opening eleven hundred libraries. Yet at the same time, the publishers on which the EKH system depended could not maintain their deliveries to him. He summarized the deteriorating situation eloquently: "Matériel difficulties, staff shortages (we are presently lacking eighty employees!), and unforeseen hitches (holidays to save coal!) make the work still more difficult for those remaining. And, on top of everything else, orders received that formerly lay in the shadows have had to be recorded. We have had to write out in the last four weeks alone fourteen hundred final government accounts in order not to lose the money."[16] Förster did not know it, but that was only the beginning.

By 1942 the situation was considerably worse. The RV had to step in and establish priorities for deliveries. Lippe, for example, was allocated nine hundred volumes for new libraries and fifteen hundred volumes for additions to existing libraries. Beratungsstellen were advised as early as May 1942 to concentrate on strengthening existing libraries rather than founding new ones. In August the recommended size for opening collections was reduced. Josef Witsch of the EKH may have been perfectly correct when, in the autumn of 1942, he emphasized that the book shortage should not be attributed to reduced production but to greatly increased demand for books, but that did not get to the Beratungsstellen the books they needed.[17]

The heavy bombing of Leipzig, center of the German book trade, just before Christmas 1943 brought the EKH to a standstill for some weeks and dealt it, and many publishers located there, a blow from

248

which they never truly recovered. Books stored at the EKH were destroyed, as were the inventories of the publishers; neither could be replaced. Deliveries were resumed at the beginning of February, but Beratungsstellen were warned that they would be in even smaller quantities. By the following December the steadily worsening military position had made lengthy delays the norm and closed off some areas of the Reich completely.[18]

The history of a box of cards ordered by the Lippe Beratungsstelle hints at the impossible conditions for libraries that prevailed in the last days of the Third Reich and provides an appropriate epitaph to the Nazi version of the EKH. The Beratungsstelle was informed on February 8, 1945, that the box—ordered at some undetermined date—had been sent. On March 31 the Beratungsstelle wrote to the EKH that it had yet to arrive. In August the box finally wandered in, but the Beratungsstelle could not pay the bill for the cards because there was no postal exchange with the Russian zone.[19]

The EKH and the Beratungsstellen were caught in a situation in which the demands placed on each exceeded the resources available. In the early phases the EKH recommended alternatives, suggesting that libraries concentrate on more easily obtained Heimat literature rather than on general literature, and sent Beratungsstellen back to deal with the local book dealers from whom they had so recently weaned them. Yet these reversals of policy could be no more than temporary expedients. The EKH steadily reduced the size of its deliveries and was ultimately forced to admit defeat. The primary problem was the paucity of production; delivery difficulties were tangential. German publishers could not produce the books needed to fill library collections when denied raw materials, deprived of personnel, and faced with damaged facilities. Beratungsstellen might request eleven new block collections, plead for fourteen additional block collections, or order individual titles, but by 1942 the EKH was forced to deny most of these requests.[20]

Although the increasingly severe book shortage was the dominating feature of public librarianship during the war years, other shortages also hampered the activity of libraries. Dermatoid for binding was in short supply. Wood needed to make book cabinets had disappeared by 1944. Coal was rationed; the binder for the Hamburg public libraries complained in February 1940 that the room in which he worked was so cold that binding materials did not respond properly. The delivery wagon that connected the branches in Hamburg had its trips reduced to two per week, and the use of private automobiles for official business was prohibited because of the lack of gasoline. The director of the Schaumburg-Lippe, who was responsible for a territory poorly served by trains, was told to use a bicycle.[21]

In the last years of the war Allied bombing had a major effect on library service, especially in the industrialized, urban areas that were the principal targets. On November 22, 1943, the quarters of the RV were completely burned in a raid on Berlin; a day later the section of the ministry in which Dähnhardt worked was also destroyed. All central records relating to public libraries were lost. The public libraries of Frankfurt/Main, Kassel, Kiel, and Potsdam were almost completely destroyed. Those in the West lost approximately a million volumes, 110,000 in Cologne alone. The 1945 class at Leipzig carried gas masks to its final examinations, which it took in an unheated room as hostile airplanes screamed overhead. The Beratungsstelle in Nuremberg, a city selected for particularly heavy attack because of its symbolic importance as the location of party rallies, was destroyed in March 1943 and all its equipment lost, including the personal handkerchiefs and aprons of the staff. After serious damage in August to the Beratungsstelle in its new location, it moved out of the city.[22]

The large cities endured the worst destruction, but even small towns were affected. In the largely rural areas administered by the Bayreuth Beratungsstelle—land located farther from the English airfields that sent the Allied bombers than most of Germany—thirty-nine of seventy-one reporting village libraries and twenty-six of thirty-nine reporting city libraries could be considered in good condition after the war. Twenty-seven Gemeinde libraries and twelve city libraries had sustained some damage. Almost all had not only been damaged but also plundered in the general breakdown of organized government. In the small Westphalian town of Gütersloh, librarian Heinrich Breenkotter had a nervous breakdown in 1941. He was told not to be in a place where there were air raid alarms, but, as he reported wryly to the Beratungsstelle, the English were not cooperating with his doctor's advice.[23]

By early 1944 the continuous Allied bombing had become so effective that public libraries, along with other cultural institutions,

250

were ordered to remove their collections to safekeeping, to the extent possible. In the prevailing conditions librarians often had some difficulty complying with this order, as in Braunschweig where the city had no trucks available, but by the end of the war the collections of most major cities in Germany had been dispersed into the countryside. Occasionally books might have departed from the city only to be destroyed on thier new, supposedly safe, sites, or to be ruined by poor storage conditions, but generally what was bunkered survived. The securing of collections did, of course, inhibit library service and tarnish the proactive image of Nazi public librarianship. The librarian in Weddel was sharply admonished by the Braunschweig Beratungsstelle that he could keep books in the cellar to protect them against air raids only if it did not interfere with normal circulation.[24]

The effects of bombing on the well-documented public libraries of Hamburg are probably only slightly greater than the impact on other large cities. Because of its strategic importance and its accessibility to England, Hamburg was bombed throughout the war. The September 30, 1941, memorandum that announced that the next meeting of branch librarians would take place on October 4, regardless of any air raid alarms the previous night, indicates how early air raids came to be treated as a routine feature of daily life in wartime Hamburg. The raids in July and August 1943 were exceptional in their destructiveness and are compared with the extraordinary bombings in 1945 of Dresden and Tokyo. These attacks cost the Hamburger Öffentliche Bücherhallen five branch libraries, two small stations, and 75,777 volumes. Librarians were on the front line, patrolling library buildings at night. Two library staff members, Maria Arpe and Ursel Wolf, were recommended for the war service cross for their heroism in saving the branch in Eilbek and their help with wounded on the night of July 27–28, 1943.[25]

It is striking that even in the midst of war, efforts were made to repair buildings and restore normal service. Library use was increasing, and librarians could see that their work had an important influence on morale. As the *Hamburger Tageblatt* commented in October 1943, "books are all that are left to us." The public was actually demanding more libraries in 1943. Hamburg opened new branches in 1944 in Winterhude, located in the southern part of the city, and in March 1945 in Eppendorf, in the northern section. The books that

251

had survived the destruction of the Hammerbrook branch in July 1943 formed the basis of the new Winterhude library. Existing branches contributed the largest part of Eppendorf's books and furniture, because by March 1945 they could no longer be obtained in any other way.[26]

To all public libraries from the largest to the smallest, the war brought an acute shortage of personnel. Men of military age were drafted immediately, and the reserves called up. This meant that many libraries and Beratungsstellen lost their directors. Their departure was particularly serious when it affected the higher administrative posts. For want of an appropriate administrator many plans had to be postponed, such as the founding of the Nuremberg Beratungsstellen. The Kreisbüchereipfleger plan could never be fully and effectively implemented when no sooner would a Kreisbüchereipfleger be chosen than he would be drafted. As more and more men were needed, age provided no protection. Wilhelm Schuster at fifty-six had the misfortune to be enrolled in the Volkssturm in the closing days of the war, sustain severe wounds, and be captured by the Russians. By the end of the war virtually all men had gone from professional life.

In the early days libraries would sometimes try to obtain deferments or concessions. In 1941 the Lippe Beratungsstelle tried to get the drafting of the furniture maker supplying its libraries delayed so that he could finish his work. At Hamburg, Dr. Joerden requested in July 1940 that the *Hausmeister* be released from the army because he was needed both in the library and at home, where he had an aging grandmother. Six months later Joerden himself had been drafted, and the acting head of the Hamburger Öffentliche Bücherhallen was pleading that he be given leave to help with the budget.[27]

War service did not always mean the front line, although many librarians were killed on duty. Wutz, director of the Bayreuth Beratungsstelle, served in a special capacity, vaguely described as the "particular purposes of the Reichsführer-SS." Pfeiffer, from the Rhenish Palatinate, was on the staff of Rosenberg, who had been given charge of the occupied areas. Joerden was offered the opportunity to be on one of the artistic commissions scavenging Europe but preferred to spend the war as a gunner. Schriewer spent the war stationed in Frankfurt/Oder and was able to remain involved in the running of the library.[28]

For the most part, however, the men had to be replaced. Occasionally the shortage gave someone like Erwin Ackerknecht, who had been excluded from public library work, the chance to practice his profession again. More usually, the departed men were replaced by women. By 1945 almost every Beratungsstelle was being run by the woman who had previously been the professional librarian on the staff. In small libraries wives often replaced their husbands when they were called up. In the later years of the war it became very difficult to find anyone suitable for the village libraries, and compromises often had to be made. The librarians of the village libraries in the part of Franconia administered by the Nuremberg Beratungsstelle in 1944 were sometimes the mandated teachers, but they were also stenotypists, clerks, cashiers, seamstresses, and forest rangers.[29]

The substitution of women for men was not welcome. Von Stengel of the Bavarian Ministry of Culture described the Beratungsstellen of Bavaria as "able to work" even though they were weaker in personnel. The Braunschweig minister of adult education was less kind. Frau Quincke, who had replaced a male director, he seems to have considered minimally adequate, even though she directed the Beratungsstelle only half-time and administered no men. But on Frau Horberth, who had been put in charge when Frau Quincke became ill, he was scathing. In January 1945 she went off to war herself, but the minister felt that even if she did return, they could not expect public library work to make progress. They needed a man with the necessary energy and organizing ability. But the loss of so many men during the war forced greater acceptance, and after the war many administrative posts were held by women.[30]

More was asked of those who did remain. In the spring of 1943 the workweek was extended to fifty-three hours in the Hamburg library, except for those under age eighteen and women protected by the mothers' protection law. No overtime was paid; employees were adjured to think of the men at the front. The Reichsstelle recognized the burdens that were placed upon the reduced staffs, but their only solution was to recommend that directors try to get library employees exempted from the emergency service being required of civil servants.[31]

The effects of personnel changes and reductions were exacerbated by augmented responsibilities for public libraries. After a very brief drop in the weeks immediately preceding and following the outbreak of the war, reading increased steadily. Official documents and messages proclaimed this fact regularly; statistics from different parts of the Reich confirm it. In Hamburg, for example, the system that circulated 543,331 volumes in 1939 circulated 560,129 in 1940 and 578,026 in 1941, increases of 3.4 and 6.4 percent, respectively. Monthly statistics comparing 1941 and 1942 show even more dramatic growth. Circulation in April 1942 was up 30 percent over that of April 1941; circulation in June 1942 was 58 percent larger than the preceding June's.[32]

In addition to the increase in reading by already existing readers, the war created new groups to be served as groups. The first and most obvious, of course, were the soldiers. Working with the party literary agencies, the public libraries packed up and sent in the course of six weeks during the fall of 1939 a total of about 8 million volumes. Some libraries waived residence rules and normal fees to make their libraries accessible to soldiers stationed locally, although this could cause problems if the soldier did not return the books before being transferred. The Hamburg administration cautioned librarians to obtain the home addresses of such soldier-readers.[33]

Other libraries might establish special collections in army quarters, rather on the pattern of the old Wanderbüchereien. The Detmold Beratungsstelle, for instance, deposited sixty-five volumes in the soldiers' home of a provincial guard unit. Service to army hospitals was often handled in the same way.[34]

Some library service was on a very informal basis. Librarians in the army would write to their former colleagues, requesting books, which they would in turn lend to their comrades in arms. Detmold sent part of a former Wanderbücherei to a guard battalion in the West at the request of a Volksschule teacher. Ackerknecht dispatched books from Stettin to Ernst Saltzwedel, its director, who had been drafted; his only condition was that Saltzwedel should not lend those that had come from Ackerknecht's personal collection.[35]

The heavy bombing that was responsible for so much physical damage to public libraries also created large numbers of refugees. Many residents of such industrialized areas as the Ruhr, especially children, were relocated in areas remote from military targets—the Upper Palatinate or Lower Bavaria, for example—where they became potential library users. These evacuees were joined in the last year of the war by ethnic Germans from Eastern Europe, fleeing the Russian armies and the wrath of their Slavic neighbors. Unwelcome for many reasons in the community, the refugees were often also un-welcome in the public library; they had not paid any of the taxes that had helped build the now-public institutions. The Reichsstelle had to issue a set of guidelines for service in districts getting many refugees. Exhortation could, however, achieve only so much in a small rural community. Readership might have suddenly doubled, but that did not mean that resources to expand collections and services had in-creased, even assuming that books were still available to be bought.[36]

People were using libraries more and reading more, but what were they reading? Not surprisingly, many sought relaxation and escape. The coarsening of taste that has been observed in other belligerent countries is very apparent. From all over the Reich the demand came for "novels with cheerful content" (Ahorn, Bavaria), "novels for women" (Halle/Westphalia), or "adventurous travel" (Hamburg). Li-brarians acknowledged this need openly, even though it ran counter to their image of the library as an educational institution. The li-brarian at Hof in Upper Franconia reported that the greatest demand was for entertaining reading "because today all people want some-thing to relax." The plea of the librarian in Gehlenbeck of the Bielefeld Beratungsstelle is even more revealing: "If it is possible, I request an increase in the entertaining group (novels for women) and young adult books. Many women ask for books that do not have a war background."[37]

Such insistent and un-Nazi frivolity was not welcome either at the Reichstelle or at the Reich Ministry of Education. In his last annual message in December 1944 Heiligenstaedt declared, "Not only do circulation statistics climb steadily, but the readers have recourse to books that are more and more substantial and serious." Someone at the Detmold Beratungsstelle underlined the statement about readers and put a question mark followed by an exclamation point in the margin.[38]

Sensible administrators tried to obscure the evidence that circula-tion statistics indirectly provided of the decline in morale and the lack of enthusiasm for the war. A report on the Hamburg public libraries in 1941 noted the strong interest in history and politics. It was, in-deed, perfectly true that history and politics were, among nonfiction,

255

second in popularity only to travel literature and technical books, but it was also true, even though unstated, that circulation was declining in this area. In 1939 history and politics had accounted for 14.6 percent of Hamburg's circulation, but in 1940 it was 13.5 and in 1941 it was down still further to 12.8 percent. Frankfurt/Oder also recorded decreasing interest in this area: from 14.9 percent in 1938/39 to 11.7 in 1941/42, 9.7 in 1942/43, and 7.1 percent in 1943/44.[39]

Facts and figures document some of the realities of wartime public librarianship, but they do not communicate the full story. During the war libraries and librarians were preoccupied with survival and with carrying out as much of their mission as they could under the formidable conditions. Librarianship, like so many areas of German society during the war, exhibits a paradoxical combination of harsher regulation, as in the strict censorship and attacks on Catholic libraries, and greater freedom, as librarians were forced to act more independently when communication became more difficult and official arrangements deteriorated. The war brought favored Nazi programs to a standstill, suspended articulation of new ideas, and turned the attention of local governments, on whom further library development depended, to more-urgent questions.

CHAPTER THIRTEEN

The Nazi
Legacy

THE NAZI ERA transformed German public librarianship, leaving little untouched. It reworked theory, purged collections, reordered administration, and revamped the activities of public libraries. National socialism replaced the old public library leadership, multiplied the number of libraries, and did its best to destroy Catholic librarianship. The years between 1933 and 1945 changed German public librarianship irrevocably. After 1945 the profession could only try to salvage what was positive, reject what was not, and assimilate the lessons of the experience.

In Nazi public librarianship positive and negative are hopelessly entangled. The Nazi regime took a moribund cultural institution and inspired it with new life. At the same time it was responsible for devastation and destruction; the traditions and humanistic values of the profession were subverted, its physical plant bombed. Every contribution had its cost. Because so many actions simultaneously brought benefit and caused harm, the Nazi record neither lends itself readily to a balance sheet approach nor accommodates other straightforward distinctions easily. Good was often done, but for the worst of reasons. A process might be admirable, but its product pernicious. Values were supposedly rooted in ancient Germanic ideals, but they had modernizing, radical consequences. Moral subtleties, professional advantages, and human costs are intertwined.

One of the first acts of the new Nazi regime was to demand the redefinition of German society in Nazi terms. For public librarianship this meant a new set of goals and a new set of values to be articulated. At the time of the seizure of power the Nazis did not really have a cultural policy, nor any program for public libraries, and Nazi leaders were not especially interested in creating them. It was left to librarians to adapt their profession to the state's new orientation, a critical task if the profession was to survive.

They accomplished the redirection of the profession by appropriating some of the more pertinent Nazi themes and giving them a specifically public library application. The political character of the public library was emphasized; the idea of the Volk was integrated into the definition of a public library. Nazi library theory ostentatiously rejected Weimar, a rejection that was in fact a repudiation of cultural diversity and led directly to the purging of collections.

During this period of examination and discussion some important pre-Nazi principles were reaffirmed. Probably the most fundamental was that the main purpose of a public library was education. Such a formulation allowed the incorporation of the idea of education for political purposes, but it placed limits on the extent of theoretical change. This affirmation of the educational function of the public library gave librarians some intellectual basis for resistance to attempts by the Propaganda Ministry to expropriate public librarianship, even if disagreement over what education was remained possible.

The revision of theory made at least one clearly positive contribution, a contribution that was not, however, any specific idea, but rather a style, an approach. National socialism exalted action, doing, vigor. This dogma brought a much needed breath of fresh air into the dusty world of public libraries, directing librarians away from their quarrels over definitions and focusing their attention on the job. It was a mood reinforced by the militaristic orientation of society, the pervasive use of military terminology, and the regime's appetite for statistics they could tout as achievements. Equally important was the stress on unity, a virtue that had been notably lacking in public librarianship. Divided and pulling in different directions, public librarians had accomplished relatively little since the beginning of the Richtungsstreit. Greater cooperation made possible a new era of accomplishment.

Associated with the redefinition of values and goals was the coordination of the profession. Dissent had to be quelled, and librarians

258

redirected and molded into a single-minded force serving the wishes of the state. Reaching this goal entailed persuading individual librarians to participate in the collective enterprise and eliminating any possible institutional rebellion.

Gaining the cooperation of librarians proved relatively easy. Individuals had a variety of motives for working with the new regime, some admirable, others more self-serving. Some librarians found the situation in 1933 so hopeless that any change was welcome, others hoped that long-standing professional objectives might be realized; there were ambitious librarians, who saw the new situation opportunistically, and there were those who recognized that only if they accommodated themselves could they continue to practice their profession. But whatever their motives, the end result was general compliance.

Although very few librarians had joined the Nazi party before 1933, committed anti-Nazis were equally rare. Librarians were predominantly women, of middle-class background, and usually either quietly conservative in their views or apolitical. They lacked any potential source of resistance; librarians had no history of organized opposition, as labor unions had, no strong faith, as Catholics had, nor any pattern of independence and individualism, like that of physicists. The few leaders who threatened to be independent were either removed or relegated to the sidelines. Within a few years new men had risen to the top of the profession.

The weakness of their institutions hindered any impulse toward group resistance. Librarians were few enough to begin with, and they did not join organizations as a matter of course. Regional associations were ephemeral. The national association, the VDV, was almost paralyzed by inner dissension. Its organizational structure was a compromise between two fundamentally irreconcilable groups. The careful distribution of offices, the equal recognition for the rival journals, and other accommodations worked together to impede the development of a unified, collegial organization. It was not difficult for the Nazi regime to transfer to state agencies the useful functions the library organizations performed and close down the organizations.

What made this small, rather insignificant profession worthy of attention was that librarians were the keepers of library collections. Librarians acquired, organized, and disseminated books and other reading material. Nazi determination to dictate what people read and, more important, what they did not read, moved librarianship from a peripheral governmental concern to a central one. Throughout the Nazi period collection policy remained at the heart of Nazi public librarianship.

Nazi collection policy was overwhelmingly negative. Although German librarians had long had fairly restrictive guidelines for collection development, the Machtergreifung introduced a completely new order of direction. All works by Marxist, pacifist, and Jewish authors were immediately banned. Elaborate, ceremonial book burnings were held, symbolizing the purification of a decayed society or the destruction of modern culture, depending on your point of view. In the confusion of the spring of 1933 independent patriotic groups campaigned against one or another work held by their local libraries; party members, emboldened by the Nazis' triumph, on their own authority told librarians what to remove. Librarians had to act quickly to block threats from outside, but they succeeded only by preparing extensive blacklists and by devising an efficient system that guaranteed rapid enforcement of any regulation. In the end they protected themselves against the caprice of self-appointed censors, but the state control that they helped construct was so thorough that it was a Pyrrhic victory.

Strengthening the Nazi orientation of collections complemented the thoroughgoing purges. Librarians were directed to purchase the classics of national socialism, books such as *Mein Kampf* and *Mythus des 20. Jahrhunderts.* Recommended lists, on which many librarians depended for book selection, abounded in accounts of the Nazi movement, pseudoscholarly analyses of history and economics written from a Nazi viewpoint, and pro-Nazi Kitsch. Librarians were quick to realize that a choice of this nature was always safe.

Probably the only good feature of this heavy-handed effort at thought control, and it was very limited in its merits, was in the impact on librarians. There is some evidence that individual librarians began to think about what culture really was. As they watched library use decline, no one was more aware than they of the costs of censorship. Their thinking had little effect in the totalitarian state, but it did heighten their awareness of the need for professional ethics and make the profession more receptive to the very different ideas introduced by the occupying forces after 1945.

Insistence on tight control over collections led to a more effective administrative network. A period of experiment in which older institutions were tested was followed by their gradual replacement. The RWEV succeeded in getting itself designated the locus of authority over public librarianship, a victory over the encroachment of the Propaganda Ministry. New provincial library agencies were added to existing ones; a nationwide network began to evolve. The Prussian provincial agency, already responsible for the two-thirds of the Reich that was Prussia, was renamed the Reichsstelle für Volksbüchereiwesen and given jurisdiction over the entire country. A detailed series of guidelines were published, covering every aspect of administration. From the beginning, policy and organization existed in a symbiotic relationship, the one reinforcing the other; the desire to accomplish a specific result stimulated the establishment of the necessary institutions, which in turn formulated even more comprehensive and radical objectives.

These fundamental structural innovations were closely related to the resolution of a number of conflicts, at various levels, over power. On the whole, the state successfully defended its sovereignty over libraries, although local party organizations usurped its prerogative in a few cases. The RWEV asserted its claims over those of the Propaganda Ministry and, as time passed, enhanced its predominance. The RV was subordinated to the RWEV, molded into an agency with only routine duties. But the success of the RWEV was less complete than it appeared. The principal beneficiary of the outcome of the contest between state and party for control of librarianship was local government rather than the RWEV. Traditionally, public libraries had been the concern of cities and villages and the failure of the Propaganda Ministry's effort guaranteed that they would remain so. Changes in the law converted their voluntary interest into a legal responsibility to support a library. This jurisdiction made local governments a factor to be reckoned with in any public library program; their financial control gave them a decisive role.

The result of the continuing importance of local governments was a bifurcated administration of public librarianship. Individual libraries were accountable to their municipal governments—but also to the Beratungsstelle of their province. Beratungsstellen answered to their provincial education ministry—but also to the RV and RWEV. Compromise enabled the system to function, although it was never optimally efficient. The administration of public librarianship in the Third Reich remained an uneasy accommodation. Public libraries were imposed by the national government on unwilling and recalcitrant localities, who might comply with the letter of the law but more often than not failed to carry out the spirit.

The gradual accretion of authority over public libraries at the national level in the hands of the RWEV occurred at the same time as a series of struggles for leadership among individuals was being resolved. By degrees, Heinz Dähnhardt, the advisor in the RWEV responsible for adult education, emerged as the single most important figure, his personal power tied to the institutional dominance of the ministry. The pre-Nazi library leaders, Schuster and Schriewer, were tried and either failed or withdrew. Some less well-established librarians, such as Narcisz and Herrmann, attempted to use the fluidity of the situation to promote themselves. Walter Hofmann used his many connections and made an especially persistent effort in the South to expand his power. In the end, though, Dähnhardt, the non-librarian, was the Reich's First Librarian.

The victory of the RWEV over the Propaganda Ministry had initially been welcomed as an affirmation of the educational character of the public library, but the subsequent history of public libraries in the Third Reich demonstrates how hollow that victory was. Program after program was instituted, by and for libraries. Many of these programs were, like administrative improvement, desirable as such, but all inescapably served fundamentally political purposes. Public libraries may have remained the administrative responsibility of the RWEV, but they steadily became less and less educational and more and more propagandistic.

Perhaps the most immediately obvious evidence of the alteration of the public library's function were the activities undertaken by individual libraries. Youth, glorified in Nazi ideology, received special attention; youth libraries proliferated, and libraries worked out cooperative efforts with the HJ. Numerous exhibits were mounted, programs presented, and book lists prepared. Such activity fulfilled a

262

dual purpose; the individual exhibit, program, or book list would have a political objective, and the fact of the effort would demonstrate the library's commitment to action. Readers' advising was given a stamp appropriate to the goals of the Nazi regime. It goes without saying that library users were pressed to read Nazi and pro-Nazi books. In addition, librarians clearly made an effort to wean readers from their preference for light, entertaining reading and to replace it with non-fiction, a fare more suitable for the subjects of the humorless Third Reich.

On a national level several major policies and projects expressed the Nazi spirit of public librarianship. An attack on Catholic libraries slowly gained momentum. First, Catholic libraries were deprived of the right to call themselves public, then their membership was regulated, finally their collections were forbidden to contain anything except specifically religious works. Their near-destruction eliminated strong competition and satisfied the need for an enemy inherent in national socialism.

Correlated with the assault on Catholic libraries was a large-scale building program. New libraries were built throughout the Reich, especially in strongly Catholic areas. Although most of the new libraries were rural and very small, this program did bring libraries to a number of towns that had not previously had one. It can be credited with having considerably expanded the availability of public library service and, just as important, greatly raised the expectations of the population, even if what some of these minuscule libraries provided was of such questionable value that many of them were closed after 1945. It again served the secondary purpose of demonstrating productivity and action.

Massive effort was devoted to strengthening library service in the border areas, where German culture was considered by definition endangered. Existing libraries were enlarged and many new ones built. A border book service had existed before 1933, but the Nazi state subsidized it far more generously than any Weimar government had; its work tied in closely with Nazi foreign policy objectives. The Grenzbüchereidienst expanded its activity, and its director became a significant factor in the planning of many Beratungsstellen.

The mixed quality of the Nazi impact on public librarianship is as apparent with respect to librarians as it is to libraries. Professional self-esteem improved, but at the same time professional independence was destroyed. The mandated development programs of the regime increased the demand for librarians. Salaries rose, the number of librarians in training grew, but the quality of education deteriorated overall. Regulations were imposed at every turn, giving librarians fewer and fewer oopportunities to exercise their professional judgment. Obedience rather than creativity was valued. Public librarianship turned inward as librarians were discouraged from seeking new ideas in the work of other countries.

Because it was out of step with Nazi ideology in several respects, the profession suffered. Librarians could not change the fact that theirs was predominantly an urban activity, and most professional librarians were employed in cities and towns, no matter how much Nazis idealized the rural life. They could not alter the composition of their profession to conform to Nazi definitions of sexual roles; it was inescapable that most librarians were women, and women, moreover, doing a professional job, rather than following the *Kinder, Kirche und Küche* precept.

All aspects of Nazi public librarianship illustrate the revolutionary zeal national socialism brought. Nazi public librarianship broke decisively with the public librarianship of the Weimar period. It demonstrated again and again its commitment to new goals. Philosophy, collections, and leadership were changed; institutional forms were drastically altered. The new regime swept all in its path. To the extent that there was resistance, it was the silent, inchoate reluctance typical of civil servants that left few traces and had minimal effect. If revolution is defined as sudden, radical, and complete change, then from the point of view of the public library Nazi Germany has to be considered a revolutionary state.

The Nazi revolution was so successful because librarians cooperated, enticed by the promise that the new order could bring to fruition some of their most cherished dreams. The Nazi regime did indeed greatly expand the numbers of libraries, create a national administrative structure, make local government responsible, and generally endorse libraries as a significant educational undertaking, but somehow the results were not quite what librarians had envisaged. It was all too possible to have form without substance. Librarians were neither the first nor the last to discover that the Nazis made unreliable allies. In the history of Nazi public libraries, nazism is the theme and professional concerns the counterpoint, the two separate yet interactive.

At the same time as the Nazi public library furnishes a model of the revolutionary public library, it provides a model of the totalitarian public library. In this model the distinguishing feature is the complete interpenetration of one system of political values. Not only were all library goals ultimately political, but on a day-to-day basis every activity, every decision had to be viewed through a political lens. By 1937 the distinction between politics and any other category in librarianship had virtually disappeared. Culture had become a component of politics. The dedication to a particular political ideology produced regulation, exaltation of the group, and emphasis on action. Statistical growth, administrative efficiency, and ceaseless publicity were other hallmarks.

Because essential characteristics of Nazi libraries are shared with the public libraries of other authoritarian regimes, a totalitarian model is more appropriate for conceptual analysis than a Fascist one. That is not to say that distinctively Nazi features were lacking. German public librarianship reflected the pervasiveness of the cult of the leader. It made every effort both to venerate Adolf Hitler, even if the means at its disposal were often no more powerful than a book list, and to translate the leader principle into patterns of library administrative organization. Public librarianship incorporated the aggressive elements in the Nazi ideology: hostility to neighbors; exaltation of the Volk. Enmity to Jews was expressed in the exclusion of Jewish writers from collections and, after Kristallnacht, of Jewish readers from libraries.

Yet even though they attained their object and converted an essentially cultural institution, somewhat incoherent of purpose, into a highly political, distinctly Nazi, and very purposeful one, Nazi leaders would probably not have considered the public librarianship of the Third Reich an unqualified success. The new-model libraries might be trying to shape values in the desired way, but the nature of the book relegated them to a largely supporting role. Other media and institutions were undeniably more effective. Even more serious, to the extent that nonpropaganda remained in collections, and much did, libraries made dangerously different viewpoints readily accessi-

ble. A Mazo de la Roche novel, apolitical in the judgment of most
U.S. citizens and Canadians, made a statement by merely portraying
a world in which Nazi values and concerns were absent. It presented
an alternative.

Nor were libraries particularly efficient. They never reached large
numbers of the population. Library use was low and, until the end of
the 1930s, declining. Germans could hold aloof from libraries in a
way that they could not avoid schools or party organizations. If they
did choose to use a library, they could evade what the government
wanted them to consume.

Nazi public librarianship bequeathed to the postwar period a
foundation of varying degrees of soundness. There were many libraries, well distributed geographically throughout Germany—if they
had not been destroyed by the war. Collections were substantial—but
they were full of propaganda and Kitsch. The profession was larger,
more respected, and more prosperous than it had ever been—although it had also been demoralized and regimented. Some of what
remained was less ambiguous. The Nazis had made much needed
reforms in administration. Their most valuable bequest, however,
was the principle that public libraries are a public responsibility and
must be supported by tax revenues. The Nazi regime asserted this
view and enforced it; its successors had only to embrace it. This is an
enduring legacy that at least partially redeems less-praiseworthy features of the Nazi record in public librarianship.

Notes

CHAPTER 1. INTRODUCTION

1. "Eröffnung von 30 Volksbüchereien in einem pfälzischen Grenzbezirk," *DB* 5 (1938): 236.

2. Among the most useful general treatments of Nazi Germany are Karl Dietrich Bracher, *The German Dictatorship: The Origins, Structure, and Consequences of National Socialism*, trans. Jean Steinberg, intro. Peter Gay (n.p.: Penguin University Books, 1978), and Richard Grunberger, *The 12-Year Reich: A Social History of Nazi Germany, 1933–1945* (New York: Holt, Rinehart, and Winston, 1979).

3. Wolfgang Thauer and Peter Vodosek, *Geschichte der öffentlichen Bücherei in Deutschland* (Wiesbaden: Otto Harrassowitz, 1978), pp. 29–31; Ladislaus Buzas, *Deutsche Bibliotheksgeschichte der neuesten Zeit (1800–1945): vol. 3, Elemente des Buch- und Bibliothekswesens*, ed. Fridolin Dressler and Gerhard Liebers (Wiesbaden: Dr. Ludwig Reichert Verlag, 1978), pp. 63–64; *Handbuch der deutschen Volksbüchereien* (Jahrbuch der deutschen Volksbüchereien 6, 1940), ed. Reichsstelle für das Volksbüchereiwesen and Reichsschrifttumskammer Gruppe Büchereiwesen (Leipzig: Einkaufshaus für Büchereien, 1940), p. 13.

4. Thauer and Vodosek, pp. 37–42.

5. Ibid., pp. 43–56; Wolfgang Thauer, ed., *Die Bücherhallenbewegung* (Wiesbaden: Otto Harrassowitz, 1970).

6. Germany, Statistisches Reichsamt, *Die deutschen Volksbüchereien nach Ländern, Provinzen und Gemeinden, 1933/34*, Statistik des Deutschen Reichs, vol. 471 (Berlin: Verlag für Sozialpolitik, Wirtschaft und Statistik in Berlin, 1935), pp. 8–11; "Contrasts in Library Service," *Bulletin of the American Library Association* 29 (May 1935): 252–55.

7. Margaret F. Stieg, "The Richtungstreit: The Philosophy of Public Librarianship in Germany before 1933," *Journal of Library History* 21 (Spring 1986): 261–76.

8. Peter Vodosek and Manfred Komorowski, eds., *Bibliotheken während des Nationalsozialismus*, Teil 1, Wolfenbütteler Schriften zur Geschichte des Buchwesens, Band 16 (Wiesbaden: Otto Harrassowitz, 1989).

9. Friedrich Andrae, comp., *Volksbücherei und Nationalsozialismus*, Beiträge zum Büchereiwesen, Reihe B, Quellen und Texte, Heft 3 (Wiesbaden: O. Harrassowitz, 1970); Englebrecht Boese, *Das öffentliche Bibliothekswesen im Dritten Reich* (Bad Honnef: Bock und Herchen, 1987).

CHAPTER 2. THE NAZI IDEA OF THE PUBLIC LIBRARY

1. At least partially because of its intellectual poverty, nazism as an ideology has attracted relatively little attention from scholars. Among the more extensive treatments is Raymond E. Murphy et al., *National Socialism: Basic Principles, Their Application by the Nazi Party's Foreign Organization, and the Use of Germans Abroad for Nazi Aims* (Washington, D.C.: Government Printing Office, 1943), prepared during the war by a special unit in the Division of European Affairs of the State Department. A useful, more recent study is Martin Broszat, *German National Socialism, 1919–1945*, trans. Kurt Rosenbaum and Inge Pauli Boehm (Santa Barbara, Calif.: Clio Press, 1966). *Mein Kampf* remains the basic document; Adolf Hitler, *Mein Kampf*, trans. Ralph Manheim (Boston: Houghton Mifflin, 1943). The chapter "Ideology and the Nationalization of the Masses," in John Hiden and John Farquharson, *Explaining Hitler's Germany: Historians and the Third Reich* (London: Batsford Academic and Educational, 1983), is a historiographical discussion of the subject.

2. Hitler, *Mein Kampf*, p. 385.

3. Murphy, pp. 5–6.

4. Ibid., pp. 6–8; G. W. F. Hegel, *Grundlinien der Philosophie des Rechtes* (Stuttgart, 1938), p. 441, as quoted in translation in Murphy, p. 7; G. W. F. Hegel, *Die Vernunft in der Geschichte* (Leipzig, 1930), p. 37, as quoted in translation in Murphy, p. 7.

5. Gottfried Feder, *The Programme of the N.S.D.A.P. and Its General Conceptions*, trans. E. T. S. Dugdale (Munich: Franz Eher Nachfolger, 1932), p. 18.

6. Ernst Rudolf Huber, *Verfassungsrecht des großdeutschen Reiches* (Hamburg, 1939), p. 51, as quoted in translation in Murphy, p. 26.

7. Huber, pp. 165–66, as quoted in Murphy, p. 25.

8. Ibid., p. 194, as quoted in Murphy, p. 34.

9. Ibid., p. 230, as quoted in Murphy, p. 37. This has interesting echoes of Rousseau's "general will." Jean-Jacques Rousseau, *The Social Contract*, trans. Wilmoore Kendall (Chicago: Henry Regnery, 1954).

10. Dietrich Strothmann, *Nationalsozialistische Literaturpolitik: Ein Beitrag zur Publizistik im Dritten Reich*, Abhandlungen zur Kunst-, Musik- und Literaturwissenschaft, vol. 13 (Bonn: H. Bouvier, 1960), p. 88.

11. Hitler, *Mein Kampf*, pp. 254–66; Feder, p. 31.

12. Hitler, *Mein Kampf*, p. 407.

13. Adolf Hitler, *The Speeches of Adolf Hitler, April 1922–August 1939*, trans. and ed. Norman Baynes (London, New York, and Toronto: Oxford University Press, 1942), p. 568.

14. Adolf Hitler, *Die deutsche Kunst als stolzeste Verteidigung des deutschen Volkes*, Hier spricht das neue Deutschland, vol. 7 (Munich: Zentralverlag der N.S.D.A.P., 1934).

15. Strothmann, p. 90; Wolf Sluyterman von Langeweyde, *Kultur ist Dienst am Leben*, 2d ed. (Berlin: Nordland-Verlag, 1940), pp. 10, 79.

16. Hans Schmidt-Leonhardt, "Kultur und Staat im Recht des neuen Reiches," in *Deutsches Kulturrecht*, ed. by Deutscher Fichte-Bund (Hamburg: Falken, 1936), p. 18.

17. See Alan Bullock, *Hitler: A Study in Tyranny*, rev. ed. (Penguin, 1962), p. 71.

18. Hitler, *Mein Kampf*, pp. 35–37.

19. Niedersächsisches Staatsarchiv, Bückeburg, Schaumburg Des L 4, Nr. 10325, blank poster.

20. Asphalt literature technically meant novels with an urban setting. It was usually used, however, with a sneer and implied writing somewhere between trash and pornography. An entire article devoted to its definition is Wolfgang Herrmann, "Was ist Asphaltliteratur?" *Volksbücherei und Volksbildung in Niedersachsen* 13 (June/July 1933): 16–21.

21. Joseph Goebbels, *Goebbels-Reden* (Düsseldorf: Droste, 1971), vol. 1, 1932–1939, pp. 108–12, 168–73.

22. Wilhelm Schuster, "Das Ende des Bildungsreiches," *DB* 1 (1934): 1–6; Franz Schriewer, "Die Volksbücherei: Möglichkeiten und Grenzen," *DB* 2 (1935): 195; G. A. Narcisz, "Die Volksbüchereien werden neu geordnet," *Volksbücherei und Volksbildung in Niedersachsen* 13 (June/July 1933): 13–16; Bayerisches Hauptstaatsarchiv, MK 41452, "Protokoll einer Arbeitsbesprechung über süddeutsche Büchereiverhältnisse, am 7. Juli 1934 in Stuttgart"; Staatsarchiv der Senat der Freien und Hansestadt Hamburg, Hamburger Öffentliche Bücherhallen, 23, "Die deutsche Volksbücherei," article written by Dr. Alfred Krebs, director, for *Hamburger Tageblatt*, sent October 23, 1935.

23. "Preußische Minister für Wissenschaft, Kunst und Volksbildung U II R Nr. 750.1, 28.12.33," *DB* 1 (1934): 11–13.

24. Schriewer, "Die Volksbücherei," p. 200; Niedersächsisches Staatsarchiv, Wolfenbüttel, 12 A Neu 13 19014, clipping from *Braunschweiger Tageszeitung*, April 6, 1937; Stadtarchiv, Kiel, 40790, Stadtbücherei Organisation, "Die neue Stadtbücherei im Kiel [1937]."

25. E. A. Fenelonov, "Soviet Public Libraries," in *Libraries in the USSR*, ed. Simon Francis (n.p.: Linnet Books and Clive Bingley, 1971), pp. 39–50; *The Public Library: Its Role in Socio-Economic and Cultural Life of the Society* (Moscow: V. I. Lenin State Library, 1974).

26. Karl Taupitz, *Das Büchereiwesen in Dorf und Kleinstadt* (Dresden: Verlag Heimatwerk Sachsen, n.d.), p. 9; "Grundsätze für den Aufbau des ländlichen Volksbüchereiwesens in der Provinz Hannover," *Volksbücherei und Volksbildung in Niedersachsen* 14 (October/November 1934): 1–2.

27. Fritz Prinzhorn, "Die Aufgaben der Bibliotheken im nationalsozialistischen Deutschland," *Zentralblatt für Bibliothekswesen* 51 (August/September 1934): 465–66; Fritz Heiligenstaedt, "Die neue deutsche Volksbücherei," *Die niedersächsische Volksbücherei* 16 (August/November 1936): 33.

28. Boese, *Das öffentliche Bibliothekwesen*, p. 89; interview with Dietrich Vorwerk, Villingen, July 25, 1985.

29. As quoted in Kummer, "Nationalsozialismus und Volksbüchereiwesen," *DB* 2 (1935): 320.

269

30. Schuster, "Das Ende des Bildungsreiches," pp. 1–6.

31. Schriewer, "Die Volksbücherei."

32. Heinz Dähnhardt, "Deutsche Büchereiarbeit von heute," *DB* 5 (1938): 646.

33. [Bernhard] Rust, "An die deutschen Volksbibliothekare," *DB* 5 (1938): 503–504.

34. Rudolf Reuter, "Die Volksbüchereien im neuen Staat," *Soziale Praxis* 42 (September 17, 1933): 1068; Narcisz, "Die Volksbüchereien werden neu geordnet," p. 14.

35. Schriewer, "Die Volksbücherei," p. 196.

36. Fritz Heiligenstaedt, "Volksbibliothekarische Zusammenarbeit," *DB* 5 (1938): 656.

37. Niedersächsisches Staatsarchiv, Wolfenbüttel, 12 A Neu 13 19015, "Das Ziel der Volksbücherei [1936]."

38. Schriewer, "Die Volksbücherei," p. 199; Taupitz, *Das Büchereiwesen in Dorf und Kleinstadt*, pp. 11–12.

39. Kummer, "Nationalsozialismus und Volksbüchereiwesen," p. 320; Generallandesarchiv, Karlsruhe, 235/6811 Konstanz, Philipp Harden-Rauch, Staatliche Volksbüchereistelle, Baden, to Ministerium für Kultus und Unterricht, July 8, 1940.

40. Nordrhein-Westfälisches Staatsarchiv, Detmold, M1 1Ju Nr. 148, Rud. Angermann, "Reinigung und Neuaufbau der Volksbüchereien," October 7, 1933.

41. Heinz Dähnhardt, "Weg und Ziel deutscher Volksbüchereiarbeit," *DB* 4 (1937): 2; Franz Schriewer, "Die deutsche Volksbücherei," *DB* 2 (1935): 300.

42. Boese, *Das Öffentliche Bibliothekwesen*, pp. 91–92.

43. Dähnhardt, "Weg und Ziel deutscher Volksbüchereiarbeit," p. 2.

44. Wilhelm Schuster, "Bücherei und Nationalsozialismus," *DB* 1 (1934): 1–9.

45. In an article published in the next issue of that volume of *DB*, Schuster was even more overtly religious. He used the three themes of the *via purgativa*, *via meditativa*, and *via unitativa* to organize his remarks. Schuster, "Das Ende des Bildungsreiches."

CHAPTER 3. POLITICS, PEOPLE, AND THE TAKEOVER OF THE PROFESSION

1. Zentrales Staatsarchiv, Potsdam, 62 DAF 3, 19359, B1. 46, clipping, *Hamburger Tageblatt*, May 16, 1933.

2. See Hiden and Farquharson, chs. 4 and 7; Ian Kershaw, *The Nazi Dictatorship: Problems and Perspectives of Interpretation* (London: Edward Arnold, 1985).

3. "Erklärung und Aufruf," in Andrae, *Volksbücherei und National Sozialismus*, pp. 54–56.

4. Robert Wohl, *The Generation of 1914* (Cambridge, Mass.: Harvard University Press, 1979); Otto Dietrich, *Mit Hitler in die Macht* (Munich, 1934), quoted in Bracher, p. 188; also Bracher, p. 343; Joachim C. Fest, *The Face of the Third Reich*, trans. Michael Bullock (Penguin, 1983), pp. 333–34.

5. Deutsches Literaturarchiv, Erwin Ackerknecht Collection, Ackerknecht to Joerden, April 26, 1933; Kindervater to Ackerknecht, June 28, 1934.

6. Deutsches Literaturarchiv, Erwin Ackerknecht Collection, Dr. Narcisz to Schuster, June 16, 1934.

7. Rudolf Joerden, "Zur neuen Einheit der Volksbüchereibewegung," *BuB* 8 (1928): 287–93; Wilhelm Schuster, "Vergangenheit, Gegenwart und Zukunft des deutschen Büchereiwesens im Spiegel der Leipziger Zentralstelle," *BuB* 8 (1928): 293–322.

8. *Auflockern;* this word can also be translated as disintegration, an interpretation that conveys a prejudice on Beer's part.

9. Johannes Beer, "Autorität und Volksbildung," *BuB* 13 (1933): 19–27.

10. Deutsches Literaturarchiv, Erwin Ackerknecht Collection, Schriewer to Schuster, February 24, 1934.

11. Deutsches Literaturarchiv, Erwin Ackerknecht Collection, Kurd Schulz to [Ackerknecht], March 26, 1933.

12. Deutsches Literaturarchiv, Erwin Ackerknecht Collection, Ackerknecht to Beer, September 17, 1932; [Schuster] to Ackerknecht, October 14, 1932; Ackerknecht to Schuster, October 20, 1932.

13. Hans Heimbach and Erwin Ackerknecht, "Rede und Antwort," *BuB* 13 (1933): 115.

14. Wolfgang Herrmann, "Der neue Nationalismus und seine Literatur," *BuB* 12 (1932): 261–73, and 13 (1933): 42–57.

15. This and the following paragraph are based on Bundesarchiv, Koblenz, R 56 V /137/141, 151; Deutsches Literaturarchiv, Erwin Ackerknecht Collection, Ackerknecht to Dr. Pauls, June 12, 1931; Johannes Beer to Ackerknecht, June 25, 1932; Ackerknecht to Beer, June 30, 1932; Ackerknecht to Schuster, September 9, 1932; Johannes Beer to E. Ackerknecht, September 15, 1932; Ackerknecht to Schuster, February 16, 1933, enclosed copy of letter from Hans Engelhardt; Schuster to Ackerknecht, February 18, 1933; Ackerknecht to Wolfgang Herrmann, February 20, 1933; Wolfgang Herrmann to Ackerknecht, February 21, 1933; Ackerknecht to Beer, March 14, 1933; Ackerknecht to W. Herrmann, January 13, 1938.

16. Deutsches Literaturarchiv, Erwin Ackerknecht Collection, Ackerknecht to Bondy, January 16, 1934. SA is the Sturmabteilung (storm troopers or Brown Shirts); SS, the Schutzstaffel or elite guard of the party.

17. Deutsches Literaturarchiv, Erwin Ackerknecht Collection, Joerden to Ackerknecht, April 23, 1933, and Joerden to Ackerknecht, July 22, 1933; interview with Rudolf Joerden, Hamburg, June 19, 1984. There were limits to Joerden's cooperation. Rather than participate in the plunder of Europe's cultural treasures, he allowed himself to be drafted into the army.

18. Deutsches Literaturarchiv, Erwin Ackerknecht Collection, Johannes Beer to E. Ackerknecht, April 28, 1933, and Ackerknecht to Schuster, April 27, 1933; Fachhochschule für Bibliothekswesen, Stuttgart, Walter Hofmann Archiv, Erich Thier to Hofmann, May 3, 1933.

19. Interview with Dietrich Vorwerk, Villingen, July 25, 1985.

20. Deutsches Literaturarchiv, Erwin Ackerknecht Collection, Ackerknecht to Dr. Haidenhain, January 31, 1931; Ackerknecht to Schuster, April 27, 1933;

Bundesarchiv, R56 v/137, "Die bisherige Büchereipolitik in Preußen, eine Ergänzung zum Abschnitt III der Denkschrift (Karl Heinl, Denkschrift betreffend Neubau des deutschen öffentlichen Büchereiwesens)"; Carl Jansen, "Wer wahren will, muss wagen; Dank an Wilhelm Schuster," *Bücherei und Bildung* 6 (July/August 1954): 661–66.

21. Völker Weimar, ed., *Franz Schriewer, 1893–1966*, Bibliographien, vol. 3 (Berlin: Deutscher Bibliotheksverband, Arbeitsstelle für das Volksbüchereiwesen, 1976); information from the family; Deutsches Literaturarchiv, Erwin Ackerknecht Collection, Ackerknecht to Dr. Georg Leyh, March 9, 1936.

22. *Biographisch Lexikon für Schleswig-Holstein und Lübeck* (Neumünster: Wachholtz, 1982), s.vv. Dähnhardt, Heinz; Berlin Documentation Center, Dähnhardt file.

23. Berlin Documentation Center, Heiligenstaedt file; Deutsches Literaturarchiv, Erwin Ackerknecht Collection, Ackerknecht to [Else] Mau, February 20, 1942.

24. Martin Broszat, *The Hitler State*, trans. John W. Hiden (London and New York: Longman, 1982), pp. 241–61. This low rate is in part attributable to the conservative, nationalistic bias of that profession.

25. Hannover, Stadtarchiv, SCO-8C, Preußische Ministerium für Wissenschaft, Kunst und Volksbildung, U II R Nr. 423.1, September 2, 1933.

26. Deutsches Literaturarchiv, Erwin Ackerknecht Collection, Ackerknecht to Schuster, September 8, 1933.

27. Interview with Lydia Gross, Kiel, May 8, 1984.

28. "Unseren jüdischen Kollegen, die unter dem Nationalsozialismus gelitten und das Leben verloren haben, zum Gedenken!" *Bucherei und Bildung* 4 (September 1952): 853–59.

29. Boese, *Das öffentliche Bibliothekwesen*, p. 206; Deutsches Literaturarchiv, Erwin Ackerknecht Collection, Ackerknecht to Leyh, July 26, 1934. Ackerknecht believed that the attacks on Fritz in 1933 had accelerated his death. There are many letters in both the Ackerknecht and Hofmann archives that touch on their respective dismissals. Fritz's removal is treated in Hans-Dieter Holzhausen, "Gottlieb Fritz und seine Entfernung aus dem Amt des Direktors der Berliner Stadtbibliothek 1933/34," in Vodosek and Komorowski, pp. 261–68.

30. This account is drawn from Bayerische Hauptstaatsarchiv, München, MK 41451; Rudolf Wille to [BSUK], September 28, 1935; Friedrich Welscher to Bezirksamt Rehau, July 7, 1933; Kath. Kuratie, Rehau, to Bezirksamt Rehau, September 12, 1933; Rudolf Wille to Bezirksamt Rehau, September 27, 1933; Ortsgruppenleiter Kummitzer to BSUK, October 11, 1933; Dr. Reismüller to BSUK, November 13, 1933; BSUK V 58852, to Regierung von Oberfranken und Mittelfranken, December 19, 1933; Dr. Moll to BSUK, March 14, 1934; MK 41452: BSUK V 13882 A.IV, May 3, 1934; Rudolf Wille to BSUK, May 23, 1934; Maurey, 1. Burgermeister Rehau, memo, May 27, 1934; Staatlichen Beratungsstelle für öffentliche Büchereien, Bayreuth, Rehau File, J[osef] W[utz] to Wille, June 25, 1936.

31. The special commissioner was formally a state official. In reality he was a party leader who acted independently of established channels. See Broszat, *The*

Hitler State, pp. 195–99. The struggle in Rehau is one example of the contest between state and party, although it is more obviously an opposition between the traditional way of doing things and the new style.

32. Wilhelm Schuster, "7. Jahresversammlung des Verbandes Deutscher Volksbibliothekare in Hannover vom 17.–19. September 1933," *BuB* 13 (1933): 342–44; Nordrhein-Westfälisches Staatsarchiv, Detmold, D III C Nr. 23 [1933], Dr. Schladebach, "Bücherei und Nationalsozialismus."

33. Deutsches Literaturarchiv, Erwin Ackerknecht Collection, Ackerknecht to Schuster, March 14, 1933.

34. "Satzung der Reichsschrifttumskammer," *DB* 1 (1934): 484–87.

35. Kurd Schulz, "8. Jahresversammlung des Verbandes Deutscher Volksbibliothekare in Danzig vom 24. bis 26. Mai 1934," *DB* 1 (1934): 282–88; Deutsches Literaturarchiv, Erwin Ackerknecht Collection, E. Saltzwedel to Ackerknecht, May 29, 1934; Fachhochschule für Bibliothekswesen, Stuttgart, Walter Hofmann Archiv, Rudolf Reuter to Hofmann, June 2, 1934.

36. Wilhelm Schuster, "Büchereipolitische Rationalisierung," *HfB* 16 (1932): 79.

37. Deutsches Literaturarchiv, Erwin Ackerknecht Collection, Ackerknecht to Schuster, May 17, 1933; Ackerknecht to Schriewer, July 26, 1940.

38. Deutsches Literaturarchiv, Erwin Ackerknecht Collection, Schuster to Ackerknecht, December 15, 1933; Nordrhein-Westfälisches Staatsarchiv, Detmold, D14 Nr. 168, Wiegand to Leweke, [1935 or 1936].

39. Deutsches Literaturarchiv, Erwin Ackerknecht Collection, Saltzwedel to Ackerknecht, June 4, 1935; Schriewer to Ackerknecht, November 5, 1934; Schuster to Ackerknecht, December 15, 1933; Schriewer to Ackerknecht, February 14, 1938.

40. Bundesarchiv, Koblenz, R56 v/140 *Die Bücherei*, advertising sheet; Staatsarchiv der Senat der Freien und Hansestadt Hamburg, Hamburger Öffentliche Bücherhallen, 12 Bd. 1, April 1931–December 1937, "Rundschreiben der Bücherhallenleitung, Nr. 25," June 3, 1935; Deutsches Literaturarchiv, Erwin Ackerknecht Collection, editor, *Die Bücherei*, to Mitarbeiter am Besprechungsteil der Zeitschrift "Die Bücherei," June 3, 1937.

41. [Franz Schriewer], "Zum neuen Jahrgang," *DB* 2 (1935): 1–3; [Hans Beyer], "Der Widerstand in den Büchereien," *Die Tat*, July 1934, pp. 314–16.

CHAPTER 4. THE NATIONAL ADMINISTRATIVE ORGANIZATION OF PUBLIC LIBRARIANSHIP

1. "Preußische Minister für Wissenschaft, Kunst und Volksbildung U II R Nr. 750.1, 28.12.33," *DB* 1 (1934): 11–13.

2. William Ebenstein, *The Nazi State* (1943; reprint New York: Octagon, 1975), pp. 45–52.

3. "Neuordnung des Büchereiwesens auch in Hessen," *DB* 1 (1934): 37; "Thüringische Landesstelle für volkstümliches Büchereiwesen," *DB* 1 (1934): 56–58; "Neuordnung des Volksbüchereiwesens in Sachsen," *DB* 1 (1934):

171–72; "Staatliche Neuordnung des Volksbüchereiwesens in Baden," *DB* 3 (1936): 427–29.

4. Deutsches Literaturarchiv, Erwin Ackerknecht Collection, Kurd Schulz to Ackerknecht, September 10, 1933.

5. Thauer and Vodosek, p. 80; Niedersächsisches Staatsarchiv, Wolfenbüttel, 12A Neu 13 19009, "An die Mitglieder der deutschen Zentralstelle für volkstümliches Büchereiwesen, Jahresversammlung 15. und 16. Januar 1931."

6. Boese, *Das öffentliche Bibliothekwesen*, p. 28; Deutsches Literaturarchiv, Erwin Ackerknecht Collection, Ackerknecht to Schuster, February 6, 1933; "Erklärung und Aufruf."

7. Boese, *Das öffentliche Bibliothekwesen*, p. 28.

8. Ibid., pp. 28–29; Andreas Kettel, *Volksbibliothekare und Nationalsozialismus* (Cologne: Pahl-Rugenstein, 1981), has a useful chronology, pp. 64–68. Fritz Heiligenstaedt and Carl Jansen, "Zur jüngsten Entwicklung im deutschen volkstümlichen Büchereiwesen," *Volksbücherei und Volksbildung in Niedersachsen* 13 (April/May 1933): 2–4, is a detailed account of the Berlin group's activities. The Schuster-Ackerknecht correspondence in the Deutsches Literaturarchiv, Erwin Ackerknecht Collection, is informative about Schuster's viewpoint because of his trust in Ackerknecht; see especially Schuster to Ackerknecht, May 2 and December 13, 1933.

9. Deutsches Literaturarchiv, Erwin Ackerknecht Collection, Schuster File, "Besprechung zwischen Prof. Bargheer (Kultusministerium) und Dr. Schuster und Dr. Herrmann (Verband deutscher Volksbibliothekare) vom 30.5.1933."

10. "Verordnung über die Aufgaben des Reichsministeriums für Volksaufklärung und Propaganda vom 30. Juni 1933," *Reichsgesetzblatt* 1 (1933): 449; Bundesarchiv, Koblenz, R 56 V/137, "Denkschrift betreffend Neubau des deutschen öffentlichen Büchereiwesens," by Karl Heinl, June 1933.

11. Jutta Sywottek, *Die Gleichschaltung der deutschen Volksbücherein 1933 bis 1937*, Archiv für Geschichte des Buchwesens, Band 24/1983, Lieferung 2 (Frankfurt am Main: Buchhändler-Vereinigung, 1983), cols. 504–13. Cols. 410–22 have an excellent account of this struggle; "Dokument 2: Karl Heinl: Denkschrift betreffend Neubau des deutschen öffentlichen Büchereiwesens, Juni 1933, Anlage I," in ibid., cols. 490–94; Bundesarchiv, Koblenz, R 56 V/166, Heinl, "Für die zuständige Eingliederung des Volksbüchereiwesens," June 19, 1934.

12. "Leitsätze, betreffend den Aufbau zentraler Organisationen im deutschen Volksbüchereiwesen," in Sywottek, cols. 505–13; Fachhochschule für Bibliothekswesen, Stuttgart, Walter Hofmann Archiv, Schuster to Hofmann, May 16, 1933; Hofmann to F. Heiligenstaedt, July 13, 1933.

13. "Dokument 6: Walter Hofmann: Leitsätze, betreffend den Aufbau zentraler Organisationen im deutschen Volksbüchereiwesen, 14.10.1933," in Sywottek.

14. Fachhochschule für Bibliothekswesen, Stuttgart, Walter Hofmann Archiv, Schuster to W. Hofmann, October 28, 1933.

15. Fachhochschule für Bibliothekswesen, Stuttgart, Walter Hofmann Archiv, W. Hofmann to W. Schuster, June 12, 1933; Deutsches Literaturarchiv, Erwin Ackerknecht Collection, Schuster file, B. A. Nr. 29133, Schuster, Beratender Ausschuß für das volkstümliches Büchereiwesen, to PMWKV, October 9, 1933.

16. Archives of the Zentralinstitut für Bibliothekswesen, Berlin, "Denkschrift zur gegenwärtigen Krise der deutschen Büchereipolitik," November 14, 1933.

17. For example, Walter Hofmann, *Die Lektüre der Frau* (Leipzig: Quelle und Meyer, 1931).

18. Fachhochschule für Bibliothekswesen, Stuttgart, Walter Hofmann Archiv, Schuster to Hofmann, June 14, 1933; [Hofmann] to Fritz Heiligenstaedt, April 27, 1933, labeled "Nicht abgegangen!"

19. "The Public Libraries Act, 1919," *Library Association Record* 22 (1919): 365–67; Erwin Ackerknecht, *Skandinavisches Büchereiwesen* (Stettin: Verlag Bücherei und Bildungspflege, 1932). Sywottek, *Die Gleichschaltung der deutschen Volksbüchereien 1933 bis 1937*, is an excellent summary of these complicated events.

20. Zentrales Staatsarchiv, Potsdam, 62 DAF 3, 19359, Bl. 46, clipping, *Hamburger Tageblatt*, May 16, 1933; Deutsches Literaturarchiv, Erwin Ackerknecht Collection, Heiligenstaedt to Ackerknecht, June 26, 1933; Ackerknecht to Heiligenstaedt, July 4, 1933.

21. "Dokument 7: Wilhelm Schuster: Entwurf für ein Büchereigesetz, 27.11.1933," in Sywottek, cols. 513–14.

22. Boese, *Das öffentliche Bibliothekwesen*, pp. 56–57.

23. Niedersächsisches Staatsarchiv, Wolfenbüttel, 12A Neu 13 19015, RWEV, Vd Nr. 237, March 2, 1935, attached conference proceedings, p. 12; RWEV, Vd Nr. 1192. I. 35, May 7, 1935, published in *DB* 2 (1935): 241; RWEV, Vd Nr. 2379/35, August 7, 1935, published in *DB* 2 (1935): 477.

24. Fachhochschule für Bibliothekswesen, Stuttgart, Walter Hofmann Archiv, Schuster to Hofmann, February 27, 1933.

25. Interview with Rudolf Joerden, Hamburg, June 19, 1984; Deutsches Literaturarchiv, Erwin Ackerknecht Collection, Schuster to Ackerknecht, December 13, 1933.

26. Ackerknecht to Meyer-Lülmann, April 18, 1934, quoted in Sywottek, col. 416.

27. Ackerknecht wrote to Schriewer that he hoped the time was not far distant when Hofmann could truly be regarded as an emeritus and the paper on which his theoretical pronouncements were published used in more practical ways; Deutsches Literaturarchiv, Erwin Ackerknecht Collection, Ackerknecht to Schriewer, January 9, 1939.

28. Deutsches Literaturarchiv, Erwin Ackerknecht Collection, Schriewer to Ackerknecht, August 4, 1934; Schriewer to Ackerknecht, October 3, 1936; Ackerknecht to Joerden, January 16, 1937; Schriewer to Ackerknecht, February 18, 1937.

29. Fachhochschule für Bibliothekswesen, Stuttgart, Walter Hofmann Archiv, [Reuter] to Walter Hofmann, May 18, 1935; Walter Hofmann to Reuter, June 23, 1936; Dähnhardt to Hofmann, June 25, 1935.

30. Deutsches Literaturarchiv, Erwin Ackerknecht Collection, Schuster, Beratender Ausschuß für das volkstümliches Büchereiwesen, to PMWKV, October 9, 1933, signed by Schuster.

31. Deutsches Literaturarchiv, Erwin Ackerknecht Collection, Ackerknecht to Joerden, September 12, 1935; Schuster to Ackerknecht, July 5, 1935.

32. Deutsches Literaturarchiv, Erwin Ackerknecht Collection, Schriewer to Ackerknecht, May 20, 1935, and Ackerknecht to Joerden, November 25, 1936; Staatliche Beratungsstelle für öffentliche Büchereien, Bayreuth [Staatliche Volksbüchereistelle, Bayreuth], to Dr. Schriewer, May 5, 1936.

33. Nordrhein-Westfälisches Staatsarchiv, Detmold, D 14 Nr. 169, B. Schladebach to Reichsstelle für volkstümliches Büchereiwesen, September 24, 1935.

34. Information from Schriewer family; letter from Jürgen Schriewer to Margaret Stieg, September 28, 1987; Deutsches Literaturarchiv, Erwin Ackerknecht Collection, Schriewer to Ackerknecht, December 1, 1936.

35. Fachhochschule für Bibliothekswesen, Stuttgart, Walter Hofmann Archiv, W. Hofmann to W. Herrmann, January 15, 1937, and June 17, 1935; Deutsches Literaturarchiv, Erwin Ackerknecht Collection, Ackerknecht to Joerden, January 16, 1937.

36. Bayerisches Hauptstaatsarchiv, München, MK 41453, "Die heutige Situation des deutschen Volksbüchereiwesens," [Fall 1936]; document given to author by Dietrich Vorwerk, copy of "Entwurf von Dr. Herrmann," undated.

37. Deutsches Literaturarchiv, Erwin Ackerknecht Collection, Ackerknecht to Joerden, December 8, 1936; Joerden to Ackerknecht, January 4, 1937; interview with Dietrich Vorwerk, Villingen, July 25, 1985.

38. Deutsches Literaturarchiv, Erwin Ackerknecht Collection, Joerden to [Ackerknecht], August 19, 1937; Ackerknecht to [Else] Mau, February 20, 1942; Ackerknecht to [Else] Mau, January 20, 1942; interview with Dietrich Vorwerk, Villingen, July 25, 1985.

39. "Richtlinien für das Volksbüchereiwesen, RWEV Vb 2799, 26. Oktober 1937," *DB* 5 (1938): 39–44; [Heinz] Dähnhardt, "Richtlinien für das Volksbüchereiwesen," *DB* 5 (1938): 130–36.

40. Bayerisches Hauptstaatsarchiv, München, MK 41453, "Die heutige Situation des deutschen Volksbüchereiwesens," [Fall 1936]; Deutsches Literaturarchiv, Erwin Ackerknecht Collection, Ackerknecht to Heiligenstaedt, August 24, 1940; Heiligenstaedt to Ackerknecht, August 27, 1940.

41. Staatliche Beratungsstelle für öffentliche Büchereien (Staatliche Volksbüchereistelle), Bayreuth, Heiligenstaedt to Josef Wutz, February 16, 1938.

42. Generallandesarchiv, Karlsruhe, 235/6811 Konstanz, Mager, Oberbürgermeister to Ministerium für Kultus und Unterricht, September 3, 1940.

43. Bayerisches Hauptstaatsarchiv, München, MK 41473, RWEV Vb Nr. 512, Karstin to Bayerische Staatsministerium für Unterricht und Kultus, March 1, 1938, Abschrift; Städtische Büchereien, Wien, Abschrift zu [RWEV] Vb Nr. 1679/41.

44. Nordrhein-Westfälisches Staatsarchiv, Detmold, D 14 Nr. 119, "Besprechung über die Arbeitsplanung der Staatlichen Volksbüchereistelle, Hagen, am 29.11.1937"; M 1 1 Ju Nr. 54, Der Regierungspräsident, II M 4969, December 22, 1937.

45. Niedersächsisches Staatsarchiv, Wolfenbüttel, 12A Neu 13 19015, RWEV, Vd Nr. 237, March 2, 1935, attached conference proceedings, p. 11.

CHAPTER 5. LIBRARY COLLECTIONS AND COLLECTION POLICY

1. An excellent, detailed account of literary control in the Third Reich is Strothmann, *Nationalsozialistische Literaturpolitik.*

2. Harold Brodkey, "Reading, the Most Dangerous Game," *New York Times Book Review,* November 24, 1985, pp. 1, 44–45.

3. Fachhochschule für Bibliothekswesen, Stuttgart, Walter Hofmann Archiv, Walter Hofmann to W. Schuster, February 24, 1933. Posters in preparation for the May book burnings called for students and citizens to "cleanse your public libraries." A Würzburg poster is reproduced in Gerhard Sauder, ed., *Die Bücherverbrennung zum 10. Mai 1933* (Munich, Vienna: Carl Hanser Verlag, 1983), p. 159. At this time the *Völkischer Beobachter* also ran almost daily a section titled "A Cultural Chamber of Horrors."

4. The term usually used was *Säuberung*, meaning cleaning or purging.

5. Erwin Ackerknecht, "Bücherei und Politik," in *BuB.* For a more detailed description of pre-Nazi collection values see Stieg, "The Richtungsstreit" and Boese, *Das öffentliche Bibliothekswesen*, pp. 215–22.

6. Gertrud E. Kallmann, "German Public Libraries and Their Principles of Book Selection," *Library Association Record* 1, ser. 4 (1934): 169–72.

7. Ibid., p. 172.

8. Christa Kamenetsky, *Children's Literature in Hitler's Germany: The Cultural Policy of National Socialism* (Athens, Ohio, and London: Ohio University Press, 1984) is a description of how these policies were applied to children's books.

9. Margaret F. Stieg, "The 1926 German Law to Protect Youth against Smut: Moral Protectionism in a Democracy," *Central European History* 23 (March 1990): 22–56.

10. Nordrhein-Westfälisches Staatsarchiv, Detmold, M1 1 JU Nr. 148, Angermann to Hrn. Regierungspräsident, October 20, 1933, "Reinigung und Neuaufbau der Volksbüchereien."

11. Kallmann, "German Public Libraries," p. 172.

12. Dietrich Aigner, "Die Indizierung 'schädlichen und unerwünschten Schrifttums' im Dritten Reich," *Archiv für Geschichte des Büchereiwesens* 11 (1971): cols. 983–1002.

13. Fachhochschule für Bibliothekswesen, Stuttgart, Walter Hofmann Archiv, "Zur Weltanschauungsfrage in den Städtischen Bücherhallen," Entwurf, dated March 19, 1933.

14. Engelbrecht Boese, "Die Säuberung der Leipziger Bücherhallen 1933–1936," *Buch und Bibliothek* 35 (1983): 283–96; Walter Hofmann, *Die deutsche Volksbücherei: Die Idee und die Aufgabe, das Werk und die Werkleute* (Bayreuth: Gauverlag Bayerische Ostmark, 1934), p. 13; Walter Hofmann, *Der Weg zum Schrifttum* (Berlin: Verlag der Arbeitsgemeinschaft, 1926), p. 121; quoted in Hofmann, *Die deutsche Volksbücherei,* p. 21; Walter Hofmann, "Die Organisation des Ausleihdienstes in der modernen Bildungsbibliotheke, III. Die Organisation," *Volksbildungsarchiv* 3 (1913): 32–33.

15. Boese, "Die Säuberung der Leipziger Bücherhallen 1933–1936," p. 284; Fachhochschule für Bibliothekswesen, Stuttgart, Walter Hofmann Archiv, Walter Hofmann to Reuter, May 12, 1933.

16. Fachhochschule für Bibliothekswesen, Stuttgart, Walter Hofmann Archiv, Rudolf Reuter to Walter Hofmann, July 19, 1933.

17. For this detailed information about Metelmann's difficulties, I am indebted to Dr. Karl-Heinz Jügelt, director of the library of the University of Rostock, who generously shared the results of his own research with me.

18. Deutsches Literaturarchiv, Erwin Ackerknecht Collection, Ackerknecht to Dr. Grabow, Oberbürgermeister, Memel, February 12, 1932; Ackerknecht to Beer, February 20, 1932.

19. Völker Dahn, "Die nationalsozialistische Schrifttumspolitik nach dem 10. Mai 1933," in Ulrich Walberer, ed., *10. Mai 1933: Bücherverbrennung in Deutschland und die Folgen* (Frankfurt am Main: Fischer Taschenbuch Verlag, 1983), p. 57.

20. Sywottek, col. 438; Aigner, col. 938; Manfred H. Niessen, "Wie es zu den Bücherverbrennungen kam," in Walberer, p. 26; Deutsches Literaturarchiv, Erwin Ackerknecht Collection, from Rita Demme, clipping from *Gen. Anz.*, February 6, 1933.

21. "Erklärung und Aufruf" in Andrae, *Volksbücherei und Nationalsozialismus*, pp. 52–56. It was originally published both in *HfB* 10 (1932/33) and *BuB* 13 (1933).

22. Wolfgang Herrmann, "Prinzipielles zur Säuberung der öffentlichen Büchereien," *Börsenblatt für den deutschen Buchhandel* 100 (May 16, 1933): 356–58.

23. Deutsches Literaturarchiv, Erwin Ackerknecht Collection, Ackerknecht to Gertrud Freuer, April 7, 1933.

24. Stadtarchiv, Duisburg, 401/3, copy, Fraktion Kampffront Schwarz-Weiss-Rot to Oberbürgermeister Duisburg, April 24, 1933; Deutsches Literaturarchiv, Erwin Ackerknecht Collection, Ackerknecht to Gertrud Freuer, April 7, 1933.

25. Staatsarchiv der Senat der Freien und Hansestadt Hamburg, Hamburger Öffentliche Bücherhallen, 3 Band 1, 24. Leitersitzung, am Sonnabend, for March 18, 1933.

26. Durlach is in Baden, which was not Prussian territory. It is clear that the Prussian decrees were being used as models.

27. Karlsruhe, Stadtbibliothek, Archiv, unlabeled file I Durlach, Volksbücherei, Bürgermeister to Bibliothekar Letzelter, April 15, 1933; Joseph Letzelter to Gebietsführer, HJ, May 14, 1933; Joseph Letzelter to Bürgermeister, Stadt Durlach, June 30, 1933; newspaper clipping, July 13, 1933.

28. The fiftieth anniversary of the book burnings stimulated research and produced an abundance of publications on the topic. Among the most important is *10. Mai 1933: Bücherverbrennung in Deutschland und die Folgen*, ed. by Ulrich Walberer, which includes a revised edition of Hans-Wolfgang Strätz's indispensable analysis of its organization, originally published as "Die studentische 'Aktion wider den undeutschen Geist' im Frühjahr 1933," *Vierteljahrshefte für Zeitgeschichte* 16 (October 1968): 347–72. The collection of documentary material edited by Gerhard Sauder, *Die Bücherverbrennung zum 10. Mai 1933*, is especially useful as is *"Das war ein Vorspiel nur . . . ," Bücherverbrennung Deutschland 1933: Voraussetzungen und Folgen* (Berlin, Vienna: Medusa, 1983).

29. Strätz, p. 354; "Wider den undeutschen Geist!" in Sauder, pp. 93–94.

30. Hans-Wolfgang Strätz, "Die geistige SA rückt ein," in Walberer, p. 98.

31. Stephan Füssel, "'Wider den undeutschen Geist': Bücherverbrennung und Bibliothekslenkung im Nationalsozialismus," in *Göttingen unterm Hakenkreuz: Nationalsozialistischer Alltag in einer deutschen Stadt, Texte und Materialien* (Göttingen, 1983), pp. 95–104.

32. Erich Kästner, "Die Verbrennung meiner Bücher," in Walberer, pp. 138–39; Oskar Maria Graf, "Verbrennt mich!" in Sauder, pp. 285–86, orig. pub. in *Volksstimme* (Saarbrücken) May 15, 1933; *New York Times*, May 10, 1933, 1:4, 10:2, 11:2, May 11, 1933, 1:1, 10:2, May 13, 7:4.

33. The instructions issued by the Hauptamt of the Deutsche Studentenschaft made it clear that the burden of real purification was not on these burnings: "Because it won't be possible to burn all the books, a limitation to the following list of writings is appropriate."

34. Strothmann, pp. 218–19.

35. Aigner, cols. 983–84.

36. Strothmann, pp. 218–20.

37. Aigner, cols. 983–84.

38. "Ungeeignetheit von Prachtwerken für Volksbüchereien: RWEV, Vd 2164/35, 29. Juli 1935," *DB* 2 (1935): 478; Nordrhein-Westfälisches Staatsarchiv, Detmold, D 14 Nr. 128, Preußische Landesstelle für volkstümliches Büchereiwesen, Rundschreiben Nr. 3/35, July 13, 1935.

39. Nordrhein-Westfälisches Hauptstaatsarchiv, Düsseldorf, Zweigarchiv Schloss Kalkum, Kunst-, Kultur-, und Heimatpflege; Erwachsenenbildung; BR 1004/815, Staatliche Volksbüchereistelle für den Regierungsbezirk Düsseldorf, September 29, 1941, to the Leiter der Volksbüchereien in den Regierungsbezirk Düsseldorf; Staatsarchiv der Senat der Freien und Hansestadt Hamburg, Hamburger Öffentliche Bücherhallen, 12 Band 3, Rundschreiben der Bücherhallenleitung, Nr. 107, June 3, 1940; Band 15, Indiziertes Schrifttum im Dritten Reich, 1934–1944, Reichsstelle für Volksbüchereiwesen, Rundschreiben Nr. 40/24/19, May 24, 1940.

40. Staatsarchiv der Senat der Freien und Hansestadt Hamburg, Hamburger Öffentliche Bücherhallen, 15, Indiziertes Schrifttum im Dritten Reich, 1934–1944, Reichsstelle für das Volksbüchereiwesen, Sonderrundschreiben, November 11, 1937; Nordrhein-Westfälisches Staatsarchiv, Detmold, D 14 Nr. 103, Heinrich Breenkotter to Dr. [Angermann], November 18, 1934, and [Rudolf Angermann] to Heinrich Breenkotter, November 19, 1934.

41. Nordrhein-Westfälisches Staatsarchiv, Detmold, M1 1 JU Nr. 148, Angermann to Hrn. Regierungspräsident, October 20, 1933, "Reinigung und Neuaufbau der Volksbüchereien"; Generallandesarchiv, Karlsruhe, Badisches Ministerium des Kultus und Unterrichts, Künste und Wissenschaften, 235/6567, Gauschulungsamt der NSDAP, Abteilung Volksbüchereien, Rundschreiben 14/35, September 19, 1935; Stadtarchiv, Hannover, XC1-10, Ausgesonderte und agbegebene [sic] Bücher der Städt. Volksbücherei, Calenbergstr. 37, March 1933; Fachhochschule für Bibliothekswesen, Stuttgart, Walter Hofmann Archiv, Walter Hofmann to Dähnhardt, December 2, 1936.

42. Stadtarchiv, Saarbrücken, G. Nr. 6419/1, Dr. Gerber, Stadtbücherei, to Dr. Gaudig, April 5, 1938; Nordrhein-Westfälisches Staatsarchiv, Detmold, D 14

Nr. 169, Dr. B. Schladebach to Reichsstelle zur Förderung des deutschen Schrifttums, February 18, 1938.

43. Interview, Anneliese Benneman, Duisburg, June 26, 1984.

44. Niedersächsisches Staatsarchiv, Wolfenbüttel, 12 A Neu 13 19014, "Neuordnung des Volksbüchereiwesens im Lande Branschweig und seine Finanzierung [1935]."

45. "Säuberung des Buchbestandes: RWEV Vd Nr. 2439 M, 14. Aug. 1935," *DB* 2 (1935): 479; Rudolf Angermann, "Säuberung nach der Säuberung: Eine dringende Aufgabe," *DB* 2 (1935): 281–83; Nordrhein-Westfälisches Staatsarchiv, Detmold, D 14 Nr. 128, Preußische Landesstelle für volkstümliches Büchereiwesen, Rundschreiben Nr. 4135, July 23, 1935.

46. Nordrhein-Westfälisches Staatsarchiv, Detmold, D 14 Nr. 119, Staatliche Volksbüchereistelle für die Provinz Westfalen to Hrn. Dr. Kratky, October 3, 1935; Staatliche Büchereistelle für den Regierungsbezirk Detmold, "Jahresberichten 1936/37 der Staatlichen Volksbüchereistelle für das Land Lippe"; D 14 Nr. 194, Dr. Wiegand to Herrn Bürgermeister Wedderwille, Barntrup, November 12, 1935; Wedderwille, Bericht, August 8, 1936.

47. Bayerisches Hauptstaatsarchiv, München, MK 41452, Staatliches Ministerium für Unterricht und Kultus to Herrn Reichs u. Preuß. Minister für Wissenschaft, Erziehung und Volksbildung, January 31, 1936; Staatsarchiv der Senat der Freien und Hansestadt Hamburg, Hamburger Öffentliche Bücherhallen, Band 15, Indiziertes Schrifttum im Dritten Reich, 1934–1944, RWEV Vb 2319/36, W5, May 10, 1937.

48. *"Das war ein Vorspiel nur . . . ,"* pp. 277–303; Raimund Kast, "Die Leihbibliotheken im Nationalsozialismus," in Vodosek and Komorowski, pp. 522–25.

49. These figures were calculated using the statistics in Germany, Statistisches Reichsamt, *Die deutschen Volksbüchereien nach Ländern, Provinzen und Gemeinden 1933/34*, and Rudolf Lawin, "Die Volksbüchereien der deutschen Gemeinden," *Gemeinde und Statistik*, Suppl. 5, 1939, to *Der Gemeindetag*. Lawin includes the very useful figure, books acquired since 1933.

For comparative purposes it is of interest to note that in 1937/38 the average annual rate of weeding in U.S. libraries serving communities of over 200,000 was between 5 and 6 percent. In all probability that 5–6 percent would have been a relatively high figure for the 1930s, as library budgets improved and librarians could discard more fully in anticipation of new money. "General and Salary Statistics—Public Libraries Serving More Than 200,000 Population," *Bulletin of the American Library Association* 33 (April 1939): 279.

50. *Jahresbericht der Stadtbüchereien und Städt. Lesehalle zu Hannover für das Jahr 1933/34, . . . 1934/35, . . . 1935/36*; Nordrhein-Westfälisches Staatsarchiv, Detmold, D 14 Nr. 103, H. Breenkotter to Staatliche Beratungsstelle für das Öffentliche Büchereiwesen in der Provinz Westfalen, March 4, 1936; Staatsarchiv der Senat der Freien und Hansestadt Hamburg, Hamburger Öffentliche Bücherhallen, 13, Jahresstatistik 1936; Boese, *Das öffentliche Bibliothekswesen*, p. 232; Boese, "Die Säuberung der Leipziger Bücherhallen 1933–1936," p. 294; Germany, Statistisches Reichsamt, *Die deutschen Volksbüchereien nach Ländern*,

Provinzen und Gemeinden 1933/34; Zentrales Staatsarchiv, Potsdam, 62 DAF 3, 19359, B1. 44. *N.S.K.*, June 10, 1933.

51. *"Das war ein Vorspiel nur . . . ,"* p. 171.

52. Stadtarchiv, Freiburg im Breisgau, V/33/2, 1920/34, "Protokoll der Sitzung des Volksbibliotheksausschuß . . . ," April 6, 1933.

53. Boese, *Das öffentliche Bibliothekswesen*, p. 236.

54. "Erklärung und Aufruf."

55. Nordrhein-Westfälisches Staatsarchiv, Detmold, D 14 Nr. 122, [Beratungsstelle, Hagen] to Hrn. Stadtvorsteher, Halle i/W., October 10, 1931; D 14 Nr. 184, Dr. B. Schladebach to Lehrer Brokhausen, Bösingfeld, June 23, 1938; Staatliche Beratungsstelle für öffentliche Büchereien, Bayreuth [Staatliche Volksbüchereistelle, Bayreuth], to Leiter, Städtische Volksbücherei, Hof, December 23, 1936.

56. Staatsarchiv der Senat der Freien und Hansestadt Hamburg, Hamburger Öffentliche Bücherhallen, 12 Band 4, Gesichtspunkte für die Aufertigung von Buchbesprechungen, January 1934; Nordrhein-Westfälisches Staatsarchiv, Detmold, D 14 Nr. 155, *Bauernpsalm: von Felix Timmermans*; Peter Langendorf, "Die neuen Maßstäbe bei der Buchauswahl in der politisch-historischen Literatur," *DB* 1 (1934): 281.

57. Carl Jansen, "Nationalpolitisches Schrifttum," *Volksbücherei und Volksbildung im Niedersachsen* 13 (1933): 27–31; Nordrhein-Westfälisches Staatsarchiv, Detmold, D 14 Nr. 1915 #2, Auswahlliste der Staatliche Volksbüchereistelle für das Land Lippe.

58. Herrmann, "Der neue Nationalismus und seine Literatur."

59. Jansen, "Nationalpolitisches Schrifttum," pp. 29–31; Strothmann, pp. 235–38.

60. Germany, Reichsstelle zur Förderung des deutschen Schrifttums, *Die ersten hundert Bücher für nationalsozialistische Büchereien*, 6th ed. (Munich: Zentralverlag der N.S.D.A.P., Franz Eher Nachfolger, n.d.); Germany, Reichsstelle für das Volksbüchereiwesen, *Reichsliste für kleinere städtische Büchereien*, 2d ed. (Leipzig: Einkaufshaus für Büchereien, 1939).

61. Stadtarchiv, Freiburg im Breisgau, V/33/4 Betrieb der Volksbibliothek, 1934/39, Carl Ehrmann to Oberbürgermeister Dr. Kerber, March 9, 1936; Stadtarchiv, Hannover, XC1-34, mimeographed letter from Börsenverein der deutschen Buchhändler to Magistrat der Stadt Hannover, May 11, 1933; "Das Einkaufshaus für Büchereien in Leipzig," *DB* 1 (1934): 392; "Regelung der Skontogewahrung an volkstümliche Büchereien," *DB* 1 (1934): 170–71; Nordrhein-Westfälisches Staatsarchiv, Detmold, M1 1 JU Nr. 54, RWEV Vd Nr. 1151 II, June 11, 1936.

62. Staatliche Beratungsstelle für öffentliche Büchereien, Bayreuth, Tirschenreuth, Meyer, Bürgermeister, to Staatliche Grenzbüchereistelle, October 30, 1936.

63. Staatsarchiv der Senat der Freien und Hansestadt Hamburg, Hamburger Öffentliche Bücherhallen, 3 Band 1, 24. Leitersitzung, am Sonnabend, for March 18, 1933; 3 Band 1, "Zurückgestellte Bücher" (attachment to 18. III. 1933. Protokolle).

64. Staatsarchiv der Senat der Freien und Hansestadt Hamburg, Hamburger Öffentliche Bücherhallen, File 14, "Umstellung der Hamburger Öffentliche Bücherhalle auf die Grundsätze und Erfordernisse der nationalsozialistischen Weltanschauung," December 10, 1935.

65. "Erklärung und Aufruf" (in Andrae), p. 55; Karlsruhe, Stadtbibliothek, Archiv, unlabeled file I Durlach, [Letzelter to Bürgermeister], April 21, 1933, copy; interview, Dietrich Vorwerk, Villingen, July 25, 1985; interview, Erika Joerden, Hamburg, June 19, 1984.

66. Deutsches Literaturarchiv, Erwin Ackerknecht Collection, Wilhelm Schuster to Ackerknecht, May 21, 1933; Fachhochschule für Bibliothekswesen, Stuttgart, Walter Hofmann Archiv, Rudolf Reuter to Walter Hofmann, July 19, 1933.

67. *New York Times*, May 11, 1933, p. 1; "An die Deutsche Studentenschaft," in Sauder, pp. 94–95.

68. The German fiscal year ran from April 1 to March 31 so 1932/33 was really very little influenced by posttakeover action.

69. *Jahresbericht der Stadtbüchereien und Städt. Lesehalle zu Hannover für das Jahr 1932/33, . . . 1933/34, . . . 1934/35, . . . 1935/36, . . . 1936/37; 50 Jahre Stadtbücherei Lingen (E-MS)*; Hansjörg Suberkrub, *Die Stadtbücherei Kiel* (Kiel: n.p., 1954); Deutsches Literaturarchiv, Erwin Ackerknecht Collection, Ackerknecht to Kurd Schulz, April 3, 1933.

70. Lotte Bergtel-Schleif, "Möglichkeiten volksbibliothekarischer Arbeit unter dem Nationalsozialismus," *Der Volksbibliothekar* 1 (April 1947): 196.

71. Hans Beyer, "Schrifttum das wir ablehnen," *DB* 1 (1934): 258.

CHAPTER 6. THE PROVINCIAL BERATUNGSSTELLEN

1. "Richtlinien für Aufbau und Arbeit der staatlichen Büchereiberatungsstellen: Vorbemerkung," *DB* 1 (1934): 30–33, a printed version of PMWKV U II R Nr. 169, May 2, 1934; "Richtlinien für das Volksbüchereiwesen; RWEV Vb 2799, 26. Oktober 1937," *DB* 5 (1938): 39–44. In its typically independent fashion, Bavaria felt it necessary to confirm and publish local Richtlinien "for the completion of the Reich Richtlinien of 1937": *Bayerischer Regierungsanzeiger* 162, June 11, 1938.

2. A detailed contemporary account of the Beratungsstellen is Franz Schriewer, *Die staatlichen Volksbüchereistellen im Aufbau des deutschen Volksbüchereiwesens* (Leipzig: Einkaufshaus für Büchereien, 1938). The statement about Westphalia's Beratungsstelle is from the Erlaß that Schriewer cited on p. 29.

3. Bayerisches Hauptstaatsarchiv, München, MK 41453, "Die heutige Situation des deutschen Volksbüchereiwesens," p. 6; Schriewer, *Die staatlichen Volksbüchereistellen*, pp. 16–38; Dokument 3: Wilhelm Schuster: Die Neuordnung des ländlichen Beratungsstellen wesens . . . , 4. 10.1933 (BA R 36/2357)," in Sywottek, col. 497. At one point the tiny Lippe Beratungsstelle sought to "cooperate" with the Hanover Beratungsstelle rather than the geographically closer Hagen Beratungsstelle because Hanover's publication gave such important help and be-

cause it had the same, non-Leipzig viewpoint. Nordrhein-Westfälisches Staatsarchiv, Detmold, D 14 Nr. 168, Wiegand to Alfred Meyer, March 1, 1943.

4. "Dokument 3: Wilhelm Schuster: Die Neuordnung des ländlichen Beratungsstellenwesens" and "Dokument 4: Wilhelm Schuster: Die Einrichtung Staatlicher Beratungsstellen in den Städten uber 20 000 Einwohner, 4.10.1933 (BA Nr. 23/33)," in Sywottek, cols. 494–500.

5. PMWKV, U II R Nr. 750.1, December 28, 1933, published in *DB* 1 (1934): 11–13; Schriewer, *Die staatlichen Volksbüchereistellen*, pp. 23–38.

6. Staatsarchiv, Bremen, 3.S.19. Nr. 154 [9], "Neuordnung zur Einrichtung einer staatlichen Beratungsstelle für das Volksbüchereiwesen vom 3.5.34"; Nordrhein-Westfälisches Staatsarchiv, Detmold, D 14 Nr. 169, Wiegand to Verband deutscher Volksbibliothekare, June 28, 1935.

7. Bayerisches Hauptstaatsarchiv, München, MK 41461, Willy Pfeiffer, Lebenslauf, December 28, 1935.

8. Bayerisches Hauptstaatsarchiv, München, MK 41452, Moll to RWEV, July 10, 1934.

9. Bayerisches Hauptstaatsarchiv, München, MK 41467, "Bayerische Staatsbibliothek, Bericht der Direktion vom 15. Nov. 1934," and MK 41467, MK 41468, Wutz, undated, untitled statement from mid-1935.

10. Bayerisches Hauptstaatsarchiv, München, MK 41467, untitled statement, probably December 21, 1934.

11. Bayerisches Hauptstaatsarchiv, München, MK 41467, SMUK. Nr. V 3098, January 19, 1935.

12. Bayerisches Hauptstaatsarchiv, München, MK 41468, Wutz to Boepple, November 26, 1935; Kurt Wiegand, "50 Jahre Beratungsstelle in Bayreuth," *Die Neue Bücherei* (1986): 116.

13. Bayerisches Hauptstaatsarchiv, München, MK 41452, Moll to RWEV, July 10, 1934; MK 41467, untitled statement, probably December 21, 1934.

14. Bayerisches Hauptstaatsarchiv, München, MK 41468, Wutz to Boepple, November 26, 1935; MK 41467, untitled statement, probably December 21, 1934.

15. Bayerisches Hauptstaatsarchiv, München, MK 41467, Josef Wutz to Staatsministerium für Unterricht und Kultus, February 3, 1935; MK 41467, untitled statement, probably December 21, 1934; Deutsches Literaturarchiv, Erwin Ackerknecht Collection, Gretl [Margarete] Schmeer to [Ackerknecht], February 5, 1935.

16. Bayerisches Hauptstaatsarchiv, München, MK 41467, W. Scheffen to Boepple, November 14, 1934.

17. Deutsches Literaturarchiv, Erwin Ackerknecht Collection, Gretl [Margarete] Schmeer to [Ackerknecht], February 5, 1935; Bayerisches Hauptstaatsarchiv, München, MK 41468, Ruckdeschel to SMUK, May 2, 1935.

18. Stadtarchiv, Freiburg im Breisgau, V/34/4, Harden-Rauch to Oberbürgermeister, Freiburg, May 12, 1934. For a detailed account of the Freiburg Beratungsstelle and its activities in the Third Reich see Konrad Heyde, "Die staatlichen Volksbüchereistellen am Beispiel Freiburg im Breisgau," in Vodosek and Komorowski, pp. 113–56.

19. Generallandesarchiv, Karlsruhe, 235/6776, Deutscher Gemeindetag, Landesdienststelle Baden, to [Badisches] Ministerium des Kultus und Unterrichts, February 6, 1935; Stadtarchiv, Freiburg im Breisgau, V/34/4, Harden-Rauch to Oberbürgermeister, December 5, 1934.

20. Stadtarchiv, Freiburg im Breisgau, V/34/4, Harden-Rauch to Oberbürgermeister, November 6, December 5, and May 12, 1934, January 22 and 28, and March 14, 1935; Generallandesarchiv, Karlsruhe, 235/6776, Gauschulungsamt NSDAP, Abt. Vbn. to [Badisches] Ministerium des Kultus und Unterrichts, April 5, 1935; 233/27961, [Badisches] Ministerium des Kultus und Unterrichts to Staatsministerium, March 13, 1936; "Satzung für die Badische Landesstelle für das Volksbüchereiwesen," *Amtsblatt des Badischen Ministeriums des Kultus und Unterrichts*, June 20, 1936. Harden-Rauch's official appointment by the party was dated March 1935, but he was functioning as if he were the director of provincial public library service as early as January.

21. Bayerisches Hauptstaatsarchiv, München, MK 41456, Boepple to Staatliche Volksbüchereistelle, September 10, 1938; Nordrhein-Westfälisches Staatsarchiv, Detmold, D 14 Nr. 148, Dähnhardt to Rang, February 15, 1941.

22. Nordrhein-Westfälisches Staatsarchiv, Detmold, M 1 II B Nr. 4437, Rang to Regierungspräsident, Minden, December 8, 1941.

23. Bayerisches Hauptstaatsarchiv, München, MK 41456, Boepple to Staatliche Volksbüchereistelle, in München, September 10, 1938; Herm. Sauter to Bayerische Staatsministerium für Unterricht und Kultus, September 20, 1938; Boepple to Gauleitung Franken der NSDAP, May 31, 1939.

24. Niedersächsisches Staatsarchiv, Wolfenbüttel, 12A Neu 13 19015, RWEV, Vd Nr. 237, March 2, 1935, attached conference proceedings; "Richtlinien für Ausbau und Arbeit . . .", and "Richtlinien für das Volksbüchereiwesen."

25. Schriewer, *Die staatlichen Volksbüchereistellen*, pp. 51–55.

26. Deutsches Literaturarchiv, Erwin Ackerknecht Collection, Gertrud Schmidt to Ackerknecht, May 8, 1938; Nordrhein-Westfälisches Hauptstaatsarchiv, Düsseldorf, BR 1004/790, Oberbürgermeister, Düsseldorf, to Regierungspräsident, Düsseldorf, 31 Nr. 1660/34, October 11, 1934.

27. "Richtlinien für das Volksbüchereiwesen."

28. Ibid.

29. Nordrhein-Westfälisches Hauptstaatsarchiv, Düsseldorf, BR 1004/804, "Aus der Arbeit der Beratungsstelle," 1936/37.

30. Bayerisches Hauptstaatsarchiv, München, MK 41474, "Arbeitsbesprechung mit dem Leiter der Staatlichen Volksbüchereistelle in München . . . ," July 15, 1938.

31. Bayerisches Hauptstaatsarchiv, München, MK 41475, "Bericht über die Zusammenarbeit mit der Reisebuchhandlung H. Graf-Augsburg," January 24, 1940; MK 41474, Hanns Graf to H. Sauter, March 30, 1938; MK 41474, Heiligenstaedt to Diederich, August 1, 1938.

32. Nordrhein-Westfälisches Hauptstaatsarchiv, Detmold, D 14 Nr. 128, RV Rundschreiben Nr. 18/38, June 21, 1938; D 14 Nr. 185, "Besichtigungsfahrt am 13. Marz 1941"; Staatliche Beratungsstelle für öffentliche Büchereien, Bayreuth (for example, "Schwarzenbach/Salle Überprufungs-Bericht, 25.–30.6.41").

33. Nordrhein-Westfälisches Hauptstaatsarchiv, Detmold, D 14, Nr. 35, "Aktennotiz Kirchborchen, Besuch in der dortigen Bücherei am 8.11.45."

34. Karl Taupitz, "Der Aufbau des Büchereiwesens in Sachsen seit der nationalsozialistischen Revolution," *DB* 4 (1937): 247; Nordrhein-Westfälisches Staatsarchiv, Detmold, D 14 Nr. 169, Wiegand to Meier, August 3, 1938.

35. Niedersächsisches Staatsarchiv, Wolfenbüttel, 12 A Neu 13 19014, Voigt to [Braunschweigisches] Ministerium für Volksbildung, November 18, 1937.

36. Nordrhein-Westfälisches Staatsarchiv, Detmold, D 14 Nr. 185, Blomberg, July 17, 1942. The very small Beratungsstelle of Schaumburg-Lippe stated in its annual report for 1939/40 that it did *not* provide technical help to libraries.

37. Nordrhein-Westfälisches Staatsarchiv, Detmold, D 14 Nr. 128, RV Rundschreiben Nr. 18138, June 21, 1938; Bayerisches Hauptstaatsarchiv, München, MK 41468, Wutz to BSUK, October 26, 1937, Anlage I.

38. "Richtlinien für das Volksbüchereiwesen"; Niedersächsisches Staatsarchiv, Wolfenbüttel, 12 A Neu 13 19011, *passim.*

39. Bayerisches Hauptstaatsarchiv, München, MK 41473, RWEV Vb Nr. 512, Baudissin to BSUK, March 1, 1938.

CHAPTER 7. THE LIBRARY DEVELOPMENT PROGRAM

1. Germany, Statistisches Reichsamt, *Die deutschen Volksbüchereien nach Ländern, Provinzen und Gemeinden 1933/34,* "Deutsches Reich," pp. 8–9; *Handbuch der deutschen Volksbüchereien* (1940), "Neugründungen," pp. 187–89, "Gesamtübersicht und Schlußzahlen," pp. 190–91; *Handbuch der deutschen Volksbüchereien; Nachtrag zum ... 1938–40,* "Neugründungen" (Leipzig: Einkaufshaus für Büchereien, 1940), pp. 70–71. The calculations that follow are based largely on information in these two compilations. Some additional information is taken from Lawin, "Die Volksbüchereien der deutschen Gemeinden."

The reliability of the raw figures cannot be verified, and they may well be overstated. For example, the 1940 *Handbuch* indicates that as of March 3, 1938, Germany had 9,765 libraries serving 41,337,792 people at a cost of RM 10,119,245, an outlay of RM 0.245 per individual served. The *Nachtrag*, published the same year but covering a later period, gives the same figures for libraries and individuals served but claims an expenditure of RM 11,484,885, or RM 0.28 per individual served. The figures are, however, almost certainly true for the relative positions they indicate.

It should be noted that many German figures are given as for 1933/34 or 1935/36. They in fact represent only one year; the German fiscal year ran from April 1 to the following March 31.

2. Schriewer, *Die staatlichen Volksbüchereistellen,* p. 18. The phrase was actually "Jedes Schuldorf eine Volksbücherei," or "for every school village, a public library." By law, every village of five hundred people was supposed to have its own school. This objective was first stated in PMWKV U II R Nr. 169, May 2, 1934, and became the slogan of the development program.

3. The main source of funding of the Beratungsstellen were their provincial administrations, but they also dispensed occasional special monies from the RWEV and, if they were located on the border, the Grenzbüchereidienst.

4. Germany, *Reichsgesetzblatt,* January 30, 1935, p. 49.

5. Staatsarchiv der Senat der Freien und Hansestadt Hamburg, Hamburger

Öffentliche Bücherhallen, File 29, "Entwurf für den Aufbau des Hamburger volkstümlichen Büchereiwesens, Anlage 1 zum Haushaltsplan 1934."

6. "Richtlinien für das Volksbüchereiwesen," pp. 39–40.

7. Franz Schriewer, *Das ländliche Volksbüchereiwesen: Einführung in Grundfragen und Praxis der Dorf- und Kleinstadtbüchereien* (Jena: Eugen Diederichs, 1937), p. 15.

8. Quality is a subjective judgment, but librarians usually include such measures as number of volumes, number of readers (especially as a percentage of the population), and circulation.

9. "Vorläufige Übersicht über den Stand des Büchereiwesens in Thüringen," *DB* 5 (1938): 726–27; Nordrhein-Westfälisches Hauptstaatsarchiv, Düsseldorf, BR 1004/183, "Jahresbericht 1935/36." The figures given in this report do not agree with those given in Lawin for the same year; the annual report gives only adult readers.

10. Niedersächsisches Staatsarchiv, Oldenburg, Best. 170-1-335 (old V.O.), Dienstvertrag, April 25, 1934; Best. 134-Nr. 3610 (IV-61-17), RWEV Vb 2769/42, Dähnhardt to Ministerium der Kirchen und Schulen in Oldenburg, July 28, 1943; Niedersächsisches Staatsarchiv, Wolfenbüttel, 12 A Neu 19015, Braunschweig Minister für Volksbildung to Heiligenstaedt, VI 808 1/40, July 20, 1940; Lübcke to Herrn Ministerpräsident Klagges, May 8, 1941; Bayerisches Hauptstaatsarchiv, München, MK 41473, Dr. Herm. Sauter to Staatsministerium für Unterricht und Kultus, November 11, 1936.

11. Franz Schriewer, "Das Zusammenwirken von Kreis, Gemeinde und Staatlicher Büchereiberatungsstelle," *DB* 3 (1936): 19–25.

12. Schriewer, *Die staatlichen Volksbüchereistelle*, pp. 79–80.

13. Ibid., p. 80; "Richtlinien für das Volksbüchereiwesen," pp. 39–40.

14. Schriewer, *Die staatlichen Volksbüchereistellen*, p. 82; Schriewer, "Das Zusammenwirken von Kreis, Gemeinde und Staatlicher Büchereiberatungsstelle"; Schriewer, *Das ländliche Volksbüchereiwesen*, p. 26.

15. Schriewer, *Die staatlichen Volksbüchereistellen*, pp. 82–83.

16. The following account is based on Staatliche Beratungsstelle für öffentliche Büchereien, Bayreuth, Tirschenreuth file: Bund Deutscher Osten to Leiter, Volksbücherei Tirschenreuth, February 13, 1935; Staatliche beauftragte Volksbüchereistelle, March 27, 1935; [Staatliche beauftragte Gauvolksbüchereistelle] to Bürgermeister, Tirschenreuth, July 8, 1935; Staatliche beauftragte Gauvolksbüchereistelle to Bezirksamt, Tirschenreuth, September 27, 1935; W. Zintl, Volksbüchereileiter, to Pg. Wutz, Leiter der Gaubücherei, September 12, 1936; Meyer, Bürgermeister Tirschenreuth, to Staatliche Grenzbüchereistelle, Bayreuth, October 20 and 30, 1936, January 9, and February 27, 1937; [Staatliche Grenzbüchereistelle] to Bürgermeister, Tirschenreuth, May 8 and August 13, 1937, November 4 and 30, 1938; Meyer, Bürgermeister Tirschenreuth, December 8, 1938; Arbeitsberichte, 1942[1]/42, 1942/43.

17. Niedersächsisches Staatsarchiv, Wolfenbüttel, 12 A Neu 13 19015, mimeographed memorandum, April 27, 1937.

18. Bayerisches Hauptstaatsarchiv, München, MK 41453, "Allgemeine Richtlinien für den Aufbau des Volksbüchereiwesens im Gau Bayerische Ostmark," [1936], printed; "Grundsätze für den Aufbau des ländlichen Volksbüchereiwesens in der Provinz Hannover."

19. Hessisches Staatsarchiv, Darmstadt, G15 Alsfeld XX, Der Reichsstatthalter in Hessen, to Kreis- und Schulämter, Kreisämter, and Herren Bürgermeister der Stadt Darmstadt, Offenbach a/M., Mainz, Worms and Giessen, May 11, 1936; Nordrhein-Westfälisches Staatsarchiv, Detmold, M1 1 JU Nr. 54, Regierungspräsident to Landräte, II M 4969, December 22, 1937.

20. Nordrhein-Westfälisches Staatsarchiv, Detmold, M1 1 JU Nr. 54, "Bericht über die amtliche Tagung über das Volksbüchereiwesen in Jena am 6. und 7. August 1937."

21. Nordrhein-Westfälisches Staatsarchiv, Detmold, D 14 Nr. 128, RV, Rundschreiben, February 27, 1937; D 14 Nr. 129, Abschrift, Arbeitsvereinbarung über die Zusammenarbeit zwischen dem Reichsnährstand und der Reichsstelle für das Volksbüchereiwesen, February 5, 1943; Niedersächsisches Staatsarchiv, Wolfenbüttel, 12 A Neu 13 19015, RWEV Vb Nr. 125 (b), January 26, 1938.

22. Bayerisches Hauptstaatsarchiv, München, MK 41456, W. Pfeiffer, Staatliche Volksbüchereistelle für die Pfalz an das Bayerischen Staatsministerium für Unterricht und Kultus, May 13, 1938.

CHAPTER 8. THE LIBRARY AND ITS READERS

1. Gustav Hoof, "Erinnerungen, Impressionen und Reflexionen rund um das Buch," in *Einst Dorfbücherei—heute Bibliothekssystem* (Cologne, 1973), p. 43, quoted in Boese, *Das öffentliche Bibliothekswesen*, p. 126.

2. Frauke Hansen, "Die 'geistige Bildung eines Volkes' oder Die Lektüre der 'Kleinen Leute' in der Volksbücherei Schöneberg," *Buch und Bibliothek* 39 (1987): 961.

3. The statistics on which the conclusions of this chapter are based must be taken with an even larger grain of salt than most. German public librarians had long taken pride in their exhaustive statistics that covered acquisitions, broken down by subject area; circulation, organized by both subject area and social status of reader; and readership, divided into economic/social status. During the Nazi period, library statistics suffered not only from the unreliable individual who did not keep proper records, who can be found anywhere, but also from political pressures. Librarians had every motive to show high circulation, circulation of preferred material, and use by those in certain categories. Even the most inquisitorial Beratungsstelle could not verify every transaction. One favorite expedient, a librarian reported, to achieve a high circulation of *Mein Kampf* was to send it out in a block loan, along with other books. It could count as circulated; whether it had been read was irrelevant. Bergtel-Schleif, pp. 200–201; interview with Rudolf and Erika Joerden, Hamburg, June 19, 1984.

4. In German political conditions it was impossible to be apolitical or open to a variety of viewpoints; that stance was a tenet of nineteenth-century liberalism and the National Liberal party.

5. Wilhelm Schuster, "Vom Geiste eines deutschen Büchereigesetzes," *DB* 1 (1934): 216.

6. *Handbuch der deutschen Volksbüchereien* (1940), pp. 172–83; Staatsarchiv der Senat der Freien und Hansestadt Hamburg, Hamburger Öffentliche

Bücherhallen, File 13, Statistikzahlen; Staatliche Beratungsstelle für öffentliche Büchereien, Bayreuth, Hof file.

7. Stadtarchiv, Kiel, 40798, Stadtbücherei Statistik, Tabelle 4, 1935/36; Stadtarchiv, Freiburg, v/34/1, "Jahresberichte 1935/36."

8. Schriewer, *Das ländliche Volksbüchereiwesen,* p. 78; Staatliche Beratungsstelle für öffentliche Büchereien, Bayreuth, files.

9. Stadtarchiv, Kiel, 40798, Stadtbücherei Statistik, Tabelle 4, 1935/36; Stadtarchiv, Freiburg, v/34/1, "Jahresberichte 1935/36."

10. Schriewer, *Das ländliche Volksbüchereiwesen,* p. 72; Stadtarchiv, Saarbrücken, G. 6418, "Statistik der Stadtbücherei Saarbrücken vom Rechnungsjahr 1936"; Gunther Tschich, "Berichte und Mitteilungen: Gemeinde- und Werkbücherei Spechthausen," *DB* 5 (1938): 370–71.

11. Bundesarchiv, Koblenz, R/56/V 166, Anordnung über die Teilnahme von Juden an Darbietungen der deutschen Kultur, November 12, 1938.

12. Walter Hofmann, "Die kleine Ausleihschule," in Walter Hofmann, *Buch und Volk: Gesammelte Aufsätze zur Buchpolitik und Volksbüchereifrage,* ed. Rudolf Reuter (Cologne: Verlag der Löwe, 1951), p. 411; E. Sulz, "Fortschritt und Reaktion in der Deutschen Bücherhallenbewegung," in *Büchereifragen,* ed. by E. Ackerknecht and G. Fritz (Berlin: n.p., 1914), pp. 17–18.

13. Taupitz, *Das Büchereiwesen im Dorf und Kleinstadt,* p. 37.

14. Wilhelm Schuster, "Der Beruf des Volksbibliothekars," *DB* 3 (1936): 31; Nordrhein-Westfälisches Staatsarchiv, Detmold, D14 Nr. 155, Einweisungsreferat, Volksbüchereistelle Hagen.

15. Bergtel-Schleif, pp. 200–201; interview with Anneliese Benneman, Duisburg, June 26, 1984; interview with Sitta Krause, Celle, May 18, 1984.

16. Walter Hofmann, "Schalter oder freie Theke?" *DB* 4 (1937): 21–30; Franz Schriewer, "'Freie' Theke oder 'pädagogischer' Schalter?" *DB* 4 (1937): 30–38.

17. "Deutscher Volksbüchereitag in Würzburg, 24.–26. September 1936," *DB* 3 (1936): 564–69; E. Schäfer, "Von der Leistungsschau der deutschen Volksbüchereien im Leipzig 1938: 1. Das Hamburger Büchereiwesen," *DB* 6 (1939): 235–40; Fachhochschule für Bibliothekswesen, Stuttgart, Walter Hofmann Archiv [Hofmann to Reichsstelle für volkstümliches Büchereiwesen], November 30, 1936.

18. Rudolf Joerden, "Neue Freihandbüchereien in Hamburg," *DB* 7 (1940): 143–47; [Kurd] Schulz, "Berichte: Eröffnung einer Freihandbücherei in Bremen," *DB* 7 (1940): 36–37; Pott, "Berichte: Aus der Arbeit einer kleinstädtischen Freihandbücherei (Glucksburg, 1792 — Einw.)," *DB* 9 (1942): 332.

19. Interview with Rudolf and Erika Joerden, Hamburg, June 19, 1984.

20. Schriewer, *Das ländliche Büchereiwesen,* p. 80; the statistics upon which the following conclusions are based come from Germany, Statistisches Reichsamt, *Die deutschen Volksbüchereien nach Ländern, Provinzen und Gemeinden 1933/34; Handbuch der deutschen Volksbüchereien* (1940); Lawin, "Die Volksbüchereien der deutschen Gemeinden," and archival sources. Staatsarchiv der Senat der Freien und Hansestadt Hamburg, Hamburger Öffentliche Bücherhallen, File 13, July 23, 1937; Stadtarchiv, Kiel, 40798, Stadtbücherei Statistik; Stadtarchiv, Hannover, XCO-3; Stadtbücherei, Lingen, Statistikbogen 1920–1949.

21. Bergtel-Schleif, p. 198.

22. Strothmann, p. 148.

23. Generallandesarchiv, Karlsruhe, 235/6559, "Jahresbericht der Städtischen Volksbibliothek," May 31, 1935; interview with Marta Höhl, Bremen, May 1984.

24. Janet L. Hannaford, "Libraries Serving More Than 200,000 Population," *Bulletin of the American Library Association* 32 (April 1938): 268.

25. Illustration in Detlev J. K. Peukert, *Inside Nazi Germany: Conformity, Opposition and Racism in Daily Life*, trans. Richard Deveson (London: B. T. Batsford, 1987), foll. p. 192; Walter Hofmann, "Das bedingte Lesegeld," in *Politik der Bücherei: Paul Ladewig und die jungere Bücherhallenbewegung*, ed. Wolfgang Thauer (Wiesbaden: 1975), pp. 83–85.

26. Erwin Ackerknecht, "Die Büchereiaufgaben der deutschen Städte (1922)" and "Werbemittel und Benutzertaktik (1917)," in Erwin Ackerknecht, *Büchereifragen*, 2d ed. (Berlin: Weidmannsche Buchhandlung, 1926), pp. 21–24, 28–56.

27. Hans Teichmann, "Arbeitsberichte: Dichtung findet neuen Lebensraum," *DB* 3 (1936): 329–32.

28. Max Wieser, "[Die Ausstellung 'Jugend und Buch' der Volksbücherei in Spandau]," *Mitteilungen und Arbeiten für das Berliner Städtischen Büchereiwesens, 1936*; reprinted in Andrae, *Volksbücherei und Nationalsozialismus*, pp. 160–64.

29. Stadtarchiv, Freiburg, V/33/6, Herausgabe von Bücherverzeichnisse 1920/43; Nordrhein-Westfälisches Staatsarchiv, Detmold, D 14 Nr. 128, RV Rundschreiben Nr. 39/8/5, March 14, 1939; Staatsarchiv der Senat der Freien und Hansestadt Hamburg, Hamburger Öffentliche Bücherhallen, File 12, Bd. 2, Rundschreiben der Bücherhallenleitung Januar 1938–April 1939, Nr. 116, April 3, 1939, Nr. 120, April 17, 1939; "Zur 'Woche des deutschen Buches'," *DB* 1 (1934): 535.

30. Nordrhein-Westfälisches Staatsarchiv, Detmold, D 14 Nr. 185, B. Example of 2. Auswahlliste der Staatlichen Volksbüchereistelle für das Land Lippe.

31. Strothmann, pp. 163–69.

32. Zentrales Staatsarchiv, Potsdam, 62 DAF 3, 19362/10, "Das Reich eröffnet zur Buchwoche 730 neue Volksbüchereien," *Völkischer Beobachter*, October 30, 1937; "Eröffnung von 30 Volksbüchereien in einem pfalzischen Grenzbezirk."

33. Staatliche Büchereistelle, Detmold, Die Woche des deutschen Buches 1938, Anlagenteil.

34. Stadtarchiv, Freiburg, V/33/4, Harden-Rauch to Oberbürgermeister, Abt. I, December 31, 1934; "Volksbücherei—'Kraft durch Freude,'" *DB* 1 (1934): 311; "Die Volksbücherei in der Ausstellung Schaffendes Volk," *DB* 4 (1937): 555–56.

35. Niedersächsisches Staatsarchiv, Wolfenbüttel, 12 A Neu 13 19015, RWEV Vd Nr. 237, March 2, 1935, attached conference proceedings, p. 7.

36. For an extensive discussion of library service to youth see Margaret F. Stieg, "The Nazi Public Library and the Young Adult," *Top of the News* 43 (Fall 1986): 45–57.

37. Karl Hobrecker, "Die neue Reichsjugendbücherei," *Das junge Deutschland* 27 (September 1933): 252–55; Kamenetsky, pp. 274–75.

38. Peter Aley, *Jugendliteratur im Dritten Reich*, Schriften zur Buchmarkt-Forschung, vol. 12 (Hamburg: Verlag für Buchmarkt-Forschung, 1967), pp. 35–41; Franz Schriewer, "Leistungszahlen der Schülerbüchereien," *Jugendschriften-Warte* 42 (July 1938): 49–51; Staatsarchiv der Senat der Freien und Hansestadt Hamburg, Hamburger Öffentliche Bücherhallen, File 13, Tätigkeitsberichte vom September 1934–September 1936.

39. "The Law for the Hitler Youth, 1 December 1936," in *The German Youth Movement 1900–1945: An Interpretative and Documentary History*, ed. Peter Stachura (New York: St. Martin's, 1981), p. 180.

40. Staatsarchiv der Senat der Freien und Hansestadt Hamburg, Hamburger Öffentliche Bücherhallen, File 12, Rundschreiben der Bücherhallenleitung, Nr. 2 January 10, 1935.

41. Nordrhein-Westfälishes Staatsarchiv, Detmold, D 14 Nr. 169, Abkommen zwischen den Staatlichen Beratungsstellen für Büchereiwesen der Provinz Westfalen, der Länder Lippe und Schaumburg-Lippe, und der Gebietsführung Westfalen der Hitler-Jugend, enclosure in letter of Fritz Reuter to Lippische Landesberatungsstelle für Volksbüchereien, April 15, 1937; "Vereinbarung zwischen der Reichstelle für das Volksbüchereiwesen und der Reichsjugendführung der NSDAP, 28," *DB* 4 (1937): 558.

42. Staatliche Volksbüchereistelle, Detmold, "Jahresbericht 1937/38"; Stadtarchiv, Saarbrücken, G Nr. 6419/1, W. Koch to Dr. Gaudig, February 16, 1938.

43. Waldemar Wenzel, "Das Gesicht einer Jugendbücherei," *DB* 6 (1939): 355; Richard Kock, "Bericht über die Zusammenarbeit der Städtischen Volksbücherei Schneidemühl mit der HJ," *DB* 4 (1937): 488–91; Erik Wilkens, "Vorlesestunden für die Hitler-Jugend," *DB* 3 (1936): 351–57; Staatliche Beratungsstelle für öffentliche Büchereien, Bayreuth, File: Altenstadt, Frau Schonberger to Staatliche Volksbüchereistelle, May 28, 1942.

44. Karl Taupitz, "Parteibibliotheken oder Volksbüchereien?" *DB* 1 (1934): 545–50; Karl Taupitz, "Die Bücherei in der Großstadt," *DB* 3 (1936): 145–58; Bayerisches Hauptstaatsarchiv, München, MK 41452, "Das Volksbüchereiwesen in der Pfalz," *Nationalsozialistische Zeitung Rheinfront*, May 4, 1934; Niedersächsisches Staatsarchiv, Wolfenbüttel, 12 A Neu 13 19015, RWEV, Vd Nr. 237, March 2, 1935, attached conference proceedings, p. 8.

45. Bayerisches Hauptstaatsarchiv, München, MK 41468, Anordnung der Gauleitung Bayerische Ostmark der NSDAP, Verordnungsblatt "Der Führerordnen," February 12, 1937; Niedersächsisches Staatsarchiv, Wolfenbüttel, 12 A Neu 13 19014, "Aufbau des Volksbüchereiwesens in Deutschland bis 1940," copy of article in *Berliner Tages-Zeitung*, September 10, 1937.

46. Staatliche Büchereistelle, Detmold, "Jahresbericht 1937/38"; Bayerisches Hauptstaatsarchiv, München, MK 41465, "Jahresbericht 1938/39 der Staatlichen Volksbüchereistelle, München"; Niedersächsisches Staatsarchiv, Wolfenbüttel, 12 A Neu 13 19014, Bericht der Staatlichen Volksbüchereistelle für das Land Braunschweig für das Jahr (1938–1939).

47. Franz Schriewer, "Kampf den Leihbüchereien!" *BuB* 13 (1933): 100–13.

48. Nordrhein-Westfälisches Staatsarchiv, Detmold, D III c Nr. 24, Leihbibliotheken in Lage [May 1934].

49. "Amtliche Erläße und Bekanntmachungen: Achte Anordnung zum Schutze des Leihbücherei-Gewerbes," *DB* 4 (1937): 269.

CHAPTER 9. LIBRARIANS AND THEIR JOBS

1. Zentrales Staatsarchiv, Potsdam, 62 DAF 3, 1963, B1. 66, E. Propach, "Volksbüchereien hüten das geistige Erbe," *N.S.K.*, November 2, 1937; *Handbuch der deutschen Volksbüchereien*, Jahrbuch der deutschen Volksbüchereien 5, 1935 (Leipzig: Kommissions Verlag; Einkaufshaus für Büchereien, 1935), p. 74; *Handbuch der deutschen Volksbüchereien* (1940), pp. 204–207; *Handbuch der deutschen Volksbüchereien; Nachtrag zum . . . 1938–40*, pp. 106–10.

2. Lawin, "Die Volksbüchereien der deutschen Gemeinden," p. 25.

3. Taupitz, "Die Bücherei in der Großstadt."

4. Staatsarchiv der Senat der Freien und Hansestadt Hamburg, Hamburger Öffentliche Bücherhallen, 12 Bd 2, Nr 4, February 5, 1939; 16 Bd 2, Dr. Krebs to Öffentliche Bücherhallen, November 22, 1943.

5. For a detailed discussion of women and the professions in Nazi Germany see Jill Stephenson, *Women in Nazi Society* (New York: Barnes and Noble, 1975), pp. 147–84.

6. *Handbuch der deutschen Volksbüchereien* (1935), pp. 75–100, 74; *Handbuch der deutschen Volksbüchereien* (1940), pp. 204–207.

7. Deutsche Staatsbibliothek, Leipzig, Walter Hofmann, "Bemerkungen zur Frage der Weiterführung der Deutschen Volksbüchereischule," typescript, January 10, 1934, pp. 1–3; Elise Hofmann-Bosse, "Die Frau im Dienst der volkstümlichen Bücherei," in *Der Volksbibliothekar: Seine Aufgabe, sein Beruf, seine Ausbildung*, ed. Hans Hofmann (Leipzig: Quelle und Meyer, 1927), pp. 30–51; Lilli Volbehr, "Anteil und Anrecht der Frau an der volksbibliothekarischen Berufsarbeit," *DB* 1 (1934): 25–30; Helga Lüdtke, "Mütter ohne Kinder: Volksbibliothekarinnen während des Nationalsozialismus," in Vodosek and Komorowski, pp. 424–39.

8. Deutsche Staatsbibliothek, Leipzig, Walter Hofmann, "Bemerkungen zur Frage der Weiterführung der Deutschen Volksbüchereischule."

9. *Handbuch der deutschen Volksbüchereien* (1935), pp. 75–100; Deutsches Literaturarchiv, Erwin Ackerknecht Collection, Johannes Beer to Ackerknecht, July 18, 1932.

10. Volbehr, p. 25; Lüdtke, p. 434.

11. Deutsches Literaturarchiv, Erwin Ackerknecht Collection, Therese Krimmer to Ackerknecht, May 3, 1925, May 1, 1929; and October 2, 1930.

12. Deutsches Literaturarchiv, Erwin Ackerknecht Collection, Ackerknecht to Rudolf Autenrieth, September 9, 1933; Boese, *Das öffentliche Bibliothekswesen*, pp. 207–208.

13. Jill McIntyre, "Women and the Professions in Germany, 1930–1940," in *German Democracy and the Triumph of Hitler: Essays in Recent German History*, ed. Anthony Nicholls and Erich Matthias, St. Antony's College, Oxford, Publications, no. 3 (New York: St. Martin's, 1972), pp. 175–213.

14. Hofmann-Bosse, p. 38; Dähnhardt, "Richtlinien für das Volksbüchereiwesen," p. 132; Schuster, "Der Beruf des Volksbibliothekars," p. 28.

15. Staatsarchiv der Senat der Freien und Hansestadt Hamburg, Hamburger Öffentliche Bücherhallen, 11, "Teilprotokoll der Verwaltungsrats-Setzung am 15. Oktober 1935"; Franz Schriewer, "Grundfragen der Kataloggestaltung," *DB* 3 (1936): 41–49; Willi Schrader, "Dies ist eine politische Bücherei!" in Grenzbüchereidienst, *Mitteilungen*, vol. 16 (Berlin: Volk und Reich Verlay), p. 65.

16. Staatsarchiv der Senat der Freien und Hansestadt Hamburg, Hamburger Öffentliche Bücherhallen, 39, Volbehr to Margarete Hildebrandt, October 28, 1942; 41, Ed. Dietten to Magistrat der Stadt Hamburg, December 16, 1934; 45, Organisationsamt, NSDAP, Gauleitung Hamburg, to Behorde für Kirche, Volkstum und Kunst, January 10, 1935.

17. Erwin Ackerknecht, "Bibliothekarische Berufsgesinnung," in Erwin Ackerknecht, *Büchereifragen*, 2d ed. (Berlin: Weidmannsche Buchhandlung, 1926), pp. 74–75; Karl Th. Bayer, "Von der Verantwortung des Bildungsbibliothekars in unserer Zeit," *Geisteskultur* 42 (1933): 132; Franz Schriewer, *Das ländliche Volksbüchereiwesen*, p. 94.

18. Deutsche Staatsbibliothek, Leipzig, Walter Hofmann, "Bemerkungen zur Frage der Weiterführung der Deutschen Volksbüchereischule," pp. 6–7; *Handbuch der deutschen Volksbüchereien* (1940), vol. 6, p. 203.

19. Bayerisches Hauptstaatsarchiv, München, MK 41468, Heiligenstaedt to Dähnhardt, April 17, 1935; Nordrhein-Westfälisches Staatsarchiv, Detmold, M1 II B Nr. 4435, Oberbürgermeister, Bielefeld, to Regierungspräsident, Minden, February 1, 1939.

20. PMWKV U II R Nr. 423, September 2, 1933, "Drei wichtige Preußische Erläße," *DB* 1 (1934): 38.

21. Martin Broszat, "Politische Denunziationen in der NS-Zeit," *Archivalische Zeitschrift* 73 (1977): 221–38; "Denunciation," in Grunberger, pp. 108–15.

22. Generallandesarchiv, Karlsruhe, 235/6818, Harden-Rauch to Ministerium für Kultus und Unterricht, December 3, 1936; Jacobi to Oberbürgermeister der Hauptstadt Mannheim, May 4, 1937; Harden-Rauch to Ministerium für Kultus und Unterricht, July 8, 1937.

23. Staatsarchiv der Senat der Freien und Hansestadt Hamburg, Hamburger Öffentliche Bücherhallen, 13, Dr. Krebs to Senator Allworden, December 13, 1937.

24. Stadtarchiv, Saarbrücken, G6418.

25. Staatliche Beratungsstelle für öffentliche Büchereien, Bayreuth, Feilitzsch file, Überprüfungsbericht, October 18, 1944; Ba[ruch] to Georg Riedel, October 27, 1945.

26. Interview with Lydia Gross, Kiel, May 8, 1984; interview with Dietrich Vorwerk, Villingen, July 25, 1985.

27. Erwin Marks, "1945—Eine Wende in unserem Bibliothekswesen," *Der Bibliothekar* 29 (May 1975): 289–96; Lüdtke, p. 432; "Zum Thema 'Volksbüchereien und Nationalsozialismus' befragt: Hedwig Bieber," in *Volksbüchereien und Nationalsozialismus: Eine Ausstellung der Stadtbibliotheken Bielefeld, Dortmund und Solingen* (Bielefeld, November 1988), pp. 23–30; interview with Dietrich Vorwerk, Villingen, July 25, 1985; interview with Rudolf and Erika Joerden, Hamburg, June 19, 1984.

28. Interview with Rudolf and Erika Joerden, Hamburg, June 19, 1984; Staatsarchiv der Senat der Freien und Hansestadt Hamburg, Hamburger Öffentliche Bücherhallen, 10 Band 1, correspondence between Krebs and Eduard Hallier.

292

29. Bergtel-Schleif, pp. 193–207.

30. Ibid., p. 206; see also Werner Jutte, "Volksbibliothekare im Nationalsozialismus," *Buch und Bibliothek* 39 (1987): 345–48.

31. Nordrhein-Westfälisches Staatsarchiv, Detmold, M1 1 JU Nr. 148, PMWKV U II R Nr. 246, May 24, 1933.

32. Thauer and Vodosek, pp. 91–94; Wilhelm Schuster, "Die Berliner Bibliotheksschule," *DB* 5 (1938): 511–22; Erich Thier, "Die Deutsche Volksbüchereischule zu Leipzig," *DB* 5 (1938): 522–26; Maria Steinhoff, "Die westdeutsche Volksbüchereischule 1928–1938," *DB* 5 (1938): 526–29; Hans-Dieter Holzhausen, "Von der Bibliotheksschule zum Universitätsinstitut: Grundzüge der Entwicklung der Berliner bibliotekarischen Ausbildungsstätte von 1930–1980," in *Bibliotheksarbeit: Hermann Wassner zum 60. Geburtstag*, ed. Peter Vodosek (Wiesbaden: Otto Harrassowitz, 1982), pp. 48–61.

33. Hans F. Abraham, "German Public Libraries as Agencies of Propaganda," typescript, June 1944, in Columbia University library.

34. Walter Hofmann, "Die Ausbildung für den volksbibliothekarischen Beruf," in his *Buch und Volk: Gesammelte Aufsätze und Reden zur Buchpolitik und Volksbüchereifrage* (1938; reprint Cologne: Verlag der Löwe, 1951), pp. 142–53; *Handbuch der deutschen Volksbüchereien* (1935), p. 72; RWEV, Vb 1141 (b), May 11, 1938, published in *DB* 5 (1938): 367.

35. *Jahrbuch der deutschen Volksbüchereien* 4, 1928/29, 1929/30 (Leipzig: Otto Harrassowitz, 1931), p. 208; *Handbuch der deutschen Volksbüchereien* (1935), p. 72.

36. Holzhausen, "Von der Bibliotheksschule zum Universitätsinstitut," p. 52.

37. Fachhochschule für Bibliothekswesen, Stuttgart, Walter Hofmann Archiv, W. Hofmann to K. Taupitz, December 12, 1935; Schuster, "Die Berliner Bibliotheksschule," p. 521.

38. "Richtlinien für die Vorbildung und Ausbildung des volksbibliotekarischen Personals," in *Der Volksbibliothekar: Seine Aufgabe, sein Beruf, seine Ausbildung*, ed. Hans Hofmann, p. 131; Thauer and Vodosek, pp. 92–93; Schuster, "Die Berliner Bibliotheksschule," p. 517; Holzhausen, "Von der Bibliotheksschule zum Universitätsinstitut," p. 53.

39. *Handbuch der deutschen Volksbüchereien* (1935), pp. 75–100.

40. Heinz Dähnhardt, "Ergänzungsbildung," *DB* 7 (1940): 202–206; "Sonderprüfung für den Dienst an volkstümlichen Büchereien: RWEV Vb Nr. 1489/38, Z (b), 28. Juni 1938," *DB* 5 (1938): 470–71; "Ergänzungslehrgange," in *Nachtrag zum Handbuch der deutschen Volksbüchereien, 1938–40*, p. 104.

41. Staatsarchiv, Bremen, 3.5.19 Nr. 154 [12], RWEV, Vb 3 426/37 (b), January 18, 1938; Nordrhein-Westfälisches Staatsarchiv, Detmold, D 14 Nr. 140, Reichsprüfungsamt für das Büchereiwesen to Herren Leiter, Volksbüchereistellen und Stadtbüchereien, May 7, 1943.

42. "Zur der Ausbildung für den höheren Volksbüchereidienst," *BuB* 7 (1927): 116–20; Bundesarchiv, Koblenz, R 56 v/137, Karl Heinl, "Denkschrift betreffend Neubau des deutschen öffentlichen Büchereiwesens," June 1933.

43. Fritz Heiligenstaedt, "Der nebenamtliche Büchereileiter," *DB* 3 (1936): 33.

44. "Volksbücherei: Kundgebung in Bayreuth," in Grenzbüchereidienst, *Mitteilungen*, vol. 14 (Berlin, 1936), p. 25; Heiligenstaedt, "Der nebenamtliche Büchereileiter," *DB* 3 (1936): 34–35.

45. Nordrhein-Westfälisches Staatsarchiv, Detmold, D 14 Nr. 153, Leiter, Staatliche Volksbüchereistelle für den Regierungs-Bezirk Minden, January 1943; D 14 Nr. 35, Aktennotiz Kirchborchen, June 20, 1944; Niedersächsisches Staatsarchiv, Wolfenbüttel, 12 A Neu 13 19011, RWEV, Vb 1668/43, September 17, 1943; Staatliche Beratungsstelle für öffentliche Büchereien, Bayreuth, Weiden file, Überprüfungs-Bericht, August 26–27, 1942.

46. Nordrhein-Westfälisches Staatsarchiv, Detmold, D 14 Nr. 147, Rang to RV, January 28, 1943.

47. *Die Arbeitslager der Volksbibliothekare 1936 und 1937* (Leipzig, 1938); Staatsarchiv der Senat der Freien und Hansestadt Hamburg, Hamburger Öffentliche Bücherhallen, 12 Bd. 1, unnumbered circular, April 2, 1937.

48. Interview with Lydia Gross, Kiel, May 8, 1984.

CHAPTER 10. PUBLIC LIBRARIANSHIP AND THE
CATHOLIC CHURCH

1. Zentrales Staatsarchiv, Potsdam, 62 DAF 3, 19359, B1. 70, H. Ruster, "Katholische Büchereiarbeit," *Germania*, October 29, 1931; Table: "Konfessionelle Büchereien in Germany," in Germany, Statistisches Reichsamt, *Die deutschen Volksbüchereien nach Ländern, Provinzen und Gemeinden, 1933/34*, pp. 60–61; Rudolf Reuter, "Die Aufgaben der Volksbücherei in der deutschen Westmark," *DB* 2 (1935): 221; Deutsches Literaturarchiv, Erwin Ackerknecht Collection, Heinrich Horstmann to Ackerknecht, November 29, 1929, and April 1, 1930; Ackerknecht to Hilde Krimmer, March 9, 1933.

2. Table: "Konfessionelle Büchereien in Germany," in Germany, Statistisches Reichsamt, *Die deutschen Volksbüchereien nach Ländern, Provinzen und Gemeinden, 1933/34*, pp. 60–61; Bayerische Hauptstaatsarchiv, München, MK 41465, "Betreffend Volksbüchereiwesen an der bayerischen Ostgrenze," April 16, 1930; Borromäus Verein, Bonn, Diözese Rottenburg, Blochingen Post Mengen, January 15, 1934.

3. Borromäus Verein, *Jahresbericht 1933*, (Bonn: Verein vom heiligen Karl Borromäus, 1934), p. 13.

4. Bayerisches Hauptstaatsarchiv, München, MK 41451, Volks-Bibliothek Eggenfelden, [catalog], June 1932; Lambert Dohmen, "Praktische Büchereiarbeit," *Die Bücherwelt* 30 (1933): 105; Erich Hodick, "Die willkommene Gelegenheit: Zerschlagung der katholischen Büchereiarbeit während des Nationalsozialismus," in Vodosek and Komorowski, p. 488.

5. Borromäus Verein, Bonn, Vertrauliche Mitteilungen, May 1933; "Leitsätze der Vortrage des 21. Kursus für Leiter und Mitarbeiter von Volksbüchereien vom 9. bis 13. Oktober 1933."

6. Josef Hackmann, "Buch und Bücherei im Aufbruch des Volkstums," *Die Bücherwelt* 30 (1933): 93–97.

7. Borromäus Verein, Bonn, "Bericht über den 22. Kursus des Borromäusvereins . . . Oktober 1934."

8. Peter Matheson, ed., *The Third Reich and the Christian Churches* (Edinburgh: T. and T. Clark, 1981), policy statement by Hitler, March 23, 1933, p. 9; Roman Catholic Conference in Berlin, April 25–26, 1933, pp. 20–21.

·9. Ibid., Concordat between the papacy and the Third Reich, July 20, 1933.

10. Deutsches Literaturarchiv, Erwin Ackerknecht Collection, Beratender Ausschuß für das volkstümliche Büchereiwesen, B.A. Nr. 24/33, "Kulturpolitische Bemerkungen zum Neuaufbau des deutschen Büchereiwesens," October 4, 1933.

11. PMWKV, U II R Nr. 750.1, December 28, 1933, published in *DB* 1 (1934): 12.

12. One example among many is Nordrhein-Westfälisches Staatsarchiv, Detmold, D 14 Nr. 124, [Angermann] to Herrn Landrat, Wiedenbrück, June 24, 1935.

13. The Bavarian Pressverein (after 1934 the Sankt Michaelsbund) libraries were not administered by the Borromäus Verein in Bonn. Agreements concluded with the Borromäus Verein did not, therefore, apply in Bavaria and had to be separately concluded. The same restrictions would eventually be applied, but when they went into effect would usually differ in Bavaria.

14. Bayerisches Hauptstaatsarchiv, München, MK 41452, Direktor Braun to sämtliche Borromäusvereine, August 23, 1935, mimeographed; Nordrhein-Westfälisches Hauptstaatsarchiv, Düsseldorf, Zweigarchiv Schloss Kalkum, BR 1011/385, Regierungspräsident, Aachen, to Landräte des Bezirks, II 4 b j 22 Nr. 419, November 6, 1935; Bayerisches Hauptstaatsarchiv, München, MK 41452, BSUK to RWEV, December 10, 1935; MK 41453, Geheime Staatspolizei, Staatspolizeistelle München, to various police and civil officials, November 18, 1936; Nordrhein-Westfälisches Hauptstaatsarchiv, Düsseldorf, Zweigarchiv Schloss Kalkum, BR 1011/385, RWEV Vd 2087, July 27, 1935.

15. For example, the Borromäus Verein libraries in the diocese of Münster received a total of RM 4,555.63 from provincial, Kreis, and local governments in 1934. Borromäus Verein, Bonn, "Aufstellung über die Beihilfen . . . in der Diözese Münster im Jahre 1934"; Bayerisches Hauptstaatsarchiv, München, MK 41451, Belz, Katholischer Pressverband, Bad-Aibling to Stadtrat Aibling, January 30, 1934.

16. Bayerisches Hauptstaatsarchiv, München, MK 41453, "Notizen über die Tagung des 'Sankt Michaelsbund zur Pflege des Katholischen Schrifttums in Bayern," July 18–20, 1936.

17. Borromäus Verein, Bonn, Generalsekretäriat des Borromäusvereins, Vertrauliche Mitteilungen, June 1933; Borromäus Verein, *Jahresbericht 1933*, p. 3.

18. Bundesarchiv, Koblenz, R 56 v/138/188, Braun to Dr. Wismann, January 30, 1934; Borromäus Verein, Bonn, Borromäus Verein und Reichsschrifttumskammer, attachment to letter from Braun to Weihbischof Wilhelm Stockums, January 4, 1936; Dr. Westhoff to Weihbischof Stockums, January 30, 1936.

19. PMWKV, U II R Nr. 750.1, December 28, 1933, published in *DB* 1 (1934): 12; Bayerisches Hauptstaatsarchiv, München, MK 41451, V 58852, December 19, 1933.

20. Bayerisches Staatsarchiv, München, LRA 152 920, BSUK to Regierungen, September 7, 1938.

21. Bayerisches Hauptstaatsarchiv, München, MK 41452, Schriewer to

RWEV, December 6, 1935; Borromäus Verein, Bonn, A. Card. Bertram to Generalvikar, Prälat Dr. David, February 27, 1937.

22. Borromäus Verein, Bonn, Briele to Braun, May 3, 1934; A. Card. Bertram to RV, September 21, 1935; Nordrhein-Westfälisches Staatsarchiv, Detmold, D 14 Nr. 119, SVBS Provinz Westfalen to Regierungspräsident Minden, October 3, 1935.

23. Borromäus Verein, Bonn, Braun to Euer Exzellenz [Stockums] February 27, 1934; Bayerisches Hauptstaatsarchiv, München, MK 41452, Fischer to BSUK, August 22, 1934.

24. Borromäus Verein, Bonn, "Gesamt-Borromäus-Verein Mitglieder, 1905–1925 [sic]"; Kursbericht 1936; "Der Borromäusverein in der Diözese Osnabrück im Jahre 1934."

25. For example, Borromäus Verein, Bonn, Speyer: Harter, Diözesanpräses to Pfarrbibliotheken, May 14, 1936.

26. Staatsarchiv, München, LRA (Schongau) 301/3, Beck, Geheime Staatspolizei, to Polizeipräsidium, München . . . , November 22, 1937.

27. Borromäus Verein, Bonn, "Gesamt-Borromäus-Verein Mitglieder, 1905–1925 [sic]."

28. Nordrhein-Westfälisches Staatsarchiv, Detmold, M1 II B Nr. 4435, RWEV Vb 1545 (b), August 14, 1940.

29. Borromäus Verein, Bonn, [Braun] to Reichsminister für Wissenschaft, Erziehung und Volksbildung, October 5, 1940; Dr. Müller to Herrn Weihbischof Dr. W. Stockums, October 26, 1940.

30. Borromäus Verein, Bonn, "Die Chronik des Generalsekretäriats seit 1919 in Stichworten," undated.

31. Bayerisches Hauptstaatsarchiv, München, MK 41451, Dr. Reismüller to BSUK, November 13, 1933; MK 41451, BSUK V 58852, December 19, 1933; Staatsarchiv, München, LRA 152 920, BSUK to Ordinariat München-Freising, May 16, 1934.

32. Staatsarchiv, München, LRA 51549, "Protokollentwurf zur Ruckgabe der Volksbibliothek," April 16, 1935; Klage des Rechtsanwaltes Franz Zeitler, Namen des Sanktmichaelsbund, gegen Marktgemeinde Kraiburg, March 7, 1935; "Beschluß des Markt gemeinderates Kraiburg," March 10, 1935; Bayerisches Hauptstaatsarchiv, München, MK 41451, Buchholzer, Generalvikar, to BSUK, January 22 and February 28, 1934.

33. Nordrhein-Westfälisches Hauptstaatsarchiv, Düsseldorf, Zweigarchiv Schloss Kalkum, BR 1004/800, "Niederschrift über die Besprechung im Reichserziehungsministerium am Freitag, den 11. Oktober 1940"; Borromäus Verein, Bonn, [Braun] to RWEV, October 5, 1940; Hodick, "Die willkommene Gelegenheit," p. 496.

34. Borromäus Verein, Bonn, "Die Chronik des Generalsekretäriats seit 1919"; Nordrhein-Westfälisches Staatsarchiv, Detmold, M1 II B Nr. 4435, RWEV Vb 1985, December 10, 1940; Borromäus Verein, Bonn, [Braun] to RWEV, October 5, 1940; Braun to die Herren Diözesanpräsides, January 16, 1941; Teusch to Büchereien des Borromäusvereins der Erzdiözese Köln, February 7, 1941; RWEV Vb 204 (b), February 11, 1941.

35. Staatsarchiv, München, LRA 152 920, Gend[armerie]-Posten Rottach-

Egern to Landrat, Miesbach, March 10, 1942; Borromäus Verein, Bonn, Dr. Frings, Erzbischof von Köln to Herrn Reichsminister, January 17, 1944.

36. Staatliche Beratungsstelle für öffentliche Büchereien, Bayreuth, Weiden file, Kreisschrifttumsbeauftragter, A. Glossmer to Gauleitung der NSDAP, Gau "Bayerische Ostmark," November 12, 1938.

37. Nordrhein-Westfälisches Staatsarchiv, Detmold, M1 II B Nr. 4435, RWEV Vb 1546 (b), June 28, 1938; M1 II B Nr. 4435, RWEV Vb 1545 (b), August 14, 1940.

38. The RWEV used the term *publish* (*veröffentlichen*) in the old-fashioned sense of "to make known." Most of these anti-Catholic policies were labeled confidential, but a copy of Vb 1545 (b), at least, was given to Braun. They were disseminated in a mimeographed form, but not printed in *DB*.

39. Nordrhein-Westfälisches Staatsarchiv, Detmold, M1 1 JU Nr. 54, [RWEV] Vb 3408, "Bericht über die Besprechung in der Staatlichen Volksbüchereistelle Hagen am 30. November 1937"; Nordrhein-Westfälisches Hauptstaatsarchiv, Düsseldorf, Zweigarchiv Schloss Kalkum, BR 1011 1385, Beratungsstelle Düsseldorf und Aachen, December 6, 1935.

40. Generallandesarchiv, Karlsruhe, 235/6865, P. B. No. 421/35, October 16, 1935.

41. Stadtarchiv, Freiburg, V/33/5, Harden-Rauch to Oberbürgermeister, Abteilung I, July 11, 1935; Harden-Rauch to Oberbürgermeister, Abteilung I, December 23, 1936; Harden-Rauch to Stadtkammerei, December 27, 1937.

42. Generallandesarchiv, Karlsruhe, 235/6776, Harden-Rauch to NSDAP Gauleitung, Gauschulungsamt, February 4, 1938; Borromäus Verein, Bonn, "Vereine und Mitglieder 1936"; "Vereine und Mitglieder 1939"; Nordrhein-Westfälisches Hauptstaatsarchiv, Düsseldorf, Zweigarchiv Schloss Kalkum, BR 1004/800, "Niederschrift über die Besprechung im Reichserziehungsministerium am Freitag, den 11. Oktober 1940."

43. Bundesarchiv, Koblenz, R 56 v/138/183, Paul Walz to Dr. Wismann, October 12, 1934; R 56 v/138/163, Hede Limbach to Paul Walz, November 6, 1934; R 56 v/138/92, Paul Walz to Reichsminister für Volksaufklärung und Propaganda, August 1, 1936.

44. Nordrhein-Westfälisches Hauptstaatsarchiv, Düsseldorf, Zweigarchiv Schloss Kalkum, BR 1004/813, Beratungsstelle für Düsseldorf und Aachen, "Jahresbericht 1935/36"; Herbert Lepper, "Von der Stadtbibliothek zur Öffentlichen Bibliothek der Stadt Aachen 1831–1977," in *Aachen: Öffentliche Bibliothek 150 Jahre* (Aachen: Öffentliche Bibliothek der Stadt Aachen, 1981), pp. 45–47; Bernhard Schlagheck, "Die ausgebaute Bücherei der Mittelstadt und ihr Aufgabenkreis," *DB* 3 (1936): 628–29.

45. Borromäus Verein, Bonn, "Statistik der Jahre 1914 bis 1939 der Borromäusvereine in der Erzdiözese *Paderborn*."

46. Nordrhein-Westfälisches Staatsarchiv, Detmold, M1 1 JU Nr. 54, Kratky to Herrn Landrat, Paderborn, March 9, 1937; Landrat, Paderborn, to [Kratky], March 30, 1937; Kratky to Bürgermeister, Paderborn, March 10, 1937; Nobelmann, Bürgermeister, Paderborn, to Kratky, March 16, 1937; Kratky to Angermann, March 18, 1937.

47. Nordrhein-Westfälisches Staatsarchiv, Detmold, M1 1 JU Nr. 54, Land-

rat, Paderborn, to Herrn Regierungspräsidenten in Minden, February 28, 1938; M1 II B Nr. 4435, RWEV Vb 3144/38, Z II c, RWEV to Herrn Regierungspräsidenten in Minden, January 27, 1939; D 14 Nr. 76, [Angermann] to Herrn Landrat, Paderborn, April 12, 1938; D 14 Nr. 103, Kosiek, Bürgermeister, Paderborn, to RWEV, December 14, 1938; M1 II B Nr. 4435, Bürgermeister, Paderborn, to Herrn Regierungspräsidenten in Minden, September 15, 1939; D 14 Nr. 82, Farber to R. Angermann, October 8, 1940.

During the early years of the war the Paderborn library continued to prosper. Its opening day collection was forty-nine hundred vols; by 1944 that had become 8,509. Readership grew, although readers regrettably continued to prefer adventure stories and light reading. Just before the end of the war, however, on March 27, 1945, the library into which so much effort had gone was completely destroyed. In July 1945 the whereabouts of the librarian were unknown. Nordrhein-Westfälisches Staatsarchiv, Detmold, D 14 Nr. 146, Paderborn 1941/42, Paderborn 1942/43; D 14 Nr. 146a, Paderborn 1943/44; D 14 Nr. 82, SD-Aussenstelle Paderborn to —, September 3, 1942; D 14 Nr. 83, Bürgermeister, Paderborn, to Staatliche Volksbüchereistelle Regierungs-Bezirk Minden, September 7, 1945.

48. Nordrhein-Westfälisches Hauptstaatsarchiv, Düsseldorf, Zweigarchiv Schloss Kalkum, BR 1004/800, W. van der Briele to Herrn Regierungspräsidenten Düsseldorf, November 12, 1940; BR 1004/813, Staatliche Volksbüchereistelle für den Regierungsbezirk Düsseldorf, "Statistik der Neugründungen, 1. April 1941 bis 31. Marz 1942"; BR 1004/813, Staatliche Volksbüchereistelle für den Regierungsbezirk Düsseldorf, "Statistik der Neugründungen, 1. April 1942 bis 31. Marz 1943"; Nordrhein-Westfälisches Staatsarchiv, Detmold, D 14 Nr. 119, Staatliche Volksbüchereistelle für die Provinz Westfalen to Herrn Regierungspräsident, Minden, Z. Hd. Dr. Kratky, March 26, 1938.

49. Hodick, "Die willkommene Gelegenheit," p. 495.

50. Stadtarchiv, Saarbrücken, G. 6263, RWEV Vd 3207, EII, EIII, M, January 9, 1936; Bayerisches Hauptstaatsarchiv, München, MK 41473, Hermann Sauter to SMUK, September 5, 1936; Generallandesarchiv, Karlsruhe, 235/6865, RWEV Vb 1315, EIb, EIIb, EIIIa, EIIIb (b), October 20, 1938; Staatsarchiv, München, LRA 152 920, Sauter to Regierung Oberbayern, July 20, 1938; Borromäus Verein, Bonn, "Die Chronik des Generalsekretäriats seit 1919."

51. Borromäus Verein, Bonn, "Die Chronik des Generalsekretäriats seit 1919."

52. Ibid.

CHAPTER 11. DEFENDING GERMAN CULTURE

1. For a general discussion of the concept of ethnicity see Anthony D. Smith, *The Ethnic Origins of Nations* (Oxford: Basil Blackwell, 1986). A useful overview is Stephen M. Horak et al., *Eastern European National Minorities, 1919–1980: A Handbook* (Littleton, Colo.: Libraries Unlimited, 1985). Other works providing background for this chapter are Peter F. Sugar, ed., *Ethnic Diversity and Conflict in Eastern Europe* (Santa Barbara, Calif., and Oxford: ABC-Clio, 1980), and Anthony Komjathy and Rebecca Stockwell, *German Minorities and the Third Reich* (New York and London: Holmes and Meier, 1980).

2. Franz Schriewer, "Buch, Volk und Menschheit," in *Kultur, Buch, und Grenze: Grundfragen und Beispiele deutscher Bücherei- und Kulturarbeit in den Grenzgebieten,* ed. Franz Schriewer (Leipzig: Quelle und Meyer, 1930), p. 8.

3. Alfred Petrau, "Der 'Grenzbüchereidienst'—seine Geschichte und seine Leistung," in *Festschrift Wilhelm Scheffen* (n.p.: Grenzbüchereidienst, n.d.), pp. 24–74; Wilhelm Scheffen, "Zwanzig Jahre 'Grenzbüchereidienst'," *DB* 7 (1940): 257.

4. Franz Schriewer, "Das Grenzbüchereiwesen im neuen Staate," in Grenzbüchereidienst, *Mitteilungen* no. 12 (n.p.: Volk und Reich Verlag, 1933), p. 12.

5. Grenzbüchereidienst, *Mitteilungen* no. 14 (Berlin: n.p, 1936): frontispiece; K. C. von Loesch, "Volk und Staat im Vorland des Rheintales," in Grenzbüchereidienst, *Mitteilungen* no. 15 (Berlin: Volk und Reich, 1938): "Die Dreivölkerecke von Aubel," p. 81.

6. Petrau, pp. 24–25.

7. "Tagungsbericht," remarks by Kunckel, in Grenzbüchereidienst, *Mitteilungen* no. 16 (Berlin: Volk und Reich Verlag, 1939), p. 19.

8. Bayerisches Hauptstaatsarchiv, München, MK 41471, Korn to Hermann Bauer, July 20, 1929. Tables in Christensen, "Das Büchereiwesen in Nordschleswig, 1.4.1930 bis 31.3.1931," in *Das Grenzbüchereiwesen im Jahre 1930/31* (Flensburg: Zentrale für Nordmarkbüchereien, 1931) show that the Zentrale für Nordmark Büchereien in Flensburg, subsidized by the Grenzbüchereidienst, was supporting some German libraries in North Schleswig, which was Danish territory. This was the only regular exception to the rule that I have identified.

9. Generallandesarchiv, Karlsruhe, 235/6559, *Die büchereipolitische Lage in Baden,* Jahresbericht 1934/35, attachment: "Aufbauplan für das Volksbüchereiwesen in Baden"; Nordrhein-Westfälisches Hauptstaatsarchiv, Düsseldorf, Zweigarchiv Schloss Kalkum, BR 1004/793, van der Briele to Regierungspräsident, May 27, 1941; Deutsches Literaturarchiv, Erwin Ackerknecht Collection, Ackerknecht to [Margarete Schmeer], December 14, 1925; Ackerknecht to Horstmann, February 26, 1931; Ackerknecht to Elisab[eth] Kiderlen, November 12, 1927.

10. Scheffen, "Zwanzig Jahre 'Grenzbüchereidienst'"; *Grenzbüchereidienst 1937; Grenzbüchereidienst 1940.*

11. Fr[itz] Heiligenstaedt, "Das Volksbüchereiwesen im nordöstlichen Grenzraum," in Grenzbüchereidienst, *Mitteilungen* no. 16, p. 37.

12. Henry Albert Phillips, *Meet the Germans* (Philadelphia, Penn., and London: J. B. Lippincott, n.d.), p. 114.

13. Ernst Otto Thiele, *Polen greift an!* (Breslau, Wilh. Gottl. Korn, 1933). The work contains some statements and pictures so outrageous they are inadvertently amusing. One such is a picture of Polish geese marching to Germany. Its caption raises the question whether the 6 million marks paid by Germany for geese should be taken from the German economy and allowed to strengthen the Polish economy.

14. For example, Heinrich Horstmann, "Die praktische Volksbüchereiarbeit im Ostgebiet," in Grenzbüchereidienst, *Mitteilungen* no. 16.

15. Franz Schriewer, "Aus der Vorgeschichte des Grenzbüchereiwesens," manuscript in possession of Jürgen Schriewer, pp. 8–9; Erwin Ackerknecht, "Deutsche Bildungspflege in Oberschlesien," in *Oberschlesien: Ein Land deutscher Kultur* (Gleiwitz: Heimatverlag Oberschlesien, 1921).

16. Wilhelm Scheffen, "Grenzbüchereiarbeit im preußischen Osten," *DB* 1 (1934): 317.

17. *Handbuch der deutschen Volksbüchereien* (1940), p. 107; *Handbuch der deutschen Volksbüchereien; Nachtrag zum . . . 1938–40*, pp. 37–43. Franz Schriewer, *Das deutsche Volksbüchereiwesen in den Gemeinden unter 5,000 Einwohnern nach Zahlen und Massen* (Berlin: Reichsstelle für volkstümliches Büchereiwesen, 1937), Tabelle 3, p. 8. Schriewer's figures in this table are collected on a slightly different basis from those of the *Handbuch*, but they are essentially comparable. Only Prussia is covered. The figures are organized by Beratungsstelle, include rural areas only (the rural-to-urban ratio was approximately thirty to one in the later period), and are for the period October to September rather than April to March.

18. Franz Schriewer, "Die Ostbücherei, alte und neue Wege," *DB* 1 (1934): 151–61.

19. Heinrich Horstmann, "Aus der Volksbüchereiarbeit in Oberschlesien," in Grenzbüchereidienst, *Mitteilungen*, vol. 13 (Berlin: Volk und Reich Verlag, 1935), pp. 45–56; G. A. Narcisz, "Volksbüchereiarbeit in Niederschlesien," in ibid., pp. 57–66; Henrich Horstmann, "Die praktische Volksbüchereiarbeit im Ostgebiet"; Friedrich Leopold, "Volksbüchereiarbeit in einer oberschlesischen Industriegemeinde," in Grenzbüchereidienst, *Mitteilungen* no. 16 (Berlin: Volk und Reich Verlag, 1939), pp. 95–103; Anne Jurgens, "Aus meiner Beratungsstellenarbeit in Oberschlesien," *DB* 2 (1935): 90–91.

20. *Encyclopaedia Britannica*, 14th ed., s.vv. "Saar (Sarre) Territory," by N.P.C.M.

21. Eva-Maria Desczyk, "Zur Bibliotheksgeschichte des Saarlandes," Student paper, Fachhochschule für Bibliothekswesen, Stuttgart, 1977.

22. Ibid.; Adolf Waas, "Unsere fahrbare Bücherei an der Saar," *HfB* 12 (1928): 138–41.

23. Bayerisches Hauptstaatsarchiv, München, MK 41461, Reichsmittel für kulturelle Fürsorge im ehemals besetzten Gebiete, 1. Halbjahr des Rechnungsjahr 1930.

24. Walther Koch, "Die Bücherei an der Saar in ihrer volkspolitischen Bedeutung," *DB* 1 (1934): 393–403; quotation on p. 402.

25. *Grenzbüchereidienst 1934*; Petrau, p. 52.

26. Stadtarchiv, Saarbrücken, G 6418, "Bericht des Kulturwartes der Deutschen Front," Otto Keller, Jägersfreude, March 5, 1935.

27. Bayerisches Hauptstaatsarchiv, München, MK 41461, "Bericht über die Grenzbüchereilage des Volksbücherei-Beratungsstelle Rheinpfalz, 6. im Lenzing 1935"; "Übersicht über der Pfalzhilfezinsen und der kulturellen Reichsmittel . . . Jahre 1928 mit 1932."

28. Table: "Deutsches Reich," in Germany, Statistisches Reichsamt, *Die deutschen Volksbüchereien nach Ländern, Provinzen und Gemeinden, 1933/34*; Schriewer, *Das deutsche Volksbüchereiwesen in den Gemeinden unter 5,000 Einwohnern nach Zahlen und Massen*, Tabelle 3, p. 8; *Handbuch der deutschen Volksbüchereien* (1940), p. 189, and *Nachtrag zum . . . 1938–40*, pp. 68–69.

29. The best account of Schleswig's physical and economic geography is in Rudolf Heberle, *From Democracy to Nazism: A Regional Case Study on Political Parties in Germany* (New York: Howard Fertig, 1970), pp. 34–39.

30. Franz Schriewer, *Bauer und Buch*, Sonderdruck aus der *Neuen Landjugend* 11 and 12 (September and October 1929) (Wittenberg: Zentralverlag für Berufs- und Fachschule, n.d.); Franz Schriewer, "Landschaft, Mensch und Buch im Grenzland Schleswig," in Franz Schriewer, ed., *Kultur, Buch und Grenze*, pp. 68–87; Petrau, p. 33; *Handbuch der deutschen Volksbüchereien* (1940), pp. 27–28, and *Nachtrag zum . . . 1938–40*, p. 19.

31. Rudolf Reuter, "Die Aufgaben der Volksbücherei in der deutschen Westmark," *DB* 2 (1935): 215–23.

32. Josef Wutz, "Von den Volksbüchereien der Bayerischen Ostmark," in Grenzbüchereidienst, *Mitteilungen* no. 14 (Berlin, 1936), pp. 61–64.

33. In 1929 the director of the Beratungsstelle in Munich commented that Czech efforts had made the Bavarian population dissatisfied with their own lack of cultural institutions and conscious of neglect. Bayerisches Hauptstaatsarchiv, München, MK 41472, Fischer to BSUK, June 20, 1929; Arthur Herr, "Sudetendeutsches Büchereiwesen und Büchereigesetz," *DB* 6 (1939): 500–10; *Handbuch der deutschen Volksbüchereien; Nachtrag zum . . . 1938–40*, p. 100; "Positive und negative Büchereipolitik," *DB* 1 (1934): 199–200.

34. Deutsches Literaturarchiv, Erwin Ackerknecht Collection, Schlüter to Oberbürgermeister, June 28, 1939; Auslandsdeutsche Büchereien, "Erster Entwurf eines Statistischen Überblicks," undated.

35. Heinz Roscher, "Deutsches Büchereiwesen jenseits der Reichsgrenzen," *DB* 1 (1934): 538; Deutsches Literaturarchiv, Erwin Ackerknecht Collection, "Deutsche Volksbücherei in Eldorado, Argentina."

36. Deutsches Literaturarchiv, Erwin Ackerknecht Collection, Karl Koberg to Ackerknecht, December 18, 1929.

37. Deutsches Literaturarchiv, Erwin Ackerknecht Collection, Ackerknecht to Lockle, February 15, 1928.

38. "Stichworte und Zahlen in Ergänzung des Jahresberichts 1935/36," *Der Auslands Deutsche* 19 (October 1936): 739–40; Borromäus Verein, "Bericht des Borromäusvereins in Bonn über Büchersendungen an auslandsdeutsche Stellen . . . 1. Januar bis 31. Dezember 1938."

39. Borromäus Verein, "Flensburger Tagung der Auslands-bibliothekare"; Deutsches Literaturarchiv, Erwin Ackerknecht Collection, Gerda von Hollander to Ackerknecht, August 25, 1934.

40. Deutsches Literaturarchiv, Erwin Ackerknecht Collection, Ackerknecht to Kock, March 4, 1927; Karl Koberg to Ackerknecht, December 18, 1929.

41. Deutsches Literaturarchiv, Erwin Ackerknecht Collection, G. von Hollander, "Deutsche Volksbüchereiarbeit in Lettland, 14/11/35."

42. Willy Salewski, "Tradition und Aufbau: Das Volksbüchereiwesen im Raum des Reichsgaues Wartheland," *DB* 8 (1941): 286; *Handbuch der deutschen Volksbüchereien; Nachtrag zum . . . 1938–40*, pp. 102–103; *Grenzbüchereidienst 1941*.

43. Zentrales Staatsarchiv, Potsdam, 62 DAF 3, 19367, Bl. 101, "Aufbau der Volksbüchereien in Ost und West: Von Straßburg bis Litzmannstadt," *Völkischer Beobachter*, December 16, 1940; 62 DAF 3 19367, Bl. 2, "22000 öffentliche Büchereien im Reich," *Deutsche Allgemeine Zeitung*, November 6, 1943.

44. *Handbuch der deutschen Volksbüchereien* (1940), p. 210, and *Nachtrag zum . . . 1938–40*, pp. 70, 100.

45. Franz Schriewer, *Vorträge: Kultur und Grenzpolitik*, "Bedingungen, Formen und Lehren der Kulturellen Grenzarbeit," November 15, 1947, privately bound volume in possession of Jürgen Schriewer.

CHAPTER 12. THE WAR YEARS

1. Zentrales Staatsarchiv, Potsdam, 62 DAF 3, 19366, Bl. 14, "Gegenwärtige Aufgaben der öffentlichen Volksbüchereien," *Deutsche Wissenschaft, Erziehung und Volksbildung*, October 20, 1939; Stadtbibliothek, Bremen, 3S. 19 Nr. 154 [12], RWEV Vb 2244/39, September 12, 1939.

2. Nordrhein-Westfälisches Staatsarchiv, Detmold, D 14 Nr. 185, Biemsen-Ahmsen, Rundschreiben, Staatliche Volksbüchereistelle für das Land Lippe, September 20, 1939.

3. Niedersächsisches Staatsarchiv, Wolfenbüttel, 12 A Neu 13 19011, RWEV Vb 1668/43, September 17, 1943.

4. Nordrhein-Westfälisches Staatsarchiv, Detmold, D 14 Nr. 168, Rundschreiben Nr. 1943/4, Entwurf; Generallandesarchiv, Karlsruhe, 235/6564, Badisches Ministerium des Kultus und Unterricht to RWEV, October 25, 1943.

5. Staatsarchiv der Senat der Freien und Hansestadt Hamburg, Hamburger Öffentliche Bücherhallen, File 12 Bd. 7, Rundschreiben Nr. 15, October 13, 1944; Hessisches Staatsarchiv, Darmstadt, G 15 Alsfeld XX, RWEV Vb 1 Nr. 2569/44 (a), October 2, 1944.

6. Fritz Heiligenstaedt, "Zur Jahreswende 1940/41," *DB* 8 (1941): 1–2; Nordrhein-Westfälisches Staatsarchiv, Detmold, D 14 Nr. 129, RV, Nr. 41/37/26, December 29, 1941; RV, Nr. 43/36/30, December [3]1, 1943; RV, Nr. 44/40/27, December 20, 1944.

7. Hessisches Staatsarchiv, Darmstadt, G 15 Alsfeld XX, RWEV Vb 1 Nr. 2569/44 (a), October 2, 1944; Nordrhein-Westfälisches Staatsarchiv, Detmold, D 14 Nr. 129, RV, Nr. 43/35, December 19, 1943.

8. Staatsarchiv der Senat der Freien und Hansestadt Hamburg, Hamburger Öffentliche Bücherhallen, File 15, RV, Nr. 39/21/15, September 20, 1939.

9. Bayerisches Hauptstaatsarchiv, München, MK 41454, RWEV V1 777/44 (b), May 31, 1944; Nordrhein-Westfälisches Staatsarchiv, Detmold, D 14 Nr. 168, B. Schladebach to Dr. Bonwetsch, May 5, 1942.

10. Staatsarchiv der Senat der Freien und Hansestadt Hamburg, Hamburger Öffentliche Bücherhallen, File 12, Bd. 2, Nr. 107, June 3, 1940.

11. Nordrhein-Westfälisches Staatsarchiv, Detmold, D 14 Nr. 149, memorandum from Dr. Angermann, Staatliche Volksbüchereistelle für die Provinz Westfalen, July 3, 1941; Staatsarchiv der Senat der Freien und Hansestadt Hamburg, Hamburger Öffentliche Bücherhallen, File 15, RV Nr. 41/26/17, August 9, 1941; RV Nr. 41/34/24, October 21, 1941; File 12, Bd. 4, Nr. 52, September 18, 1941.

12. Staatsarchiv der Senat der Freien und Hansestadt Hamburg, Hamburger Öffentliche Bücherhallen, File 15, RV Nr. 40/10/10, February 26, 1940; RV Nr. 40/24/19, May 24, 1940; RV Nr. 42/14/13, May 21, 1942.

13. Bayerisches Hauptstaatsarchiv, München, MK 41454, Rosa Kästner to the National Sozialistische Deutsche Arbeiter Partei Gauleitung, München, January

2, 1944; MK 41454, Springer, Gauamtsleiter to Rosa Kästner, January 4, 1944; MK 41454, RWEV V1 777/44 (b), May 31, 1944.

14. Nordrhein-Westfälisches Staatsarchiv, Detmold, M1 II B Nr. 4435, "Zeitgerechte Erneuerung der Buchbestände der Volksbüchereien," April 9, 1940; D 14 Nr. 129, RV Nr. 43/7/6, May 13, 1943; Staatsarchiv der Senat der Freien und Hansestadt Hamburg, Hamburger Öffentliche Bücherhallen, File 12 Bd. 3, Nr. 24, July 10, 1939.

15. Nordrhein-Westfälisches Staatsarchiv, Detmold, M1 II B Nr. 4335 Vb 1937, E II a (b), October 15, 1940; Bayerisches Hauptstaatsarchiv, München, MK 41456, BSMUK to RWEV, October 28, 1940.

16. Nordrhein-Westfälisches Staatsarchiv, Detmold, D 14 Nr. 172, Förster to Staatliche Volksbüchereistelle für das Land Lippe, April 4, 1940.

17. Nordrhein-Westfälisches Staatsarchiv, Detmold, D 14 Nr. 173, RV to Herren Leiter der Staatlichen Volksbüchereistellen, May 22, 1942; Josef Witsch, "Die Herbstveranstaltungen des deutschen Schrifttums und die deutsche Volksbücherei," *DB* 9 (1942): 263–68.

18. Nordrhein-Westfälisches Staatsarchiv, Detmold, D 14 Nr. 173, EKH to Herren Gaubeauftragten des Börsenvereins der deutschen Buchhändler zu Leipzig, December 18, 1944.

19. Nordrhein-Westfälisches Staatsarchiv, Detmold, D 14 Nr. 173 [Staatliche Volksbüchereistelle für das Land Lippe] to EKH, March 31, 1945.

20. Nordrhein-Westfälisches Staatsarchiv, Detmold, D 14 Nr. 133, Bastian to Staatliche Volksbüchereistelle für den Regierungs-Bezirk Minden, March 12, 1942; Rang to RV, September 22, 1942; D 14 Nr. 173, Witsch to Dr. B. Schladebach, January 31, 1942.

21. Nordrhein-Westfälisches Staatsarchiv, Detmold, D 14 Nr. 133, Rang to RV, June 24, 1942; M1 II B Nr. 4437, RWEV V1 Nr. 1155/44, July 1, 1944; Staatsarchiv der Senat der Freien und Hansestadt Hamburg, Hamburger Öffentliche Bücherhallen, File 12, Bd. 3, Nr. 89, February 23, 1940; File 12, Bd. 3, Nr. 42, September 1939; Niedersächsisches Staatsarchiv, Bückeburg, Schaumburg Des L 4 Nr. 10322, Landrat, Kreis Bückeburg, to Leiter, Volksbüchereistelle für Schaumburg-Lippe, January 22, 1941.

22. Nordrhein-Westfälisches Staatsarchiv, Detmold, D 14 Nr. 129, RV, unnumbered memorandum, January 2, 1944; Boese, *Das öffentliche Bibliothekswesen*, p. 333; Bayerisches Hauptstaatsarchiv, München, MK 41457, telegram from [Kafitz] to Stengel, BSUK, March 10, 1943; Franz Kafitz to Regierungspräsident Ansbach, March 11, 1943; Franz Kafitz to V[on] Stengel, BSUK, August 30, 1943; interview with Hanna Bieger, Flensburg, August 9, 1987.

23. Staatliche Beratungsstelle für öffentliche Büchereien, Bayreuth, File BSUK, 1945–1954, Ba[ruch] to BSUK, November 9, 1945, Übersicht; Nordrhein-Westfälisches Staatsarchiv, Detmold, D 14 Nr. 103.

24. Stadtarchiv, Kiel, 40790, clipping from *Deutsche Wissenschaft, Erziehung und Volksbildung*, vol. 9, p. 175 [1943]; Niedersächsisches Staatsarchiv, Wolfenbüttel, 12 A Neu 13 19012, Flechsig to Klagges, September 28, 1944; 12 A Neu 13 19020, Becker, librarian of Weddel, to Herrn Braunschweigischen Minister für Volksbildung, August 24, 1944; Braunschweigischer Minister für Volksbildung to Lehrer Becker, Weddel, VI 874/44, September 8, 1944.

25. Staatsarchiv der Senat der Freien und Hansestadt Hamburg, Hamburger Öffentliche Bücherhallen, File 12 Bd. 4, Nr. 56, September 30, 1941; File 16 Bd. 2 [Report], January 25, 1944, Hamburger Öffentliche Bücherhallen; File 16 Bd. 2, to Verwaltung für Kunst- und Kulturgelegenleiten, from B[öhmer], February 21, 1944. Gordon Musgrove, *Operation Gomorrah: The Hamburg Firestorm Raids* (London, New York, and Sydney: Jane's, 1981), and Martin Middlebrook, *The Battle of Hamburg: Allied Bomber Forces against a German City in 1943* (New York: Charles Scribner's Sons, 1980) treat the 1943 bombing of Hamburg in detail.

26. Staatsarchiv der Senat der Freien und Hansestadt Hamburg, Hamburger Öffentliche Bücherhallen, File 24, *Hamburger Tageblatt*, "Zu den alten Lesern kamen jetzt viele neue," September 7, 1943; File 16 Bd. 2, M. F. to Dr. Krebs, August 27, 1943; File 23, notice to *Hamburger Fremdenblatt, H. Tageblatt, H. Anzeiger*, April 19, 1944; File 38, "Bericht über die Einrichtung der öffentlichen Bücherhallen B."

27. Nordrhein-Westfälisches Staatsarchiv, Detmold, D 14 Nr. 168, Wiegand to Wehrbezirkskommando, January 11, 1941; Staatsarchiv der Senat der Freien und Hansestadt Hamburg, Hamburger Öffentliche Bücherhallen, File 1b Bd. 1, Joerden to Verwaltung für Kunst- und Kulturangelegenheiten, July 31, 1940; File 1b Bd. 1, B[öhmer] to Verwaltung für Kunst- und Kulturangelegenheiten, November 4, 1940.

28. Bayerisches Hauptstaatsarchiv, München, MK 41456, "Das Volksbüchereiwesen in der Bayerischen Ostmark im Jahre 1939/40"; "Das Volksbüchereiwesen im der Pfalz im Jahre 1941/42"; interview, Rudolf Joerden, Hamburg, June 19, 1984.

29. Deutsches Literaturarchiv, Erwin Ackerknecht Collection, 40641, 1942, Mappe II, Ackerknecht to Grimm, September 10, 1942; Bayerisches Hauptstaatsarchiv, München, MK 41456, "Das Büchereiwesen in Mittelfranken und Mainfranken im Jahre 1943/44."

30. Bayerisches Hauptstaatsarchiv, München, MK 41475, Stengel, BSUK, to Bayer, Staatsminister des Innern, March 6, 1943; Niedersächsisches Staatsarchiv, Wolfenbüttel, 12 A Neu 13 19016, Braunschweigischer Minister für Volksbildung to Dr. Benecke, Deutschen Gemeindetag, January 19, 1945.

31. Staatsarchiv der Senat der Freien und Hansestadt Hamburg, Hamburger Öffentliche Bücherhallen, File 12 Bd. 4, Rundschreiben Nr. 5, April 12, 1943; File 12 Bd. 3, Rundschreiben Nr. 98, May 3, 1940; Nordrhein-Westfälisches Staatsarchiv, Detmold, D 14 Nr. 129, RV Nr. 41/11–, April 8, 1941.

32. Staatsarchiv der Senat der Freien und Hansestadt Hamburg, Hamburger Öffentliche Bücherhallen, File 13, "Statistikzahlen der Hamburger Öffentlichen Bücherhallen in den Kriegsjahren [1942]"; "Statistikzahlen der Hamburger Öffentlichen Bücherhallen in den Kriegsjahren," stamped September 5, 1942.

33. Nordrhein-Westfälisches Staatsarchiv, Detmold, D 14 Nr. 128, "Nachrichten aus den deutschen Volksbüchereien," December 1939; Richtlinen für die Büchersammlung der NSDAP; RV Rundschreiben Nr. 39/25/19; Staatsarchiv der Senat der Freien und Hansestadt Hamburg, Hamburger Öffentlichen Bücherhallen, File 12 Bd. 4, Nr. 26, November 18, 1942.

34. Nordrhein-Westfälisches Staatsarchiv, Detmold, D 14 Nr. 169, B. Schladebach to Heiligenstaedt, December 2, 1939.

35. Ibid.; Deutsches Literaturarchiv, Erwin Ackerknecht Collection, Ackerknecht to Saltzwedel, October 23, 1939.

36. Nordrhein-Westfälisches Staatsarchiv, Detmold, D 14 Nr. 128, RV, Nr. 43/17–, September 18, 1943; Niedersächsisches Staatsarchiv, Bückeburg, Schaumburg Des L 4 Nr. 10322, mimeographed memorandum, October 14, 1943, Hille.

37. Staatliche Beratungsstelle für öffentliche Büchereien, Bayreuth, File Ahorn, Arbeitsbericht, 1943/44; Nordrhein-Westfälisches Staatsarchiv, Detmold, "Besuch der Bibliothekarin Haeger in Halle i. W. am 14.1.44"; Staatsarchiv der Senat der Freien und Hansestadt Hamburg, Hamburger Öffentliche Bücherhallen, File 20 Bd. 2, "Die Öffentlichen Bücherhallen im Kriege [1941]"; Staatliche Beratungsstelle für öffentliche Büchereien, Bayreuth, File Hof, Jahresbericht 1943/44; Nordrhein-Westfälisches Staatsarchiv, Detmold, D 14 Nr. 146, "Jahresstatistik, Gehlenbeck (Kreis Lübbecke) 1942/43."

38. Nordrhein-Westfälisches Staatsarchiv, Detmold, D 14 Nr. 129, RV Nr. 44/40/27, December 20, 1944.

39. Staatsarchiv der Senat der Freien und Hansestadt Hamburg, Hamburger Öffentliche Bücherhallen, File 20 Bd. 2, "Die öffentliche Bücherhallen im Kriege [1941]"; File 13, "Statistikzahlen der Hamburger Öffentlichen Bücherhallen in den Kriegsjahren"; *Jahresbericht der Stadtbücherei Frankfurt/Oder, 1.4.43–31.3.44* (Frankfurt/Oder, 1944); *Zusammenfassung und Erschliessung des stadt- und heimatgeschichtlichen Schrifttums* (Frankfurt/Oder, 1943).

Bibliography

INTERVIEWS

Anneliese Benneman, Duisburg, June 26, 1984
Lydia Gross, Kiel, May 8, 1984
Hans Ludwig and Frau Hofman, Marbach am Neckar, July 15, 1985
Martha Höhl, Bremen, May 1984
Alfred and Frau Jennewein, Stuttgart, July 14, 1985
Rudolf and Erika Joerden, Hamburg, June 19, 1984
Sitta Krause, Celle, May 18, 1984
Adolf von Morzé, Berlin, May 21, 1984
Jürgen Schriewer and Hanna Bieger, Flensburg, August 9, 1987
Dietrich Vorwerk, Villingen, July 25, 1985

MANUSCRIPTS AND ARCHIVES

Bayreuth. Staatliche Volksbüchereistelle für öffentliche Büchereien
Berlin Documentation Center
Bonn. Borromäus Verein
Bremen. Staatsarchiv; Stadtbibliothek
Bückeburg. Niedersächsisches Staatsarchiv
Darmstadt. Hessisches Staatsarchiv
Detmold. Nordrhein-Westfälisches Staatsarchiv
Duisburg. Stadtarchiv
Düsseldorf. Nordrhein-Westfälisches Hauptstaatsarchiv, Zweigarchiv Schloss
    Kalkum
Freiburg. Staatsarchiv; Stadtarchiv
Hamburg. Senat der Freien und Hansestadt Hamburg, Staatsarchiv
Hanover. Staatsarchiv; Stadtarchiv; Stadtbibliothek
Heidelberg. Stadtbücherei
Karlsruhe. Generallandesarchiv; Stadtbibliothek
Kiel. Stadtarchiv
Koblenz. Bundesarchiv
Leipzig. Deutsche Staatsbibliothek

Lingen. Stadtbücherei
Marbach am Neckar. Deutsches Literaturarchiv, Erwin Ackerknecht Collection
München. Bayerisches Hauptstaatsarchiv; Staatsarchiv; Stadtarchiv
Oldenburg. Niedersächsisches Staatsarchiv
Potsdam. Zentrales Staatsarchiv
Saarbrücken. Stadtarchiv
Stuttgart. Fachhochschule für Bibliothekswesen, Walter Hofmann Archiv
Washington, D.C. National Archives
Wien. Städtische Büchereien
Wolfenbüttel. Niedersächsisches Staatsarchiv

PRINTED MATERIALS

Aachen: Öffentliche Bibliothek 150 Jahre. Aachen: Öffentliche Bibliothek der Stadt Aachen, 1981.

Abel, Heinrich. "Hitler-Jugend und öffentliche Bücherei." *DB* 4 (1937): 41–43.

Abraham, Hans F. German Public Libraries as Agencies of Propaganda. Typescript, June 1944.

Ackerknecht, Erwin. "Bibliothekarische Berufsgesinnung." Orig. pub. 1925; reprinted in *Büchereifragen.* 2d ed. Berlin: Weidmannsche Buchhandlung, 1926.

———. "Bücherei und Politik." Orig. pub. 1924; reprinted in *Büchereifragen.* 2d ed. Berlin: Wiedmannsche Buchhandlung, 1926.

———. "Die Büchereiaufgaben der deutschen Städte (1922)." In *Büchereifragen.* 2d ed. Berlin: Weidmannsche Buchhandlung, 1926.

———. *Büchereifragen.* 2d ed. Berlin: Weidmannsche Buchhandlung, 1926.

———. "Deutsche Bildungspflege in Oberschlesien." In *Oberschlesien: Ein Land deutscher Kultur.* Gleiwitz: Heimatverlag Oberschlesien, 1921.

———. "Werbemittel und Benutzertaktik (1917)." In *Büchereifragen.* 2d ed. Berlin: Weidmannsche Buchhandlung, 1926.

———. "Zur Psychologie der Schundliteratur." Orig. pub. 1919; reprinted in *Büchereifragen.* 2d ed. Berlin: Weidmannsche Buchhandlung, 1926.

Ackerknecht, E., and G. Fritz. *Büchereifragen.* Berlin: n.p., 1914.

Ahlers, Otto. "Zum Aufbau eines deutschen Büchereiwesens im Generalgouvernement." *DB* 8 (1941): 334–37.

Aigner, Dietrich. "Die Indizierung 'schädlichen und unerwünschten Schrifttums' im Dritten Reich." *Archiv für Geschichte des Büchereiwesens* 11 (1971): 933–1034.

Akerman, Achim von. "Berichte: Aus der Arbeit der staatlichen Volksbüchereistelle für den Reg.-Bez. Hohensalza." *DB* 8 (1941): 395–96.

Aley, Peter. *Jungendliteratur im Dritten Reich.* Schriften zur Buchmarkt-Forschung, vol. 12. Hamburg: Verlag für Buchmarkt-Forschung, 1967.

"Allgemeine Lagerbericht der Teilnehmer." In *Die Arbeitslager der Volksbibliothekare 1936 und 1937.* Leipzig: n.p., 1938.

"Amtliche Bekanntmachungen." *DB* 5 (1938): 367–68.

"Amtliche Erlässe und Anordnungen." *DB* 4 (1937): 219–27.

"Amtliche Erlässe und Bekanntmachungen." *DB* 3 (1936): 141–42, 236–40, 421–31, 478–80.

Bibliography

"Amtliche Erlässe und Bekanntmachungen." *DB* 4 (1937): 269–70, 340.

"Amtliche Erlässe und Mitteilungen." *DB* 2 (1935): 275–80, 390, 477–80.

"Amtliche Verfügungen." *DB* 5 (1938): 470–73.

"Amtliche Verfügungen: Richtlinien für das Volksbüchereiwesen." *DB* 5 (1938): 39–46.

"Amtliche Verfügungen: Umsatzsteuer bei Museen, Büchereien und Schwimmbädern." *DB* 5 (1938): 188.

"An die Deutsche Studentenschaft." In *Die Bücherverbrennung zum 10. Mai 1933.* Ed. Gerhard Sauder. Munich and Vienna: Carl Hauser Verlag, 1983.

"An unsere Bezieher." *DB* 5 (1938): unnumbered.

Andrae, Friedrich. "Einleitung." In *Volksbücherei und Nationalsozialismus.* Comp. Friedrich Andrae. Wiesbaden: O. Harrassowitz, 1970.

———, comp. *Volksbücherei und Nationalsozialismus.* Beiträge zum Büchereiwesen. Reihe B. Quellen und Texte. Heft 3. Wiesbaden: O. Harrassowitz, 1970.

———, ed. *Bibliothek '76: Rückschau und Ausblick: Ein Freundensgabe für Werner Mevissen zu seinem 65. Geburtstag am 16. April 1976.* Bremen: Stadtbibliothek, n.d.

Angermann, Rudolf. "Säuberung nach der Säuberung: Eine dringende Aufgabe." *DB* 2 (1935): 281–83.

"Anordnung des REM über die Einziehung des ausgesonderten Schrifttums vom 10.5. 1937." In *Volksbücherei und Nationalsozialismus.* Comp. Friedrich Andrae. Wiesbaden: O. Harrassowitz, 1970.

"Arbeitsberichte: Ausstellung der staatlichen Grenzbüchereistelle Bayreuth auf der 'Ostmarkschau 1937' in Weiden." *DB* 4 (1937): 268–69.

Die Arbeitslager der Volksbibliothekare 1936 und 1937. Leipzig, 1938.

Arendt, Hannah. *The Origins of Totalitarianism.* New ed. San Diego, New York, and London: Harcourt Brace Jovanovich, 1973.

Ashby, Robert F. "The German Public Library." *Library Association Record* 39 (1937): 379–84.

"Die Aufgaben des Besprechungsteiles in unserer Zeitschrift." *DB* 5 (1938): 9–11.

"Aus der Ansprache des Gauhauptmanns der Sudentenlandes Dr. A. Kreissl bei der Eröffnung der neuen Stadtbücherei in Komotau am 14. September 1940." *Nachrichten aus den deutschen Volksbüchereien* (October 1940): 1–7.

"Aus der Beratungsstellenarbeit." *DB* 1 (1934): 172–73.

"Aus der Büchereiarbeit." *DB* 3 (1936): 143–44, 189–91.

"Aus der Fachschaft—für die Fachschaft." *DB* 1 (1934): 69, 197–201, 250–54, 309–12, 389–92, 580–84.

"Aus der Fachschaft—für die Fachschaft." *DB* 2 (1935): 44–47, 90–95, 183–91, 235–40, 390–91, 480–86.

"Die Ausbildung akademischer Anwärter für den Beruf des Volksbibliothekars in Preußen." *DB* 1 (1934): 38.

Ayçoberry, Pierre. *The Nazi Question: An Essay on the Interpretations of National Socialism.* Trans. Robert Hurley. New York: Pantheon, 1981.

Bayer, Karl Th. "Von der Verantwortung des Bildungsbibliothekars in unserer Zeit." *Geisteskultur* 42 (1933): 130–35.

Becker, Heinrich. *Zwischen Wahn und Wahrheit.* Berlin: Verlag der Nation, 1972.

Beer, Johannes. "Autorität und Volksbildung." *BuB* 13 (1933): 19–27.

———. "Buchauswahl vom volksbibliothekarischen Standpunkt aus." *Die Volks-bücherei im Rhein-Main-Gebiet* 2 (June 1939): 1–5.

———. "Deutsche Volksbüchereistatistik in den Verwaltungsjahren 1932/33 bis 1934/35." *DB* 2 (1935): 393–401.

"Begrüßungen." In Grenzbüchereidienst, *Mitteilungen*, vol. 17. N.p., n.d.

"Begrüßungsansprachen." In Grenzbüchereidienst, *Mitteilungen*, vol. 15. Berlin: Volk und Reich Verlag, 1938.

Beintker, ———. "Bücherei im Arbeitsdienst." *DB* 1 (1934): 333–40.

Bergtel-Schleif, Lotte. "Möglichkeiten volksbibliothekarischer Arbeit unter dem Nationalsozialismus." *Der Volksbibliothekar* 1 (April 1947): 193–207.

"Bericht aus der Büchereiarbeit." *DB* 3 (1936): 91–95.

"Berichte: Aus dem Volksbüchereiwesen der Provinz Hannover." *DB* 6 (1939): 233–34.

"Berichte: Die Entwicklung des Danziger Volksbüchereiwesens in Stadt und Land." *DB* 5 (1938): 163–65.

"Berichte: Die Verankerung des Grenzbüchereiwesens an der Saar nach der Rückgliederung." *DB* 6 (1939): 378–79.

"Berichte: Von der Leistungsschau der deutschen Volksbüchereien in Leipzig 1938." *DB* 6 (1939): 235–40.

"Berichte und Mitteilungen." *DB* 4 (1937): 402–403.

"Berichte und Mitteilungen: Bericht über die Zusammenarbeit der städtischen Volksbücherei Schneidemühl mit der HJ." *DB* 4 (1937): 488–95.

"Berichte und Mitteilungen: Neuordnung des Werkbüchereiwesens in Sachsen." *DB* 5 (1938): 375–76.

"Berichte und Mitteilungen: Zur zweiten Ausgabe der Reichsliste für Dorf-büchereien." *DB* 5 (1938): 372–73.

Beyer, Hans. "Das Reich sozialistischer Volksordnung." *DB* 1 (1934): 203–209.

———. "Schrifttum das wir ablehnen." *DB* 1 (1934): 255–59.

[Beyer, Hans]. "Der Widerstand in den Büchereien." *Die Tat* 26 (July 1934): 314–16, and (August 1934): 398–400.

Biographisch Lexikon für Schleswig-Holstein und Lübeck. Neumünster: Wach-holtz, 1982. S. vv. Dähnhardt, Heinz.

Birdsall, William F. "The Political Persuasion of Librarianship." *Library Journal* 113 (June 1, 1988): pp. 75–79.

Boese, Engelbrecht. "Die Bestandspolitik der öffentlichen Büchereien im Dritten Reich." *Bibliotheksdienst* 17 (1983): 263–82.

———. *Das öffentliche Bibliothekswesen im Dritten Reich.* Bad Honnef: Bock und Herchen, 1987.

———. "Die Säuberung der Leipziger Bücherhallen 1933–1936." *Buch und Bibliothek* 35 (1983): 283–96.

———. "Walter Hofmanns 'Institut für Leser- und Schrifttumskunde', 1926–1937." *Bibliothek: Forschung und Praxis* 5 (1981): 3–23.

Bollmus, Adalbert. "Die Stadtbücherei Drossen nach der Neuordnung." *DB* 2 (1935): 237–39.

Bongard, Hans. "Grundlinien deutscher Kulturpolitik an der Saar." In *Die*

Bibliography

Grundlagen des Saarkampfes. Ed. Adolf Grabowsky and Georg Wilhelm Sante. Berlin: Carl Heymanns Verlag, 1934.

Borromäus Verein. *Jahresbericht 1933.* Bonn: Verein vom heiligen Karl Borromäus, 1934.

Bouhler, —. "Die Arbeit der Prüfungskommission zum Schutze des NS-Schrifttums." *DB* 1 (1934): 534.

Bracher, Karl Dietrich. *The German Dictatorship: The Origins, Structure, and Consequences of National Socialism.* Trans. Jean Steinberg. N.p.: Penguin University Books, 1978.

Brady, Robert A. *The Spirit and Structure of German Fascism.* New York: Viking, 1937.

Braun, —, and — Eggebrecht. "Gegenentwurf." *BuB* 7 (1927): 118–20.

Briele, Wolfgang van der. "Der heutige Stand des Volksbüchereiwesens im rheinischen Grenzgebiet (Reg.-Bez. Düsseldorf und Aachen) und der weitere Aufbau eines Öffentlichen Büchereiwesens." *DB* 1 (1934): 542–44.

Brodkey, Harold. "Reading, the Most Dangerous Game." *New York Times Book Review,* November 24, 1985, pp. 1, 44–45.

Broszat, Martin. *German National Socialism, 1919–1945.* Trans. Kurt Rosenbaum and Inge Pauli Boehm. Santa Barbara, Calif.: Clio Press, 1966.

———. *The Hitler State: The Foundation and Development of the Internal Structure of the Third Reich.* Trans. John W. Hiden. London and New York: Longman, 1982.

———. "Politische Denunziationen in der NS-Zeit." *Archivalische Zeitschrift* 73 (1977): 221–38.

Brown, Eileen. "War Damage, 1939–1945, and Postwar Reconstruction in Libraries of the Federal German Republic and England: A Comparison." *Journal of Librarianship* 7 (October 1975): 288–307.

"Bucheinkauf für die volkstümlichen Büchereien." *DB* 1 (1934): 487.

"Die Bücher der Volksbücherei." *Die Volksbücherei im Rhein-Main-Gebiet* 6 (August 1944): 19–25.

"Bücherschau: Bücher gegen das Reich." *DB* 1 (1934): 298–99.

Bullock, Alan. *Hitler: A Study in Tyranny.* Rev. ed. N.p.: Penguin, 1962.

Busse, Kurt. "Die Werkbücherei als sozialpolitische Aufgabe der Betriebe." *DB* 8 (1941): 357–60.

Buzas, Ladislaus. *Deutsche Bibliotheksgeschichte der neuesten Zeit (1800–1945).* Vol. 3: *Elemente des Buch- und Bibliothekswesens,* ed. Fridolin Dressler and Gerhard Leibers. Wiesbaden: Dr. Ludwig Reichert Verlag, 1978.

Carnovsky, L. "Libraries in Nazi Germany." *Library Journal* 59 (November 15, 1934): 893–94.

Christensen, —. "Das Büchereiwesen in Nordschleswig." In *Das Grenzbüchereiwesen im Jahre 1930/31.* Flensburg: Zentrale für Nordmarkbüchereien, 1931.

Christensen, Fritz. "Deutsche Büchereien in Nordschleswig." *DB* 2 (1935): 49–55.

"Contrasts in Library Service." *ALA Bulletin* 29 (May 1935): 252–55.

D'Agata, Brigitte Prorini, and Gustav Rottacker. "Zur geschichtlichen Entwicklung des Öffentlichen Bibliothekswesens in Stuttgart." In *Biblio-*

thekarische Arbeit zwischen Theorie und Praxis: Beiträge zum bibliothekarischen Fachwissen und Berichte über bibliothekarische Aktivitäten. Festgabe für Wolfgang Thauer. Ed. Peter Vodosek. Stuttgart: Fachhochschule für Bibliothekswesen, 1976.

Dahn, Völker. "Die nationalsozialistische Schrifttumspolitik nach dem 10. Mai 1933." In *10. Mai 1933: Bücherverbrennung in Deutschland und die Folgen.* Ed. Ulrich Walberer. Frankfurt am Main: Fischer Taschenbuch Verlag, 1983.

Dähnhardt, Heinz. "Der Aufbau des Volksbüchereiwesens." *Volksbücherei und Volksbildung in Niedersachsen* 15 (April/May 1935): 1–3.

———. "Aufbau und Organisation des öffentlichen Büchereiwesens." *DB* 2 (1935): 306–19.

———. "Deutsche Büchereiarbeit von heute." *DB* 5 (1938): 644–56.

———. "Ergänzungsbildung." *DB* 7 (1940): 202–206.

———. "Das Grenzbüchereiwesen einst und heute." In *Festschrift Wilhelm Scheffen.* N.p.: Grenzbüchereidienst, 1941.

———. "Richtlinien für das Volksbüchereiwesen." *DB* 5 (1938): 1–7; 130–36.

———. "Volksbücherei und Gemeinde." *DB* 3 (1936): 1–6.

———. "Das volkstümliche und öffentliche Büchereiwesen." *Deutsche Wissenschaft, Erziehung und Volksbildung* 1 (1935): 18–19.

———. "Weg und Ziel deutscher Volksbüchereiarbeit." *DB* 4 (1937): 1–5.

———. "Zur Entwicklung des öffentlichen Büchereiwesens." *DB* 8 (1941): 305–308.

Dahrendorf, Ralf. *Society and Democracy in Germany.* New York and London: W. W. Norton, 1979.

Desczyk, Eva-Maria. Zur Bibliotheksgeschichte des Saarland: Die staatliche Büchereien und die öffentlichen Bibliotheken von den Anfangen bis zur Gegenwart. Student paper, Fachhochschule für Bibliothekswesen, Stuttgart, 1977.

"Deutscher Volksbüchereitag in Würzburg, 24.–26. September 1936." *DB* 3 (1936): 564–69.

Diere, Horst. "Das Reichsministerium für Wissenschaft, Erziehung und Volksbildung: Zur Entstehung, Struktur und Rolle der zentralen schulpolitischen Institution im faschistischen Deutschland." *Jahrbuch für Erziehungs- und Schulgeschichte* 22 (1982): 108–20.

Dohmen, Lambert. "Praktische Büchereiarbeit." *Die Bücherwelt* 30 (1933): 105–109.

Donath, Helmut. "Berichte: Aus der Büchereiarbeit im Protektorat." *DB* 8 (1941): 150–51.

Dosa, Marta L. *Libraries in the Political Scene.* Contributions in Librarianship and Information Science, 7. Westport, Conn., and London: Greenwood Press, 1974.

"Drei wichtige preußische Erlässe. *DB* 1 (1934): 38–40.

Ebenstein, William. *The Nazi State.* 1943. Reprint. New York: Octagon, 1975.

"Das Einkaufshaus für Büchereien in Leipzig." *DB* 1 (1934): 392.

Emrich, —. "Der Aufbau des Volksbüchereiwesens im Gau Saarpfalz." *DB* 5 (1938): 33–38.

Bibliography

Encyclopaedia Britannica. 14th ed. S.vv. "Saar (Sarre) Territory" by N.P.C.M.

Engelhardt, W. "Hitlerjugend in der Jugendbücherei." *DB* 4 (1937): 175–79.

Engelhardt, Wolfgang. "Eine HJ-Schulungsbücherei." *DB* 3 (1936): 419–21.

Erckmann, Rudolf. "Probleme und Aufgaben unseres Schrifttums." *DB* 8 (1941): 308–16.

"Ergänzungslehrgange." In *Nachtrag zum Handbuch der deutschen Volksbüchereien, 1938–40.* Leipzig: Einkaufshaus für Büchereien, 1940.

"Erklärung und Aufruf des Verbandes Deutscher Volksbibliothekare." *BuB* 13 (1933): 97–98.

"Erlässe und Bekanntmachungen." *DB* 8 (1941): 214–15, 342–43.

"Erlässe und Mitteilungen." *DB* 7 (1940): 235–38.

"Erlässe und Verordnung." *DB* 7 (1940): 118–19, 155.

"Erlässe und Verordnungen." *DB* 7 (1940): 40–42, 188–90.

"Eröffnung von 30 Volksbüchereien in einem pfälzischen Grenzbezirk." *DB* 5 (1938): 236.

"Erwin Ackerknecht an den Leiter der Abteilung für Schul- und Bildungswesen des Deutschen Gemeindetages, Albert Meyer-Lülmann, 19.6.1937." In Jutta Sywottek, *Die Gleichschaltung der deutschen Volksbüchereien 1933 bis 1937.* Frankfurt am Main: Buchhändler-Vereinigung, 1983.

Esterquest, Ralph. "Statistical Contribution to the Study of Libraries in Contemporary Germany." *Library Quarterly* 11 (January 1941): 1–35.

Euringer, Richard. "Volksbücherei und Politik." *DB* 3 (1936): 13–17.

Ewig, Karl. "Arbeitsbericht: Zwanzig Jahre nebenamtliche Volksbüchereiarbeit." *DB* 3 (1936): 322–28.

Feder, Gottfried. *The Programme of the N.S.D.A.P. and Its General Conceptions.* Trans. E. T. S. Dugdale. Munich: Franz Eher Nachfolger, 1932.

Fenelonov, E. A. "Soviet Public Libraries." In *Libraries in the USSR* Ed. Simon Francis. N.p.: Linnet Books and Clive Bingley, 1971.

Fest, Joachim C. *The Face of the Third Reich.* Trans. Michael Bullock. N.p.: Penguin, 1983.

Feuchtwanger, E. J., ed. *Upheaval and Continuity: A Century of German History.* London: Oswald Wolff, 1973.

Fiehler, —. "Die Gemeinden und das Buch." *DB* 6 (1939): 67–71.

Fliege, Werner. "Fünf Jahre ländliche Büchereiarbeit." *DB* 1 (1934): 580–82.

Francis, Simon, ed. *Libraries in the USSR* N.p.: Linnet Books and Clive Bingley, 1971.

Fritsch, —. "Zur Neuordnung des Schundkampfes." *Die Rheinprovinz* 11 (1935): 479–81.

F[ritz], G. "Zur Frage der Ausbildung für den höheren Volksbüchereidienst." *BuB* 7 (1927): 116–18.

Fritz, Gottlieb, and Erwin Ackerknecht. "Zum Abschied." *BuB* 13 (1933): 329–30.

Fritz, Gottlieb, and Otto Plate. *Volksbüchereien (Bücher- und Lesehallen): Ihre Richtung und Verwaltung.* Berlin and Leipzig: Walter de Gruyter, 1924.

Fuhr, Otto. "Die Arbeitseinrichtungen der Volksbüchereistelle und die Einzelbücherei." *Die Volksbücherei im Rhein-Main-Gebiet* 6 (August 1944): 13–18.

75 Jahre Stadtbücherei Hamm, 1895–1970. Hamm: Franz Berges, 1970.

Füssel, Stephan. "'Wider den undeutschen Geist': Bücherverbrennung und Bibliothekslenkung im Nationalsozialismus." In *Göttingen unterm Hakenkreuz: Nationalsozialistischer Alltag in einer deutschen Stadt, Texte und Materialien.* Göttingen, 1983.

"General and Salary Statistics—Public Libraries Serving More Than 200,000 Population." *Bulletin of the American Library Association* 29 (April 1935): 200–203, and 33 (April 1939): 279–83.

"General and Salary Statistics—Public Libraries Serving 100,000 to 199,999 Population." *Bulletin of the American Library Association* 29 (April 1935): 204–207, and 33 (April 1939): 284–88.

General and Salary Statistics—Public Libraries Serving 35,000 to 99,999 Population." *Bulletin of the American Library Association* 29 (April 1935): 208–210, and 33 (April 1939): 290–93.

"General and Salary Statistics—Public Libraries Serving 10,000 to 34,999 Population. *Bulletin of the American Library Association* 29 (April 1935): 211–13, and 33 (April 1939): 294–97.

Germany. *Reichsgesetzblatt,* 1935.

———. Reichsschrifttumskammer. *Liste 1 des schädlichen und unerwünschten Schrifttums.* Berlin: Reichsdruckerei, Stand von Oktober 1935.

———. ———. *Liste des schädlichen und unerwünschten Schrifttums.* Leipzig: Druck von Ernst Hedrich Nachf., n.d. Stand von 31. Dez. 1938.

———. Reichsstelle für das Volksbüchereiwesen. *Nachtrag.* Leipzig: Einkaufshaus für Büchereien, 1940.

———. ———. *Reichsliste für kleinere städtische Büchereien.* 2d ed. Leipzig: Einkaufshaus für Büchereien, 1939.

———. Reichsstelle zur Förderung des deutschen Schrifttums. *Die ersten hundert Bücher für nationalsozialistische Büchereien.* 6th ed. Munich: Zentralverlag der N.S.D.A.P., Franz Eher Nachfolger, n.d.

———. Statistisches Reichsamt. *Die deutschen Volksbüchereien nach Ländern, Provinzen und Gemeinden 1933/34.* Statistik des Deutschen Reichs, vol. 471. Berlin: Verlag für Sozialpolitik, Wirtschaft und Statistik in Berlin, 1935.

"Geschichte und Volkserziehung." *DB* 1 (1934): 291–93.

Glaser, Hermann. *The Cultural Roots of National Socialism.* Trans. Ernest A. Menze. Austin: University of Texas Press, n.d.

Goebbels, Joseph. *Goebbels-Reden.* Band 1: 1932–1939. Düsseldorf: Droste Verlag, 1971.

Graf, Oskar Maria. "Verbrennt mich!" In *Die Bücherverbrennung zum 10. Mai 1933.* Ed. Gerhard Sauder. Munich and Vienna: Carl Hauser, 1983.

Green, Muriel M. "Observations Arising from an Anglo-German Exchange." *DB* 5 (1938): 283–86.

Gregor, Helena. *Die nationalsozialistische Bibliothekspolitik in den annektierten und besetzten Gebieten, 1938 bis 1945.* Berlin: Deutscher Bibliotheksverband, Arbeitsstelle für das Bibliothekswesen, 1976.

Grenzbüchereidienst, 1933. N.p., n.d.

Grenzbüchereidienst, 1934. N.p., n.d.

Grenzbüchereidienst, 1936. N.p., n.d.

Grenzbüchereidienst, 1937. N.p., n.d.

Grenzbüchereidienst, 1940. N.p., n.d.

Grenzbüchereidienst, *Mitteilungen* no. 12. N.p.: Volk und Reich Verlag, 1933.

Grenzbüchereidienst, *Mitteilungen* no. 13. Berlin: Volk und Reich Verlag, 1935.

Grenzbüchereidienst, *Mitteilungen* no. 14. Berlin: n.p., 1936.

Grenzbüchereidienst, *Mitteilungen* no. 15. Berlin: Volk und Reich Verlag, 1938.

Grenzbüchereidienst, *Mitteilungen* no. 16. Berlin: Volk und Reich Verlag, 1939.

Grenzbüchereidienst, *Mitteilungen* no. 17. N.p., n.d.

Das Grenzbüchereiwesen im Jahre 1930/31. Flensburg: Zentrale für Nordmarkbüchereien, 1931.

Grosse, Franz. "Zur Statistik des Deutschen Gemeindetages über das Volksbüchereiwesen in den Städten mit über 20 000 Einwohnern." *DB* 6 (1939): 510–15.

Grunberger, Richard. *The 12-Year Reich: A Social History of Nazi Germany, 1933–1945.* New York: Holt, Rinehart, and Winston, 1979.

"Grundlisten für das volkstümliche Büchereiwesen in Preußen. I. Ostliste." *DB* 1 (1934): 40–41.

"Grundsätze für den Aufbau des ländlichen Volksbüchereiwesens in der Provinz Hannover." *Volksbücherei und Volksbildung in Niedersachsen* 14 (October/November 1934): 1–2.

Haasbauer, Anton. "Das Volksbüchereiwesen der Ostmark." In Grenzbüchereidienst, *Mitteilungen*, vol. 17.

Hachmann, Josef. "Buch und Bücherei im Aufbruch des Volkstums." *Die Bücherwelt* 30 (1933): 93–97.

Handbuch der deutschen Volksbüchereien. Jahrbuch der deutschen Volksbüchereien 5, 1935. Leipzig: Einkaufshaus für Büchereien in Kommission, 1935.

Handbuch der deutschen Volksbüchereien. Jahrbuch der deutschen Volksbüchereien 6. Leipzig: Einkaufshaus für Büchereien, 1940.

Handbuch der deutschen Volksbüchereien. Nachtrag. Leipzig: Einkaufshaus für Büchereien, 1940.

Hannaford, Janet L. "Libraries Serving More Than 200,000 Population." *Bulletin of the American Library Association* 32 (April 1938): 268.

Hansen, Frauke. "Die 'geistige Bildung eines Volkes' oder Die Lektüre der 'Kleinen Leute' in der Volksbücherei Schöneberg." *Buch und Bibliothek* 39 (1987): 960–66.

Hardach, Karl. *The Political Economy of Germany in the Twentieth Century.* Berkeley, Los Angeles, and London: University of California Press, 1980.

Harden-Rauch, Philipp. "Die Zusammenarbeit der staatlichen Volksbüchereistellen mit Partei und Staat." *DB* 6 (1939): 516–21.

Heberle, Rudolf. *From Democracy to Nazism: A Regional Case Study on Political Parties in Germany.* New York: Howard Fertig, 1970.

Heiligenstaedt, Fritz. "Abkommen zwischen der staatlichen Beratungsstelle für Volksbüchereiwesen in der Provinz Hannover und der Kulturabteilung der Gebietsführung Niedersachsen der Hitler-Jugend." *DB* 4 (1937): 43–44.

———. "Betrifft Schwarze Listen." *Volksbücherei und Volksbildung in Niedersachsen* 13 (June/July 1933): 21–22.

———. "Das Buch im neuen Staat." *Volksbücherei und Volksbildung in Niedersachsen* 13 (1933): 31–33.

———. [Comment on U II R 750]. *Volksbücherei und Volksbildung in Niedersachsen* 13 (1933/34): 51–53.

———. "Gemeindliche Kulturarbeit im Kriege." *Die Kulturverwaltung* 4 (April/June 1940). Sonderdruck.

———. "Das ländliche Volksbücherei im neuen Staat." *Volksbücherei und Volksbildung in Niedersachsen* 13 (1933): 37–40.

———. "Der nebenamtliche Büchereileiter." *DB* 3 (1936): 33–41.

———. "Der nebenamtliche Büchereileiter." *Volksbücherei und Volksbildung in Niedersachsen* 15 (December 1935/January 1936): 51–57.

———. "Die neue deutsche Volksbücherei." *Die niedersächsische Volksbücherei* 16 (August/November 1936).

———. "Die Neuordnung des gemeindlichen Volksbüchereiwesens." *Die Kulturverwaltung* 1 (1937): 262–66.

———. "Um Gegenwart und Zukunft der deutschen Volksbüchereien." *DB* 4 (1937): 237–43.

———. "Der Volksbibliothekar im neuen Staat." *Volksbücherei und Volksbildung in Niedersachsen* 13 (1933): 25–27.

———. "Volksbibliothekarische Zusammenarbeit." *DB* 5 (1938): 656–70.

———. "Das Volksbüchereiwesen im nordöstlichen Grenzraum." In Grenzbüchereidienst, *Mitteilungen* no. 16. Berlin: Volk und Reich Verlag, 1939.

———. "Vom Geist der Grenze im deutschen Volksbüchereiwesen." In Grenzbüchereidienst, *Mitteilungen* no. 16. Berlin: Volk und Reich Verlag, 1939.

———. "Zum Bestandaufbau." *Volksbücherei und Volksbildung in Niedersachsen* 15 (April/May 1935): 4–7.

———. "Zur Jahreswende 1940/41." *DB* 8 (1941): 1–2.

———. "Zur Überwachung des Bestandaufbaus durch die Beratungsstellen." *DB* 2 (1935): 211–15.

Heiligenstaedt, Fritz, and Carl Jansen. "Zur jüngsten Entwicklung im deutschen volkstümlichen Büchereiwesen." *Volksbücherei und Volksbildung in Niedersachsen* 13 (April/May 1933): 3.

Heimbach, Hans, and Erwin Ackerknecht. "Rede und Antwort." *BuB* 13 (1933): 113–15.

Heinl, Karl. "Denkschrift betreffend Neubau des deutschen öffentlichen Büchereiwesens im Rahmen des die Neugestaltung des gesamten deutschen Volks- und Kulturlebens umfassenden nationalpädagogischen Programms der Reichsregierung. Juni 1933." In Jutta Sywottek, *Die Gleichschaltung der deutschen Volksbüchereien 1933 bis 1937*. Frankfurt am Main: Buchhändler-Vereinigung, 1983.

———. "Denkschrift über die zuständige Eingleiderung des Volksbüchereiwesens in das Reichsministerium für Volksaufklärung und Propaganda, Juni 1934." In Jutta Sywottek, *Die Gleichschaltung der deutschen Volksbüchereien 1933 bis 1937*. Frankfurt am Main: Buchhändler-Vereinigung, 1983.

Herr, Arthur. "Sudetendeutsches Büchereiwesen und Büchereigesetz." *DB* 6 (1939): 500–10.

———. "Zur Charakteristik des sudetendeutschen Büchereiwesens." *DB* 5 (1938): 639–43.

Herrmann, Wolfgang. "Deutscher Sozialismus." *DB* 1 (1934): 37–56.

———. "Der neue Nationalismus und seine Literatur." *BuB* 12 (1932): 261–73, and 13 (1933): 42–57.

———. "Prinzipielles zur Säuberung der öffentlichen Büchereien." *Börsenblatt für den deutschen Buchhandel* 100, May 16, 1933): 356–58.

———. "Was ist Asphaltliteratur?" *Volksbücherei und Volksbildung in Niedersachsen* 13 (June/July 1933): 16–21.

———. "Werbeveranstaltung des Grenzbüchereidienst E.V. Berlin." *DB* 4 (1937): 230–33.

Heyde, Konrad. "Die Staatlichen Volksbüchereistellen am Beispiel Freiburg im Breisgau." In *Bibliotheken während des Nationalsozialismus.* Ed. Peter Vodosek and Manfred Komorowski. Wiesbaden: Otto Harrassowitz, 1989.

Hiden, John, and John Farquharson. *Explaining Hitler's Germany: Historians and the Third Reich.* London: Batsford Academic and Educational, 1983.

Hirschfeld, Gerhard, and Lothar Kettenacker, eds. *Der Führerstaat: Mythos und Realität.* Stuttgart: Klett-Cotta, 1981.

Hitler, Adolf. *Die deutsche Kunst als stolzeste Verteidigung des deutschen Volkes.* Hier spricht das neue Deutschland, vol. 7. Munich: Zentralverlag der N.S.D.A.P., 1934.

———. *Mein Kampf.* Trans. Ralph Manheim. Boston: Houghton Mifflin, 1943.

———. *The Speeches of Adolf Hitler, April 1922–August 1939.* Trans. and ed. Norman Baynes. London, New York, and Toronto: Oxford University Press, 1942.

Hobrecker, Karl. "Die neue Reichsjugendbücherei." *Das junge Deutschland* 27 (September 1933): 252–55.

Hodick, Erich. "Die willkommene Gelegenheit: Zerschlagung der katholischen Büchereiarbeit während des Nationalsozialismus." In *Bibliotheken während des Nationalsozialismus.* Ed. Peter Vodosek and Manfred Komorowski. Wiesbaden: Otto Harrassowitz, 1989.

Hofer, Walther. *Der Nationalsozialismus: Dokumente, 1933–1945.* Frankfurt am Main: Fischer Taschenbuch Verlag, 1983.

Hofmann, Hans. "Kulturabbau und Büchereien." *Zentralblatt für Bibliothekswesen* 49 (1932): 410–17.

———, ed. *Der Volksbibliothekar: Seine Aufgabe, sein Beruf, seine Ausbildung.* Schriften zur Büchereifrage. Leipzig: Quelle und Meyer, 1927.

Hofmann, Hans E. *Walter Hofmann, 1879–1952.* Biobibliographien, vol. 2. Berlin: Deutscher Bibliotheksverband, Arbeitstelle für das Bibliothekswesen, 1976.

Hofmann, Walter. "Die Ausbildung für den volksbibliothekarischen Beruf." Orig. pub. 1938; reprinted in *Buch und Volk: Gesammelte Aufsätze und Reden zur Buchpolitik und Volksbüchereifrage.* Ed. Rudolf Reuter. Cologne: Verlag der Löwe, 1951.

———. "Bücher des Lebens: Ein Grundproblem der Bücherauswahl der volkstümlichen Bücherei." Orig. pub. 1922; reprinted in *Buch und Volk: Gesammelte Aufsätze zur Buchpolitik und Volksbüchereifrage.* Ed. Rudolf Reuter. Cologne: Verlag der Löwe, 1951.

———. *Die deutsche Volksbücherei: Die Idee und die Aufgabe, das Werk und die Werkleute.* Bayreuth: Gauverlag Bayerische Ostmark, 1934.

317

————. "Die Erlebensnahe: Grundsätze für die Auswahl der Bildungsmittel." Orig. pub. 1919; reprinted in *Buch und Volk: Gesammelte Aufsätze zur Buchpolitik und Volksbüchereifrage.* Ed. Rudolf Reuter. Cologne: Verlag der Löwe, 1951.

————. "Das Gedächtnis der Nation." *Neue Literatur* 34 (1933): 3–13.

————. "Die gesellschaftliche Funktion der öffentlichen Bücherei." Orig. pub. 1925; reprinted in *Buch und Volk: Gesammelte Aufsätze zur Buchpolitik und Volksbüchereifrage.* Ed. Rudolf Reuter. Cologne: Verlag der Löwe, 1951.

————. "Grenzen der Volksbildungsarbeit." Orig. pub. 1920; reprinted in *Buch und Volk: Gesammelte Aufsätze zur Buchpolitik und Volksbüchereifrage.* Ed. Rudolf Reuter. Cologne: Verlag der Löwe, 1951.

————. "Die Kernbestände der volkstümlichen Bücherei: Ein Problem des Bestandaufbaus der Volksbücherei, dargestellt am Beispiel der Städtischen Bücherhallen zu Leipzig." Orig. pub. 1924; reprinted in *Buch und Volk: Gesammelte Aufsätze zur Buchpolitik und Volksbüchereifrage.* Ed. Rudolf Reuter. Cologne: Verlag der Löwe, 1951.

————. "Die kleine Ausleihschule." In *Buch und Volk: Gesammelte Aufsätze zur Buchpolitik und Volksbüchereifrage.* Ed. Rudolf Reuter. Cologne: Verlag der Löwe, 1951.

————. "Leitsätze, betreffend des Aufbau zentraler Organisationen im deutschen Volksbüchereiwesen, 14.10.1933." In Jutta Sywottek, *Die Gleichschaltung der deutschen Volksbüchereien 1933 bis 1937.* Frankfurt am Main: Buchhändler-Vereinigung, 1983.

————. "Leitsätze zur Politik der deutschen Volksbücherei in der Epoche der deutschen Revolution." In *Volksbücherei und Nationalsozialismus.* Comp. Friedrich Andrae. Wiesbaden: O. Harrassowitz, 1970.

————. Die Lektüre der Frau. Leipziger Beiträge zur Grundlegung der praktischen Literaturpflege, 5. Heft 1. Leipzig: Quelle und Meyer, 1931.

————. "Die Nebengebiete und die dienende Technik in der volkstümlichen Bücherei." Orig. pub. 1925/26; reprinted in *Buch und Volk: Gesammelte Aufsätze zur Buchpolitik und Volksbüchereifrage.* Ed. Rudolf Reuter. Cologne: Verlag der Löwe, 1951.

————. "Die Organisation des Ausleihdienstes in der modernen Bildungsbibliotheke, III. Die Organisation." *Volksbildungsarchiv* 3 (1913): 31–132.

————. *Die Praxis der Volksbücherei.* Leipzig: Quelle und Meyer, 1926.

————. "Schalter oder freie Theke?" *DB* 4 (1937): 21–30.

————. "Um Buch und Volk." Orig. pub. 1916; reprinted in *Buch und Volk: Gesammelte Aufsätze zur Buchpolitik und Volksbüchereifrage.* Ed. Rudolf Reuter. Cologne: Verlag der Löwe, 1951.

————. "Volksbildung, Volksbücherei, Volkswerdung: Leitsätze." *HfB* 16 (1932/33): 337–49.

————. "Vom 'richtigen' Buch." *DB* 4 (1937): 524–30.

————. *Der Weg zum Schrifttum.* Berlin: Verlag der Arbeitsgemeinschaft, 1926.

————. "Zur Reform des Bibliothekswesens." *Blätter für die gesamten Sozialwissenschaften* 4 (1908): 147–51, 164–67.

Hofmann-Bosse, Elise. "Die Frau im Dienst der volkstümlichen Bücherei." In

Bibliography

Der Volksbibliothekar: Seine Aufgabe, sein Beruf, seine Ausbildung. Ed. Hans Hofmann. Leipzig: Quelle und Meyer, 1927.

Hohl, Martha. *75 Jahre Stadtbibliothek Bremen: Entwicklung und Perspektiven.* Bremen: Buchbinderei der Stadtbibliothek, n.d.

Holzhausen, Hans-Dieter. "Gottlieb Fritz und seine Entfernung aus dem Amt des Direktors der Berliner Stadtbibliothek 1933/34." In *Bibliotheken während des Nationalsozialismus.* Ed. Peter Vodosek and Manfred Komorowski. Wiesbaden: Otto Harrassowitz, 1989.

————. "Von der Bibliotheksschule zum Universitätsinstitut: Grundzüge der Entwicklung der Berliner bibliothekarischen Ausbildungsstätte von 1930–1980." In *Bibliotheksarbeit: Hermann Wassner zum 60. Geburtstag.* Ed. Peter Vodosek. Wiesbaden: Otto Harrassowitz, 1982.

Horak, Stephen M. et al. *Eastern European National Minorities, 1919–1980: A Handbook.* Littleton, Colo.: Libraries Unlimited, 1985.

Horstmann, Heinrich. "Aus der Volksbüchereiarbeit in Oberschlesien." In Grenzbüchereidienst, *Mitteilungen* no. 13. Berlin: Volk und Reich Verlag, 1935.

————. "Die praktische Volksbüchereiarbeit im Ostgebiet." In Grenzbüchereidienst, *Mitteilungen* no. 16. Berlin: Volk und Reich Verlag, 1939.

Hoyer, Walter. "Die Aufgaben des Besprechungsteiles in unserer Zeitschrift." *DB* 5 (1938): 9–12.

————. "Die Durchdringung der Großstadt durch die Bücherei." *DB* 6 (1939): 137–67.

————. "Grundsätze zur Auswahl der Dichtung." *DB* 1 (1934): 260–69.

Hüttenberger, Peter. *Bibliographie zum Nationalsozialismus.* Arbeitsbücher zur modernen Geschichte, Band 8. Göttingen: Vandenhoeck und Ruprecht, 1980.

International Encyclopedia of the Social Sciences. London and New York: Macmillan and Free Press, 1968. S.vv. National Socialism.

Jacobsen, Hans-Adolf. *Hans Steinacher: Bundesleiter des VDA 1933–1937. Schriften des Bundesarchiv, 19.* Boppard am Rhein: Harold Boldt Verlag, 1970.

Jahresbericht der Stadtbücherei Frankfurt/Oder, 1.4.43–31.3.44. Frankfurt/Oder: n.p., 1944.

Jahresbericht der Stadtbüchereien und Städt. Lesehalle zu Hannover für das Jahr 1932/33. N.p.: n.d.; . . . *für das Jahr 1933/34.* N.p.: n.d.; . . . *für das Jahr 1934/35.* N.p.: n.d.; . . . *für das Jahr 1935/36.* N.p.: n.d.; and . . . *für das Jahr 1936/37.* N.p.: n.d.

Jansen, Carl. "Die Bücherei im Arbeitsdienst." *DB* 1 (1934): 6–21.

————. "Nationalpolitisches Schrifttum." *Volksbücherei und Volksbildung in Niedersachsen* 13 (1933): 27–31.

————. "Rudolf Angermann zum Gedächtnis." *Bücherei und Bildung* 6 (September/October 1954): 853–54.

————. "Unser neues Handbuch." *DB* 8 (1941): 277–80.

————. "Wer wahren will, muss wagen; Dank an Wilhelm Schuster." *Bücherei und Bildung.* 6 (July/August 1954): 661–66.

Joerden, Rudolf. "Neue Freihandbüchereien in Hamburg." *DB* 7 (1940): 143–47.

————. "Sekretär, Geschaftsführer, Referent . . . Heinrich Beckers Anteil an der Büchereigeschafte." *Buch und Bibliothek* 25 (1973): 140–43.

————. "Über die Funktion der öffentlichen Büchereien." In *Bibliothekarischen Arbeit zwischen Theorie und Praxis: Beiträge zum bibliothekarischen Fachwissen und Berichte über bibliothekarischen Aktivitäten.* Festgabe für Wolfgang Thauer. Stuttgart: Fachhochschule für Bibliothekswesen Stuttgart, 1976.

————. "Vor fünfzig Jahren: Anmerkungen zum Thema Arbeiter und Bibliothek." *Buch und Bibliothek* 27 (1975): 316–21.

————. "Zur neuen Einheit der Volksbüchereibewegung." *BuB* 8 (1928): 287–93.

Johannsen, —. "Deutsche Kulturarbeit in der Nordmark." In Grenzbüchereidienst, *Mitteilungen,* vol. 17, pp. 81–91. N.p., n.d.

Johannsen, Hans-Peter. "Berichte: Die Nordmarkbüchereien." *DB* 9 (1941/42): 330–31.

Jurgens, Anne. "Aus meiner Beratungsstellenarbeit in Oberschlesien." *DB* 2 (1935): 90–91.

Jutte, Werner. "Volksbibliothekare im Nationalsozialismus." *Buch und Bibliothek* 39 (1987): 345–48.

Kallmann, Gertrud E. "German Public Libraries and Their Principles of Book Selection." *Library Association Record* 1, ser. 4 (1934): 169–72.

————. "The Public Library System in Germany Today." *Library Association Record* 2, ser. 4 (1935): 145–48.

Kamenetsky, Christa. *Children's Literature in Hitler's Germany: The Cultural Policy of National Socialism.* Athens, Ohio, and London: Ohio University Press, 1984.

Kast, Raimund. "Die Leihbibliotheken im Nationalsozialismus." In *Bibliotheken während des Nationalsozialismus.* Ed. Peter Vodosek and Manfred Komorowski. Wiesbaden: Otto Harrassowitz, 1989.

Kästner, Erich. "Die Verbrennung meiner Bücher." In *10. Mai 1933: Bücherverbrennung in Deutschland und die Folgen.* Ed. Ulrich Walberer. Frankfurt am Main: Fischer Taschenbuch Verlag, 1983.

Kauder, Viktor. "Das deutsche Büchereiwesen im ehemaligen Polen." *DB* 6 (1939): 599–604.

Kehr, Helen, and Janet Langmaid. *The Nazi Era, 1919–1945: A Select Bibliography of Published Works from the Early Roots to 1980.* London: Mansell, 1982.

Kershaw, Ian. *The Nazi Dictatorship: Problems and Perspectives of Interpretation.* London: Edward Arnold, 1985.

Kettel, Andreas. *Volksbibliothekare und Nationalsozialismus.* Pahl-Rugenstein Hochschulschriften, Gesellschafts- und Naturwissenschaften. vol. 72. Cologne: Pahl-Rugenstein, 1981.

Keuth, Rosemarie. *Fünfzig Jahre Bibliotheksarbeit an der Saar.* Mimeographed, n.d.

Kirchner, Joachim. "Schrifttum und wissenschaftliche Bibliotheken im nationalsozialistischen Deutschland." *Zentralblatt für Bibliothekswesen* 50 (August–September 1933): 514–25.

Klingbeil, Lore. "Das Volksbüchereiwesen des Kreises Stuhms." In Grenzbüchereidienst, *Mitteilungen,* vol. 16. Berlin: Volk und Reich Verlag, 1939.

Bibliography

Klotzbücher, Alois, ed. *Von Büchern und Bibliotheken in Dortmund: Beiträge zur Bibliotheksgeschichte einer Industriestadt.* Dortmund: Ruhfus, 1982.

Koch, Walther. "Die Bücherei an der Saar in ihrer volkspolitischen Bedeutung." *DB* 1 (1934): 393–403.

———. "Grenzbüchereiarbeit im Saargebiet." In *Kultur, Buch und Grenze: Grundfragen und Beispiele deutscher Bücherei- und Kulturarbeit in den Grenzgebieten.* Ed. Franz Schriewer. Leipzig: Quelle und Meyer, 1930.

———. "Wie Büchereien im Saarland sichergestellt wurden." *DB* 7 (1940): 170–75.

Kock, Richard. "Bericht über die Zusammenarbeit der Städtischen Volksbücherei Schneidemühl mit der HJ." *DB* 4 (1937): 488–95.

———. "Die Neuordnung der Beratungstellen." *DB* 1 (1934): 18–28.

———. "Die Parole der Woche in der Volksbücherei." *DB* 5 (1938): 271–75.

———. "Das Volksbüchereiwesen der Grenzmark Posen-Westpreußen." In Grenzbüchereidienst, *Mitteilungen,* vol. 16. Berlin: Volk und Reich Verlag, 1939.

Komjathy, Anthony, and Rebecca Stockwell. *German Minorities and the Third Reich.* New York and London: Holmes and Meier, 1980.

Kossow, K. "Deutsche Geschichte fürs traute Heim." *DB* 1 (1934): 458–63.

Kossow, Karl. "Alter und neuer Lesesaal." *DB* 3 (1936): 241–51.

Kruger, Gerhard. "Die parteiamtliche Prüfungskommission." *DB* 8 (1941): 105–108.

Kruse, H. "Die deutschen Bibliotheken in der volksdeutschen Arbeit." *Deutschtum im Ausland* 22 (1939): 443–51.

Kummer, —. "Der planmassige Einsatz des deutschen Buches." *DB* 3 (1936): 17–19.

———. "Nationalsozialismus und Volksbüchereiwesen." *DB* 2 (1935): 319–25.

Kummer, Rudolf. "Die wissenschaftliche Bibliothekswesen im nationalsozialistischen Deutschland." *Zentralblatt für Bibliothekswesen* 55 (September/October 1938): 399–413.

Ladewig, Paul. *Politik der Bücherei.* Leipzig: Ernst Wiegand, 1917.

Das Land Bremen und seine drei grössen Bibliotheken: Universitätsbibliothek Bremen. Stadtbibliothek Bremerhaven. Stadtbibliothek Bremen. Bremen: Universität Bremen, 1977.

Langenbücher, Hellmuth. "Graphische-schematische Darstellung der staatlichen und parteilichen Organisation im Hinblick auf die Welt des Buches." In *Volksbücherei und Nationalsozialismus.* Comp. Friedrich Andrae. Wiesbaden: O. Harrassowitz, 1970.

Langendorf, Peter. "Die neuen Maßstäbe bei der Buchauswahl in der politisch-historischen Literatur." *DB* 1 (1934): 270–81.

Langfeldt, Johannes. "Grundfragen der Rassen- und Vererbungslehre als Voraussetzungen für den Volksbibliothekar bei der Beurteilung von rassekundlichen Büchern." *DB* 1 (1934): 325–32.

Laqueur, Walter, ed. *Fascism: A Reader's Guide.* Berkeley and Los Angeles: University of California Press, 1978.

"The Law for the Hitler Youth, 1 December 1936." In *The German Youth Movement 1900–1945: An Interpretative and Documentary History.* Ed. Peter Stachura. New York: St. Martin's, 1981.

Lawin, Rudolf. "Die Volksbüchereien der deutschen Gemeinden." *Gemeinde und Statistik*: Beilage to *Der Gemeindetag* 5 (1939).

Lehmann, Stephen. Review of *10. Mai 1933: Bücherverbrennung in Deutschland und die Folgen* and *Bücherverbrennung: Zensur, Verbot, Vernichtung unter dem Nationalsozialismus in Heidelberg. Library Quarterly* 54 (April 1984): 197–98.

Leopold, Friedrich. "Volksbüchereiarbeit in einer oberschlesischen Industriegemeinde." In Grenzbüchereidienst, *Mitteilungen* no. 16. Berlin: Volk und Reich Verlag, 1939.

Loesch, K. C. von. "Volk und Staat im Vorland des Rheintales." In Grenzbüchereidienst, *Mitteilungen* no. 15. Berlin: Volk und Reich Verlag, 1938.

Loesch, Karl C. von. "Österreich im Reich." In Grenzbüchereidienst, *Mitteilungen*, vol. 16. Berlin: Volk und Reich Verlag, 1939.

Lüdtke, Helga. "Mütter ohne Kinder: Volksbibliothekarinnen während des Nationalsozialismus." In *Bibliotheken während des Nationalsozialismus*. Ed. Peter Vodosek and Manfred Komorowski. Wiesbaden: Otto Harrassowitz, 1989.

Luft, Robert. "Das Bibliothekswesen in Böhmen und Mähren während der Nationalsozialistischen Herrschaft 1938–1945." *Bohemia* 30 (1989): 295–342.

McIntyre, Jill. "Women and the Professions in Germany, 1930–1940." In *German Democracy and the Triumph of Hitler: Essays in Recent German History.* Ed. Anthony Nicholls and Erich Matthias. New York: St. Martin's, 1972.

Marks, Erwin. "1945—Eine Wende in unserem Bibliothekswesen." *Der Bibliothekar* 29 (May 1975): 289–96.

Marwinski, Felicitas. *Die Freie Öffentliche Bibliothek Dresden-Plauen und Walter Hofmann. Der Bibliothekar,* Beiheft, vol. 6. Leipzig: VEB Bibliographisches Institut, 1983.

Mascher, Bruno. "Zehn Jahre 'Volk ohne Raum'." *DB* 3 (1936): 378–80.

Mason, Tim. "Intention and Explanation: A Current Controversy about the Interpretation of National Socialism." In *Der Führerstaat: Mythos und Realität.* Ed. Gerhard Hirschfeld and Lothar Kettenacker. Stuttgart: Klett-Cotta, 1981.

Matheson, Peter, ed. *The Third Reich and the Christian Churches.* Edinburgh: T. and T. Clark, 1981.

Matzerath, Horst. *Nationalsozialismus und Kommunale Selbstverwaltung.* Stuttgart: W. Kohlhammer, 1970.

Mau, Else. "Lesesaalarbeit—ihre Wege und Ziele." *DB* 8 (1941): 385–90.

Menze, Ernest A. *Totalitarianism Reconsidered.* Port Washington, N.Y.: Kennikat Press, 1981.

Michlenz, —. "Aus der Büchereiarbeit: Aus der Arbeit der Bücherei Inschwalde, Kr. Cottbus." *DB* 3 (1936): 189–90.

Middlebrook, Martin. *The Battle of Hamburg: Allied Bomber Forces against a German City in 1943.* New York: Charles Scribner's Sons, 1980.

"Minister Goebbels in Weimar am 31. Oktober 1937." *DB* 4 (1937): 523.

Mirbt, Rudolf. "Deutsche Büchereien im Ausland." *Klingsor* 15 (1938): 352–54.

"Mitteilungen." *DB* 4 (1937): 227–36, *DB* 5 (1938): 188–92, and *DB* 9 (1942): 238–43.

Bibliography

"Mitteilungen: Vereinbarung zwischen der Reichsstelle für das Volksbüchereiwesen und der Reichsjugendführung der NSDAP." *DB* 4 (1937): 558.

"Mitteilungen: Volksbüchereitagung des Gaues Saarpfalz." *DB* 5 (1938): 236–37.

Morzé, Adolf von. "Chicago-Leipzig 1931 bis 1933." *Buch und Bibliothek* 31 (1979): 859–73.

Mühle, Wolfgang. "Bemerkungen zur imperialistischen Theorie und Historiographie der deutschen Volksbücherei." In *Bibliotheksarbeit heute*, Folge 4. Leipzig: Verlag für Buch- und Bibliothekswesen, 1967.

———. *Zur alteren Bücherhallenbewegung als Beginn der deutschen Volksbücherei im Zeitalter des Imperialismus.* Berlin: Zentralinstitut für Bibliothekswesen, 1968.

Müller, Georg Wilhelm. *Das Reichsministerium für Volksaufklärung und Propaganda.* Schriften zum Staatsaufbau, 43. Berlin: Junker und Dunnhaupt, 1940.

Müller, Herbert. "Die Werbung der Volksbücherei." *DB* 8 (1941): 210–13.

Müller, Paul. "Berichte: Aus der Arbeit in den neuen Ostgauen." *DB* 8 (1941): 338–39.

Murphy, Raymond E. et al. *National Socialism: Basic Principles. Their Application by the Nazi Party's Foreign Organization, and the Use of Germans Abroad for Nazi Aims.* Washington, D.C.: Government Printing Office, 1943.

Musgrove, Gordon. *Operation Gomorrah: The Hamburg Firestorm Raids.* London, New York, and Sydney: Jane's 1981.

"Nachrichten." *DB* 1 (1934): 482–84.

"Nachrichten aus der Fachschaft." *DB* 1 (1934): 531–33.

Narcisz, G. A. "Franz Schriewer/Das ländliche Büchereiwesen." *DB* 5 (1938): 136–39.

———. "Die Neuaufbau der Breslauer Volksbüchereien." *DB* 5 (1938): 559–70.

———. "Volksbüchereiarbeit in Niederschlesien." In Grenzbüchereidienst, *Mitteilungen* no. 13. Berlin: Volk und Reich Verlag, 1935.

———. "Die Volksbüchereien werden neu geordnet." *Volksbücherei und Volksbildung in Niedersachsen* 13 (June/July 1933): 13–16.

Neumann, Franz. *Behemoth: The Structure and Practice of National Socialism, 1933–1944.* New York: Octagon Books, 1983.

"Neuordnung des Büchereiwesens auch in Hessen." *DB* 1 (1934): 37.

"Neuordnung des Volksbüchereiwesens in Sachsen." *DB* 1 (1934): 288–91.

Niessen, Manfred H. "Wie es zu den Bücherverbrennungen kam." In *10 Mai 1933: Bücherverbrennung in Deutschland und die Folgen.* Ed. Ulrich Walberer. Frankfurt am Main: Fischer Taschenbuch Verlag, 1983.

Noakes, J., and G. Pridham, eds. *Nazism, 1919–1945.* Vol. 2: *State, Economy and Society, 1933–1939: A Documentary Reader.* Exeter Studies in History, vol. 8. Exeter, Eng.: University of Exeter, 1984.

Orlow, Dietrich. *The History of the Nazi Party.* 2 vols. Pittsburgh, Penn.: University of Pittsburgh Press, 1969–1973.

Payr, Bernhard. "Fünfzig wesentliche Bücher des Jahres 1935 für Volksbüchereien." In *Volksbücherei und Nationalsozialismus.* Comp. Friedrich Andrae. Wiesbaden: O. Harrassowitz, 1970.

——. "Fünfzig wesentliche Bücher des Jahres 1936 für Volksbüchereien." *DB* 4 (1937): 5–14.

——. "Fünfzig wesentliche Bücher des Jahres 1938 für Volksbüchereien." *DB* 6 (1939): 8–17.

Petrau, Alfred. "Der 'Grenzbüchereidienst'—seine Geschichte und seine Leistung." In *Festschrift Wilhelm Scheffen*. N.p.: Grenzbüchereidienst, n.d.

Petzold, Joachim. "Die Aufgaben des nationalsozialistischen Büchereiwesens." *DB* 5 (1938): 212–16.

Peukert, Detlev J. K. *Inside Nazi Germany: Conformity, Opposition and Racism in Daily Life*. Trans. Richard Deveson. London: B. T. Batsford, 1987.

Pfeiffer, Willi. "Aktualität und Aktivität in der Volksbücherei." *DB* 6 (1939): 428–37.

Phillips, Henry Albert. *Meet the Germans*. Philadelphia and London: J. B. Lippincott, n.d.

Pirtle, Wayne G. A History of Adult Education in Germany, 1800–1933. Ph.D. diss., University of California, Berkeley, 1966.

Pott, ——. "Berichte: Aus der Arbeit einer kleinstädtischen Freihandbücherei (Glucksburg, 1792 Einw.)." *DB* 9 (1942): 332.

"Praxis der staatlichen Zensur am Beispiel der Behandlung antisowjetischer und russischer Literatur." In *Volksbücherei und Nationalsozialismus*. Comp. Friedrich Andrae. Wiesbaden: O. Harrassowitz, 1970.

"Preußisches Minister für Wissenschaft, Kunst und Volksbildung U II R Nr. 750.1, 28.12.33." *DB* 1 (1934): 11–13.

Prinzhorn, F. *Die Aufgaben der Bibliotheken im nationalsozialistischen Deutschland*. Leipzig: Eichblatt Verlag (Max Zedler), 1934.

Prinzhorn, Fritz. "Die Aufgaben der Bibliotheken im nationalsozialistischen Deutschland." *Zentralblatt für Bibliothekswesen* 51 (August/September 1934): 465–71.

Propach, E. "Volksbüchereien hüten das geistige Erbe." *N.S.K.*, November 2, 1937.

Propach, Elisabeth. "Vom neuen Sehen." *DB* 1 (1934): 447–55.

Prove, Karl-Heinz. *Von der ersten Lesergesellschaft zur Stadbücherei*. Mainfränkische Hefte, vol. 48. Würzburg: Freunde Mainfränkischer Kunst und Geschichte, 1967.

"The Public Libraries Act, 1919." *Library Association Record* 22 (1919): 365–67.

The Public Library: Its Role in the Socio-Economic and Cultural Life of the Society. Moscow: V. I. Lenin State Library, 1974.

Rang, Bernhard. "Sexuelle Frage und Volksbücherei." *DB* 1 (1934): 455–58.

Rantzau, Otto zu. *Das Reichsministerium für Wissenschaft, Erziehung und Volksbildung*. Schriften der Hochschule für Politik, Der organisatorische Aufbau des Dritten Reiches, Heft 38. Berlin: Junker und Dunnhaupt, 1938.

"Regelung der Skontogewahrung an volkstümliche Büchereien." *DB* 1 (1934): 170–71.

"Das Reich eröffnet zur Buchwoche 730 neue Volksbüchereien." *Völkischer Beobachter*, October 30, 1937.

Reuter, Rudolf. "Die Aufgaben der Volksbücherei in der deutschen Westmark." *DB* 2 (1935): 215–23.

————. "Berufsausbildung des Volksbibliothekars in Deutschland." In *Otto Glauning zum 60. Geburtstag*. Leipzig: Hadl, 1938.

————. "Der Büchereiaufbau im Westen." In Grenzbüchereidienst, *Mitteilungen*, vol. 15. Berlin: Volk und Reich Verlag, 1938.

————. "Einheitsbücherei-Volksbücherei." *DB* 3 (1936): 97–108.

————. "Die Volksbücherei im rheinischen Grenzland." *DB* 5 (1938): 724–26.

————. "Die Volksbüchereien im neuen Staat." *Soziale Praxis* 42 (1933): 1065–69.

Richter, —. "Berichte: Eröffnung der Deutschen Bücherei der Hauptstadt Prag." *DB* 8 (1941): 108–109.

Richter, Karl. "Aus der Arbeit der Städtischen Bücherei Sebnitz (Sachsen)." In Grenzbüchereidienst, *Mitteilungen*, vol. 16. Berlin: Volk und Reich Verlag, 1939.

"Richtlinien für Aufbau und Arbeit der staatlichen Büchereiberatungsstellen: Vorbemerkung." *DB* 1 (1934): 30–33.

"Richtlinien für das Volksbüchereiwesen. Entwurf des Reichs- und Preußischen Ministeriums für Wissenschaft, Erziehung und Volksbildung, März 1937." In Jutta Sywottek, *Die Gleichschaltung der deutschen Volksbüchereien 1933 bis 1937*. Frankfurt am Main: Buchhändler-Vereinigung, 1983.

"Richtlinien für das Volksbüchereiwesen; RWEV Vb 2799, 26. Oktober 1937." *DB* 5 (1938): 39–44.

"Richtlinien für die Bestandsprüfung in den Volksbüchereien Sachsens." In *Volksbücherei und Nationalsozialismus*. Comp. Friedrich Andrae, Wiesbaden: O. Harrassowitz, 1970.

"Richtlinien für die Vorbildung und Ausbildung des volksbibliotharischen Personals." In *Der Volksbibliothekar: Seine Aufgabe, sein Beruf, seine Ausbildung.* Ed. Hans Hofmann. Leipzig: Quelle und Meyer, 1927.

Rischer, Walter. *Die nationalsozialistische Kulturpolitik in Düsseldorf, 1933–1945*. Düsseldorf: Michael Tritsch, 1972.

Robenek, Brigitte. *Geschichte der Stadtbücherei Köln von den Anfangen im Jahre 1890 bis zum Ende des Zweiten Weltkrieges*. Kölner Arbeiten zum Bibliotheks- und Dokumentationswesen, vol. 3. Cologne: Greven, 1983.

Roscher, Heinz. "Deutsches Büchereiwesen jenseits der Reichsgrenzen." *DB* 1 (1934): 537–42.

————. "Heinrich Becker aus anderer Sicht: Anmerkungen zu einem Nachruf." *Buch und Bibliothek* 25 (1973): 213.

Rosenbaum, Gertrud. "Das Kasperletheater und Vorlesestunden in dem Hamburger öffentlichen Bücherhallen im Kriegswinter 1939/40." *DB* 8 (1941): 33–35.

Rosenberg, Alfred. *Der Sumpf: Querschnitte durch das Geistes "Leben der November"—Demokratie*. Munich: Franz Eher Nachfolger, 1939.

Rothfeder, Herbert P. "Amt Schrifttumspflege: A Study in Literary Control." *German Studies Review* 4 (February 1981): 64–78.

Rothfels, Hans. *The German Opposition to Hitler: An Assessment*. Trans. Lawrence Wilson. London: Oswald Wolff, 1978.

Rousseau, Jean-Jacques. *The Social Contract*. Trans. Wilmoore Kendall. Chicago: Henry Regnery, 1954.

"Rundschreiben der Reichsstelle für das Volksbüchereiwesen Nr. 39/31/15 vom 20.9.1939 an die Leiter der Staatl. Volksbüchereistellen u. Städt. Volksbüchereien, die Ausrichtung auf die aussenpolitische Lage betreffend." In *Volksbücherei und Nationalsozialismus.* Comp. Friedrich Andrae. Wiesbaden: O. Harrassowitz, 1970.

Ruppe, Hans. "Bericht über die Tatigkeit der Staatlichen Volksbüchereistelle in Wien." In Grenzbüchereidienst, *Mitteilungen*, vol. 17, pp. 68–74. N.p., n.d.

Rust, [Bernard]. "An die deutschen Volksbibliothekare." *DB* 5 (1938): 503–504.

Salewski, [Willy]. "Berichte: Das Büchereigebaude der Gauhauptstadt Posen." *DB* 8 (1941): 152–53.

———. "Berichte: Eröffnung der Städtischen Volksbücherei der Gauhauptstadt Posen." *DB* 8 (1941): 32.

———. "Berichte: Die ersten Ergebnisse der Büchereiarbeit im Regierungsbezirk Posen (Warthegau)." *DB* 9 (1942): 232–34.

———. "Berichte: Lehrgang der Staatlichen Volksbüchereistelle in Posen." *DB* 8 (1941): 213–14.

———. "Tradition und Aufbau: Das Volksbüchereiwesen im Raum des Reichsgaues Wartheland." *DB* 8 (1941): 280–86, 329–34.

Saltzwedel, Ernst-Wilhelm. "Aus der Beratungspraxis." *DB* 2 (1935): 207–11.

Sander, Richard. "Die Landesbibliotheken und ihre Aufgaben." *Zentralblatt für Bibliothekswesen* 54 (September/October 1937): 485–97.

"Satzung der Reichsschrifttumskammer." *DB* 1 (1934): 484–87.

"Säuberung des Buchbestandes: RWEV Vd Nr. 2439 M, 14. Aug. 1935." *DB* 2 (1935): 479.

Sauder, Gerhard, ed. *Die Bücherverbrennung zum 10. Mai 1933.* Munich and Vienna: Carl Hauser Verlag, 1983.

Schäfer, E. "Von der Leistungsschau der deutschen Volksbüchereien im Leipzig 1938: 1. Das Hamburger Büchereiwesen." *DB* 6 (1939): 235–40.

Scheffen, Wilhelm. *Büchereiarbeit im Grenzland.* Sonderdruck aus der *Zeitschrift für Selbstverwaltung.* Berlin: 1930.

———. "Grenzbüchereiarbeit im preußichen Osten." *DB* 1 (1934): 313–25.

———. "Grenzbüchereidienst." *DB* 2 (1935): 249–50.

———. "Grenzbüchereidienst in der Zeitwende." In Grenzbüchereidienst, *Mitteilungen*, vol. 12. Berlin: Volk und Reich Verlag, 1933.

———. "Vorwort." In Grenzbüchereidienst, *Mitteilungen*, vol. 16. Berlin: Volk und Reich Verlag, 1939.

———. "20 Jahre Grenzbüchereiarbeit." In Grenzbüchereidienst, *Mitteilungen*, vol. 17. N.p., n.d.

———. "Zwanzig Jahre 'Grenzbüchereidienst'." *DB* 7 (1940): 257–63.

———, ed. "Grenzbüchereitagung Schneidemühl vom 7. bis 11. Juni 1938." In Grenzbüchereidienst, *Mitteilungen*, vol. 16. Berlin: Volk und Reich Verlag, 1939.

Scheffen-Doring, Luise. "Reisebericht." In Grenzbüchereidienst, *Mitteilungen*, vol. 14. Berlin: n.p., 1936.

———. "Tagungsbericht." In Grenzbüchereidienst, *Mitteilungen*, vol. 16. Berlin: Volk und Reich Verlag, 1939.

Schinkel, Friedrich. "Einkaufshaus für Büchereien G.m.b.H." *DB* 3 (1936): 25–27.

Schippel, K. "Die Volksbüchereiarbeit des Deutschen Schulvereines Sudmark." *DB* 5 (1938): 714–19.

Schlagheck, Bernhard. "Die ausgebaute Bücherei der Mittelstadt und ihr Aufgabenkreis." *DB* 3 (1936): 625–34.

———. "Die ortliche Verankerung des Grenzbüchereiwesens." In Grenz-büchereidienst, *Mitteilungen*, vol. 15. Berlin: Volk und Reich Verlag, 1938.

Schmidt-Leonhardt, Hans. "Kultur und Staat im Recht des neuen Reiches." In *Deutsches Kulturrecht.* Ed. Deutscher Fichte-Bund. Hamburg: Falken Verlag, 1936.

Schoenbaum, David. *Hitler's Social Revolution: Class and Status in Nazi Germany, 1933–1939.* New York and London: W. W. Norton, 1980.

Schrader, Willi. "Dies ist eine politische Bücherei." In Grenzbüchereidienst, *Mitteilungen*, vol. 16. Berlin: Volk und Reich Verlag, 1939.

Schriewer, Franz. *Bauer und Buch.* Sonderdruck aus der *Neuen Landjugend* 11 und 12 (September and October 1929). Wittenberg: Zentralverlag für Berufs- und Fachschule, n.d.

———. "Buch, Volk und Menschheit." In *Kultur, Buch und Grenze: Grundfragen und Beispiele deutscher Bücherei- und Kulturarbeit in den Grenzgebieten.* Ed. Franz Schriewer. Leipzig: Quelle und Meyer, 1930.

———. "Das deutsche Büchereiwesen im Bilde der Landschaft." *DB* 3 (1936): 545–622.

———. "Die deutsche Volksbücherei." *DB* 2 (1935): 298–305.

———. *Das deutsche Volksbüchereiwesen in den Gemeinden unter 5,000 Einwohnern nach Zahlen und Massen.* Berlin: Reichsstelle für volkstümliches Büchereiwesen, 1937.

———. "'Freie' Theke oder 'pädagogischer' Schalter?" *DB* 4 (1937): 30–38.

———. "Das Grenzbüchereiwesen im neuen Staat." In Grenzbüchereidienst, *Mitteilungen*, vol. 12. N.p.: Volk und Reich Verlag, 1933.

———. "Grundfragen der Kataloggestaltung." *DB* 3 (1936): 41–49.

———. "Grundgedanken der Technik für eine Dorfbücherei." *DB* 2 (1935): 11–19.

———. "Kampf den Leihbüchereien!" *BuB* 13 (1933): 110–13.

———. *Das ländliche Volksbüchereiwesen: Einführung in Grundfragen und Praxis der Dorf- und Kleinstadtbüchereien.* Jena: Eugen Diederichs, 1937.

———. "Landschaft, Mensch und Buch im Grenzland Schleswig." In *Kultur, Buch und Grenze: Grundfragen und Beispiele deutscher Bücherei- und Kulturarbeit in den Grenzgebieten.* Ed. Franz Schriewer. Leipzig: Quelle und Meyer, 1930.

———. "Die Ostbücherei, alte und neue Wege." *DB* 1 (1934): 151–61.

———. "Prinzip und Form grenzländischer Büchereiorganisation." In *Kultur, Buch und Grenze: Grundfragen und Beispiele deutscher Bücherei- und Kulturarbeit in den Grenzgebieten.* Ed. Franz Schriewer. Leipzig: Quelle und Meyer, 1930.

———. "Reorganisation—warum und wie?" *DB* 2 (1935): 3–10.

————. "Das Schulerbüchereiwesen." *DB* 2 (1935): 350–51.

————. *Die staatlichen Volksbüchereistellen im Aufbau des deutschen Volksbüchereiwesens.* Leipzig: Einkaufshaus für Büchereien, 1938.

————. "Die Volksbücherei: Möglichkeiten und Grenzen." *DB* 2 (1935): 193–202.

————. "Warum Grenzbüchereidienst?" In Grenzbüchereidienst, *Mitteilungen*, vol. 13. Berlin: Volk und Reich Verlag, 1935.

————. "Warum staatliche Stellen für das Volksbüchereiwesen?" *DB* 3 (1936): 6–13.

————. "Was heisst Volkstum in der Bücherei?" *DB* 1 (1934): 441–47.

————. "Zum neuen Jahrgang." *DB* 2 (1935): 1–3.

————. "Das Zusammenwirken von Kreis, Gemeinde und Staatlicher Büchereiberatungsstelle." *DB* 3 (1936): 19–25.

————, ed. *Kultur, Buch und Grenze: Grundfragen und Beispiele deutscher Bücherei- und Kulturarbeit in den Grenzgebieten.* Leipzig: Quelle und Meyer, 1930.

Schroder, Wilhelm. "Grenzcharakter und Büchereiarbeit in Ostpreußen." In *Kultur, Buch und Grenze: Grundfragen und Beispiele deutscher Bücherei- und Kulturarbeit in den Grenzgebieten.* Ed. Franz Schriewer. Leipzig: Quelle und Meyer, 1930.

Schulenburg, — von der. *Praktische Büchereiarbeit im Kreise Northeim.* Berlin: n.p., 1943.

Schulz, Kurd. "8. Jahresversammlung des Verbandes deutscher Volksbibliothekare in Danzig von 24. bis 26. Mai 1934." *DB* 1 (1934): 282–88.

————. "Berichte: Eröffnung einer Freihandbücherei in Bremen." *DB* 7 (1940): 36–37.

————. "Erziehung zur Dichtung—Aufgabe der Volksbücherei." *DB* 8 (1941): 2–7.

————. "Zur gegenwärtigen Lage der Dorfbüchereiarbeit." *DB* 2 (1935): 202–207.

Schurer, Heinz. *Public Libraries in Germany.* German Educational Reconstruction, no. 5. London: James Clark, 1946.

Schuster, Wilhelm. "Arbeitsberichte: Die Dichterlesungen der NS-Kulturgemeinde und die Berliner Volksbüchereien." *DB* 3 (1936): 332–33.

————. "Die Berliner Bibliotheksschule." *DB* 5 (1938): 511–22.

————. "Der Beruf des Volksbibliothekars." *DB* 3 (1936): 28–33.

————. "Bücherei und Nationalsozialismus." *DB* 1 (1934): 1–9.

————. "Büchereipolitische Rationalisierung." *HfB* 16 (1932): 77–79.

————. "Die Einrichtung staatlicher Beratungsstellen in den Städten über 20 000 Einwohner, 4.10.1933." In Jutta Sywottek, *Die Gleichschaltung der deutschen Volksbüchereien 1933 bis 1937.* Frankfurt am Main: Buchhändler-Vereinigung, 1983.

————. "Das Ende des Bildungsreiches." *DB* 1 (1934): 1–6.

————. "Entwurf für ein Büchereigesetz, 27.11.1933." In Jutta Sywottek, *Die Gleichschaltung der deutschen Volksbüchereien 1933 bis 1937.* Frankfurt am Main: Buchhändler-Vereinigung, 1983.

————. "Facharbeitsstelle des Verbandes deutscher Volksbibliothekare,

9.10.1933." In Jutta Sywottek, *Die Gleichschaltung der deutschen Volksbüchereien 1933 bis 1937*. Frankfurt am Main: Buchhändler-Vereinigung,
1983.

———. "Freie Volksbildungsarbeit im Grenzland." In *Kultur, Buch und Grenze:
Grundfragen und Beispiele deutscher Bücherei- und Kulturarbeit in den
Grenzgebieten*. Ed. Franz Schriewer. Leipzig: Quelle und Meyer, 1930.

———. "Historische und andere Irrtumer in der Kritik der Volks-
bildungsbewegung." *BuB* 7 (1927): 367–88.

———. "Masse und Volk, Gruppe und Einzelner in ihren Beziehungen zu Volkserziehung und Bücherei." In *Volksbücherei und Nationalsozialismus*. Comp.
Friedrich Andrae. Wiesbaden: O. Harrassowitz, 1970.

———. "Das neue deutsche Volksbüchereiwesen." *Zentralblatt für Bibliothekswesen* 53 (1936): 144–54.

———. "Neue Wege der Bestandserschliessung in den Bücherverzeichnissen."
DB 1 (1934): 28–36.

———. "Die Neuordnung des ländlichen Beratungsstellungswesens als Grund-
lage einer staatlichen Büchereipolitik." In Jutta Sywottek, *Die
Gleichschaltung der deutschen Volksbüchereien 1933 bis 1937*. Frankfurt am
Main: Buchhändler-Vereinigung, 1983.

———. "Die Neuordnung des Preußischen Büchereiwesens." *DB* 1 (1934): 9–17.

———. "7. Jahresversammlung des Verbandes Deutscher Volksbibliothekare in
Hannover vom 17.–19. September 1933." *BuB* 13 (1933): 342–44.

———. "Volksbildung im Grenzland als angewandte vergleichende Volks- und
Kulturkunde." In *Kultur, Buch und Grenze: Grundfragen und Beispiele
deutscher Bücherei- und Kulturarbeit in den Grenzgebieten*. Ed. Franz
Schriewer. Leipzig: Quelle und Meyer, 1930.

———. "Die Volksbücherei im neuen Reich." *DB* 1 (1934): 342–48.

———. "Volksbücherei und Revolutionspädagogik." *BuB* 11 (1931): 89–94.

———. "Vom Geiste eines deutschen Büchereigesetzes." *DB* 1 (1934): 209–18.

———. "Die Zusammenarbeit der Stadtbibliothek mit den Volksbüchereien."
Zentralblatt für Bibliothekswesen 55 (October 1938): 457–67.

———. "Zur Geschichte des lesenden Volkes und seiner Büchereien." *DB* 5
(1938): 703–14.

60 Jahre: Verein für Volksbildung eV. Reutlingen: N.p., 1978.

Simon, Wilhelm. "Büchereiarbeit in einer Bergstadt des Oberharzes." *DB* 4
(1937): 132–37.

Smith, Anthony D. *The Ethnic Origins of Nations*. Oxford: Basil Blackwell,
1986.

Smith, Woodruff. "The Colonial Novel as Political Propaganda: Hans Grimm's
Volk ohne Raum." *German Studies Review* 6 (May 1983): 215–35.

"Sogenannte 'Schwarze Liste' und Empfehlungslisten für die Umstellung der
Volksbüchereibestände." In *Volksbücherei und Nationalsozialismus*. Comp.
Friedrich Andrae. Wiesbaden: O. Harrassowitz, 1970.

"Sonderprüfung für den Dienst an volkstümlichen Büchereien: RWEV Vb Nr.
1489/38, Z (b), 28. Juni 1938." *DB* 5 (1938): 470–71.

Sonnichsen, —. "Meine Arbeit im Dienste der deutschen Bücherei." *DB* 2 (1935):
223–24.

Bibliography

"Staatliche Neuordnung des Volksbüchereiwesens in Baden." *DB* 3 (1936): 427–29.

Stachura, Peter. *The German Youth Movement 1900–1945: An Interpretative and Documentary History*. New York: St. Martin's, 1981.

Stansch, Hildegard. "Was fördern wir vom Mädelbuch?" *DB* 8 (1941): 390–94.

Starzacher, Karl. "Der Sinn der Dorfgemeinschaftsarbeit." In Grenzbüchereidienst, *Mitteilungen*, vol. 17. N.p., n.d.

———. "Die geschichtliche Entwicklung Kärntens mit besonderer Rücksichtigung der Entstehung der Volksgrenze in Kärnten." In Grenzbüchereidienst, *Mitteilungen*, vol. 17. N.p., n.d.

Steinert, Marlis G. *Hitler's War and the Germans: Public Mood and Attitude during the Second World War*. Trans. and ed. Thomas E. J. DeWitt. Athens: Ohio University Press, 1977.

Steinhoff, Maria. "Die Westdeutsche Volksbüchereischule 1928–1938." *DB* 5 (1938): 526–29.

Stephenson, Jill. *Women in Nazi Society*. New York: Barnes and Noble, 1975.

Stern, Fritz. *The Politics of Cultural Despair: A Study in the Rise of the Germanic Ideology*. Berkeley, Los Angeles, and London: University of California Press, 1974.

"Stichworte und Zahlen in Ergänzung des Jahresberichts 1935/36." *Der Auslands Deutsche* 19 (October 1936): 739–40.

Stieg, Margaret F. "The Nazi Public Library and the Young Adult." *Top of the News* 43 (Fall 1986): 45–57.

———. "The 1926 German Law to Protect Youth against Smut: Moral Protectionism in a Democracy." *Central European History* 23 (March 1990): 22–56.

———. "The Richtung[s]streit: The Philosophy of Public Librarianship in Germany before 1933." *Journal of Library History* 21 (Spring 1986): 261–76.

Stolc, Jozef. "Kleine Beiträge: Die Gemeindebücherei in der Slowakei." *DB* 9 (1942): 316–20.

Strätz, Hans-Wolfgang. "Die studentische 'Aktion wider den undeutschen Geist' im Frühjahr 1933." *Vierteljahrshefte für Zeitgeschichte* 16 (October 1968): 347–72.

Strothmann, Dietrich. *Nationalsozialistische Literaturpolitik: Ein Beitrag zur Publizistik im Dritten Reich*. Abhandlungen zur Kunst-, Musik- und Literaturwissenschaft, vol. 13. Bonn: H. Bouvier, 1960.

Studentkowski, Werner. "Partei und Volksbücherei." *DB* 4 (1937): 285–91.

Suberkrub, Hansjörg. *Die Stadtbücherei Kiel*. Kiel: n.p., 1954.

Sugar, Peter F., ed. *Ethnic Diversity and Conflict in Eastern Europe*. Santa Barbara, Calif., and Oxford: ABC-Clio, 1980.

Sulz, E. "Fortschritt und Reaktion in der Deutschen Bücherhallenbewegung." In *Büchereifragen*. Ed. E[rwin] Ackerknecht and G[ottlieb] Fritz. Berlin: n.p., 1914.

Sywottek, Jutta. *Die Gleichschaltung der deutschen Volksbüchereien 1933 bis 1937*. Separatausdruck aus Archiv für Geschichte des Buchwesens (AGB), Band 24/1983, Lieferung 2. Frankfurt am Main: Buchhändler-Vereinigung, 1983.

"Tagungsbericht." In Grenzbüchereidienst, *Mitteilungen*, vol. 16. Berlin: Volk und Reich Verlag, 1939.

"Tagungsplan." In Grenzbüchereidienst, *Mitteilungen*, vol. 16. Berlin: Volk und Reich Verlag, 1939.

T[aupitz] K. "Neuordnung des Volksbüchereiwesens in Sachsen." *DB* 1 (1934): 288–89.

Taupitz, Karl. "Der Aufbau des Büchereiwesens in Sachsen seit der national-sozialistischen Revolution." *DB* 4 (1937): 243–58.

———. "Die Bücherei in der Großstadt." *DB* 3 (1936): 145–58.

———. *Das Büchereiwesen in Dorf und Kleinstadt*. Dresden: Verlag Heimatwerk Sachsen v. Baensch Druckerei, n.d.

———. "Parteibibliotheken oder Volksbüchereien?" *DB* 1 (1934): 545–50.

———. "Die politische Aufgabe der Grenzbücherei." In Grenzbüchereidienst, *Mitteilungen*, vol. 15. Berlin: Volk und Reich Verlag, 1938.

———. "Über den Begriff der Volksbücherei." *DB* 6 (1939): 1–8.

Teichmann, Hans. "Arbeitsberichte: Dichtung findet neuen Lebensraum." *DB* 3 (1936): 329–32.

Thauer, Wolfgang. "Wechsel und Stetigkeit im Buchbestand." *DB* 8 (1941): 316–28.

———, ed. *Die Bücherhallenbewegung*. Beiträge zum Büchereiwesen, Reihe B, Quelle und Texte, Heft 4. Wiesbaden: Otto Harrassowitz, 1970.

———, ed. *Politik der Bücherei: Paul Ladewig und die jungere Bücherhallen-bewegung*. Wiesbaden: Otto Harrassowitz, 1975.

Thauer, Wolfgang, and Peter Vodosek. *Geschichte der öffentlichen Bücherei in Deutschland*. Wiesbaden: Otto Harrassowitz, 1978.

Thiele, Ernst Otto. *Polen greift an!* Breslau: Wilh. Gottl. Korn, 1933.

Thier, Erich. "Die Deutsche Volksbüchereischule zu Leipzig." *DB* 5 (1938): 522–26.

———. "Lenkung des Berufsnachwuchs." *DB* 8 (1941): 273–76.

Thierbach, Hans. "What the Nazis Say about American Libraries: A German View of American Public Libraries as Instruments in the Shaping of Political Control." *Saturday Review of Literature* 25 (November 21, 1942): 3–5, 16.

Thompson, Lawrence. "New Problems for German Librarians." *Library Quarterly* 11 (January 1941): 102.

"Thüringische Landesstelle für volkstümliches Büchereiwesen." *DB* 1 (1934): 56–58.

Tschich, Gunther. "Berichte und Mitteilungen: Gemeinde- und Werkbücherei Spechthausen." *DB* 5 (1938): 369–72.

———. "Was die deutsche Volksbücherei im letzten Jahr gefördert hat." *DB* 3 (1936): 49–54.

"Ungeeignetheit von Prachtwerken für Volksbüchereien: RWEV Vd 2164/35, 29. Juli 1935." *DB* 2 (1935): 478.

"Unseren jüdischen Kollegen, die unter dem Nationalsozialismus gelitten und das Leben verloren haben, zum Gedenken!" *Bücherei und Bildung* 4 (September 1952): 853–59.

"Verband deutscher Volksbibliothekare: Zum Umbau des deutschen Volksbüchereiwesens." *BuB* 13 (1933): 169–70.

"Vereinbarung zwischen der Reichstelle für das Volksbüchereiwesen und der Reichsjugendführung der NSDAP, 28." *DB* 4 (1937): 558.

"Verordnung über die Aufgaben des Reichsministeriums für Volksaufklärung und Propaganda vom 30. Juni 1933." *Reichsgesetzblatt* 1 (1933): 449.

40 Jahre Stadtbücherei Siegburg. N.p., n.d.

Vodosek, Peter. "Arbeiterbibliothek und öffentliche Bibliothek: Zur Geschichte ihrer Beziehung von der ersten Hälfte des neunzehnten Jahrhunderts bis 1933." *Buch und Bibliothek* 27 (April 1975): 321–28.

———, ed. *Bibliotheksarbeit: Hermann Wassner zum 60. Geburtstag.* Wiesbaden: Otto Harrassowitz, 1982.

Vodosek, Peter, and Manfred Komorowski, eds. *Bibliotheken während des Nationalsozialismus*, Teil 1. Wolfenbütteler Schriften zur Geschichte des Buchwesens, Bd. 16. Wiesbaden: Otto Harrassowitz, 1989.

Volbehr, Lilli. "Anteil und Anrecht der Frau an der volksbibliothekarischen Berufsarbeit." *DB* 1 (1934): 25–30.

"Die Volksbücherei in der Ausstellung Schaffendes Volk." *DB* 4 (1937): 555–56.

"Volksbücherei—'Kraft durch Freude'." *DB* 1 (1934): 311.

"Volksbücherei: Kundgebung in Bayreuth." In Grenzbüchereidienst, *Mitteilungen*, vol. 14. Berlin: n.p., 1936.

"Das Volksbüchereiwesen in der Pfalz." *Nationalsozialistische Zeitung Rheinfront*, May 4, 1934.

"Vorläufige Übersicht über den Stand des Büchereiwesens in Thüringen." *DB* 5 (1938): 726–27.

"Vorwort." In Grenzbüchereidienst, *Mitteilungen* no. 15. Berlin: Volk und Reich Verlag, 1938.

Waas, Adolf. "Unsere fahrbare Bücherei an der Saar." *HfB* 12 (1928): 138–41.

Walberer, Ulrich, ed. *10. Mai 1933: Bücherverbrennung in Deutschland und die Folgen.* Frankfurt am Main: Fischer Taschenbuch Verlag, 1983.

"Das war ein Vorspiel nur . . ." Bücherverbrennung Deutschland 1933: Voraussetzungen und Folgen. Berlin and Vienna: Medusa, 1983.

Weber, Gertrud. "Gemeinsame Büchereistatistik der Grenzgebiete: Versuch und Ziel." In *Kultur, Buch und Grenze: Grundfragen und Beispiele deutscher Bücherei- und Kulturarbeit in den Grenzgebieten.* Ed. Franz Schriewer. Leipzig: Quelle und Meyer, 1930.

Weiland, Werner. "Arbeitsberichte: Planmässige Aufbauarbeit und der 20-pf-Kopfsatz." *DB* 4 (1937): 39–41.

Weimar, Völker, ed. *Franz Schriewer, 1893–1966.* Bibliographien, vol. 3. Berlin: Deutscher Bibliotheksverband, Arbeitsstelle für das Volksbüchereiwesen, 1976.

Wentzcke, —. "Skizze zum Lichtbildervortrag." In Grenzbüchereidienst, *Mitteilungen* no. 15. Berlin: Volk und Reich Verlag, 1938.

Wenzel, Waldemar. "Das Gesicht einer Jugendbücherei." *DB* 6 (1939): 355–60.

Wermke, Ernst. "Die deutschen Bibliotheken im Osten." *Zentralblatt für Bibliothekswesen* 51 (August/September 1934): 471–86.

"Wichtige Neuordnung im Volksbüchereiwesen." *DB* 2 (1935): 241.

"Eine wichtige Verordnung über den Aufbau des Volksbüchereiwesens." *Volksbücherei und Volksbildung in Niedersachsen* 14 (December 1934/January 1935): 14.

Bibliography

"Wider den undeutschen Geist." In *Die Bücherverbrennung zum 10. Mai 1933*. Ed. Gerhard Sauder. Munich and Vienna: Carl Hauser Verlag, 1983.

Wiegand, Kurt. "50 Jahre Beratungsstelle in Bayreuth." *Die Neue Bücherei* (1986): 113–28.

Wieser, Max. "Aufruf an die Volksbibliothekare, 25. Marz 1933." In *Volksbücherei und Nationalsozialismus*. Comp. Friedrich Andrae. Wiesbaden: O. Harrassowitz, 1970.

———. "Die Ausstellung 'Jugend und Buch' der Volksbucherei in Spandau." In *Volksbücherei und Nationalsozialismus*. Comp. Friedrich Andrae. Wiesbaden: O. Harrassowitz, 1970.

Wilke, —. "Die grenzpolitische Arbeit der HJ im Westen und ihre Zusammenarbeit mit der Volksbücherei." In Grenzbüchereidienst, *Mitteilungen*, vol. 15. Berlin: Volk und Reich Verlag, 1938.

Wilkens, Erik. "Die Leistungen der Büchereien eines Landkreises (Northeim/Hann.) im Kriegsjahr 1941/42." *DB* 9 (1942): 320–22.

———. "Das Ostlandlager." In *Die Arbeitslager der Volksbibliothekare 1936 und 1937*. Leipzig: n.p., 1938.

———. "Vorlesestunden für die Hitler-Jugend." *DB* 3 (1936): 351–57.

Wille, [Rudolf]. "Ein Büchereileiter erzählt aus seiner Arbeit." In Grenzbüchereidienst, *Mitteilungen* vol. 14. Berlin: n.p., 1936.

Witsch, Josef. "Die Herbstveranstaltungen des deutschen Schrifttums und die deutsche Volksbücherei." *DB* 9 (1942): 263–68.

Wohl, Robert. *The Generation of 1914*. Cambridge, Mass.: Harvard University Press, 1979.

"Ein Wort zu den 'Prachtwerken.'" *DB* 1 (1934): 166–68.

Wulf, Joseph, ed. *Literatur und Dichtung im Dritten Reich: Eine Dokumentation*. Frankfurt am Main, Berlin, and Vienna: Ullstein, 1983.

Wunder, Gerd. "Die fachliche und politische Weiterbildung der im Beruf stehenden Volksbibliothekare." *DB* 4 (1937): 95–100.

Wutz, Josef. "Von den Volksbüchereien der Bayerischen Ostmark." In Grenzbüchereidienst, *Mitteilungen* no. 14. Berlin: n.p., 1936.

Zifreund, V. "Wege und Ziele der sudetendeutschen Volksbüchereiarbeit." In *Aus dem Volksbüchereiwesen der Gegenwart*. Ed. Hans Rosin. Stettin: Verlag Bücherei und Bildungspflege, 1930.

Zimmer, —. "Warum Grenzbüchereidienst." *Westdeutsche Blätter für Büchereiberatung* 7 (1936): 9–11.

"Zu den alten Lesern kamen jetzt viele neue." *Hamburger Tageblatt*, September 7, 1943.

"Zum neuen Jahrgang." *DB* 2 (1935): 1–3.

"Zum Thema 'Volksbüchereien und Nationalsozialismus' befragt: Hedwig Bieber." In *Volksbüchereien und Nationalsozialismus: Eine Ausstellung der Stadtbibliotheken Bielefeld, Dortmund und Solinger*. Bielefeld, November 1988.

"Zur der Ausbildung für den höheren Volksbüchereidienst." *BuB* 7 (1927): 116–20.

Zusammenfassung und Erschliessung des stadt- und heimatgeschichtlichen Schrifttums. Frankfurt/Oder: n.p., 1943.

————. "Wiedereröffnung der Stadtbücherei Frankfurt-Oder." *DB* 1 (1934): 404–405.

"22 000 öffentliche Büchereien im Reich." *Deutsche Allgemeine Zeitung,* November 6, 1943.

Index

Aachen, 131, 209–10

Ackerknecht, Erwin, 39, 40, 65, 172, 237; accepts apprentices at Stettin, 18; advises Deutsche Gemeindetag, 68–69; and attack by Nazis on Rostock library collection, 87–88; and Auslandsdeutsche libraries, 23; as leader of profession, 38, 43; dismissal, 46–47; leader of Alte Richtung, 7; on attracting readers, 161; on circulation decline, 107; on hopes of younger librarians, 35; on librarians' qualifications, 180; on VDV, 50; opinion of Franz Schriewer, 42; opinion of Fritz Heiligenstaedt, 4, 74; opinion of Heinz Dähnhardt, 44; opinion of Herrmann review, 38; opinion of Johannes Beer, 36; opinion of Walter Hofmann, 62, 69, 275 (n. 27); opinion of Wilhelm Scheffen, 220; sends books to Saltzwedel, 254; wartime reappointment to public library, 253

Acquisitions lists, 163

Activism, 27, 146, 258

Administrative structure, 261; in operation, 97–99

Adult readers. *See* Readers: adult

Air raids, 241, 243, 250–51

Allenstein, 109

Allied bombing. *See* Air raids

All Quiet on the Western Front, 61, 86, 95

Alte Richtung, 6–8, 151, 282–83 (n. 3); ideas, 7–8

Altkämpfer, 37; definition, xv

Altona, 130

Angermann, Rudolf, 42, 76, 82–83, 96, 98, 118, 211

Anschluss: definition, xv

Anti-Catholicism, 9, 213, 230, 263

Anti-French feelings, 229

Anti-Polish feelings, 223–24, 299 (n. 13)

Anti-Semitism, 15, 247

Anti-Soviet literature, 245

Anzengruber, Ludwig, 157

Application of policies: local variations, 214

Armed services libraries, 248

Armee hinter Stacheldraht, 235

Arpe, Maria, 251

Asphalt literature, 90; definition, 269 (n. 20)

Aufruf an die Volksbibliothekare. *See* Erklärung und Aufruf

Aumund, 100

Auslandsdeutsche, 233; definition, xv

Auslandsdeutsche libraries, 233–36; and Machtergreifung, 237–40; Argentina, 236; Belgium, 236; Bolivia, 236; collections, 235; during World War II, 238–39; Guatemala, 236; Korea, 236; lack of organizational framework, 235–36; Poland, 237; Romania, 236; United States, 236

Ausschuss zur Neuordnung der Berliner Stadt- und Volksbüchereien, 59–60

Index